Homelessness, Housing, and Mental Illness

Homelessness, Housing, and Mental Illness

RUSSELL K. SCHUTT

with Stephen M. Goldfinger

HARVARD UNIVERSITY PRESS
Cambridge, Massachusetts
London, England
2011

Library of Congress Cataloging-in-Publication Data

Schutt, Russell K.
Homelessness, housing, and mental illness / Russell K. Schutt with
Stephen M. Goldfinger.
p. cm.
Includes bibliographical references and index.
ISBN 978-0-674-05101-0 (alk. paper)
1. Mentally ill homeless persons—United States.
2. Group homes for people with mental disabilities—United States.
I. Goldfinger, Stephen M. II. Title.
[DNLM: 1. Mental Disorders—United States.
2. Homeless Persons—psychology—United States.
3. Housing—United States.
4. Social Problems—United States. WM 140 S396h 2011]
HV3006.A4S383 2011
362.2—dc22 2010018566

To Elizabeth and Julia

Contents

Illustrations

Figures

Tables

Preface

THERE WAS A TIME, not so long ago, when the sight of homeless persons on city streets shocked the conscience of American citizens. Newspaper stories announced "A High Tide of Homelessness . . ." (Rule 1984), "the alarming increase in homelessness" (Griesbach et al. 1984), the "cancer of homelessness has spread" (McQuiston 1984). The barracks-style accommodations quickly opened by cities and charities were termed "emergency" shelters—not just because they offered beds to people in crisis but because they were seen as an emergency solution to a temporary social problem (Kaufman 1992): "most shelter providers looked forward to the day when they could go out of business or convert their structures to affordable housing" (p. 477).

But homelessness did not diminish, and the "shelter industry" flourished. Stories about homeless persons receded from the front pages (Kaufman 1992, 482), reappearing during the holidays in the spirit of Charles Dickens's *A Christmas Carol*. Charitable organizations, church members, and student groups added "helping the homeless" to their missions. Government agencies developed regulations for shelter management and rules for service provision. Social researchers investigated the dimensions of this new social problem. Homelessness had become an expected part of community life, in cities large and small, in rural areas, throughout the United States.

Of course this change in the social world of the 1980s was neither as complete nor abrupt as implied by the "emergency" rhetoric. The United

States has always had homeless persons, and there have been other historical periods when the size of that population swelled and its visibility increased. But since the Great Depression of the 1930s, homeless persons
had comprised a tiny part of the population, and were found mainly in
urban Skid Row districts, invisible to the larger community. Even the term
"Skid Row" conjured an image of individuals who had "skidded" to the
bottom of the social ladder like logs rushing down the Seattle street where
the term had its origins. Homelessness was a problem of some individuals
who had fallen on hard times, who lived apart from the community.

Homelessness in the 1980s seemed different: the rapid increase in numbers outpaced local efforts to provide emergency shelter, while the homeless population's diversity—single mothers with young children, Vietnam
veterans, persons whose behavior seemed bizarre, as well as apparent substance abusers—required something other than a "one size fits all" service
response. Social researchers were soon asked to provide systematic descriptions of the homeless population and to count its size, first in collaboration with local service agencies and then with federal funding. The National Institute of Mental Health (NIMH) awarded its first research grant
focused on homelessness in 1982, followed by a series of additional grants
to individual investigators. In 1989 NIMH established a new program on
homelessness and severe mental illness headed by Irene Levine, PhD, and
funded ten additional research studies about homeless persons (Straw et
al. 1997, 20).

Surveys focused on the single adult homeless population identified a
substantial fraction—between 20 percent and 50 percent—as suffering
from severe and persistent mental illness (Schutt and Garrett 1992). Many
others were chronic substance abusers, with about half of those who were
seriously mentally ill also suffering from substance abuse. Explaining
homelessness in the 1980s would require understanding changes in mental
health services as well as changes in the low-income housing market. Responding to homelessness would require new approaches in health services as well as additional funds for affordable housing.

The 1987 Stewart B. McKinney Homeless Assistance Act (P. L. 100–77)
represented the first major federal commitment to fund housing and services for homeless persons. The McKinney Act authorized a total of
$1.059 billion for programs to help homeless persons in 1987 and 1988,
with $542 million actually appropriated (Congressional Quarterly 1990,
677–78). The Act included $30 million for a Mental Health Services for
the Homeless Block Grant and, ultimately (over three years), $13.9 mil-
lion for Community Mental Health Services Demonstration Projects for
Homeless Individuals Who Are Chronically Mentally Ill (Straw et al.

1997, 21–22). The demonstration projects indicated the importance of comprehensive supportive services for homeless persons with mental illness as well as the critical need for them to have permanent housing in order to improve outcomes.

When Congress reauthorized the McKinney Act in 1990, it appropriated $6 million for additional demonstration projects to test hypotheses about the value of different combinations of service and housing interventions. An innovative Memorandum of Understanding between the U.S. Department of Housing and Urban Development (HUD) and the Department of Health and Human Services (which includes NIMH) provided for HUD to contribute $10 million to support the housing component of these interventions for three years (Straw et al. 1997, 22–23).

NIMH quickly developed a Request for Applications to solicit rigorous evaluation research proposals from teams of investigators around the United States. Investigators were required to describe client characteristics and treatment implementation and use an experimental design to test the effectiveness of the proposed interventions among subgroups of the homeless mentally ill persons studied (Straw et al. 1997, 23).

In September 1990 NIMH announced the results of the competition for research funding: its expert panels had recommended funding six projects in five different cities (Straw et al. 1997, 23). Each of these projects took advantage of the interagency agreement with HUD and so included some type of housing opportunity as well as a service intervention. All anticipated following homeless persons recruited for the projects for at least one year.

The project team formed in Boston at the request of the Massachusetts Department of Mental Health in order to develop a proposal for a McKinney grant decided to compare the value of group homes to independent apartments, taking into account participants' housing preferences. There was no question in our minds that homeless persons need housing, whether or not they have been diagnosed with severe mental illness. But prior research and clinical experience left us less certain about the type of housing that would be most helpful to individuals who had been homeless and were recipients of mental health services. We knew that many state mental health agencies placed most patients who were homeless or had been discharged from psychiatric hospitals into group homes, where they were supervised by a full-time staff. Some agencies provided some of their patients the option of living in their own apartments, with varying levels of services provided by the agency. We also knew that most homeless persons sought to live on their own, but many psychiatrists and other clinicians assumed these persons needed the type of services that were available in group homes. It was time to test these opposing perspectives.

The research teams that successfully sought funding in San Diego and Baltimore proposed giving some persons federal Section 8 housing vouchers in addition to case management services, thus allowing a comparison of the value of easy access to housing with the value of special case management services. In New York City one team planned to provide enhanced support services to homeless persons with mental illness during the "critical time" of six months after they moved out of a shelter into independent housing. Another New York City research team focused on a drop-in center for persons living on the streets.

Stephen M. Goldfinger, MD, our team's principal investigator, had recently arrived at the Massachusetts Mental Health Center to manage outpatient services. Previously, at San Francisco General Hospital, he had established a national reputation as an expert on problems in coordinating services for homeless persons with mental illness. In his new role, he quickly realized the severity of the problems confronted by the large numbers of homeless persons in the MMHC caseload. Larry J. Seidman, PhD, a project co-investigator, directed neuropsychology training and assessment at Mass Mental. He was aware of the importance of cognition for community functioning and was at the cutting edge of what was then an emerging understanding of the contribution of different brain regions to particular dimensions of cognitive functioning.

As a methodologist, I brought to the project team expertise in the assessment of needs and perspectives of shelter users and shelter staff, as well as research connections with many local agencies and shelters. The methods we developed are described in detail in the appendix, which is necessary reading for those who seek to understand the foundation for the results that I present. As a sociologist, my contribution on the co-investigator team was to focus attention on the social processes that would shape reactions to housing, relations with service providers, and opportunities in the larger community. From my perspective, our project's research design provided an opportunity to investigate the most important sociological questions: how much does social structure contribute to explaining individual behavior, and how do social processes shape this contribution? These are the questions that underlie this book.

Co-investigator Barbara E. Dickey, PhD, brought to the project expertise in health care economics. Clinical psychologist Walter E. Penk, PhD, was at the time an administrator in the Massachusetts Department of Mental Health and also brought to the project his expertise in personality assessment. Co-investigator Sondra Hellman, RN, CS, directed outpatient services at MMHC, while co-investigator Martha O'Brien, RN, managed housing operations for DMH's Metro Boston Region. Harvard Medical

School's Department of Social Medicine agreed to provide three anthropologists to serve as ethnographers in our project's group homes, one of whom, Norma Ware, PhD, subsequently joined the project team as a co-investigator.

Our initial grant provided $3.1 million from NIMH for research and case management services and led to an additional $10 million from HUD to fund the project's housing. (Some of the $10 million was already dedicated to Metro Boston housing programs.) With this funding, we rapidly expanded our project team to include eight master's level case managers and a case management supervisor, a research director, a services and recruitment coordinator, a neuropsychological evaluator, a project administrative assistant, and several research assistants. The Department of Mental Health began negotiations to develop and manage the new housing. For a total of five years, we immersed ourselves in project management, research design, and data collection. In 1994–1995, project funds allowed me to focus full time on the analysis of project data and the preparation of project articles. Project team members also secured supplementary funding to support surveys of staff and clients in the shelters from which we would recruit participants (UMass Boston, Russell Schutt, Principal Investigator[PI]), perform personality assessments (UMass Boston, Russell Schutt, PI), assess long-term housing outcome evaluation (UMass Boston, Russell Schutt, PI), evaluate housing and service cost assessment (NIMH, Barbara Dickey, PI), and perform a three-year follow-up neuropsychological assessment (NARSAD, Brina Caplan, PI). My continuing analyses of project data after the NIMH funding ended were facilitated by the Commonwealth of Massachusetts/Harvard Medical School Research Center (Larry J. Seidman, PI).

The federal funds we received have had multiple benefits. First and foremost, our project succeeded in securing funds with which to house 118 persons who had been homeless for periods that often exceeded ten years. Most of these project participants were still housed at the grant's end (for each subject, 1.5 years after initial housing placement). According to conditions stipulated by the federal government, these participants were then to be continued in DMH-funded housing. Later chapters describe participants' reactions to the project housing.

My colleagues and I have used the data we collected as the basis for two dozen articles and book chapters. These scholarly works answer questions about housing preferences, service satisfaction, housing retention, neuropsychological functioning, service costs, and consumer empowerment. Each makes a contribution to an important area of scholarship pertaining to mental illness and/or mental health services. Each takes advantage of a singularly strong feature of the extensive data we collected on our project participants. Due to the composition of our project team, the disciplinary foci of these articles and book chapters range from sociology, psychiatry, and psychology to anthropology and health policy.

But there is a whole that is much greater than the sum of these parts. My purpose in *Homelessness, Housing, and Mental Illness* is to present that whole. A researcher on consumer preferences may know we reported that our participants desired to live independently (Schutt and Goldfinger 1996), but she may not know that we also found that consumer preferences to live independently did not predict ability to live independently (Goldfinger et al. 1999). A student may have learned of the high rate of substance abuse in our sample (Goldfinger et al. 1996) but may not have read subsequently about the implications this had for gains in cognitive functioning (Caplan et al. 2006). Readers of *Evaluation and Program Planning* may know that our participants were very satisfied with the housing they received but would not know that housing satisfaction did not predict housing retention during or after the project (Schutt et al. 1997). Empowering social processes in our group homes have been described (Ware 1999), but other processes that undermined consumer empowerment have not yet been reported. Most importantly, our many separate analyses have not permitted attention to the larger sociological question of how social structure influences individual behavior.

This central question underlies many divergent currents in social thought and a good deal of social research. In order to answer it, I will weigh the relative importance for individual behavior of social situations—what people encounter—and individual dispositions—what they bring to social situations. Because we have been able to learn so much about the role of and interplay between situation and disposition in the setting we studied, our conclusions about housing outcomes have much more general implications. And there has been no social issue to which alternative situational and dispositional perspectives have been applied with more fervor than mental health services. Between a medical model of mental illness, with a focus on neurochemical processes and pharmacological cures, and a sociocentric model that emphasizes labeling processes and the effects of stigma, lies a wide chasm that has too often been avoided by those who contribute to scholarship on each side.

The diverse disciplinary backgrounds of our co-investigator team and the mixed methods we developed were never compatible with an either/or perspective. Building on this legacy, I have maintained a commitment to integrated scholarship and have used *Homelessness, Housing, and Mental Illness* to make many linkages between medical and social processes. My goal is to chart a more productive direction for social theory that recognizes that "social facts" never exist apart from psychological processes or physical bodies. Understanding the social world requires an integrated perspective, no matter how great the value in focusing attention on particular dimensions when we seek to answer narrow research questions. Just as recent discoveries in behavioral genetics have convinced many biologically oriented investigators that the action of genes can be expressed in interaction with social processes, so progress in sociological theory requires attention to the opportunities for and constraints on individual action that stem from psychological orientations and biological processes.

This book is not the first scholarly work to call for more integrated theorizing about mental illness. Like Bernice Pescosolido's (1992) "social organization strategy" and Bruce Link et al.'s (1989) "modified labeling perspective," the analytic framework developed in *Homelessness, Housing, and Mental Illness* contributes to an enriched and more consciously interdisciplinary sociological perspective whose time has come.

If *Homelessness, Housing, and Mental Illness* helps urban policy makers and mental health service providers develop new opportunities for housing homeless persons suffering from severe mental illness, it will have contributed to righting some of the unintended wrongs of prior social policy. If *Homelessness, Housing, and Mental Illness* contributes to the slowly increasing body of research about housing homeless persons with mental illness, it will have helped achieve the original goals of the Boston McKinney Project. But if, in addition, *Homelessness, Housing, and Mental Illness* convinces some readers of the value of integrated biopsychosocial perspectives on human behavior, it will have become part of a foundation for more ambitious social theory and more effective social programs.

Of course this preface, like the book itself, has a glaring omission from its discussion of homelessness and mental health services. Although I use various strands in economic and political theory to construct my explanations, I give very limited attention to the economic and political processes that shape labor and housing markets and resources and so constrain the major options for social programs and policies. This omission is intentional and reflects the basic parameters of the Boston McKinney Project: the combined $13.1 million that we received for our project allowed us to provide comfortable housing to all of our project participants without regard to their economic resources. This local infusion of federal funds forestalled what might in other contexts have become political battles over scarce resources. As is so often the case in evaluation projects, we had, for a time, an artificial laboratory in which some social processes were controlled so that others could be examined with greater intensity. I hope that the knowledge our project produced about social processes will make our neglect of economic and political processes understandable.

Inevitably, some will find another glaring omission in this book: I issue no call to action or suggestions for advocacy. I have identified many implications for social policy in the final chapter, but I take the position that these are issues for deliberative bodies to debate and for executive agencies to implement. By the time you finish *Homelessness, Housing, and Mental Illness,* I hope that you will understand my commitment to further research rather than public action. Many aspects of the problem of homelessness, like other complex social problems, are not so obvious after all. Some of the key assumptions that have guided new policies seem in light of our findings to be questionable. The views of mental health clinicians no less than those of advocates for mental health service consumers often reflect only partially the complex social processes in which they are embedded. Research like ours that allows some aspects of those processes to be controlled and other aspects to be deconstructed and reexamined yields a more comprehensive understanding that can produce more effective social policy. We could not be omniscient and all-knowing observers of this social world, but I believe that *Homelessness, Housing, and Mental Illness* offers new insights for social theory and new directions for social policy.

Russell K. Schutt

Acknowledgments

THE BOSTON MCKINNEY PROJECT was funded by the National Institute of Mental Health in 1990, #1R18MH4808001, and by the U.S. Department of Housing and Urban Development. I am profoundly grateful for the opportunity that these funds provided to investigate intensively social processes for an extended period of time and to help improve understanding of how best to help homeless persons with serious mental illness. Our proposal would not have been successful without the inspired leadership of Stephen M. Goldfinger, MD, who was the project's Principal Investigator, nor without the exceptional team of co-investigators assembled by Steve and the Massachusetts Department of Mental Health to craft the proposal and lead the project. In addition to me, the co-investigators were Larry J. Seidman, PhD, Barbara Dickey, PhD, Sondra Hellman, RN, Walter E. Penk, PhD, Martha O'Bryan, RN, and Norma Ware, PhD (who joined us after the grant was funded). I am grateful for the opportunity to work with each of them, and particularly to the ensuing years of intensive working and learning with Steve and Larry. Steve Goldfinger gave valuable feedback on many chapters, and his insights about mental health services helped particularly to shape the conclusions chapter. Larry Seidman's leadership of the project's neurocognitive assessment component, our coauthorship of several articles and this book's chapter on functioning, as well as our ongoing collaboration in research have provided the necessary foundation for our contributions in this book to scholarship on cognitive functioning

The team of junior (at the time) medical anthropologists we recruited for the project created an ethnographic record that proved to be essential for understanding the effect of the housing we provided, as reflected in this book. I am grateful to Norma Ware, PhD, the senior member of the team, and to Joshua Breslau, MPH, PhD, and Tara Avruskin, BA. There would have been no project data without talented research staff, and so I am also grateful for the research leadership of and years of friendship with Winston Turner, PhD, and George Tolomiczenko, PhD, as well as for other team members, including So-Young Lee, Tatjana Meschede, and Stewart Chalin. Bev Brooks and Mark Abelman played key roles in the delivery of project support services. Lois Mastrangelo provided consistent and good-humored administrative support.

I am most grateful to the Boston McKinney Project research participants, who agreed to be interviewed and observed for eighteen months (and some of them 18 years later in my long-term followup study) and thereby allowed many others to learn from their experiences as they moved into new housing and adapted to a new community. Also critical to the project's success were the many house staff employed during the project, the team of Clinical Homeless Specialists we hired to provide intensive case management services to project participants, and many Department of Mental Health case managers and other staff who responded to our participants' needs.

The Massachusetts Mental Health Center (MMHC), the Harvard Medical School, the Massachusetts Department of Mental Health and its Metro Boston office, several nonprofit service providers, including Vinfen, Inc., Bay Cove Human Services, and North Suffolk Human Services, and, later, the Beth Israel Deaconess Medical Center provided indispensable institutional resources for the project. I am grateful to each of these organizations and particularly to Miles F. Shore, MD, MMHC Director at the time the project began (and to his successor, Ming T. Tsuang, MD) and to Gerald J. Morrissey, director of the Metro Boston area of DMH. I was able to conduct the long-term housing followup study (chapter 10) thanks to the support of the current Metro Boston DMH director, Cliff Robinson, and his wonderful director of housing, Louise Marks, MSW.

Several students in the UMass Boston Graduate Program in Applied Sociology worked as research assistants on the original project or on several extensions of the project. They interviewed shelter staff and homeless persons in shelters, they entered and coded data, they conducted personality assessments and long-term follow-up interviews, and they coded ethnographic notes and case records. Some have joined me in related presentations, reports, or publications. I am profoundly grateful to each and every one of them—to an extent that is not recognized adequately by this simple listing of their names (or by the extent of my anxiety that I may have left some out). First and most recently, Anne Remington, who managed my long-term follow-up study and helped with the book's reference list, and Sonia Shirali, Jillian Doucette, Robin Myers, and Andrea Gnong, and Julia Schutt, who helped to code the ethnographic data.

My survey in the DMH shelters was made possible by Gerald J. Morrissey, former director of the Metro Boston Region of the Massachusetts Department of Mental Health, and other Metro administrators and staff, including Martha O'Bryan, Peggy Lester, Lucy Proia, and Bia Van Le, as well as LaMotte Hyman and the Metro Boston Homeless Outreach Team, the directors and staff of the DMH transitional shelters, and Walter E. Penk, Bill Alexander, John Flaherty, Stephanie Howard, Douglas Klayman, Jackie McKinney, Lydia Todd, and Dian Webber conducted interviews in the DMH shelters.

My contributions to the McKinney Project have been assisted by support from project funds—including a full-year paid sabbatical leave thanks to Stephen M. Goldfinger, MD (and the University of Massachusetts Boston)—as well as by several small grants from UMass Boston. I continue to be grateful to the University of Massachusetts Boston for these forms of support as well as for the professional environment it has provided throughout my academic career. I owe a special debt to Larry J. Seidman, PhD, who has supported my work in his role as Director of the Commonwealth of Massachusetts/Harvard Medical School Research Center. The book has benefited greatly from the extraordinary scholarly resources maintained by the librarians at Harvard University, as well as by those at UMass Boston—with special thanks to Janet Stewart for help with tracking down government documents.

I also have benefited from the assistance of the experts and program and shelter directors who helped me to build the research foundation for my contributions to the McKinney Project, including Richard Weintraub, Barbara Blakeney, RN, Suzanne Gunston, BSN, RN, Deborah Milbauer, LCSW, MPH, John O'Brien, and Ellen Bassuk, MD. The journal editors and reviewers whose feedback on many articles helped to sharpen my thinking about homelessness and mental illness also deserve a share of my gratitude.

My ongoing work with McKinney data has also benefited greatly from the supportive environment provided by successive chairs of Harvard's psychiatry departments at the Massachusetts Mental Health Center and the Beth Israel Deaconess Medical Center. In addition to Miles F. Shore, MD, and Ming T. Tsuang, MD, PhD, ScD, these are James C. Beck, MD, PhD, Mary Anne Badaracco, MD, and David C. Jimerson, MD.

I have incurred special debts in the process of writing this book. Most importantly, I am grateful to my editor at the Harvard University Press, Michael Aronson, for recognizing the book's potential and for providing ongoing advice and support, and to his talented assistants, first Hilary Jacqmin and then Heather Michele Hughes. Book production was managed artfully by Michael Haggett, production editor at Westchester Book Services and copy edited skillfully by Elissa L. Schiff. For detailed comments about particular chapters, the entire manuscript, or the prospectus and for their encouragement, I am profoundly grateful to Kai T. Erikson, Gerald Grob, Allan V. Horwitz, Joshua Breslau, Bernice Pescosolido, Susan L. Gore, Anthony F. Lehman, Dennis McCarty, Barbara Dickey, Sondra Hellman Caplin, James A. Hilliard, Mildred A. Schwartz, and the two anonymous reviewers of the entire manuscript recruited by Mike Aronson. Stephen M. Goldfinger, MD, sent comments on many chapters. Most importantly, his leadership during the Boston McKinney Projects for five years means that his commitment to improving housing and services for homeless persons with severe mental illness suffuses the entire book. Miles F. Shore, MD, deserves special acknowledgment as the illustrious leader of the Massachusetts Mental Health Center when the McKinney Project was funded and as a consistent source of advice and support as I developed the book project. I am also grateful to the University of Massachusetts Boston for providing a sabbatical semester as I began writing the book.

As always, I am grateful for the love and support of my wife, Elizabeth, and our daughter, Julia, and for the comments they both provided on book chapters.

Homelessness, Housing, and Mental Illness

CHAPTER ONE

A Point of Departure

SALLY PARKE[1] HEAVED two bags full of personal belongings into the back of a taxi in downtown Boston, slid into the back seat, and asked the driver to take her to 111 Cottage Avenue, in Dorchester. After preparing, and waiting, for five months, the actual six-mile trip on this warm April afternoon in 1991 seemed a bit anticlimactic. But when the cab drove up to her new home, Sally felt a surge of enthusiasm: she was leaving homelessness behind her at last. She paid the cabbie, dragged her bags up the stairs, and paused before opening the front door. This was not just any house—it was a nice, big colonial surrounded by a lawn in a quiet neighborhood. A familiar voice called out "Welcome to your new house, Sally." It was Charlene, but in this setting she sounded like an old friend rather than the coordinator at the shelter Sally had just left.

Fred Fielding had arrived a few hours earlier. His new case manager drove him directly to the house from his former shelter on an island in Boston's harbor. Fred had already had time to wander through the house and select a bright, airy bedroom on the third floor. Charlene introduced Sally to Fred and to the four house staff members who were sitting around the large dining room table. Sally recalled having seen Fred at the community mental health center where she received her medications each day, but she said nothing. By the time two more new tenants had arrived, and they all had enjoyed a house-warming pizza dinner, old encounters seemed far less important than new opportunities.

It was another two weeks until the rest of the Dorchester tenants had moved in, bringing the total to eight tenants and five daytime staff (with three more part-time staff during the evenings and through the night). By that time the tenants had all selected their bedrooms (two men shared one of them), divided up kitchen counter space and refrigerator shelves, and chosen preferred seats in the living areas. Staff, working in an office near the kitchen, had developed a fondness for the TV room on the first floor.

Over the next fifteen months a total of 118 homeless persons moved out of shelters financed by the Massachusetts Department of Mental Health (DMH) into permanent housing funded by the U.S. Department of Housing and Urban Development (HUD). Some moved into spacious multibedroom homes like the one at 111 Cottage Avenue; others found themselves in an apartment building on a floor that had been converted into a set of connected residences. About half moved into independent apartments without resident staff, albeit in buildings that already housed many elderly or disabled persons on government subsidies. A project ethnographer's initial observations in one McKinney apartment describes their typical amenities:

> His apartment, a studio, is surprisingly [in the words of a project ethnographer] large. There is a kitchen, a small living area equipped with table and chairs, a small sofa and easy chair, coffee table, TV, and clock radio. In the bedroom alcove there is a double bed and dresser; the bathroom is beyond. The place feels new and clean.

Although $10 million from HUD was to pay housing costs (including initial renovations) for only one and a half years, agreements signed by DMH guaranteed the tenants housing as long as necessary. When a new tenant asks whether the housing is permanent and is told that it is, "he is obviously relieved. 'Thank God,' he says."

Residential mobility is the norm, not the exception, in the United States. In the fifteen months before the 1990 U.S. Census, one-third of renter households in Massachusetts moved (U.S. Census Bureau 2008). But the 118 participants in the Boston McKinney Project had not just crossed a physical boundary in their move to a new home, nor had they just exchanged one set of neighbors for another. Much more significant than the few miles their moves had entailed was the social barrier they crossed from homelessness to being housed.

Returning to the Community

This is where our story begins, on the border between homelessness and housing, in the transition from institutional living to community residence. For periods ranging from a few months to more than ten years, Sally, Fred, and the other project participants had spent most of their nights in a homeless shelter or on the streets. In the institutional parlance, they were "guests" in a transitional status until they found more permanent accommodations. But in reality they had been living on the outskirts of human society and beyond the awareness of most Boston residents. Their shelters were on an island in Boston Harbor, in the basement of a public hospital building, in a mental health center's former gymnasium. These shelters were considerably better than other alternatives available to their "guests"— boxes in alleys, bathrooms in bus stations, beds in chaotic mass shelters; but even these special shelters for persons deemed seriously mentally ill were not places in which adults would "choose" to live. So to leave those shelters behind was to secure a place in the larger society—to become, again, part of a normal community.

The social significance of this residential transition was multiplied by the tenants' continuing status as Department of Mental Health clients. Although most would have been inpatients in a state psychiatric hospital thirty years previously, decades of deinstitutionalization ensured that inpatient status was a temporary experience for all but a very few public-sector clients (Upshur et al. 1997). Almost all of the project participants had been institutionalized at some point, but as soon as they had been "stabilized," they returned to the shelter, the streets, a friend's or family member's place; only rarely did they return to their own home in their own community. So by moving into a community residence provided by the Boston McKinney Project, each participant was doing his or her part to complete the process initiated with so much enthusiasm by passage of the federal Community Mental Health Centers Act in 1963 (Upshur et al. 1997, 200). Those who had left the back wards of hospitals only to find themselves in the back alleys of cities were finally able to walk in their own front door.

What were the consequences of this move back into housing, of this return to the community? To say that the participants were no longer homeless is to state the obvious, but that makes it no less important. For those who seek to help the homeless, there is no more necessary or laudable an achievement. Yet for those who seek to learn the lessons of this experience and to build more effective social policy, resting content with the knowledge that we had at least temporarily ended the homelessness of our participants is at best a failure of imagination; at worst, it is a lack of humanitarian concern. Did the participants change in other ways? Did they remain housed? Was everyone affected in the same way? How effective was the effort to develop community in the group homes? All of these questions must be addressed.

So when as social scientists we stand at this boundary between homelessness and housing, we must expand our vision to include past events, current processes, and a range of future possibilities. What from afar seems to be an imposed binary transition in a singularly important social status becomes, up close, part of an ongoing process in which people shape and are shaped by their social situations. We have much to learn from standing at this boundary, asking these questions, and examining these processes. We will return to this boundary repeatedly in *Homelessness, Housing, and Mental Illness*. We will learn much from what we find at this juncture: about our project participants' prior experiences and current desires; about the situation of being homeless that 5.3 percent of American adults had experienced at some point by 1990 (Jencks 1994, 106); and about the ways in which individuals are changed by and adapt to their circumstances.

Creating a Community

But our project participants did not just move from one social situation—living in a shelter—to another—residing in a home. Our design required that half the participants move into group homes, like the one at 111 Cottage Avenue, and the other half move into independent apartments. The social situation in the group homes included between seven and ten housemates, all drawn from the three shelters, as well as about ten staff—with some on duty at all times—and one project coordinator who visited each group home at least weekly. The independent apartments were all in large buildings with other low-income tenants, many of whom were elderly and/or disabled and therefore receiving housing subsidies. These buildings also included at least two, and sometimes as many as ten other project participants. All project participants were assigned a case manager who called or visited at least weekly to provide assistance and assess needs. However, the independent apartment residents had neither roommates nor residential staff, and they received no visits from the project coordinator. In these respects their new homes involved living independently in the community as do other single adults. How they spent their days, what they did in their apartments, whom they saw, and which friendships they made were largely up to them.

For the new tenants in independent apartments, "community" was outside their front door, in the surrounding neighborhood and in the opportunities it provided. But for those like Sally and Fred who moved into group homes, "community" also had another meaning: it was the goal and expectation of project staff that each group home would develop as a community, with mutually supportive relations between and among residents, shared decision making, and over the course of the project, decreasing need for staff input. In fact, these were not to be traditional service-oriented group homes in which staff plan activities, manage chores, administer medications, and do little to overcome resident passivity (Bigelow 1998; Suto and Frank 1994). The McKinney group homes were to be "evolving consumer households," with weekly tenant meetings to manage household affairs, rules determined by group consensus, and individual autonomy to decide daily activities and schedules.

So "community" has two meanings in *Homelessness, Housing, and Mental Illness*. It refers first to the larger social context surrounding the homes into which participants moved. It is this meaning that popular parlance most often attaches to "community," and it is in this sense that project participants returned to the community after many years of living apart. The second meaning of "community" in this book is even more important, for it focuses attention on the ability of participants to become active agents in shaping their futures rather than passive recipients of changes designed by others. Would the eight to ten participants in each group home create a community of peers as part of the foundation for their new future?

There was no guarantee that either effort would succeed. Although the project participants had moved into geographically and politically demarcated communities, the social gap between participants and their neighbors did not vanish. To have a history of street living, to be supported by government subsidies, to live with peers or elderly and disabled persons in a community of families and working adults is certainly to be set apart. Intensive, assertive case management programs to keep people with psychiatric disabilities living in the community provided more comprehensive services than those designated for our independent living (IL) residents (Carling 1995, 189).

Nor were the stars all aligned to ensure the success of community-building within the group homes. The closest model for the evolving consumer households (ECH) were the "intentional communities" founded by religious sects, communalists, utopian socialists, and escapists of various sorts in attempts to build tight-knit communities of believers to ward off or even transform the larger society (Kanter 1972; Vaisey 2007). None of these efforts has succeeded for long, but the extent that they do succeed is in no small part a result of shared beliefs and of restrictions imposed on outside influence. Efforts by psychiatrists to build intentional "therapeutic communities" have remained on the margins of mental health services (Rapoport 1960). The ECH tenants, by contrast, had not chosen to live in a group home and were united only by their desire for a stable residence. Far from being designed to keep the external world at bay, the ECH model was intended to facilitate integration with it. Thus, ECH tenants were to chart a new direction in group living.

Investigating Communities

The 118 McKinney project participants crossed one other boundary when they moved from various shelters into their new housing. Because they each agreed to become a research subject for the next eighteen months, we do not have to wonder how they managed in their new homes or what became of their goal of independence. With funding from the National Institute of Mental Health and other sources, our research team was able to ask participants about their experiences in the shelters, observe their behavior in the new houses, find out where they spent each day, and periodically record their attitudes. We learned about their homelessness in the past and the housing they hoped for in the future. We asked clinicians to assess their functioning and researchers to test their thinking.

We did not just observe our project participants passively but assessed them repeatedly. Although this level of scrutiny itself was unusual compared with many research projects, our participants also agreed to one other critical condition: they would not be allowed to choose the type of housing—group home or individual apartment—that they would receive. Sally and Fred moved into 111 Cottage Avenue not because it was their preferred mode of housing but because "the computer" had assigned them to the next available group home on the basis of a random process. And because of this, because neither the participants nor their clinicians were able to choose group or independent living, those who moved into one type of housing were, on average, the same at the time of their move as those who moved into the other type of housing.

This process of random assignment makes for quite a contrast with usual processes of housing acquisition. People living in the community normally move into housing that they have chosen—within the limitations of their economic resources, their awareness of alternatives, and various other constraints and preferences. People dependent on organized systems of care, whether the care involves mental health, criminal justice, or education, are often placed in housing on the basis of what the system determines that they "need"—subject to resource and other constraints. Not uncommonly some combination of what clients want and what they are judged to need shapes the type of housing they receive. But in none of these situations is the type of housing that people receive a matter solely of chance.

So our research design broke the usual links among housing preferences, needs, and type of housing received. During the eighteen months that they were enrolled in our study, we did not have to wonder whether participants did better in one type of housing because it was what they wanted, rather than what a clinician decided they needed. Nor were participants' housing assignments shaped by the amount of money they had in the bank, their earnings potential, or their review of rental ads. We leveled the economic playing field among participants as well as the usual association of desires and needs with the housing actually obtained. It is for this reason that we can focus attention on whether living in group or independent housing itself made a difference in the lives of residents.

Modeling Community Processes

Individuals' behavior is shaped by both their dispositions and the situations they encounter. Figure 1.1 diagrams these alternatives as influences stemming from persons and situations, that is, the relative influence on current behavior of individuals' preexisting dispositions as compared to the multitude of situational influences that come from without, rather than from within. When we wonder what in the past led to behavior in the present, we must weigh the influence of disposition and situation. When we ponder prospects for the future, we must balance individuals' desires against the situational constraints they face.

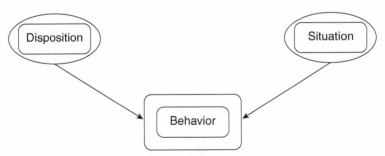

Figure 1.1. Dispositional and situational influences on behavior.

The alternative influences in figure 1.1 pertain in one way or another to the explanation of most social processes involving homelessness. With respect to the risk of becoming homeless, Johnson et al. (1997) posed these alternatives as *social selection* (or social disability or downward drift) theories (individual influence) and *social adaptation* (or social causation) theories.

David A. Snow, Leon Anderson, and Paul Koegel (1994) drew the same contrast between their favored social adaptation explanation of alcoholism and psychosis among homeless persons and the alternative social selection explanation: "much of the drinking behavior on the streets, including that which has gone awry. . . . represents ways in which individuals who find themselves trapped in demeaning social contexts attempt to stand 'apart from the role and the self' implied. . . . behaviors among the homeless . . . are frequently perceived as indicative of underlying dysfunctions" (p. 472).

These alternatives also figure in the disciplinary debate between economics and sociology about the meaning of consumer (and presumably any other) preferences. Ernst Fehr and Herbert Gintis (2007, 44) provide a pithy summary of these alternatives: "Homo Sociologicus, a creature who follows prevailing social norms without regard to self-interest" as compared to "Homo Economicus, a creature who is rational and purely self-regarding." So from this (exaggerated caricature of a) "sociological" perspective, the social situation is everything, the individual nothing; whereas from the standpoint of this (exaggerated caricature of an) "economic" perspective, the individual's dispositions are everything, the situation nothing. If these alternatives are considered as a research question, the issues become: "To what extent does society shape individuals' preferences, and how does it do so?" (Fehr and Gintis 2007, 45). In the earlier conception of sociologist Dennis Wrong (1961), the question is whether sociologists' "oversocialized conception" of people has banned from social theory recognition of individuals' diverse motives.

Thus, figure 1.1 provides a framework for considering alternative perspectives on preferences as well as on homeless persons' behavior. Psychiatrist Richard Lamb (1984, 901) pointed to individual disability behind homeless persons' service preferences: "[W]e are working with persons whose lack of trust and desire for autonomy cause them to not give their real names, to refuse our services, and to move along because of their fear of closeness, of losing their autonomy, or of acquiring a mentally ill identity."

By contrast, sociologist Catherine Ross (Ross et al. 2002, 77) emphasized psychological effects of dangerous situations: "rational actors making judgments under conditions of uncertainty theoretically should be more suspicious the higher the prevalence of true threat and the higher the cost of misplaced trust relative to the costs of erroneous mistrust."

The contrast between individualistic and situational perspectives extends to the design of a response to homelessness among persons diagnosed with serious mental illness. If the cause of the problem is largely situational, then the solution is structural, and support services are a secondary concern. As expressed by Blanch et al. (1988), the goal of residential services should be to assist all people with psychiatric disabilities to choose, obtain, and maintain normal housing.

But if individual disabilities have considerable influence, then services must be an important element in the response. "Normalized housing seems an unassailable goal for some individuals, but clinical realities can prevent its attainment. Although some individuals will initially benefit from normalized housing, others may require various degrees of structure, interpersonal intensity, and support" (Lipton et al. 2000, 486).

I will return to this conceptual model and to these alternative perspectives throughout *Homelessness, Housing, and Mental Illness*. I will examine in more detail the situation in the DMH shelters, the meaning of consumer preferences, the impact of disabilities, and the way in which our alternative housing structures and the social processes within them channeled and changed these influences. If this examination is successful, the conclusions derived should provide new insights into the meaning of and possibilities for the development of communities.

But too narrow a focus on individuals can miss the influence of the broader environment on the dispositions of the homeless and the situations they experience. Figure 1.2[2] models a broader focus in which patterns of interaction between patient and doctor, customer and salesman, or tenants and landlords are shaped by the social environment comprised of individuals, with their various motives and means, and the institutional environment that includes organizations, cultural values, and systems of stratification. People visit a doctor both because they believe they are sick and because the role of doctor is sanctioned by health care institutions. People purchase a particular car when they have the necessary desire and funds and because the auto industry and local dealerships provide a means to realize individuals' preferences. Children play in a school playground because of a seemingly innate desire to engage with their peers and the temporal and physical structure provided by the educational system. And community members move into a new residence based on their preferences and resources as well as the opportunities provided by the local housing market.

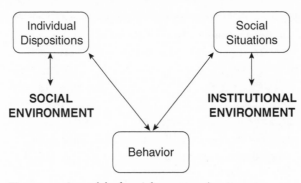

Figure 1.2. A model of social processes in context.

A single snapshot cannot reveal how social processes develop over time. Therefore figure 1.2 also focuses attention on the feedback processes that shape the social and institutional environments that result in patterned social interaction in the first place. In other words, in order to understand social processes at one point in time we need to know how individuals were affected by social processes in the past and by organizations that were influenced by those processes. A patient's interaction with a doctor may be particularly positive because of feelings generated by that individual's last interaction or by the support provided by another member of the patient's social network. A doctor's interaction with a patient may be shaped by a hospital quality-improvement program begun in response to an advocacy organization reacting to patients disgruntled by previous interactions. To analyze social processes from the formation of a social protest to the growth of a community requires identifying these different entities and pathways, examining their influences, and understanding their interactions.

Although *Homelessness, Housing, and Mental Illness* focuses on only a small portion of this comprehensive model, the elements of my investigation of social process should be understood within this larger context. Figure 1.1 highlights an aspect of social reality that underlies a difficult policy question: To what extent are individuals or situations responsible for particular social patterns? Figure 1.2 reminds us that we cannot hope to understand this reality or to answer this question without investigating the more complex relationships it identifies: The behavior we observe at one point in time may reflect individual dispositions that were in turn shaped by feedback from past situations.

Throughout the book, I test for effects of the different situations we imposed—our group and individual housing alternatives—on attitudes and behavior. We will also learn at points about the impact of the larger social and institutional environment. The resulting analyses answer, for this context, three interrelated research questions:

1. How do people choose a social environment?
2. How is the social environment constructed?
3. What is the impact of the social environment?

These are not the only questions suggested by figure 1.2, but the social environment and related processes are the factors on which our research design focused. Because we largely held the institutional environment constant during the project, my analyses of its effects are necessarily limited. Because we provided only specific housing alternatives, we constrained participants' ability to influence their social situation and so cannot assess the extent to which our participants might have developed group living arrangements or found independent apartments on their own—although within the context of the group homes I explore the extent to which participants developed "community" and so constructed their social environment in that sense.

Overview of the Project

The contributions made by *Homelessness, Housing, and Mental Illness* result both from the distinctive features of our research project and from the way I have used these features in this book.

Randomized design with longitudinal follow-up. Randomization allowed us to distinguish the influence of people's housing preferences from the influence of the type of housing that they received. Neither consumers' desires to live independently nor clinicians' concerns that they have group support had any bearing on the type of housing into which subjects moved. Randomization—using chance, the toss of a coin, to assign participants to treatment conditions—allowed us to test whether living in group or independent housing influenced outcomes over and above any influence of housing preferences or clinician-assessed needs. In the usual operation of service systems, the type of housing that people receive is shaped to some extent by their preferences as well as by clinicians' evaluations of their needs—as well as by the availability of particular housing opportunities. The funding for our two houses and our ability to assign participants to them randomly allowed us to overcome this constraint. The value of randomization is described in detail in the methodological appendix.

But this randomized design would have had little value for understanding community processes if we had just checked in with people after they had completed the eighteen months in their new housing. Whatever physical structures people confront, whatever social structures are defined in staff manuals, people are active agents in the creation of the social world that they experience. We can understand the meaning of "community" for our research participants only by learning how they contributed to its creation over time. By following every research participant for eighteen months after the move into housing, by checking in with some many years later, and by observing them within houses as well as testing them at multiple time points, we were able to move away from still photos of our participants at a particular time to a moving picture of their social experience.

Mixed methods. We cannot hope to understand the social world as people experience it if we only ask them questions whose answers we code on an arbitrary scale from 1 to 5. Nor can we hope to capture the complex ways in which people may orient themselves to the social world by classifying them only in predefined medical categories, personality types, or socioeconomic strata. Qualitative research methods help investigate alternative meanings and explore social processes. Yet understanding a complex social reality and testing alternative explanations also require methods that transcend the limitations of what can be observed directly or personally reported. Systematic measurement and structured comparisons allow rigorous assessment of differences between people and the consequences of social structures. It is because the Boston McKinney Project used methods ranging from experimental design, structured surveys, and diagnostic interviews to ethnographies and observer reports that *Homelessness, Housing, and Mental Illness* became possible. Using mixed methods allows us to see the big picture and identify unobserved processes. The appendix on methodology provides more details on the specific different methods used.

Multisite comparisons. The six different McKinney projects were funded by NIMH in order to provide different perspectives on the same research question, so there was much to be gained by coordinating these projects. Although one project soon ended because of organizational difficulties, NIMH sponsored meetings among investigators from the remaining five projects to share experiences and coordinate methods. The five research teams agreed to use a core set of measures and to share results with each other. (The methodological appendix provides more details about the other McKinney projects.) As a result, *Homelessness, Housing, and Mental Illness* includes some comparative information about homeless persons and treatment effects in Boston and the other cities that hosted McKinney projects. I also compare our results to those obtained in other investigations of housing for homeless persons.

No methods can discern every feature of or process in the social world, nor can results obtained with one sample be generalized with confidence to all other times and places. For these reasons, *Homelessness, Housing, and Mental Illness* raises more questions than it answers, and it leaves answering them to future investigations that will provide comparable insights into other settings with different people. It is important to bear in mind that we have focused attention on only one segment of the homeless population and one type of response to their needs. Yet our investigation of housing 118 homeless persons diagnosed with serious mental illness has some very tangible advantages that allow an important contribution to sociological scholarship.

Social theory. "Community" is a central concept in sociology; in fact, it could be argued that it was *the* central concept at the time of the discipline's founding. Each of the theorists whose work provided the enduring foundation for the discipline, from Ferdinand Tönnies and Emile Durkheim to Karl Marx and Max Weber, were concerned by what they perceived as the eclipse of traditional communities in the modernizing societies of late nineteenth or early twentieth century Europe. They differed in their descriptions of the past, in their prognoses for the future, in the particular aspects of the trends that they highlighted, and in the methods that they used; but each theorist, in his own way, viewed investigation of the decline of community as a means for elucidating the impact of social structure and elaborating the social processes through which that impact occurred. And each saw the fundamental challenge for modern society as replacing the "ties that bind" individuals within community structures.

In the ensuing century, this central foundation has given rise to a remarkable array of theoretical approaches and empirical investigations. Some theories have attempted to explain individual behavior on the basis of individual motives, whereas others focus on the decisive impact of group process. Behavior within psychiatric hospitals and other "total institutions" has been explained as, in part, resulting from separation from the larger community. The social ties that comprise community experience have been linked to psychological well-being and community control. Behavioral difficulties of individuals have been explained with stigmatizing processes that exclude people from social groups. The concept of community itself has been reconsidered and reinvigorated by this body of scholarship. I will draw on much of this theorizing and associated research to develop a comprehensive explanation for the social processes in the Boston McKinney Project housing.

Interdisciplinary scholarship. Homelessness is a human problem; "community" is a lived experience. To understand these features of the social world we must learn how people think about their experiences, what motivates them to act, how they interact with others, and what happens when they take medications, consume addictive substances, or become hospitalized. We need for this purpose the insights of sociology and psychology, of psychiatry and medicine, for we need to understand thoughts as well as behavior, minds as well as bodies. Although the research questions that are the focus of *Homelessness, Housing, and Mental Illness* are squarely within the discipline of sociology, I frequently cross disciplinary boundaries in order to develop comprehensive answers to these questions. Oftentimes, the book's chapters will show how psychological experience must be understood within a social context and how "social facts" are constituted in part by psychological processes. This approach is possible due to the interdisciplinary team that designed the Boston McKinney Project and the resulting rich array of measures and methods that it included. We measured social support and cognitive functioning, service usage and medication dosage, personality and psychiatric diagnosis, personal preferences and clinical assessments, and self-reported and observed behavior. Throughout *Homelessness, Housing, and Mental Illness,* I will draw on theories and measures from different disciplines to investigate the social world.

Applied research. The National Institute of Mental Health funded our project because we proposed to help answer an important question for social policy: What type of housing would be most helpful for persons who have been homeless and have been diagnosed as severely mentally ill? Our research thus falls squarely within the category of evaluation research, which applies the methods of social research to questions about public policy. In many project publications, the Boston McKinney Project research team has provided practical answers to many different versions of this basic evaluation research question. By crossing repeatedly in this book the inchoate but symbolically significant boundary between basic and applied social science, I have attempted to enrich scholarship and raise scholarly standards. I have not been content with a demonstration that two measures have a statistically significant correlation or that a hypothesis derived from an accepted theory is not supported by the evidence. Instead, I have also considered whether responses in formal interviews were consistent with patterns of social interaction and how group process influenced achievement of service goals.

I do not find merit in the assertion that social science is best served when researchers ignore the practical origins of their research questions or the policy implications of their results. The connection between social science and society is a two-way street that functions best when traffic flows easily in both directions. Because *Homelessness, Housing, and Mental Illness* builds on a solid body of social science research and theory, it has many implications for social policy. Because *Homelessness, Housing, and Mental Illness* emerges from applied research about practical problems, I have had to draw on a range of methods and a mix of social theories. Ultimately, the project's applied concerns force ongoing attention to what can be learned about peoples' lives as they experience them and to what can improve them.

It is fitting that issues related to homelessness and mental illness provide the substantive focus of an attempt to build integrated social theory that is both interdisciplinary and applied, for the 1980s conjunction of these problems can be understood as, in part, a result of the divergence of psychiatric and sociological perspectives. The policy of deinstitutionalization—closing state psychiatric hospitals—was motivated in part by psychiatrists' beliefs in the efficacy of newly discovered psychotropic medications. If medication could control symptoms of mental disorder, why could patients not return to the community and control their illness with visits to a doctor and continued medication—just as others control chronic physical ailments? There was little attention to the likely effect of social context on treatment compliance, or drug efficacy, or on the social side effects of psychotropic medication.

Drawing on an entirely different disciplinary tradition, sociologists like Erving Goffman were appalled by the oppressive conditions they observed in state psychiatric hospitals and by the conjunction they found between these conditions and the lethargic and bizarre behaviors of psychiatric patients. If ending this apparently iatrogenic situation removed the cause of psychiatric symptoms, why should patients not be reintegrated in community settings? There was little attention to the possibility that endogenous neurobiological processes might themselves limit social functioning.

The unintended consequences of the resulting policy of deinstitutionalization did not become apparent to the American public until another well-intentioned social policy transformed many U.S. cities. Demolition of Skid Row districts and their marginal single-room occupancy hotels was touted as a progressive step to improve city centers and attract higher-income residents. But one effect of this transformation was to displace the most precariously housed individuals and to limit options for keeping them out of the public eye. The concept of community integration was replaced by the reality of community displacement. It is through applied research like the Boston McKinney Project that a more comprehensive understanding of the effects of programmatic alternatives can be gained and thus more effective social policy developed.

Overview of the Book

This first chapter has introduced the research project, the research questions, and the conceptual models and research methods that have shaped the entire book. It can serve as a point of reference in subsequent chapters.

"Community" has been a central sociological concept since the discipline's founding. More recently, sociologists have focused attention on the factors that influence the development of social ties, the fundamental "glue" that holds communities together. Chapter 2 draws on the rich literature about these issues to explicate our goal of building community in the group homes and to anticipate the social processes that my colleagues and I hoped it would generate. I also introduce the approaches community psychiatrists have developed to further integration in communities through models of supported housing for individuals. Throughout chapter 2 the different styles of social organization that Ferdinand Tönnies captured in his distinction between community—*Gemeinschaft*—and society—*Gesellschaft*—provide a point of reference.

Chapter 3 reviews the history of homelessness and mental illness in the United States in order to link our research questions and answers to the context of the American social and mental health service institutions that shaped them. The situation in the shelters from which we recruited participants and the dispositions of the guests who used the shelters are described. The description draws on an ethnographic study in one of the shelters (Desjarlais 1997) and on surveys conducted with both shelter staff and shelter guests.

The analyses in chapter 4, on residential preferences and housing satisfaction, help to answer the first of the three general research questions: *How do people choose their social environment?* Two specific questions are asked that are at the heart of attempts to provide consumer-driven services and to normalize mental health treatment: "What do consumers of mental health services want?" and "How do they react to the services they receive?" To many service recipients and their advocates, the answers to these questions should be as obvious as they are to business people who design a product: what consumers prefer is by definition what they need, and they will be most satisfied if this is what they receive.

But these "obvious" answers challenge the professional ideology that has dominated mental health services in particular, and health care more generally, throughout the past century. The presumption that "the doctor knows best" was more than an ideology of a bygone elitist period; it was and still is an institutionalized pattern supported by training programs, professional associations, ethical codes, and popular culture. Nor has popular support for professional standards simply been replaced by enthusiasm for market-based solutions. Graduate schools continue to train doctors and other health care professionals; a medical license is still required to dispense medication; and there are regular program reviews to maintain professional standards. The professional model still casts a long shadow over institutionalized expectations. So the Project team also measured the housing recommended for project participants by informed clinicians and, in chapter 4, I compare their recommendations to the consumer's own preferences. This contrast between consumer preferences and clinician recommendations serves as a key analytic distinction throughout the book.

The center of figure 1.2 is the focus of chapter 5, on social relations in the group homes that describe participants' behaviors as they interacted with each other, participated in meetings, engaged with house staff, and attempted to develop a community. The empowerment coordinator who visited the group homes and encouraged this process has a key role in this chapter, but the primary focus is on how—or how much—a new social structure emerged from tenants' interaction with each other and with house staff. Together with the next three chapters, the analysis in chapter 5 helps to answer the second research question: *How is the social environment constructed?*

Both the causes and effects of substance abuse and mental illness, even the meaning of these maladies among persons who are homeless, are continuing sources of debate in the popular press as well as among social scientists. Given apparently high rates of substance abuse and disordered behavior among homeless single adults, the debate has focused on the question of whether these are consequences of the deprived situation in which homeless persons live or individual pathologies that increase vulnerability to housing loss. Prior research has also explored the behavioral consequences of substance abuse and mental illness, as well as the consequences of the conjunction of the two. I examine these issues in chapters 6 and 7 with quantitative analyses of our multiple measures as well as with a qualitative description of the impact of substance abuse and psychiatric symptoms on social interaction in our group homes.

A rapidly growing body of neuropsychological research has identified different dimensions of cognitive functioning and distinguished them from psychiatric symptoms. With McKinney co-investigator Larry Seidman, I examine in chapter 8 our project participants' neuropsychological functioning and test for changes in cognitive functioning over time as a result of experience in the project's alternative housing environments. We also describe the participants' daily functioning as they organized and carried out chores and other living tasks and examine the relations among these various aspects of functioning and the challenges posed by substance abuse and mental illness.

Chapters 9 and 10 analyze the two central outcomes of the Boston McKinney Project—consumer empowerment and housing retention—to answer the third research question: *What is the effect of the social environment?* Both chapters supplement the analysis of new data with a review of pertinent findings presented in chapters 4–8. Chapter 9 focuses on the project's attempt to "empower" tenants in the group homes, first reviewing previous research specifically on empowerment and then introducing our project's extensive ethnographic data about the empowerment process. Chapter 10 adds a unique, integrated analysis of housing loss that ties together the processes depicted in the preceding chapters. It focuses attention on the influence of the project's housing alternatives on housing retention in comparison to the influence of consumer housing preferences, clinician recommendations, substance abuse, mental illness, and cognitive functioning. This analysis includes housing outcome data collected almost 20 years after the project began as well as some comparative data on housing retention in the other four McKinney projects.

Chapter 11 returns to the theorizing in chapter 12, and revisits the historical review in chapter 3. I review the conceptual models in this chapter and their implications for mental health services in light of our findings and offer policy recommendations, theoretical implications, and suggestions for further research.

Research findings are only as good as the research methods on which they are based. The appendix provides the necessary methodological background for my presentation of research findings throughout the book. First, attention focuses on the rationale for our use of a randomized, experimental design; it then emphasizes the value of the measures collected. The multiple disciplines represented in the research team, our $3.1 million research grant from the National Institute of Mental Health (and some additional supplementary funding), and the dedication of our large project staff allowed collection of an exceptionally large and complex set of measures. My review of related literature indicates what the instrument package can contribute as well as what questions cannot be answered. Because the analysis I present is longitudinal, I also document our success in retaining project participants throughout the research process. The descriptions of both our project participants and the process by which we selected them allow points of comparison to other studies of homeless persons diagnosed with serious mental illness.

CHAPTER TWO

Community in Theory

W HEN THEY MOVED into permanent housing, the McKinney subjects returned to the community and achieved, for themselves, the
primary goal of deinstitutionalization. The contrast between the situation
that characterized their immediate past and the one that was imminent in
their future was dramatic. No matter how comfortable and safe the DMH
shelters were relative to the streets and mass shelters, they harbored a
seemingly self-perpetuating cycle of community disengagement and individual disempowerment.

As we learn in the next chapter, this was not how the shelters' homeless
"guests" said they wanted to live. Nor was a relatively permanent shelter
life acceptable to the mental health agency that funded the DMH shelters
to provide "transitional" accommodations. But what type of goal did "returning to the community" represent? Would community integration best be
achieved by placing homeless persons diagnosed with serious mental illness directly in apartments, so that they could live on their own and come
and go as they pleased? In this way project participants would live like
most others and attain in their living arrangements the goal of normaliza-
tion of treatment. Or would there be value in their continuing to live with
others and attempting to develop shared responsibilities and a sense of community within the group housing? The group housing arrangement would
distinguish residents from most others in the surrounding community—it
would not be entirely normal—but it would provide professional and

social supports that could in turn improve residents' ability to manage in that larger community.

Although our project was the first to use an experimental, randomized design to compare direct placement in independent apartments to group-home living, the relative merits of independent and group living have long been debated. In a volume summarizing findings from the National Institute of Mental Health–funded "Neighborhood and Family Services Project" in the 1970s, psychiatrist and Maryland mental health agency administrator Stanley R. Platman (1982) referred to both positions in this debate: "Although it is important for the neighborhood to integrate this population into the social and recreational network of the community, it is also important to recognize that the chronically mentally ill may require and want their own support system" (p. 200).

In their introduction to that same book, editors David E. Biegel and Arthur J. Naparstek (1982) put these alternatives in a broader, historical perspective: "At times the community has been the problem, at other times it has been the solution" (p. xix).

In terms of our project, the question is: Could enhanced support within the community of the group homes help to solve problems posed by the larger community outside of those homes?

This chapter examines the concept of community both as sociologists have used it to characterize one type of social organization and as psychiatrists have highlighted it as a goal for the residential placement of persons with chronic mental illness. A review of the history of "intentional communities" and "therapeutic communities" will anticipate the possibilities for and limitations of the McKinney group homes. Describing how researchers have understood the needs of persons with psychiatric disabilities living in community settings will identify some of the challenges McKinney participants might be expected to face in meeting those needs.

The Ideal of Community

The ideal of community served early sociologists both as a point of departure when explaining societal change and as a point of emphasis when differentiating sociology from other disciplines. In his 1887 treatise, *Community and Civil Society,* Ferdinand Tönnies (2001) defined community, *Gemeinschaft,* as "based on the idea that in the original or natural state there is a complete unity of human wills . . . direct mutual affirmation found in most intense form in relations between mother and child, man and wife, and siblings. . . . Community life means *mutual* possession and enjoyment, and possession and enjoyment of goods held *in common*" (pp. 22, 36).

The early twentieth-century American sociologist Charles Horton Cooley (1962) claimed a necessary connection between human beings and group living. "Human nature is not something existing separately in the individual, but a *group nature*. . . . Man does not have it at birth; he cannot acquire it except through fellowship, and it decays in isolation" (Kanter 1972, 30).

What drew the early sociologists' attention was not simply this appealing *Gemeinschaft* imagery of community but its increasing absence in the newly industrializing and urbanizing Europe and the United States. Tönnies (2001, 52) described social relations in modern society, *Gesellschaft,* as "the exact opposite of what happens in *Gemeinschaft*": ". . . everyone is out for himself alone and living in a state of tension against everyone else. . . . Nobody wants to do anything for anyone else." Concern about the loss of community and its consequences has remained high on the disciplinary agenda ever since.

Forming Communities

The ideal of *Gemeinschaft*-type communities has stimulated research by sociologists who seek to identify the conditions for its emergence. Some psychiatrists have seen therapeutic potential in this ideal and have tried to develop special communities to achieve that potential.

Sociology

It was in the interstices of modern society, not in its primary structures, that American sociologists continued to find evidence of, and hope for, the community ideal. Rosabeth Kanter's (1972) historical study of "intentional communities"—communes and utopias—set the agenda for most subsequent investigations. Defining these communities as "voluntary, value-based, communal social orders," Kanter (1972, 2, 3) found that their key goals were "harmony, brotherhood, mutual support, and value expression," while "[m]aintaining the sense of group solidarity is as important as meeting specific goals." Like Tönnies's *Gemeinschaft* ideal, the utopian communities valued "mutually expressive, supportive, value-oriented, emotion-laden, personally-directed, loving social relations" (Kanter 1972, 148–49).

Several features appeared consistently in the most successful communes. In order to maintain themselves for a long period, communes needed an elaborate ideology, strong leaders as well as high levels of member participation in decisions, fixed daily work routines and personal conduct rules, and ideological conversion as a prerequisite for admission (Kanter 1972, 127). Stephen Vaisey (2007) tested more systematically some of these potential internal influences on developing *Gemeinschaft*-like communities. In a sample of fifty urban communes ideological unity was associated strongly with the *Gemeinschaft* quality of the communes, but frequent social interaction, strong leadership, and time commitments were also necessary. Social homogeneity of the membership, in terms of age, education, and social class, had no relationship with communes' *Gemeinschaft* qualities.

Rosabeth Kanter (1972, 148–49) also examined the ways in which communes interacted with the larger social environment. Commune boundaries had to be somewhat permeable, allowing friends, family members, goods, and/or services to enter and leave; like all organizations, they experienced pressures to conform to extant structures around them; they often suffered value indeterminacy due to a multiplicity of ends and/or an emphasis on means rather than ends; and their perpetuation could be endangered by problems in leader succession and member recruitment (Kanter 1972, 150–57). These "*Gesellschaft* elements," although necessary, tended to undermine maintenance of the community ideal.

These analyses suggest the importance of both internal and external processes in affecting the survival of intentional communities. The external processes can be understood in terms of figure 1.2. A small, homogeneous population, particularly one with only kin-based, ideological, and affective ties, is fertile social soil for a *Gemeinschaft* style of community. By contrast the social environment created by a large, heterogeneous population with diverse roles and instrumentally based ties is consistent with a *Gesellschaft* style of community, therefore lessening the survival chances of the *Gemeinschaft* style.

The institutional environment—the world of business and industry, of educational establishments and state legislatures, of organized charities and established religion—generates pressures that can undermine *Gemeinschaft*. Tönnies's model of *Gesellschaft*—modern society—presupposed development of an institutional environment, for there was little of that in early human societies. The institutional environment creates pressures for *institutional isomorphism* or conformity to the patterns and norms of prevailing institutions (DiMaggio and Powell 1983). Whether they are communes or churches, organizations that need credit must conform to certain accounting requirements in order to qualify for a bank loan. Whether they are charities, schools, or small businesses, organizations that seek to be certified as legitimate and trustworthy must open their books and agree to review by representatives of the institutional environment. Government policies and the legal system enshrine and enforce these pressures.

So in a larger social world characterized by *Gesellschaft* patterns of social organization, any effort to develop and maintain a *Gemeinschaft*-style community will face many challenges. As Kanter's research on communes suggests, and as investigations by other sociologists on related organizational processes confirm, no organization or community can escape these environmental pressures (Gouldner 1954; Lipset, Trow, and Coleman 1962; Russell 1985; Schutt 1986). Both the imposing state psychiatric hospitals of the nineteenth century and the emergency mass shelters of the late twentieth century were products of the institutional environments at the times they were founded.

Of course the very concept of an "intentional community" can be thought of as an oxymoron that further highlights the disjuncture between the ideal of community and the reality of modern society.[1] True communities arise from ongoing face-to-face interaction among community members that is not "intentional" at all. To seek community through conscious effort is to recognize that it is no longer a naturally occurring form of social organization. But that is what must be done if members of modern societies are to achieve the *Gemeinschaft* ideal.

Psychiatry

The ideal of *Gemeinschaft*-like communities also captured the attention of psychiatrists after World War II. Based on their experience with group-oriented treatment of traumatized soldiers, some British hospital-based psychiatrists developed a model of treatment and rehabilitation that came to be known as the "therapeutic community" approach (Rapoport 1960). Rather than emphasizing the relationship between patient and therapist, the therapeutic community approach highlighted the importance of the total social environment and the value of patients helping each other to heal.

> [T]he hospital is seen not as a place where patients are classified and stored, nor a place where one group of individuals (the medical staff) gives treatment to another group of individuals (the patients) according to the model of general medical hospitals; but as a place which is organized as a community in which everyone is expected to make some contribution towards the shared goals of creating a social organization that will have healing properties. (Rapoport 1960, 10)

Principles espoused for therapeutic communities echoed sociologists' descriptions of intentional communities. Rex Haigh (1999) highlighted their "five universal qualities":

1. Attachment: an emphasis on belonging in the group.
2. Containment: provision of a safe environment for unconventional behavior.
3. Communication: openness about feelings and interchange with all group members.
4. Involvement: learning through living in the group and confronting problems openly in meetings.
5. Agency: encouraging empowerment through democratic, egalitarian decision making.

Research suggested more positive outcomes for in-hospital and community-based treatment programs having qualities like those valued in therapeutic communities (Moos 1997). The therapeutic-community approach—"community as method"—has also been used to treat substance abuse, again with some positive reports of outcomes (Hanson 2002; Yablonsky 1989).

Modeling Community

Communities and organizations can and do seek to limit environmental influences that disrupt the social patterns that founders and members desire to maintain. As represented by the reverse arrow from behavior to social situations in figure 1.2, people may "push back" against environmental influences. As reflected in the research on communes, one way to limit environmental influence is *boundary management:* members are admitted to the community only if they meet requirements or are expelled when they violate collective expectations. Alternatively, the community or organization can limit undesirable environmental influence with social control efforts that maintain desired patterns of social interaction within the organization irrespective of initial member diversity. The positive effect of strong leadership for the survival of intentional communities reflects the value of these social control efforts (Kanter 1972).

Socialization of members is a more flexible approach to limiting environmental influence than either boundary management or overt social control by leaders. If socialization processes are effective, members from diverse backgrounds with different orientations can be "molded" by community or organizational processes to the type of strong ideological beliefs that were so effective in maintaining *Gemeinschaft* within Kanter's (1961) sample of intentional communities and Vaisey's (2007) urban communes.

These problems and possibilities are summarized in figure 2.1. Tönnies's *Gemeinschaft* model of community is adapted to a relatively

Functional Differentiation

		Low	High
	Homogeneous	Community (Gemeinschaft) (Mechanical Solidarity) (A)	Social Control or Socialization (B)
	Heterogeneous	Boundary Management (C)	Society (Gesellschaft) (Organic Solidarity) (D)

Social Diversity (Low / High)

Figure 2.1. Organizational implications of functional differentiation and social diversity.

homogeneous social environment in which functional differentiation is low (cell A). This is Emile Durkheim's "mechanical solidarity": similar people perform similar functions. By contrast, Tönnies's *Gesellschaft* model of "society" presumes social diversity and functional differentiation—Durkheim's "organic solidarity" on the basis of interdependence (cell D). In this framework, the social transition that the early sociologists were observing from traditional patterns of community-based social organization to modern society represented a shift in the dominant patterns of social relations from cell A in figure 2.1—"community" to cell D—"society."

When the larger social world is characterized by social heterogeneity, it creates a challenge for communal organization. Communities may try to maintain the conditions for *Gemeinschaft* organization through boundary management: excluding potential members or expelling current members who are not "like" others in critical respects (cell C). On the other hand, when society provides different functions that need to be performed and yet the population tends to be homogeneous, society can attempt to adapt members to different roles through socialization or overt social control (cell B). This can lead to a stable, reinforcing social pattern if members are socialized to desire different roles and/or if they feel required to fulfill different roles due to the threat of sanction (social control).

Organizations may use various combinations of explicit social control efforts, socialization, and boundary management as they seek to maintain or develop a *Gemeinschaft* style. Although members may have to spend their days engaged in diverse roles, they still may be required to wear identical clothing, listen to their leader's inspirational speeches, read the same religious tracts, and obey the same rules. Such explicit social control both encourages conformity and can gradually change member dispositions through a process of socialization. Members who resist these strategies may ultimately be expelled, thus increasing member homogeneity. The two axes in figure 2.1 thus represent potentially interrelated continua, rather than simply four discrete and mutually exclusive states.

Groups can use several internal social control processes to improve cohesiveness: promoting cooperation, punishing lack of cooperation, and encouraging sharing of resources (Cacioppo and Patrick 2008, 206, 207). These processes can "affect behavior by shaping norms, enforcing patterns of social control, providing or not providing opportunities to engage in particular behaviors, and either producing or reducing stress" (Cacioppo and Patrick 2008, 101) If they fail at this task, membership apathy and withdrawal from interaction are likely (Mills 1984, 96–98; Turner 1988, 69).

Laboratory experiments indicate how social control processes can shape group cohesion. Although a majority of persons will cooperate to achieve group goals if others do, a considerable minority—perhaps one-third—will not contribute to the group themselves if left to their own devices: they are "free riders." If this occurs—if there are many "free riders"—group cooperation declines over time as others decide that it is not worth their while to contribute. However, if the "free riders" are punished for their deviance, cooperation within the group can be maintained (Fehr and Gintis 2007, 50). Members develop a sense of equity or fair treatment (Hatfield 1983). This social control process is most effective when relations within the group persist over time, and so members learn what they can expect for cooperation or deviance (Fehr and Gintis 2007, 57). "[I]nteractions will, over time and when repeated, develop their own frameworks that are unique to the setting where the interaction occurs. . . . Actors thus have a fund of shared cognitions about the world [and each others' roles in it] that greatly facilitates interaction" (Turner 1988, 105, 115).

Boundary management through selective admission and/or expulsion can also increase intragroup homogeneity and thus the potential for group cohesion (Festinger, Schachter, and Back. 1950, 174–75). Groups with strong boundaries set themselves apart from their environment and thereby can increase member commitment (Kanter 1983).

Both boundary management and overt social control efforts are limited as strategies for maintaining community in the face of social heterogeneity. Boundary management is only as effective as the organization's ability to attract enough of the appropriate type of members and to exclude those who prove not to fit in. These practices are of limited value in a very diverse social environment or when external regulations prevent enforcing the desired entry or expulsion standards. Strong overt social control efforts that require similar behavior in a diverse membership can create grievances that undermine organizational continuity (Schutt 1986).

In theory, socialization processes can avoid the problems with boundary management and social control strategies by shaping member orientations to match collective needs. The "oversocialized" conception that has guided much sociological theory presumes that people are almost infinitely malleable through socialization processes (Wrong 1961). Viewed in terms of figure 1.2, this is equivalent to believing that the influence of the "social situations" easily overwhelms that of preexisting individual "dispositions." Rosabeth Kanter (1972) captured the essence of this perspective in a statement about the utopian communities she studied:

> The primary utopian idea is human perfectibility. Utopians believe that tension, conflict, and disharmony derive from the environment, from social conditions outside the individual, not from sources within him. Societies, not people, are the cause of human problems. People are basically good but have been corrupted by society. Inner conflicts are merely a reflection of environmental tensions. It would thus be possible to perfect man and to bring about a higher order of human life by establishing the right environmental conditions. (33)

There was little question that many communitarians believed that this potential for situational influence extended to the "problem" of mental illness (Kanter 1961, 236–237):

> Utopian visions of social reconstruction supply an antidote to the pervasive assumption that "sick" or deviant individuals are both the source and the symptom of social problems. ... ... Social problems, according to this view, are a function of structural defects in society and can be solved only by constructing a new society or by reshaping social institutions. (236–37)

This utopian view of community as a solution to social problems and the recognition that community processes could shape individual behavior led many enthusiasts to overlook the potential problems with intentional communities. The same social processes that can support individuals can also give rise to conflict and distress (Moos 1997, 173). As one somewhat relevant example, Amy Siskind (2003) chronicled the degeneration of a radical therapeutic community of psychoanalysts and patients in New York City into a repressive, hierarchical organization in which members' actions and talk were closely monitored, nonmarital sexual relations were encouraged, and parent–child relations were distorted.

So the sociological literature on the value of "community" provides a scholarly foundation for the policy of offering "evolving consumer households" and for the hope that they would develop as *Gemeinschaft* communities that would benefit project participants. At the same time the literature suggests organizational challenges and larger social processes that could undermine the development of these nascent communities, as they have undermined so many efforts to maintain *Gemeinschaft* communities in modern society.

Community and Social Ties

If our participants were to achieve even a semblance of community within the group homes, they would have to develop social ties among themselves. After all, "community" is a social process, not a physical location. What matters for a community are ongoing and intersecting social ties, not simply close quarters. What distinguishes a community is the engagement of participants as whole individuals, not temporary transactions for limited purposes. What matters in community success is concern for achieving common goals, not actions taken on the basis of self-interest.

None of the community-friendly features of social relations are typical in organizations like shelters, and all of them are undermined by the experience of homelessness and the symptoms of mental illness. Shelter residents have smaller social support networks than housed persons (Solarz and Bogat 1990); symptoms of schizophrenia interfere with initiating social contact (Friedrich et al. 1999, 514); overall social support is reduced among homeless persons with mental illness (Calsyn and Winter 2002). There is considerable evidence that persons who are homeless and mentally ill receive less social support than their housed counterparts (Goering et al. 1992; Tessler et al. 1992; Eyrich, Pollio, and North 2003; Busch-Geertsema 2005) and that social support declines with length of homelessness and with longer episodes of inpatient care (Segal and Holschuh 1991; Lam and Rosenheck 1999).

If these social support deficits only undermined the development of community, clinicians seeking to help homeless mentally ill persons function on their own might be able to ignore them. Yet a sustained body of research indicates that lower levels of social ties are associated with poorer individual functioning and worse prognosis (Cacioppo and Patrick 2008). In fact social ties are so necessary for individual well-being that their absence invariably indicates future problems, if not current difficulties (Cacioppo and Patrick 2008, 15). Although intense social ties are a necessary element of *Gemeinschaft*-like communities, participants in *Gesellschaft*-like forms of social organization must also be able to maintain some meaningful social ties.

Society and Social Ties

Community psychiatrists who have turned away from therapeutic community-style rehabilitation still recognize the importance of building social ties in order to improve the ability of persons with serious mental illness to live successfully in modern *Gesellschaft*-like community settings. Paul Carling (1995), a leading proponent of community-based rehabilitation, asserted that "[p]eople cannot thrive or even survive in communities without a long-term network of friends and family" (p. 42). His antidote to the social isolation experienced so often by consumers of mental health services living on their own is to develop "circles of support" connecting peers, professionals, and others in "reciprocal, respectful relationships" that are, whenever possible, "freely given" (Carling 1995, 50–51, 251–52). From this perspective, group homes can seem to undermine community integration by segregating service consumers in their own groups and reinforcing skills needed for group living rather than those required for independent functioning in the community (Carling 1992, 26).

Supported housing is the approach to housing for mental health service consumers that has emerged from efforts to realize the potential of direct integration into the larger community. Three central principles of supported housing are designed to maximize community integration (Carling 1992, 30):

1. Consumers choose their own living situations.
2. Consumers live in normal, stable housing, not in mental health programs.
3. Consumers have the services and supports required to maximize their opportunities for success over time.

Underlying this approach is the assumption that erasing the structural distinction between consumers of mental health services and others in the community will enhance their ability to live like others in the community and develop the social ties required to do so successfully (Carling 1995, 255).

Researching Social Ties

A basic human need for group attachment is the *paramount factor* motivating social interaction; it is sufficient to ensure that social ties of some sort will emerge when people are placed in frequent contact with one another (Turner 1988, 38). Therefore, understanding how social ties develop and what effects they have will help anticipate the challenges faced by those of our participants who were assigned to independent apartments in community settings as well as those living in the group homes.

Feeling lonely is associated with being depressed and, like depressed feelings, is associated with a reduced sense of personal control (Cacioppo and Patrick 2008, 83). Protracted loneliness can cause distorted social cognition and less ability to acknowledge others' perspectives, thus eliciting less favorable views from and rejection by others and so even more social withdrawal and more pessimistic social expectations (Hawkins and Abrams 2007; Cacioppo and Patrick 2008, 16, 34, 103). As a result of negative feedback, as chronically lonely people become older, they report more marital strife, run-ins with neighbors, and other objective stressors (Cacioppo and Patrick 2008, 31, 102). In mental health services, the lack of mutually beneficial peer relations is associated with becoming dependent, passive service recipients (Weinberg and Marlow 1983).

Whereas negative social ties appear to have long-term deleterious effects (Coyne and Downey 1991; Rosenfield and Wenzel 1997), positive social ties are associated with better mental health and more positive affect (Wellman and Wortley 1990; Walker, Wasserman, and Wellman 1993; Nelson et al. 1998). "A well-regulated, socially contented person sends social signals that are more harmonious and more in sync with the rest of the environment" (Cacioppo and Patrick 2008, 19).

In general, social networks among persons with chronic mental illness are smaller, more conflict prone, and more dependent on family or professionals than friends compared to those among persons in the general population (Goering et al. 1992). Individuals with schizophrenia have problems in social functioning (Wykes 1998) and tend to become "desocialized" as others reject contact with them because of those problems (Hogarty and Flesher 1999). However Henderson's (1992, 90) research review concluded that social support has a "quite modest" effect in lessening depression, and Monroe and Johnson (1992, 102) caution that "there may be unique properties of support that are relevant only for particular kinds of disorders."

Evidence for mental health benefits of social support among homeless and homeless mentally ill persons is mixed. The longer persons with serious mental illness have been homeless and the more severe their illness, the more isolated they are (Lam and Rosenheck 1999; Goldberg et al. 2003). The result can be a cascade of detrimental effects, including less likelihood of achieving stable housing (Calsyn and Winter 2002), more frequent hospitalization (Goering et al. 1992), and less use of services (Lam and Rosenheck 1999). Both Sarason et al. (1990, 97–128) and Schutt et al. (1994) found that perceived social support was associated with better health outcomes among homeless persons. However, Sarason and her colleagues also found that this effect did not occur with objective measures of social support (and see De Silva et al. 2005), and La Gory, Ritchey, and Mullis (1990) concluded that social support was not correlated with reduced feelings of distress among homeless persons.

Research on adults who are homeless also identifies negative effects of social support, as relations with others may undermine feelings of self-worth or competence (Swann and Brown 1990). These negative social relations usually reflect the ways that alcohol and drug abusers help each other to maintain their habits (Portes and Landolt 1996; Portes 1998; Hawkins and Abrams 2007; Tyler 2007). Kawachi and Berkman (2001) also point to the potential for social support generating more dependency. Such negative effects may tend to obscure the more positive effects of other types of social support in research in which they are not distinguished.

In contrast to this considerable research on the relation between individuals' social support and their mental health, there has been little evidence on the effect of social ties at the community level, and it has not consistently supported the presumed positive association between social ties and mental health (Guest et al. 2006). Ziersch et al. (2005) reported that persons in Australia in more socially connected neighborhoods had better mental health, but Whitley and Prince (2005, 245) found that a poor community in London with a high rate of mental illness still had a high level of "social capital." When asked, community residents "generally argued that these positive contextual factors could not overcome negative individual-level factors, such as poverty and unemployment, which they ascribed as having a higher impact on their mental health."

Social support research thus identifies many potential benefits of social ties but also raises questions about the relative importance of social ties as an influence on the functioning of homeless persons and persons with severe mental illness. A theoretical model of the development of social ties will help to clarify the bases of these mixed findings.

Modeling Social Interaction

Social interaction is not itself a characteristic of individuals; instead, it is "a situation where the behaviors of one actor are consciously reorganized by, and influence the behaviors of, another actor, and vice versa." (Turner 1988, 13–14). Developing and maintaining social interaction requires

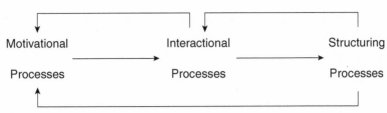

Figure 2.2. The elements of social interaction. Source: Turner 1988, figure 2.1.

both individual motivation to engage in interaction and group process to reinforce the interaction. Jonathan Turner's (1988, 15) theory of social interaction elaborates these requirements in a model that highlights the ongoing feedback between motivational and interactional processes and between interactional processes and "structuring processes" (group reinforcement) (see fig. 2.2).

Turner's model highlights the questions that must be answered in order to understand social interaction in our group homes: Did residents want to interact with others? What types of social interaction developed? How did experiences of interaction influence motivation for interaction in the future? How did patterns of social interaction shape the structure of the homes? How did the group home social structure (including the staff and other features that the residents did not initially control) influence residents' motives and their patterns of social interaction? I will address these questions in terms of the three basic stages in Turner's model.

Motivational Processes

Chapter 3's view of shelter living will provide abundant evidence of diminished motivation for social ties, including findings from a survey in the shelters that confirmed the McKinney participants' initial disinterest in living with others. Would a change in physical environment increase motivation for social engagement? Could social experiences in the new housing result in positive feedback that would in turn increase motivation to engage in social interaction? Or would difficulties with substance abuse, psychiatric symptoms, or functioning reinforce the negative lessons about social interaction learned in the shelter and on the streets?

Turner's (1988, 59) theory of social interaction provides some bases for optimism about the prospects for social interaction among the evolving consumer household (ECH) residents. Turner posited that the need for group attachment stems from the need for a sense of group inclusion, for a sense of trust, and for a sense of ontological security—that is, the belief that things are as they seem. When these three needs are not met, the result is anxiety—"a sense of diffuse discomfort and disequilibrium with the environment" (Turner 1988, 61). Anxiety in turn leads to efforts to reduce it, to create a shared account of the world and its meaning (Turner 1988, 57–58, 64–65).

The ECH environment had the potential to dramatically increase the satisfaction of each of these needs and thus reduce anxiety. By providing a small, stable group of residents who had to carry out tasks together, it offered tangible evidence of group inclusion. By allowing repeated interaction with the same residents over a long period of time, it presented the possibility of restoring trust in others. By creating a physically secure and predictable environment, ECH living seemed likely to facilitate a much greater sense of security than was possible in the shelter environment.

However, the value of social interaction identified in research on other populations cannot be assumed to apply to persons like those who participated in the Boston McKinney Project. Homeless persons often see even their families of origin as a source of problems (Timmer, Eitzen, and Talley 1994, 111–14). Those with a history of substance abuse might want to break their ties to former social networks so as to increase their chance of maintaining sobriety (Busch-Geertsema 2005; Hawkins and Abrams 2007, 2034; and see Mohr et al. 2001). Stephen Segal (1979) concluded that inpatients who were severely behaviorally disturbed often needed to maintain their distance from others, seeking only to maintain comfortable and self-respecting conditions without additional social support. The combined effects of prolonged homelessness, chronic mental illness, severe substance abuse, and/or social stigma could reduce motivation for social interaction to a level so low that it could not be rekindled.

Interactional Processes

Social interaction can be analyzed at both the individual and group levels. At the individual level, successful interaction creates social connectedness: "the construction and successful maintenance of reciprocal interpersonal relationships" (Ware et al. 2007, 471). Several personal competencies help to sustain social connectedness: the ability to communicate effectively, the integrity that leads to being viewed as trustworthy, and the capacity to be empathic and committed to others (Ware et al. 2007, 471). Within the context of ECH living, connectedness in this sense would involve identifying with the group of co-tenants.

At the group level, social cohesion is achieved when interpersonal interactions maintain strong membership attractions and attachments (Friedkin 2004). Thus, "members of a highly cohesive group, in contrast to one with a low level of cohesiveness, are more concerned with their membership and are therefore more strongly motivated to contribute to the group's welfare, to advance its objectives, and to participate in its activities" (Cartwright 1968, 91; Friedkin 2004, 412). This type of group process can help to reinforce desired behaviors and to model methods of coping with stress that arise in the process of seeking to change behavior (Levy 1983).

Member attitudes and behaviors in the aggregate create group cohesiveness through qualities that members bring to the group as well as through feedback from experiences in interaction within a group (Festinger, Schachter, and Back 1950, 274; Mills 1984, 29–31; Friedkin 2004, 410, 411). But since bases of differentiation among members continually arise, through the pull of different pursuits and the impact of divergent backgrounds and perspectives, if there is no process of interpersonal influence, if group members are not susceptible to influence by others, individual attitudes and behaviors are likely to become inconsistent with those of other group members (Friedkin 2004, 415, 419).

"Interpersonal agreements and coordinated behaviors are rarely an automatic result of internalized norms; instead, they must be continually produced (usually with much effort) through interpersonal interactions" (Friedkin 2004, 418–19).

Group cohesion is enhanced by a range of factors (Festinger, Schachter, and Back 1950, 164–65). Physical proximity and frequency of contact are critical influences (Festinger, Schachter, and Back 1950, 161); our ECHs provided these features in abundance. Group cohesion is also increased by group attractiveness, which in turn reflects the number of friends in the group and other features, and by the importance of the group's goals to its members (Festinger, Schachter, and Back 1950, 164–65). We would have to learn how friendships evolved in the group homes and how members reacted to the consumer empowerment goal. Most importantly, group cohesion is shaped by the homogeneity of members' interests and outlooks (Festinger, Schachter, and Back 1950, 163) and is undermined by the formation of factions or cliques (Festinger, Schachter, and Back 1950, 164). We would have to see if such processes developed in the group homes.

Structuring Processes

As patterns of repeated interaction become routine, and participants accept the ratio of resources they exchange with others as fair, group social structure emerges. "Social structure depends upon 'habits,' or routinized behavioral sequences where, without great mental and interpersonal effort, actors do pretty much the same thing in time and space. In the context of interaction, routines involve repetitive sequences of mutual signaling and interpreting that are customary and habitual for the parties involved" (Turner 1988, 163).

However, when participants do not accept resource exchanges as fair, social relations are not likely to stabilize, and the social structure may continue to fluctuate (Turner 1988, 170). An unstable social structure can exacerbate the stresses inherent in living with co-residents who evince significant social-skills deficits (Depp, Scarpelli, and Apostoles 1983; Hogan and Carling 1992).

But structuring does not simply develop as a result of participants' experiences in interaction. To a large extent new structures are shaped by pre-existing patterns in ongoing social structures. Although our McKinney group homes were an original design, both the staff and tenants within them had experience with traditional service roles, which would inevitably influence their reactions to the ECH experience.

Since the Progressive movement of the early twentieth century, relations between recipients and providers in health and human service organizations have been conducted in the shadow of the "professional attributes" model. Sociologists who developed a standard description of this model in the mid-twentieth century identified its key elements as the requirement of advanced education, the reliance on abstract theories, control by peers, adherence to an ethical code, and commitment to client service (Hughes 1963). Although this model focused attention on the contrast between the professions and other occupations—from semiskilled factory workers to white-collar office staff—it also implied a complementary model of professionals' clients: clients lacked the advanced education required to understand their condition and they could not evaluate professionals' work, yet they could trust professionals to provide services in a disinterested and ethical manner. In brief, clients were dependent on professional expertise.

The professional attributes model is broadly institutionalized in society, meaning that it is reflected in both structural patterns and cultural beliefs. Its influence appears in the role of professional associations, the prestige of professional schools, the incomes of successful practitioners, and in the outrage (or cynicism) that greets violations of these norms. The fact that this model does not describe adequately the bases of professionals' power makes it no less important. The fact that professions achieve these attributes through a process of political struggle does not diminish the model's social impact. The fact that professionals can be motivated by mundane considerations of self-interest rather than by lofty principles of altruistic service only highlights for practitioners the model's social value. The fact that other occupations seek to reap the rewards of professionalism by breaching the model's painstakingly constructed boundaries only emphasizes its appeal (Barber 1963; Larson 1977).

Of course no one would apply the label of "profession" to the occupation of residential staff in a group home. Like case aides in welfare agencies, like paralegals in law offices, like patient navigators in hospitals and teachers' aides in schools, residential staff serve as intermediaries between clients and professional occupations and as sometimes aspirants to professional status. But like these other "semiprofessional" and "paraprofessional" occupations, residential staff labor in the shadow of the professional model and so their work can only be understood within that context (Schutt 1986). Like the clinicians who deliver professional services to group home residents, residential staff members are expected to maintain standards of ethical conduct and altruistic service. Even more than clinicians, residential staff are required to be on call almost continuously during their working hours. Yet in spite of the importance of their position for effective service delivery, these paraprofessionals must defer to professional expertise and can only envy professional rewards.

To say that this intermediary occupational position creates the basis for dissatisfaction is only to state the obvious. To anticipate that lessening residential staff functions would increase the relative importance of professional clinicians is to perceive the reality of work and occupations. To question whether it would be possible to replace staff with tenants and thereby remove key occupational rewards is to recognize a key challenge that our housing model faced.

House staff play a critical role in house organization and thus in any structuring process. Based on their experiences in the shelters McKinney participants might have been expected to have been initially dependent on staff as well as somewhat distrustful of them. However, the group homes were to provide a markedly different environment for interaction with staff; a difference that was magnified by project efforts to reduce the role of staff and to increase tenant responsibilities. Could this different environment result in a restructuring of previous patterns of social interaction?

Findings about the role of group home staff in internal house social relations have been inconsistent (Greenfield 1992). Kruzich (1985) found that higher levels of staff-resident interaction were associated with higher levels of integration in community residential facilities, but Weinberg and Marlowe (1983) identified negative effects of resident dependence on staff rather than peers. Goering et al. (1992) found that having more support from friends compared to staff and family members was associated with more support satisfaction and less self-reported need for support. Rahav et al. (1995) found that residential programs using a therapeutic community model with high levels of both group pressure and staff control were more effective in reducing depression and increasing functioning than less intense models (and see Gunderson 1980), but Blankertz and Cnaan (1994) reported that a psychosocial rehabilitation orientation was more success-ful than a more intense therapeutic community approach in helping clients move toward independent living.

The concept of person-environment fit can explain many of these incon-sistent findings (Coulton, Holland, and Fitch 1984; Downs and Fox 1993; Hohmann, 1999). Person-environment fit occurs when an individual has the ability and/or disposition to benefit from a particular environment; if such interactions occur, differences in aggregate resident characteristics be-tween group homes may account for some of the inconsistent findings about their effects (Wing and Brown 1970, 181; Segal and Kotler 1989; Moos 1997, 173).

Diagnosis and functional ability seem particularly important factors in person-environment fit. Relatively well-functioning consumers with non-psychotic diagnoses tend to do better in programs that emphasize social interaction and self-direction, whereas more impaired and psychotic con-sumers respond better in highly structured programs having limited expec-tations and little expression of anger (Moos 1997, 215–17). These more impaired consumers appear to be overstimulated by an environment em-phasizing social interaction, and some have concluded they derive little benefit from psychosocial rehabilitation opportunities (Van Putten 1973; Van Putten and Spar 1979; Depp et al. 1983; Falloon and Marshall 1983).

Individuals who abuse substances seem to benefit from more structured programs. Nuttbrock et al. (1997) found that an intensive therapeutic com-munity approach benefited severely mentally ill drug abusers. Other stud-ies that have not measured mental illness have found that substance abus-ers benefit from higher levels of staff control, order, and organization (Bale et al. 1984; Friedman, Glickman, and Kovach 1986; Friedman and Glick-man 1987; see also Hurlburt, Hough, and Wood 1996).

Interactions involving other personal characteristics also suggest the importance of person-environment fit. Residents who are severely cogni-tively impaired (particularly in executive functioning) may not be able to respond appropriately to social stimuli (Seidman et al. 1992; Lysaker et al. 1995; Green 1996). As a result, residents with low levels of cognitive abil-ity may react adversely to a socially stimulating environment that is asso-ciated with improved outcomes among residents having more cognitive ability (see Oldham and Gordon 1999). Negative attitudes toward social interaction, perhaps reflecting an antisocial personality, are another possi-ble barrier to deriving gains from group home social dynamics (Morse et al. 1994). Sanders et al. (1967) noted that "[h]igh reactivity level male pa-tients, however, tended to respond to social stress [from the treatment program] with increased defensiveness and psychopathology, and were consequently unable to learn appropriate social behaviors" (298).

The potential for effects of community-level social capital on individuals will become clearer when researchers distinguish what has come to be termed "bonding" from "bridging" social capital (Almedom 2005; Stafford et al. 2008). Bonding social capital refers to social ties that strengthen relations among individuals in a group—the key feature of *Gemeinschaft* communities. Bridging social capital refers to social ties that connect individuals in one group to those in other groups or to larger social structures. In mental health services relations between peers may provide bonding social capital, whereas relations with staff may be required to create bridging social capital (Busch-Geertsema 2005, 216; Hawkins and Abrams 2007, 238).

Would our attempt to develop "community" in the group homes result in more supportive social ties—in "bonding" social capital? Would the move back to the community result in any "bridging" social capital between our participants and others in the community? More importantly would such ties have tangible benefits for our participants?

Implementing the Models

The contracts developed between housing providers for our group homes (ECHs) and independent apartments (ILs) show the contrasting approaches we would compare. The ECH contract emphasized tenant meetings and peer support (Bycoff and Powers 1991).

MASTER AGREEMENT

The *Evolving Consumer Household* will provide an alternative to the traditional group home program. The *ECH* will provide permanent housing to the homeless adults having long-term and persistent mental illness, as defined by the Project specifications, and who may, as well, have concomitant substance abuse and personality disorder. The focus of the *ECH* will be to provide, at all stages of its development, an opportunity for consumer-tenants to maximize their adjustment to their life-long illnesses and to improve the quality of their lives within a milieu predicated on the philosophies of consumer empowerment, self-help, and recovery. Initially, the program will resemble a traditional community residence for individuals with chronic mental illness. Twenty-four hour supervision with awake overnight staff is provided at its inception. All consumer-tenants shall have passed a Safety Screen and signed a consent to participate, both measures developed and determined by the Project's specifications. Further, all consumer-tenants will be capable of self-preservation, demonstrating the ability to get out of the residences within 2.5 minutes in the event of a fire or an alarm. . . . The *ECH* shall arrive at its most consumer-run functioning within the third year of operation. Realization of this goal will be dependent on the residents' capacity to manage household responsibilities safely and effectively. Outside assistance, support, and consultation will be available to residential staff and to consumer-tenants as requested.

The principles of operation are as follows:

1. The locus of control for operating the *ECH* will be centered on the consumer-tenants. They, collectively, will help set household routine, establish staff priorities, determine the degree and nature of services they desire, and in collaboration with the Project's interactive groups, set the policies and procedures for their specific *ECH*.

2. The essential goal of the residence, established at the outset, shall be to have program residents take over all staff functions. As consumers feel willing and able, they will systematically assume all house operational responsibilities initially held by paid residential staff. Early on, consumer-tenants will begin to take over such functions as shopping, cleaning, and preparing meals. Later, they may assume responsibility for their own overnight coverage, purchasing supplies, arranging for household repairs, and paying utilities and other bills. Finally, with consumer-tenants on-going negotiation of the group's division of responsibilities and duties, all paid staff will be eliminated and the *ECH* will be indistinguishable from other groups of adult roommates sharing living quarters in the community.

Those who so choose shall be assisted in transition to a residential setting of their choice when it is available, appropriate, safe and affordable. Consumer-tenants who leave the *ECH* shall have the option of continuing support and services at their assigned center that are consistent with their needs at that time. When available and appropriate, the consumer-tenant may return to the DMH shelter. Any terminations from the *ECH* shall be accomplished through a by-case process which . . . will ensure protection of all consumer-tenant rights.

The IL contract with the Boston Housing Authority stipulated conditions much like those expected in a regular lease (Bunte, Morrissey, and Jones 1991). Like the ECH contract, it also included provisions for terminations in exceptional cases and some expectation of engagement with clinical support.

MEMORANDUM OF AGREEMENT
BETWEEN
BOSTON HOUSING AUTHORITY
AND
DEPARTMENT OF MENTAL HEALTH
AND
. . . COUNSELING CENTER

. . . Counseling Center agrees:

1. To establish and operate a supported housing program (the "Supported Housing Program") serving twenty-five (25) homeless individuals who have agreed to participate in the NIMH Study, who have demonstrated stability, and who require mental health and community services in order to adhere to the terms of their Leases with the Authority, including the provision and coordination of all support services necessary to assist Residents to properly maintain their Units and comply with the terms of their leases with the Authority;

. . .

4. Upon termination of this Agreement, a resident shall be permitted to remain in his or her Unit as a tenant of the Authority. . . .

6. To assign to each Resident a Clinical Homeless Specialist, whose position is funded by the NIMH Grant, and who shall work directly with the Resident and regularly visit the Resident in his or her Unit pursuant to the Resident's Individual Treatment Plan. . . .

12. To assist the Authority, upon the Authority's request, in removing from the Units any Resident who, in the sole discretion of the Authority, is deemed to have disturbed the peace and quiet enjoyment of other Authority tenants or who poses a significant risk to the health, safety, or well-being of other Authority tenants, or whose other violations of his or her Lease have resulted in a lawful eviction action by the Authority.

Conclusions

The goal of building community in the McKinney group homes was to develop a social structure that would engage participants in social relations and provide many opportunities for mutual support and problem solving. This approach continued a long tradition of building communities to enhance individual functioning, both among consumers of mental health services and others seeking to recapture the supportive ties found in traditional small human communities. Research on other efforts to build communities or otherwise strengthen social bonds suggests that this approach could have positive benefits for participants.

In comparison to traditional group homes, the ECH model was intended to provide a much more supportive environment for building a community. The program's "empowerment coordinator" was to visit the group homes weekly in order to facilitate group meetings and encourage collective decision making, explicitly avoiding the tendency to simply provide medications and meals with little other stimulation that is characteristic of many traditional group homes. The project's expectations that tenants would become self-medicating, shop on their own or as a group, carry out chores and design social activities each contrasted sharply with the passivity often expected of mental health service consumers.

Yet the design of our group homes created unique challenges for strengthening bonding social capital and building community. Tenants did not join the homes in order to achieve some larger collective goal but simply to gain stable housing. The homes were not "intentional" and so they would lack, at least initially, the "voluntary, value-based" nature of the communities Kanter (1972) studied and the "ideological unity" that Vaisey (2007) found to be so important. Tenants were to be socially diverse, although not functionally differentiated, and so internal group dynamics were likely to create pressures for increasing boundary management (see table 2.1). Housing staff were assigned initially to each group home at all times, and so their presence might diminish the mutually supportive relations that help to make consumer/survivor initiatives effective. Necessary and ongoing relations with the larger environment through case management and other mental health services and through potential daily interactions with others had the potential of undermining development of an internally cohesive community.

Prospects for developing supportive social ties in the larger communities in which participants would be living—"bridging social capital"—were even less certain. Lacking work and other routines that would engage them regularly with other community members, struggling with substance abuse habits and symptoms of mental illness, the residents faced many impediments to developing meaningful social ties with new neighbors or other community members. Project participants assigned to independent living would be in government subsidized buildings with other participants and other disabled and/or elderly persons, further diminishing the ease of establishing social ties with others in the surrounding community. The prospects for developing supportive ties in the community seemed likely to depend on preexisting relations with family and friends as well as with the possibility for engaging in activities in the community with building-mates. Case managers funded by the project represented the only specific social relationship planned by the project, and even this relationship would be shaped by professional role expectations. In spite of these concerns the Independent Living housing model represented an ambitious attempt to normalize, as much as feasible, the living conditions of project participants randomized to this condition.

Which type of housing would be most effective in restoring social connections and community engagement among the McKinney Project participants? The *Gemeinschaft*-like evolving consumer household model had more than a century of enthusiastic theorizing supporting it, but systematic research about the potential of such an approach had raised too many questions to allow confidence that it would be the answer to the problems experienced by homeless mentally ill persons. The *Gesellschaft*-like logic of our independent living model minimized the situational differences between our participants and other community residents, but prior research made it seem unlikely that this structural change would be sufficient to generate new supportive social ties. Only time—and ongoing, carefully designed data collection—would tell which model would be more successful.

CHAPTER THREE

From Back Wards to Dark Hallways

T HE STARTING POINT for our research, homeless mentally ill persons in publicly funded shelters, also represented an ending point for previous mental health policy. The publicly funded psychiatric institutions that nineteenth-century reformers enthusiastically developed had mostly been abandoned as social monstrosities. Juxtaposed with this policy change, unfortunately, new urban renewal strategies sharply reduced housing options for indigent and disabled single adults. Although there were many beneficiaries of these trends, including the budgets of state governments and the quality of life of young professionals seeking urban residences, our project participants, like thousands of other homeless mentally ill persons, were not among them.

The intersection of these policy changes generated homelessness among poor persons with serious mental illness and created pressure for new approaches. Understanding these changes provides a necessary foundation for appreciating the dilemmas involved in responding to the homeless and the challenges faced by efforts at community integration. It is only after reviewing social theory in the last chapter and relevant history in this chapter that it will be time to analyze the history of the McKinney participants' housing experiences.

Mental Health Services

Some members of every society are defined as mentally ill. Underlying this label is the distinction of particular behaviors and feelings as abnormal in a particular societal context. In hunter-gatherer societies the normality of community was unquestioned, and so this labeling process was relatively straightforward. If community social patterns that had persisted for tens of thousands of years were not normal, then the concept of normality itself would have no meaning (Thomas 2006). But as communities grew and diversified, the possible meanings of normality multiplied, and so the equation of community with normality became problematic. Who was defined as mentally ill and the social response to that label then varied over time and across social groups.

The Origin of State Hospitals

Persons considered insane in the American colonies were often sustained by their families and maintained within their communities, with town funds sometimes used to build separate rooms to confine "lunatics" on their family's land (Grob 1994, 9–17). By the eighteenth century, however, confinement was increasingly used to keep persons judged seriously mentally ill apart from the larger community, often in jails or poorhouse cellars (Rothman 1990, 30–45; Grob 1994, 17–18). In subsequent decades American communities paid local families to care for insane persons who lacked supportive family or friends, or confined them in jails. The result, as described in a report by reformer Dorothea Dix to the Massachusetts Legislature, was "Insane persons confined within this Commonwealth, in cages, stalls, pens! Chained, naked, beaten with rods, and lashed into obedience" (Tiffany 1890, 76).

The use of both family-based and punitive responses to mental illness diminished in the nineteenth century due to increasing awareness of their inefficacy and the additional strains and population that accompanied urbanization and industrialization (Grob 1994, 25). In an iconic moment in 1792 that challenged the presumed efficacy of confinement, physician and superintendant Philippe Pinel removed chains and shackles from "maniacs" in two Paris asylums and noted that their violent behavior declined (Moos 1997, 5). Subsequently, he urged empathic communication with troubled patients rather than physical restraint. At about the same time, Quaker William Tuke opened the York Retreat as an alternative to English "madhouses," removing inmates' chains and providing a caring family environment. After the Quakers transferred this "moral treatment" to a new hospital in Boston, Charles Dickens (1996 (1850), 39) observed during a visit in 1842 that it was "a hundred times more efficacious than all the straight-waistcoats, fetters and handcuffs, that ignorance, prejudice, and cruelty have manufactured since the creation of the world." Returning from England after her own convalescence, Dorothea Dix began a campaign that ultimately succeeded in establishing state-funded asylums for seriously mentally ill persons throughout the United States (Tiffany 1890, 134; Grob 1994, 53).

But there was another factor in the growing appeal of asylum apart from the community. As the nineteenth century progressed politicians and reformers alike worried that the growing strains of the American republic were undermining communities and creating insanity among some of its citizens. The "well-ordered institution" "was to bring discipline to the victims of a disorganized society" and to "introduce regularity into chaotic lives" (Rothman 1990, 138). The orderly architecture of the asylums, their physical isolation, their rules, their "orderly and disciplined routine, a fixed, almost rigid calendar, and . . . daily labor" were to create community apart from society (Rothman 1990, 141–45). Hospital superintendents touted high rates of success for their "moral treatment" (Grob 1994, 83).

The number of state psychiatric hospitals rose exponentially. From 15 percent in 1840, the percentage of mentally ill persons cared for in psychiatric hospitals in the United States climbed to 70 percent by 1890 (Segal and Aviram 1978), with the hospital growth rate not leveling off until the 1940s (Dowdall 1996, 33). More than 500,000 persons were inpatients in state psychiatric hospitals in 1955 (Upshur et al. 1997, 200). Professional enthusiasm for insane asylums did not last anywhere near as long. In an 1876 report Northampton (Massachusetts) Lunatic Hospital superintendent Pliny Earle (1887) exposed faulty measurement and analysis as behind the statistics used by others to demonstrate frequent asylum cures. Rapidly increasing inpatient counts, higher proportions of chronic patients, overburdened state budgets, and a bureaucratic penchant for order conspired to shift the institutional ethos from recovery to custody (Rothman 1990, 265–74; Grob 1994, 91–93). For almost a hundred years, many state psychiatric hospitals provided little more than a place to keep chronic patients away from the community.

The Demise of State Hospitals

Like the degrading conditions they had replaced, the state psychiatric hospitals became a social situation ripe for public exposure (Grob 1994,

203–7). It mattered little whether or not they had from their inception reflected a flawed vision (Foucault 1965) or how many persons they had actually helped (Grob 1994, 100–101), for the realities of public psychiatric institutions in the twentieth century would have shocked Philippe Pinel, William Tuke, and Dorothea Dix (Grob 1994, 171). Observing for one year in a state psychiatric hospital, sociologist Erving Goffman (1961, xiii) found a "total institution" "where a large number of like-situated individuals, cut off from the wider society for an appreciable period of time, together lead an enclosed, formally administered round of life." Goffman (1961, 14) characterized "inmates" admitted to such an institution not as undergoing treatment or reaching some rehabilitative goals but as undergoing "a series of abasements, degradations, humiliations, and profanations of self."

This was not all there was to be learned from the history of institutionally based psychiatric care. Careful research provided more indications of negative situational effects on patient behavior but also evidence of therapeutic possibilities. In a study of three psychiatric hospitals in which staff were encouraged to provide a more enriched social environment, Wing and Brown (1970, 177–94) found increased patient social activity. After social conditions again deteriorated, patients' clinical gains were reversed. "Somewhere between [the] extremes" of over- and understimulating environments, they concluded, "lies the optimum social environment, in which the behaviour and expectations of others are clearly evident, predictable and not too demanding (though also not too permissive)" (Wing and Brown 1970, 181). Yet these indications of some potential for institutionally based improvements were overwhelmed by the growing anti-institutional chorus (Dowdall 1996, 142–43).

It was not only the growing recognition of the demeaning social conditions in public psychiatric hospitals that explain their subsequent demise. Belief among psychiatrists in the importance of environmental influence and the value of community-based care grew during World War II and with the founding of the National Institute of Mental Health in 1949 (Grob 1994, 211–15). The advent of psychotropic drugs encouraged many to believe that former inpatients could manage in community settings while receiving medications on an outpatient basis (Grob 1994, 228–31; Jencks 1994, 26). Psychodynamic psychiatrists found that new "milieu therapies" could aid even chronic patients (Grob 1994, 231). The civil rights and consumer rights movements of the 1960s increased sympathy for demands to reduce institutional restrictions and professional prerogatives (Grob 1994, 231). By the end of the 1970s, backed by favorable Supreme Court decisions, involuntary commitment for more than a few days had been abolished by almost all states, except in cases of imminent danger to self or others (Jencks 1994, 29). Costs of care were also a key issue. Since Dorothea Dix's legislation to begin national funding was vetoed by President Franklin Pierce in 1854, state governments had paid for public psychiatric hospitals (Tiffany 1890, 194). Many state officials now believed that Social Security and Medicaid provisions would reduce costs of care provided in community settings—although careful cost-benefit analyses left this issue unresolved (Lerman 1984, 221–23; Jencks 1994, 26–27).

Given public sanction by the Community Mental Health Act of 1963, the movement to deinstitutionalize psychiatric care rapidly gained momentum (Grob 1994, 258; Schutt 2003, 5). During the 1960s and 1970s the number of persons in state mental hospitals fell by 73 percent (Mapes 1985), while the Veterans Administration reduced its psychiatric beds by 52 percent (Hope and Young 1986). Between 1965 and 1977 New York State released more than 126,000 state hospital patients in the New York City area and in the early 1980s turned away an estimated 8000 new potential patients with more restrictive admission criteria (Hopper 2003, 77). From 1955 to 1973 California's inpatient census dropped from 37,000 to 7000 (Segal and Aviram 1978). The number of individuals in Massachusetts public psychiatric hospitals fell from 24,000 in the mid-1960s to just 2400 in the mid-1980s (Kaufman 1992, 473). Overall the number of psychiatric patients in state hospitals declined by 100,000 from 1975 to 1990 (Jencks 1994, 40).

Some even termed this period "The Golden Age of the Community Mental-Health Movement" (Segal and Aviram 1978). In 1961 a joint congressional commission issued a report urging "Action for Mental Health." In 1962 those on a cabinet committee appointed by President Kennedy who favored community-based care prevailed over those oriented to a more traditional medical model. The 1963 Community Mental Health Centers Act called for development of a nationwide system of community-based facilities that would largely replace state institutions. In 1968 the Lanterman-Petris-Short Act increased the stringency of criteria for involuntary psychiatric hospitalization (Segal and Aviram 1978).

Yet in spite of these hopeful signs an adequate new system of outpatient psychiatric care for the poor did not develop to replace the end of so much of the inpatient care system (Grob 1994, 262). Rather than transferring state funds from psychiatric hospitals to community care, states mostly maintained their now depopulated, but still costly, hospitals and instead cut supplementary payments to disabled Social Security Income recipients (Jencks 1994, 39). Changes in federal funding programs and dollars resulted in reductions in the mental health budgets of many states in the 1980s (Rochefort 1993, 72). After the Massachusetts state psychiatric hospital census had declined by more than 20,000 persons, only 2400 beds were available in community facilities (Kaufman 1992). And across the United States, reflecting ongoing fiscal pressures, only 789 of an intended 2000 community mental health centers were built (Mapes 1985). Overall, community-based care arrangements were grossly inadequate for the demands created by deinstitutionalization (Lamb 1984; Bassuk and Lamb 1986). A perfect storm was brewing that would create widespread homelessness among seriously mentally ill persons.

Provisions for the Poor

Provisions for the poor had been intertwined with those for indigent mentally ill persons until the large-scale development of public psychiatric hospitals in the nineteenth century. It was when the homelessness crisis of the 1970s and 1980s erupted that these two groups again found themselves sharing, to a large extent, the same social space.

England's Elizabethan Poor Law of 1601 imposed a tax on residents to support provisions for indigent persons who had lived in a community for at least three years. The 1662 Law of Settlement and Removal required expulsion of vagrants from communities after forty days unless they paid ten pounds per year. Community members were allowed to register their house as common lodging and receive funds to support dependent boarders. These provisions were adopted in the American colonies and remained in force until the early nineteenth century (Booth 1969, 214; Crouse 1986, 11–24; Hopper 2003, 27).

Many larger towns and cities used poorhouses to provide lodging to paupers and to ensure some control over their circumstances; often, movement into a poorhouse was required as a condition of receiving public relief. Work requirements were often imposed on the able-bodied, and discipline was strict (Crouse 1986, 24–26; Hopper 2003, 27–29). Yet services were mostly lacking, administrators were often corrupt, and staff were few (Katz 1986). Subsequent efforts to separate out able-bodied men and deny them relief led to a system of emergency lodging for them in urban police stations in even more squalid conditions (Hopper 2003, 20–24).

Both poorhouses and station houses had been abandoned as lodging options for indigent persons by the twentieth century (Hopper 1990). In their place cities opened Municipal Lodging Houses for indigent men. Also known as "flophouses," a combination of squalid conditions and work re-quirements kept use to a minimum, except in times of economic depres-sion (Hopper 1990, 21–23). During the postwar economic recovery of the 1950s and the relatively prosperous 1960s, the remaining single adult in-digent population (often isolated, elderly, homeless alcoholic men) were mostly out of sight in "grubby niches of central business districts" known as "Skid Row" (Hopper 2003, 45; see also Bahr 1973).

Intersecting Policies for Poor and Mentally Ill

The "perfect storm" arrived with housing and economic changes through the 1970s and 1980s. Urban renewal policies and increased demand for better housing in city centers led to the rapid destruction of cheap single room occupancy (SRO) hotels in these "grubby niches" (Burt 1992, 33). In the second half of the 1970s the number of SRO rooms in New York City plummeted by 30,000 (Montgomery 1981). Boston lost 94 percent of its rooming houses at about the same time (Burt 1992, 33). In Chicago, cubicle hotels accommodated 8000 homeless men, but by 1980 these hotels had been demolished (at which time two of the hotels were replaced by a 1200-unit luxury apartment complex) (Rossi 1989, 182). Similar declines in SRO lodging occurred across the United States (Redburn and Buss 1986, 97–99), although Christopher Jencks's (1994, 61–74) careful analysis sug-gests that the SRO destruction did not contribute much to homelessness until the numbers of extremely poor persons began to climb in the 1980s. A one-third reduction in the value of General Assistance benefits, the only source of public assistance available to indigent able-bodied men, contrib-uted to the affordability problem (Rossi 1989, 192; Hopper 1990) as did a decline in the availability of rental units affordable to poor persons (Burt 1992, 44–46). The crisis for extremely poor and disabled adults was exac-erbated by a changing labor market that offered fewer opportunities for casual, unskilled labor—the primary means of support for many Skid Row residents (Lee 1980; Rossi 1989, 186; Jencks 1994, 53). Adults who had been or would have been in psychiatric hospitals in previous years were particularly vulnerable to these changes (Burt 1992, 120).

Of course, alcoholism had been a concomitant of life on Skid Row for decades. This did not change much as Skid Row accommodations became less available. But the problem of addiction was magnified in the mid-1980s by the advent of crack—a much cheaper form of cocaine. By the decade's end, two-thirds of single adult shelter users in New York City who agreed to provide an anonymous urine sample tested positive for cocaine; a reason-able nationwide estimate at the time for crack use among homeless single adults in urban areas is somewhat lower—between one-quarter and one-third (Burt 1992, 118; Jencks 1994, 42–43).

We can understand the changing social dynamics that produced this crisis with the "homelessness equation" (Schutt and Garrett 1992, 3):

$$\text{Homelessness} = f \text{ (Poverty/Housing,} \\ \text{Disability/Supports)}$$

The two ratios in this equation express the economic and social factors that shape the size of the homeless population. In terms of economics, the number of homeless persons tends to rise with the ratio of poverty to housing: the more poor persons and the smaller the supply of housing they can afford, the more people are at risk for homelessness. In terms of social factors the number of homeless persons tends to rise with the ratio of the number of disabled persons to the availability of support services for them: the more disabilities and the fewer the support services, the more people are at risk for homelessness. Both factors in this equation changed in magnitude during the 1970s and 1980s with deinstitutionalization (increasing the number of disabled persons in relation to available services) and reduction in the supply of affordable housing. It is when both ratios rise sharply that a "perfect storm" occurs.[1]

Profile of Homeless Adults

As the number of single adult persons (and families) who were homeless skyrocketed in the 1980s, surveys revealed that a substantial proportion were seriously mentally ill (Burt 1992, 108–109). The lifetime risk of homelessness among persons hospitalized with a psychotic disorder for the first time was five times that for the general population, and their initial homelessness usually preceded their first hospitalization (Herman et al. 1998). Homeless persons in Los Angeles who had had a previous psychiatric hospitalization had been homeless nearly twice as long as the rest of the sample (Gelberg et al. 1988). One survey assessed over 50 percent of the single adult homeless population as having a severe psychological disorder (Kahn et al. 1987). Among 10,340 adult public mental health patients who had received treatment at least once for schizophrenia, bipolar disorder, or major depression in fiscal year 1999–2000, 15 percent had been homeless within the preceding year (Folsom et al. 2005, 372). Among state hospital patients in the New York City area, 19 percent had been homeless in the preceding three months, with 28 percent having been homeless at some prior point (Susser, Lin, and Conover 1991). Estimates based on multiple studies suggest that in the late 1980s and early 1990s about one-third of homeless adults were chronically mentally ill, one-third were alcohol dependent, and perhaps 10 percent to 20 percent were dependent on illegal drugs, with about a 50 percent overlap between substance abuse and chronic mental illness (Burt 1992, 115–20).

When the scope of mental health problems is expanded beyond diagnostic criteria for chronic mental illness, prevalence estimates rise. Both Rossi's (1989, 149) Chicago study and my (Schutt et al. 1994, 137) Boston shelter surveys found symptoms of depression 2.4 times higher among homeless adults compared to a national probability sample. A 1996 nationwide survey of persons using homeless assistance programs indicated a total of 66 percent with alcohol, drug and/or mental health problems in the last month and 86 percent on a lifetime basis (Burt 2001, 102).[2]

In addition to lower levels of economic resources and higher rates of disabilities than the housed population, single adults who were homeless in the 1980s and 1990s were also more likely to be African American. Although there had always been some black Skid Row residents, their presence was often unacknowledged in descriptions of the more numerous homeless elderly white alcoholics. This demographic picture was increasingly outdated from the mid-1960s to the mid-1980s, as the percentage of black men between 25 and 54 who did not work for pay rose from 5 percent to 15 percent (compared to an increase among white men from 3 percent to 5 percent) (Jencks 1992, 35), and the percentage of blacks living in poverty in 1990 was three times that of whites (Hopper 2003, 157). In the mid-1960s one-quarter of New York City's male Bowery residents had been African American, but this fraction rose to more than two-thirds of regular users of New York City's Men's Shelter by the early 1980s (Hopper 2003, 154, 156). In 1985–1986 in Chicago 53 percent of homeless persons were black, compared to 35.5 percent of the 1980 Chicago population (Rossi 1989, 123). In 1990 the U.S. Census Bureau found that 41 percent of shelter users and 39 percent of homeless persons found on streets and in abandoned buildings were black (Hopper 2003, 156).

The Emergency Response

The increasing numbers of homeless persons visible on city streets created a sense of emergency among many human service providers, concerned citizens, and politicians. Emergency shelters were the first response, but their numbers often fell short of the demand. In New York City a judge ruled in December 1979 in favor of the homeless plaintiffs in a Legal Aid class action suit, *Callahan v. Carey,* ordering city and state officials to provide enough shelter beds to meet the need. A 1980 lawsuit protesting conditions at one of these shelters resulted in a negotiated settlement (Hopper 2003, 92–93). As numbers of homeless men continued to increase in 1981, a state Supreme Court justice ordered city and state officials to open immediately a new facility to relieve overcrowding (Montgomery 1981). A 1981 study by New York City's Community Service Society estimated 36,000 homeless persons, as compared to just 3200 beds in public shelters (Bird 1981). By 1989 the city was home to 326 shelters with 30,000 beds, of which 15 shelters and 8000 beds were for single adult men (Gounis 1992).

The service crisis was no less severe in other cities, and emergency shelters were the usual response—even without legal action like that in New York (Bassuk and Lauriat 1986; Rossi 1989, 97–99). In Boston the number of shelter beds rose from 972 in 1983 to 3422 in 1991 (Argeriou 1992, 459), while throughout Massachusetts, the number of state-funded shelters increased from 2 in 1983 to 130 in 1989 (Tiernan 1992, 648). The Department of Housing and Urban Development (1989) reported that in 1988 there were 5400 shelters in the United States. By the late 1980s shelters and soup kitchens in the United States were servicing 200,000 to 300,000 persons each day (Jencks 1994, 103).

The quality of the accommodations in these shelters lagged far behind their quantity. Sociologist Peter Rossi (1989, 35) characterized the social organization of New York City shelters as "like a minimum-security prison." Anthropologist Kim Hopper (2003, 95–96) described the social atmosphere in New York City's Men's Shelter as one of intimidation, threats, and brutality enforced by staff who knew that working in a shelter was the civil service equivalent of being sent to Siberia. In 1982 at the city's shelter adjacent to a psychiatric hospital, Hopper (2003, 99) listened as a worker "proudly displayed the orderly way in which 'we cattle them' into the showers; he referred to the turnstile controlling entry into the intake area as 'the cattle gate, so to speak.'" In the words of a guest in a New England shelter, "it's . . . a prison, basically, that's all it is. I mean, there's one or two nice workers there, but you really take your life in your hands, not only crime, but whether you have your freedom the next morning" (Wagner 1993, 103).

There was more behind these depressing shelter features than the tendency to dispense with niceties in the rush to deal with an emergency.

Sociologist James Wright (1989, 148) reported "a subtle, certainly unspoken feeling [among policymakers] that if the shelters are made *too* nice, it will only encourage homelessness." Social work scholar David Wagner (1993, 102) found that many shelter staff were untrained and punitive, caring more about their own comfort than that of their clients (and see Axleroad and Toff 1987, 21).

Service systems in the surrounding communities seemed all too willing to leave shelters, as much as possible, to deal with their guests' panoply of problems by themselves. An Institute of Medicine (1988, 35) research committee concluded that "in most cities there is no system" for responding to homeless persons' health and social problems. Medical anthropologist Paul Koegel (1987, 41–50) recorded what he considered an apt description of what system there was: "the service delivery system for the homeless [is] a pinball machine, with homeless individuals as pinballs which bounce, almost randomly, from one community agency to another."

Yet even as the emergency shelter system continued to fail tests of its adequacy as a response to the problems of homeless persons, particularly those diagnosed with serious mental illness, new approaches were being developed at the organizational level and refined and funded at the state and federal levels (Redburn and Buss 1986, 38–39; Liebow 1993, 124–125). In 1987 the Massachusetts state legislature allocated $300 million for Governor Michael Dukakis's Comprehensive Plan for Services to the Chronically Mentally Ill (Kaufman 1992, 477). In the same year the U.S. Congress enacted the Stewart B. McKinney Homeless Assistance Act funding a wide range of programs and establishing the Interagency Council for the Homeless to review, improve, and publicize available programs (Schutt and Garrett 1992, 218–19). In fiscal year 1988, the Massachusetts legislature appropriated $48.11 million for homeless services, designated a state coordinator, a gubernatorial task force, and an interagency council, and mandated collection of data to track progress (Toff 1988a). Cities and states from New York City and St. Louis to Seattle also designed new initiatives (Hope and Young 1986, 47–50).

At the shelter level efforts to move beyond mass emergency shelters went in two directions. Some emphasized reducing rules, increasing client autonomy, and building peer support. The St. Joseph's shelter in the Los Angeles area required adherence to only minimal rules to maintain security, was opened to clients during the day, and encouraged stable social groups, a sense of community, and resource sharing (Wolch and Dear 1993, 246–59). The Refuge in Washington, DC required single homeless women to adhere to only a few rules and did not require a focus on particular goals; in the words of sociologist Elliott Liebow (1993, 122–23), staff "let Betty be

Betty." Cincinnati's Drop-Inn Center had no admission requirements, maintained a democratic governing board composed of residents, staff, and volunteers, and employed recovering alcoholics and other nonprofessionals as staff (Hope and Young 1986, 107–18).

Other shelters sought to develop a more professional service model. Pasadena's Union Station emphasized changing client lifestyles and behaviors, with counseling and referral to rehabilitation programs, as well as frequent twelve-step AA and NA programs for addicts (Wolch and Dear 1993, 146–49). Bridge House in Washington, DC sought to change homeless women through taking detailed histories, developing personal contracts with individual goals, and emphasizing attendance at group meetings and individual meetings with staff to evaluate progress toward goals (Liebow 1993, 123). It was felt that "[t]o let Betty be Betty, to be herself, to do things on her own schedule, was to be [complicit] in her dependency and failure."

These two organizational alternatives, client empowerment and professional service, also shaped the housing alternatives in the Boston McKinney Project.

The Mental Health Shelters

The Massachusetts Department of Mental Health (DMH) opened the first of its three shelters in Boston for homeless persons judged to be mentally ill in 1981 (Desjarlais 1997, 32). All three of these shelters emphasized stability and safety as well as connections through staff to mental health services; one had a special focus on persons dually diagnosed as substance abusers and mentally ill and therefore emphasized addiction services. Many shelter guests were referred by staff at Boston's large generic shelters for homeless adults, most often by psychiatric nurses assigned to health clinics in the shelters by the DMH. Others were engaged on the streets by a DMH-funded Homeless Outreach Team, which included DMH outreach psychiatrists who met with homeless persons. Some were referred by staff at one of Boston's community mental health centers.

Like other shelters, the DMH shelters sought to prevent their "guests" from getting too comfortable, barring access during the day (except in cases of physical illness) and allowing each guest no more than a bed and small storage area. The shelters' posted rules served as constant reminders of their institutional character (Desjarlais 1997, 83):

SHELTER RULES:

Guest responsibilities:

1. Leave the shelter on time, 9:30 am
2. Store all personal belongings in your locker
3. Keep bed area neat and clean
4. Shower every other day
5. Wash and dry clothes weekly
6. Clean-up after eating and smoking
7. Smoke only in designated areas
8. Participate in shelter chores
9. Respect the privacy of other guests
10. Return to the shelter by 9 pm, unless you have a pass until midnight

There is to be no:

1. Violent behavior
2. Threatening of staff or guests
3. Abusive language
4. Possession of weapons or harmful implements
5. Damaging of shelter property, or staff or client property
6. Stealing
7. Use of alcohol, or illegal substances
8. Smoking in dorms, or non-smoking areas
9. Food or drinking in the dorms
10. Loitering on the ground floor between 9:30 am and 3:30 pm

The shelter's physical organization also conveyed an institutional feel: "Upon stepping into the shelter, people first encountered 'the staff desk,' immediately to the left of the entrance. . . . Residents and staff alike understood that the desk area was off-limits to residents" (Desjarlais 1997, 82).

Yet the DMH shelters differed in their guests and their services from large generic "emergency" shelters. The DMH shelters were opened in order to remove persons with serious mental illness from mass shelters and to provide a more stable, service-oriented environment. They provided health services, offered some organized activities, allowed stays of indefinite length, and encouraged exploration of residential alternatives. Guests were viewed as particularly vulnerable to the stresses of homelessness, and extra attention was given to services that might lessen the ill effects of life on the streets.

The shelter's weekday schedule mixed attention to basic needs with some service-oriented expectations.

The weekday shelter schedule (Desjarlais 1997, 87–89)

8:00	Awaken for free breakfast in the cafeteria
9:30	Leave the shelter unless physically unwell
9:30–3:30	Attend jobs, treatment, roam streets or hang out
3:00	Wait in the lobby
3:30	Shelter doors open: "The shelter is now open."
4–7	Psychiatric nurse dispenses medication
4:45	Line up in front of cafeteria doors
5:00	Cafeteria opens for dinner
5:30	Cafeteria closes
7:00–7:20	Token store opens, "The token store is now open!"
7:55	Gather in TV room to watch lottery drawing on TV
9:00	Shelter doors close

Personal backgrounds of shelter guests were diverse, but indications of personal vulnerabilities appeared repeatedly in autobiographical narratives recorded by project ethnographers. Sam was raised in foster homes, sent to boarding schools, and adapted to institutional living. But he was put in the stockade while in the Army and was hospitalized after discharge. "He seems to take it all quite in stride, never really picking up his head to notice what is happening." John's "behavior issues" led his parents to send him to a seminary, which he left to enlist in the Air Force, which he then quit to work at a series of odd jobs before moving into a shelter. When Ben was young, he "used to run red lights without looking as a game." Peter used to hang out at bus stations, thinking only "where's the package store," but began fearing gangs of kids who robbed and beat homeless people after the stations closed. Anthony spoke of "all the terrible things that were done to him as a child by his parents." Gerry had traveled across the United States by bus, stopping to earn a bit of cash and then moving on, before ending up nights in a mass shelter and days wandering the streets. Roweena left her second husband for the streets, and Harv left his wife, kids, and a home for a bottle and the shelters. Jake had been a trucker who did "lots of drugs" to keep himself awake, then got "real manicky." He had lived in an abandoned warehouse for three years with a dozen cats, but then the warehouse was torn down.

One project participant insisted that his homelessness was "just an experiment" to see what it was like: "Some people just want to be homeless. That was true for me. I was tired of people with houses, and I just wanted to see what homelessness was like. . . . I might go homeless again, if I got too annoyed by psychiatry, or felt threatened."

Ethnography of a Mental Health Shelter

As our project began, anthropologist Bob Desjarlais observed at one of the DMH shelters and got to know many of its guests. "Their ways of talking or acting," he reported, "often perplexed or frightened others; known to be 'crazy' or 'mentally ill,' they were stigmatized for their oddness and came to live on the margins of everyday social life. . . . suffering "intense pain and isolation" (Desjarlais 1997, 44).

He observed a widely shared pattern of orientation and behavior that he labeled "struggling along":

> To "struggle along" was to proceed with great difficulty while trying at times to do away with or avoid the constraints and hazards strewn in one's path. . . . Often the trick was to find a balance between sensory overflow (which could include "hearing voices") and walking around in a stupor. . . . A good day for someone who is struggling along, . . . might be a smooth one, where difficulties can be temporarily overcome, where a few bucks are earned, where the voices are not too bad, where tension is relieved through pacing, and where there are enough cigarettes to last the day." (Desjarlais 1997, 19, 22)

Patterns of social interaction among residents were hesitant, partial, and often prematurely terminated: "[T]he social life there was such that people enjoyed contact and quick exchanges with others but tended not to sit down and participate in extensive conversations. . . . Some held onto utterly private visions and spoke at times in unique, monologic languages comprehensible to themselves alone" (Desjarlais 1997, 168, 174–75).

It would be oversimplifying to conclude that the shelter and its guests had reached an equilibrium in which degrading institutional expectations matched guests' impaired capacities and diminished hopes. Some guests, particularly those who were new to the shelter, engaged with the surrounding world more actively, evincing a sense of goals and some orientation to the future (Desjarlais 1997, 21). For most, however, particularly as they grew accustomed to the shelter, just "struggling along" became "the primary mode of existence" (Desjarlais 1997, 19).

It also would be oversimplifying to view the institution's control of the situation as total. For example the shelter's guests managed to create personal spaces where none had been intended. "Residents and other inhabitants of the mental health center made use of its secretive, labyrinthine form, which offered obscure nooks and crannies. They could take cover . . . and go unnoticed" (Desjarlais 1997, 70).

But in most respects, in fact overwhelmingly so, the shelter was an institution, not a home; staff, not "guests," were firmly in control.

Some aspects of the spatial design appeared to promote the kind of "therapeutic environment" found or intended in many psychiatric hospitals and asylums, in which an air of consistency, unambiguity, harmonious proportions, simplicity of function, and clarity of purpose is sought after. Other aspects reflected the staff's interest in creating an ambiance of personal rationality and industry. (Desjarlais 1997, 86)

Survey of Mental Health Shelter Guests

Surveys conducted just before we began to recruit shelter guests for our project provided more information about these special shelters—both about the similarities and differences between the DMH shelter guests and those using other large Boston shelters and about the differences between the DMH shelter that catered to substance abusers and the other large DMH shelter (Schutt and Goldfinger 1992).[3]

Individuals using the generic shelters who reported never having had psychiatric treatment did not differ in most background characteristics from those who reported having been treated for psychiatric problems, nor did they differ from those staying in either the central DMH shelter or the dual-diagnosis DMH shelter. However, compared to the generic shelters, the DMH shelters had a higher percentage of whites among their guests (60–70 percent) than did the generic shelters (30–40 percent). Also, DMH shelter users were less likely to have friends in Boston and were much more likely to have been homeless for one or more years than those using the generic shelters. Almost all DMH shelter users reported staying at the shelter often, compared to fewer than 60 percent of the generic shelter users—consistent with the more stable expectations for the DMH shelters.

What primarily distinguished the groups were their benefits and health. Those with psychiatric treatment histories were more likely to have health insurance (about 60 percent) than the generic shelter users without prior psychiatric treatment (40 percent), and the DMH shelter users were much more likely to be receiving benefits (80 percent) than the generic shelter users, irrespective of their psychiatric history (about 40 percent)—and they were less likely to be employed (5 percent compared to 20 percent). The greatest differences between the DMH and generic shelter users were lower rates of feeling depressed and (self-reported) drug abuse by the DMH shelter users. These survey data cannot indicate whether these differences resulted from selective recruitment of less depressed persons and those who were not drug users or to the more supportive situation the DMH shelters provided, but they are consistent with an interpretation that the

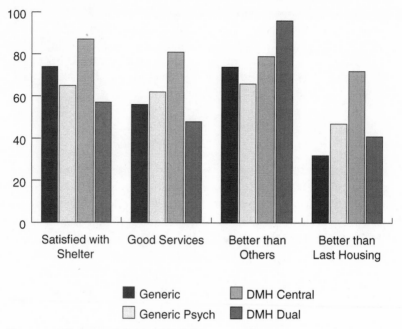

Figure 3.1. Shelter satisfaction by shelter.
Note: Central DMH shelter $N = 31$; dual-diagnosis DMH shelter $N = 28$; generic shelter psych $N = 52$; generic shelter, no psych $N = 162$. Source: Adapted from Schutt (2003, 9).

more stable DMH shelter environment helped to lessen feelings of distress and discourage drug abuse.

Figure 3.1 provides some direct evidence of a more positive environment at the DMH central city shelter—the one where Desjarlais conducted his observations—compared to the DMH shelter for the dually diagnosed and both of the generic shelters. Guests at the central city DMH shelter were more satisfied with the shelter and its services and more likely to feel it compared favorably to their last regular housing than the other three groups. The central city DMH shelter guests were also more likely to rate the shelter as better than other shelters, although this particular positive attitude was exceeded by the dual-diagnosis shelter guests. The ability of the central city shelter guests to carve out their own space in and around the shelter may have given that shelter a considerable advantage for guests' subjective feelings compared to the dual-diagnosis shelter, where such opportunities for personal privacy and limited control did not exist.

In spite of their relative satisfaction with their shelter experience, guests in the DMH shelters were eager to move. About 80 percent said they wanted to move, that it was extremely or very important to them to move, and that they would want to move even if they were required to take their psychotropic medicine. More than half said they wanted to "move out now," and another one in ten wanted to move out within one month, but almost one-third wanted to stay for at least another six months (and one in ten wanted to stay for years).

Independent living was the clear preference of a majority of shelter residents. Almost three-quarters did not like the idea of living with other former shelter residents or of living with staff—about half disliked both arrangements "a lot," and one-third were particularly adamant, stating that it would not even be "OK" if staff lived with them in a regular house. Nonetheless, almost two-thirds of the shelter residents reported that they would want to keep in touch with shelter staff after moving. The idea of staying in touch with other shelter residents after moving out was less popular: just over one-third liked the idea, and almost half disliked the idea.

When preferences for living with staff and living in a group were cross-tabulated, the resulting categories indicate the potential reactions to our project's ECH and IL housing options. The most popular option, preferred by 50 percent of the DMH shelter guests, was to live independently without either staff or other residents ("no group, no staff") (see fig. 3.2). By contrast, only one in five DMH shelter residents preferred the model

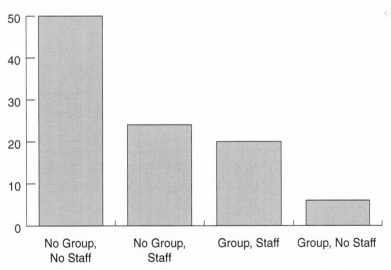

Figure 3.2. DMH shelter guests' housing preferences, group and staff.
Note: N = 66.

that our ECH housing was to begin with—"staff" and other residents ("group")—and just 6 percent preferred the model that it was to "evolve" to: collectively managing their housing without staff. Almost one-quarter preferred to have on-site staff support without a group—an option we did not provide. These distributions suggest that it is misleading to simply compare, or to measure, preference for group living compared to independent living. Living with staff was more acceptable than living with other service consumers.

Survey of Shelter Staff

When shelter staff were asked about guests' readiness for independent living, they estimated that fewer than one in five were ready to live on their own without help. Staff thought somewhat more were ready for independent living with help (44 percent) than were not ready to live on their own (38 percent).

In interviews staff emphasized the small proportion of shelter guests who were capable of living on their own and also explained why support services would be necessary for most:

> Three people I would think are truly able to live on their own. I would prefer to see them in a group home. I would hate to see them go from this many people to being alone and wonder what might happen when they are alone. We can be our own worst enemies, totally alone by ourselves.
>
> I don't think many [can live independently], just a few. Most of them need help. A lot of our clients are hearing voices and they need to be reassured that it is not true. I think they need a lot of help.
>
> A lot of them now have payees. If they were to live independently they should keep the payees because they are tempted to . . . , most of them have a drug and alcohol problem and they are tempted to spend it on that rather than on rent. They definitely need help. They should have a lot of visits. They are not going to take their meds. A lot of them deny the illness they have. (Schutt 2003, 9)

Some staff rated more shelter guests as ready for independent living but still emphasized their need for support services. As one explained, "It seems like that people who have been here from six months to a year it would be easier for them [to live on their own] as opposed to those who have been here three years, because they get comfortable. We are trying our best to let them do chores; give them tokens so that they can get ready."

One staff member emphasized the difficulty of using client preferences to decide whether the client was capable of independent living.

Without a group home I'd say 10 percent [can live independently]. The people who are opting to live alone are not always the wellest; sometimes they are the craziest people. They are going out and somehow gotten themselves apartments and have moved into it and you predict it won't be long. You give them six months and then there will be a hospitalization or something. So the ones that [sic] are actually capable of it are not the ones who ask for it.

Many staff emphasized the importance of providing structure for shelter guests through written rules.

Yes, we have a lot of rules and regulations. We have limit setting here. I think it is appropriate for the guests that we are dealing with—they need these rules and regulations, and some people tend to do better in a placement where they have structure.

It's very hard to get someone who is addicted or someone who is mentally ill to respond to limiting rules and societal norms, and if the objective is to move people back into society and hopefully society expands and relaxes so that everyone is accepting, and we are living as a group and still around and shutting off people, they need to know and understand rules, because rules will also be an integral part of society. And so that's the first thing people need to understand.

The results of the shelter surveys provide important background on the starting point for the Boston McKinney Project. The three DMH shelters from which we recruited participants provided a somewhat more stable environment than the generic shelters, but one that in its structure and its clientele seemed at risk of becoming another long-term, albeit inexpensive, institutional environment. We found in this environment, through the surveys, evidence of the central dilemma on which our project focused: homeless persons with mental illness sought to live independently, but staff who worked with them felt they mostly were not ready to do so. However, the contrast between these two perspectives was not quite as sharp as it first appeared: many guests were interested in staff support, even though they rejected living with other guests, and staff did believe that some guests were capable of managing on their own.

Conclusions

Our research is not the first to describe the dilemmas created by shelter living or the problems confronted by housing providers, nor is *Homelessness, Housing, and Mental Illness* the only scholarly work to highlight this challenge for social theory and public policy. Collectively this has been termed the problem of "shelterization." Charles Booth (1969, 233) claimed to have observed it in 1902 London: if "a man of simple vagabond habits is enabled to pass on from casual ward to refuge, and from one refuge to another . . . he will make no effort to improve." In the United States, Nels Anderson suggested that poorly designed relief measures could have disabling iatrogenic efforts (Hopper 2003, 51). In the midst of the Great Depression, American sociologists Sutherland and Locke (1936; cited in Hopper 2003, 49) claimed,

> After an initial period of disorientation, the newly homeless man shrugs off his discomfort and settles into the stuporous regimen of the shelter in the constant company of lost men.

In the midst of the more recent homeless crisis, New York City shelter observer Kostas Gounis (1992, 692) concluded,

> The shelter manufactures violence, hopelessness, and all the symptoms of social pathology that the authorities attribute to the very victims of these processes as self-inflicted.

Timmer et al. (1994, 184) posed the question bluntly:

> Are shelters and their services necessary stopgaps (if not perfect, at least benign) or debilitating, dependency-creating institutions? . . . Shelters may in fact harm those they intend to serve.

Did the situation of shelter living explain the patterns of behavior described by Desjarlais (1997) and the orientations identified in the surveys, and the conclusions of these other researchers, or did it instead reflect individuals' preexisting afflictions? Would it be more reasonable to propose that both situation and individual contributed, in an ongoing feedback loop? With our momentary snapshot in this chapter, we will not be able to come to a firm conclusion. But this picture should make it clear just how far from a normal "community" the shelter environment was. Sally, Fred, and their peers embarked on an ambitious journey when they left this institutional environment.

All this was in the past, as our project participants left the shelters behind and moved into their new housing. But history had not ended: the conflicting pressures on mental health services, the inadequacies of income supports, the scourges of substance abuse, and even the experiences of the DMH shelters each remained as part of the larger social context in which our participants tried to build new communities.

The future offered a different vision, of integration in a functioning community within the group homes and participation as residents of larger communities outside of the independent apartments. Would either of these new housing opportunities overcome the problems observed in the shelters and evidenced in the shelter guests' behavior? Would independent living, which is what most of the shelter guests wanted, lead to the problems that shelter staff feared? These questions are largely answered in the next four chapters.

CHAPTER FOUR

Satisfying Wants and
Meeting Needs

"WILL I GET AN APARTMENT of my own?" DMH shelter residents who passed the safety screen understood that the type of permanent housing they would receive from the project was to be decided like a lottery—by "a computer." Our project recruitment coordinator reported that "overwhelmingly, participants wanted to 'win' an apartment and/or studio." She quickly realized that she had to use the project's housing readiness sessions to take the "yech" out of "ECH."

This difficulty was no surprise after the preliminary shelter survey (discussed in chapter 3), nor was it inconsistent with previous housing preference surveys among similar groups. Yet the predictable and understandable enthusiasm of shelter residents for living on their own also reemphasized the paradox in the shelter staff survey results: shelter guests did not want, by and large, what shelter staff thought they needed. And in case this seems like a problem only with shelter staff attitudes, it is important to recognize that this paradox has appeared repeatedly when groups of patients and other service consumers have demanded more influence over decisions traditionally made by doctors or other professionals (Eraker, Kirscht, and Becker 1984; Minsky, Riesser, and Duffy 1995; Lovell and Cohen 1998).

This chapter first reviews the larger debate over consumerist and professional orientations as they have been formalized in social theories and reflected in policy alternatives. It then describes the McKinney project par-

ticipants' residential preferences and clinicians' residential recommendations and shows how the orientations of both groups can help us understand subsequent housing retention and satisfaction. This chapter thus
affords a very unique perspective on service consumers' service preferences: usually, the housing or other situations that people experience are
determined by what they want and by what other people (such as clinicians, realtors or salespersons) think they "need," as well as by the resources
available to people for getting what they want.

The McKinney Project's research design allowed distinction of the influence of these different factors. Participants were assigned to group or individual housing randomly, thus preventing either the participants' own
preferences or the recommendations of clinicians from influencing the type
of housing they received. Sufficient housing resources were provided for
all participants, thus removing the effect of individual resources. These
design features enabled both describing consumer preferences and clinician recommendations and identifying their effects.

Participant Preferences and Clinician Recommendations

If our project participants had been single working adults seeking a new
home or apartment and they were offered a place to live that didn't match
their preferences, they most likely would have just said "No thank you"
and continued their search. This is normal consumer behavior in the mar-
ketplace. This is why consumer satisfaction is so important for retail businesses and why, from the standpoint of maximizing sales, "the customer is
always right." But if our participants had been patients seeking help from
a doctor for a mysterious ailment, their approach likely would have been
quite different. We would not have been surprised to hear them say, "Doc,
tell me what is wrong with me" or ask, "What treatment do I need?"

These markedly different but equally predictable approaches to help-
seeking reflect the institutionalization of both the customer-seller model
and the very different patient-doctor model. Of course an experienced
consumer knows that the seller will likely try to influence her preferences,
perhaps emphasizing the beautiful view or showing another, less-desirable
apartment in comparison, and that the seller may be motivated by greed or
reputation. And a savvy patient may understand that a doctor's suggestion
of a particular drug may be motivated by the visits of a pharmaceutical
company representative or the conferences that company sponsors. But
even when we recognize that the consumer and medical decision-making

models are not diametrically opposed, we still tend to believe that consumers should be able to choose what they want (and can afford), whereas patients should do what their doctor tells them, within reason. We may question whether the professional model applies to residential house staff, but doctors still appear as prime exemplars of the second model (see discussion in chapter 2).

These same two models underlie divergent theories of decision making that will help us to understand housing preferences. In a rather oversimplified overview of these different theories, economist James Duesenberry (1960, 233, as quoted in Becker 1996, 17) suggested that "economics is all about choices, while sociology is about why people have no choices." Economists' rational choice theory is grounded in analysis of the consumer-seller relationship. According to rational choice theory consumers calculate and weigh potential costs and benefits before making a decision that maximizes their self-interest (Coleman 1990). It is the individual consumer who makes the decision, based on a knowledgeable assessment of the consequences of his or her choice. In theory a rational choice model can explain decisions about diverse choices ranging from purchasing an automobile or a home to choosing a school or a health clinic or deciding whether to do what a teacher or doctor recommends.

Many theorists have recognized limitations of the rational choice model. Economist Gary Becker (1996) noted the influence of past experiences and social relations on choices, while still supporting the basic rational choice approach. Organizational theorist James March (1978) pointed out that "[p]references are neither absolute, stable, consistent, precise nor exogenous (unaffected by the choices they control)." Psychologists Tversky and Shafir (1992) noted many complications, including delayed decisions when choices conflict. These modifications of and challenges to rational choice theory suggest it is unreasonable to simply assume that consumers will make rational choices, irrespective of their mental health status.

In contrast the medical model assumes that it is doctors, not patients, who decide what treatment patients should receive. According to the medical model, the system of medical education ensures that doctors are best able to evaluate medical problems and socializes them to serve their patients' medical needs. It is the medical profession itself that maintains a professional ethics code meant to ensure adherence to these standards (Freidson 1988). Of course today we are all too skeptical to think that doctors have *only* their patients' best interests at heart or that patients should not have the final say about their care. But it is useful to have the traditional medical model in mind as we review different explanations of help-seeking.

Advocates for homeless persons diagnosed as seriously mentally ill have argued for a rational choice perspective on their housing needs—that consumers should have "decision-making power" (Chamberlin and Schene 1997) and clinicians (Daniels and Carling 1986) should make "placements . . . on the basis of what consumers say they want, rather than 'what we think they need.'" Anthropologist Paul Koegel (1987, 41–50) came to the same conclusion: "[H]omeless and homeless mentally ill women should be given what they want and ask for, not what *we* think they need or should have."

By contrast, the medical model guides many clinicians' perspectives on housing options: "[M]ainstream housing where persons live alone in their own apartments and have to manage by themselves is beyond the capability of the great majority of this population" (Lamb 1990).

Kim Hopper (2003, 114) heard New York City shelter staff come to the same "medical model" conclusions: "It was the oft-repeated complaint of service providers at the time that the problem with the street dwellers was their unwillingness to accept assistance. This unwillingness was variously attributed to their impaired judgment or eccentric outlook. Either way, it was alleged, pathology trumped need." The late Howie the Harp (1988), subsequently a paid consumer consultant on the Boston McKinney Project, put the divergence simply: "[T]he mental health system . . . believe[s] that we are not capable of living independently."

When we turn to recent theories of help-seeking, we find movement away from the stark contrast between the rational choice and medical models. The "health belief model" is an early theory of individual help-seeking that reflects rational choice assumptions. According to this model, an individual's propensity to seek health care or follow medical advice is maximized by her perceptions of susceptibility to a disease and its likely severity and by the anticipated benefits of and barriers to taking action (Becker and Maimon 1975)—in other words, decisions about health care are made for rational reasons. A more recent version, the "Health Decision Model," adds influences on health beliefs to its model of health decisions. In the Health Decision Model, background factors such as education and health insurance and current social interaction shape experience with and knowledge about health. Experience and knowledge are both expected to influence general health beliefs and health care preferences (Eraker, Kirscht, and Becker 1984). In this way the Health Decision Model recognizes the importance of social factors without altering the basic assumption that decisions are made on rational grounds.

Research in the general population has identified some of the influences predicted by the Health Decision Model. Use of mental health services is higher among those who report physical and mental health problems. The propensity to seek help for health and substance abuse problems also increases with the perceived severity of the disorder and its adverse social and health consequences (Longshore et al. 1997; Hajema, Knibbe, and Drop 1999). These influences interact with others: when the health problem is more severe, individuals are more likely to seek help irrespective of their other characteristics or social network involvements (Frank and Kamlet 1989).

Background factors are an expected influence in the Health Decision Model. Most studies of psychiatric help-seeking find that likelihood of seeking help for psychiatric problems increases with education (Kulka, Veroff, and Douvan 1979), perhaps because of a concomitant increase in an introspective, individualistic "psychological orientation" (Greenley and Mechanic 1976). In addition the propensity to seek help from professionals increases with age and is higher among women than among men (McKinlay 1972; Frank and Kamlet 1989).

By contrast more sociological—social structural—perspectives on help-seeking emphasize the role of social networks, the influence of emotions, and the interdependence of different decisions (Pescosolido 1992). For example, Pescosolido's (1992) "social organization strategy" assumes that health care decisions must be understood as an ongoing series of steps rather than as discrete events. Her framework broadens the focus of analysis from decisions about formal medical care to the entire range of options that consumers consider when they respond to health problems. It expects that individuals make health care decisions in interaction with others and that they do so within the context of a particular time and place (Stoner 1985). This perspective is well suited to the investigation of our participants' housing preferences as they moved into a new social context and interacted with other residents and project staff for the next year and a half.

Research Background

If consumers and providers of mental health services agreed about the type of housing consumers need, the different perspectives underlying their preferences would have little consequence for housing policy. But even many years after the "consumer rights revolution" in mental health services, there is little agreement between consumers and clinicians about housing needs. Survey research on consumer housing preferences and clinician housing recommendations reveals a clear divergence.

Preferences and Recommendations

Most studies of residential preferences among mentally ill and homeless mentally ill persons have referred only to the general choice between traditional group homes and independent living (IL) facilities, and they have found a widespread preference for independence (Thomas 1987; Blanch et al. 1988; Barrow et al. 1989; Carling 1990; Elliott, Taylor, and Kearns 1990; Goering, Paduchak, and Durbin 1990): if they are asked, between 50 percent and 90 percent of mental health service consumers say that they prefer independent living (Keck 1990; Neubauer 1993; Tanzman 1993; Yeich and Mowbray 1994; Holley, Hodges, and Jeffers 1998).

But the strength of this preference for independent living varies with the nature of the group home presented as an alternative and with prior residential experiences (Goering, Paduchak, and Durbin 1990; Friedrich et al. 1999). Minsky, Riesser, and Duffy (1995) found that about one-third of consumers preferred living with family members and one-third preferred roommates of one's choice, but just 8 percent wanted to live with other mental health consumers. Among homeless women in Toronto, Goering, Paduchak, and Durbin (1990) found that most strongly preferred to live in independent residences.

A few surveys have distinguished preferences for staff support from preferences for group living; these surveys have found that it is primarily the idea of living with other consumers of mental health services that people object to—many persons living with mental illness express an interest in some form of staff support (Keck 1990). Support from visiting staff is accepted, even desired, by between two-thirds and three-quarters of consumers (Tanzman 1993; Minsky, Riesser, and Duffy 1995; Owen et al. 1996).

Clinicians' housing recommendations diverge sharply from most service consumers' housing preferences. Although relevant survey research has been limited, results indicate that clinicians recommend some type of supported group living for between 60 percent and 80 percent of consumers (Minsky, Riesser, and Duffy 1995; Holley, Hodges, and Jeffers 1998). This disjuncture between individual preferences and clinician recommendations raises the question of whether the level of support some consumers prefer is considerably lower than the level of support they need. Other research on outpatients with schizophrenia found that those who assessed their own daily functioning skills much more positively than did their case managers actually performed more poorly than did those whose self-assessments were more similar to that of their case managers (Bowie et al. 2007). Persons with schizophrenia (Amador et al. 1994) or bipolar disorder (Pini, Cassano, and Dell'Osso 2001) who do not recognize illness-related impairments in their lives are less likely to maintain treatment, including psychotropic medication (Kikkert et al. 2006), accept advice proffered by professionals or family members, or function well in the community (Haywood et al. 1995).

In the case of housing preferences there is some indication that the desire for autonomous living is associated with impairments that interfere with client autonomy, contrary to rational choice theory predictions (Morse et al. 1994). Depp, Scarpelli, and Apostoles (1983, 280) found that "[c]andidates [for housing] would often affirm they could do something, yet, on actual observation of performance in the preplacement sessions, would be found to need training. Lovell and Cohen (1998) reported that some homeless consumers used their new housing as a source of goods to be resold to support a drug habit, rather than as a means for becoming residentially stable.

There is also some evidence that clinicians' housing recommendations reflect assessments of clinical need, as expected by a medical model of decision making. Dixon et al. (1994) found that psychotic symptoms and a diagnosis of schizophrenia were associated with clinicians' judgments that a client was unsuited for a Section 8 independent housing certificate.

If, consistent with the medical model, a discrepancy involving consumer preference for independence and clinician recommendation of support indicates greater consumer vulnerability, it should be associated with higher rates of housing loss. By contrast if a rational choice perspective on consumer housing preferences is warranted, housing loss should be minimized when service consumers receive the housing they want.

Satisfaction

Satisfaction with health care is associated consistently with treatment retention (Denner and Halprin 1974; Attkisson and Zwick 1982) and with self-reported symptom improvement (Attkisson and Zwick 1982; Lebow 1983; Nguyen et al. 1984). Satisfied consumers of mental health services may not have had better experiences according to some external measure, but they tend to feel they are doing better and return for more services. In a mental health system dominated by voluntary community-based services, satisfaction must therefore be a key goal.

Consumer satisfaction is tied to consumer preferences by its definition: "the extent to which treatment fulfills the wants, wishes, and desires for treatment of the client." (Lebow 1982, 1983; Polowczyk et al. 1993). Consumer satisfaction ". . . is of fundamental importance as a measure of the quality of care because it gives information on the provider's success at meeting those client values and expectations which are matters on which the client is the ultimate authority" (Donabedian 1980, 25).

In spite of this preference-oriented definition of satisfaction, previous research provides only limited indication that service satisfaction reflects the extent to which service preferences have been fulfilled. Satisfaction tends to be higher among consumers of mental health services who have lower treatment expectations or ideals (Lebow 1983), yet service experiences do not have consistent relations with service satisfaction (Bene-Kociemba, Cotton, and Fortgang 1982; Lebow 1983; Lehman and Zastowny 1983; Olfson 1990; Huxley and Warner 1992). With respect to health care in general, Williams (1994, 512) concluded that "[E]valuations of care may have little, if anything, to do with the care itself." Rather than viewing themselves as "consumers," recipients of health care, Williams surmised, see themselves as "patients," as expected by the medical model (Williams 1994).

Research on satisfaction with housing yields some evidence of dissatisfaction resulting from the apparent discrepancy between housing desired and received. Both Minsky, Riesser, and Duffy (1995) and Seilheimer and Doyal (1996) found that housing satisfaction was positively associated with more independent housing. Srebnik et al. (1995) reported that the *number* of available housing options was correlated with satisfaction with housing received, but they did not distinguish the *type* of housing actually received. Marshall et al. (1996) identified a positive effect on satisfaction of becoming housed, but also without consumers taking into account the type of housing received. They also (Marshall et al. 1996) found that housing status influenced homeless persons' housing satisfaction but not their life satisfaction, whereas Calsyn et al. (1995) reported that housing status was unrelated to either overall life satisfaction or housing satisfaction.

Consumer satisfaction appears to have more to do with individual orientations and attitudes than with the services actually received. Housing satisfaction declines in association with poor coping skills and negative feelings (Earls and Nelson 1988; Elliott, Taylor, and Kearns 1990; Champney and Dzurec 1992), whereas it increases with feelings of self-efficacy (Seilheimer and Doyal 1996). Service satisfaction varies inversely with indications of an antisocial, psychosomatic, and less trusting disposition (Distefano, Pryer, and Garrison 1981; Lebow 1983) and is less likely among psychotic patients than in those suffering from affective disorders (Lebow 1983; Lehman and Zastowny 1983; but see Distefano, Pryer, and Garrison 1980). In general, satisfaction in its various dimensions seems to increase with positive feelings and social support and to decline with severity of mental disorder. Sociodemographic characteristics seem largely unrelated to service satisfaction (Denner and Halprin 1974; Distefano, Pryer, and Garrison 1980, 1981; Urquhart et al. 1986).

Findings

Our project participants expressed in our surveys a marked preference for independent living, while our project clinicians recommended most consumers for group homes. In both respects our baseline findings were similar to those I obtained in the shelter surveys (see chapter 3), but our project design enabled us to learn much more about the meaning and consequences of these divergent preferences.

Looking Ahead

Our baseline survey was conducted after potential participants had enrolled in the project, at a time when they knew that they were soon going to receive permanent housing. This context made the survey less of an academic exercise than the typical survey, although our participants also were told that their expressed preferences would not determine the housing that they received.

Consumer Preferences

Interest in moving out of the shelter into some type of housing was almost universal (see fig. 4.1). Half of the project participants said they were excited about moving and a total of 83 percent said they wanted to move, whereas just 17 percent indicated that they were somewhat or very unsure about moving. Ninety-two percent of them said they wanted to move, even if they were required to take psychotropic medication in order to do so. Nonetheless, almost half expressed a desire to keep in touch with other shelter residents after their move. When asked about the type of residence to which they would like to move, respondents chose independent living by a wide margin: 87 percent chose an apartment over a large group, and 78 percent chose an apartment over living with a small group. Living with a small group also was the overwhelming choice compared to a large group (Schutt and Goldfinger 1996).

In spite of their strong preference for independent living, many consumers were interested in having assistance from staff after moving into their own home: about half wanted full- or part-time staff to help out in the residence, and almost two-thirds wanted to keep in touch with shelter staff as detailed in figure 4.1. About one-third rejected staff help for anything but the most difficult problems (Schutt and Goldfinger 1996).

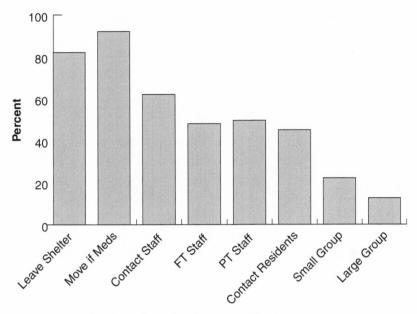

Figure 4.1. Baseline housing preferences. Note: $N = 102$–112.

Clinician Recommendations

The two clinician raters viewed consumer housing needs much differently than did the consumers themselves. Neither clinician believed that most consumers could manage in Independent Living even with case management, although Clinician B—a psychiatric nurse—was more conservative (see fig. 4.2). The ECH model seemed much more viable to both clinicians, with Clinician A—a psychiatric social worker—recommending this option as appropriate for almost all the participants. Both clinicians felt that only half of the participants could manage without full-time staff in their housing, and they both felt that most participants—almost all, in the case of Clinician B—would need at least part-time staff. Overall, they recommended fewer than one-third of the participants for independent living, with Clinician B rejecting this option for nine out of ten (Goldfinger and Schutt 1996). As figure 4.2 reminds us, consumer housing preferences were almost the reverse: nine in ten preferred Independent Living.

Discrepancies between clinician ratings and consumer preferences varied with the specific question asked (see fig. 4.2). Consumers' wish for part-time staff fell between the two raters' evaluations of which residents needed such support. However, what is most dramatic is the substantial disparity between clinicians and consumers in overall housing preference (Goldfinger and Schutt 1996). Even clinician A, who was more likely to favor

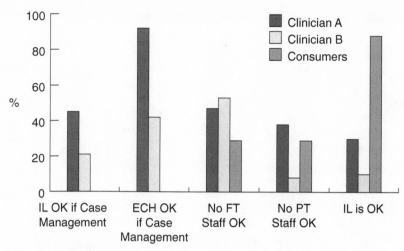

Figure 4.2. Clinician housing recommendations and consumer housing preferences. Note: $N = 109-112$.

independence, recommended independent living ("IL") for just one-third as many consumers as preferred independent living for themselves (30 percent compared to 87 percent).

The divergence in the consumer and clinician perspectives is even more apparent when consumer and clinician responses to the questions about housing options are combined into overall indexes (and the two clinicians' ratings are averaged). When these indexes are dichotomized, just over half of the consumers wanted strongly to live in their own apartment and yet were rated by the clinicians as needing a group home as shown in figure 4.3. By contrast, just over one-quarter of the consumers wanted to live independently and were recommended for that option by the clinicians. Fewer than one in five consumers preferred a group home in agreement with the clinicians, and just 5 percent sought to live in a group home even though the clinicians rated them as ready for independent living.

Explaining Preferences

Regression analyses of the baseline survey data suggest that consumers' residential preferences reflected what, in their own thinking, was a rational choice, but this evaluation was not shared by the clinicians.

The strongest independent predictor of consumer preference for a traditional group home was their response to the questions concerning ability to manage the tasks of independent living: it was the participants who felt they would have the most difficulty with chores who had the strongest pref-

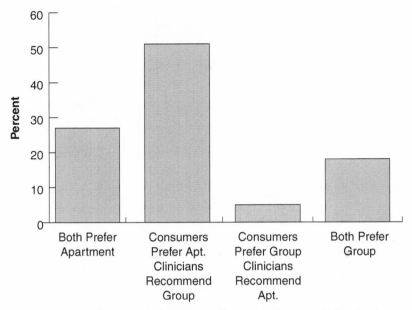

Figure 4.3. Overall consumer housing preferences and averaged clinician housing recommendations. Note: *N* = 108.

erence for group living (see fig. 4.4). In this respect the consumer preferences were "rational." In addition, preference for living in a staffed, group home was higher among those with more self-reported social ties. No other indicators of clinical status or functional ability were associated independently with the overall residential preference index. Men were also more interested than women in the group home option. Clinician residential recommendations had no association with the residential preferences of the consumer they rated.

Satisfaction

Before they moved, more than three-fourths of project participants reported that they were satisfied with the shelter, its services, and most of its features (see fig. 4.5). On a 4-point scale few chose the "very satisfied" rating, and satisfaction was noticeably lower in terms of the degree of privacy in the shelter and the kinds of people staying there, as compared to other shelter features. Nonetheless the DMH shelters seemed overall to have provided an environment that was viewed positively by those about to move into their own housing.

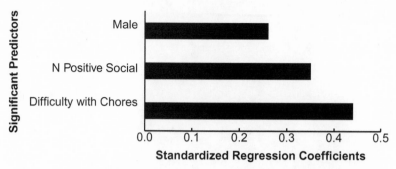

Figure 4.4. Regression analysis: Baseline preference for staffed group home. Note: $R^2 = .42$, $N = 100$. Other variables controlled but not statistically significant: race, age, education, diagnosis, lifetime substance abuse, psychiatric symptoms, clinician housing recommendation, number of negative social contacts.

Learning from Experience

The project changed the orientations of shelter staff, shelter guests, and of the new tenants as they gained experience in their homes. The project's empowerment coordinator encouraged these changes in remarks to staff and to the McKinney tenants in each new ECH. In her talks to new tenant ECH groups she often said that the essence of the desired change was,

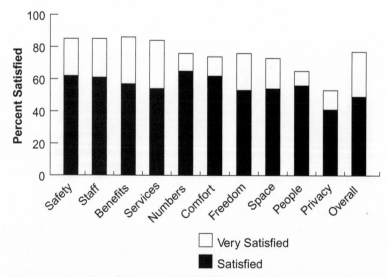

Figure 4.5. Baseline shelter satisfaction. Note: $N = 100-112$.

You're in charge now. It's gonna take time for each of you to decide what you want. What you can do is think about changing your medical appointments or your pharmacy to something here in town, so you don't have to travel so far. Think about everything you do or have to do and ask yourself, how is it for you? Does it feel like something's a pain in the ass? If so, don't feel it can't be fixed. We're here to help you be creative and innovative, to make something convenient instead of an inconvenience.

Shelter Staff Perspectives

The Boston McKinney Project dramatically changed the constraints and opportunities faced by staff and guests in the DMH special shelters. As housing was developed for the project and shelter guests were recruited over a two-year period from all three special shelters, permanent housing became an immediate possibility rather than an abstract goal.

Six months after the project began, 85 percent of staff in the three DMH shelters participated in a survey I conducted. At that time, satisfaction with the McKinney project varied substantially among the three shelters (see fig. 4.6). Satisfaction with the project was highest at the small "West" shelter, where 86 percent of staff expressed satisfaction with it, and 43 percent

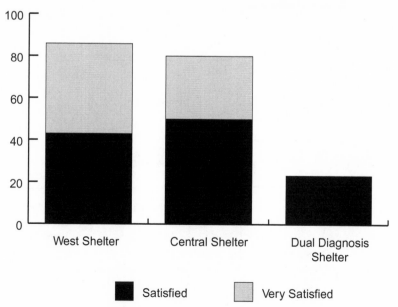

Figure 4.6. Shelter staff project satisfaction after six months. Note: West $N = 7$; Central $N = 20$; Dual Diagnosis $N = 22$.

were "very satisfied." Overall staff satisfaction with the project was about as high at the downtown "Central" shelter, although compared to the West shelter more were just satisfied with it, rather than very satisfied. At the dual-diagnosis shelter, however, the level of satisfaction among staff was sharply lower: only 50 percent of staff staff were satisfied with the project and none of these were "very" satisfied.

Many staff comments at the Central and West shelters indicated a dramatic effect of the project on staff and guest orientations (Schutt 2003, 9):

> Housing before the grant was very, very slow and people lived here for years. . . . We had people here—that one guy has been here for four years now and that's not good. So it's good, it's positive, it's fast and they don't get comfortable here. And *finally* we are a transitional shelter, not a permanent living situation. . . . People who come in are told right from the beginning that we have this housing grant and you can go for it and that you don't have to stay here very long. They accept that and they know that they are here just for a short time and that you will be moving on quickly. . . . Before, oh sure, we can house you. Two years later they were still sitting here.

A change in management philosophy supported the new staff approach at one DMH shelter.

> One thing we have changed in the shelter is the shelter was modeled after an inpatient unit. So in the beginning of the shelter the staff was treating the guests as in an inpatient unit where we would be doing the laundry, cleaning the tables, taking care of trash. . . . This is ridiculous. We are not an inpatient unit, we are supposed to be a six-month transitional shelter. That means that they come in for six months and they get services, they learn how to do, we try to teach them certain skills so that when they get out into the house with other residents they know how to behave. We didn't want to kick them out from the shelter, . . . but we wanted to make it uncomfortable enough that they say I don't want to stay out till 11 o'clock, I will do my chore.

Staff reports on the orientations of guests to the new housing opportunities were often very positive (Schutt 2003, 10).

> I think in terms of the guests, the guests are very interested in this, they are excited. Guests are meeting with people, they are really happy. I have another guest who is being considered for the project and he is really excited about it and really thinks it's going to be great.
>
> They are very excited about it. This is one thing that they were very skeptical [about] in the beginning because they have been promised so much. After the interviews and everything the first people were called and they see, yes, it is going to happen. So they look at it as a positive thing. So I'd say they're excited about it, moving out of here. They hate living here.

Knowing that permanent housing was available seemed to shelter staff to exert a profound change in shelter guest attitudes and behavior. Shelterization was less evident in guest attitudes (Schutt 2003, 10):

> [They] tell each other what is going on with them on the grant, which before everybody would be sitting alone, smoking and now you find everybody having a little discussion here. And when you listen carefully, the majority [is] about the grant.
>
> Some say: I have seen the place, do I really deserve something like this? [It's] because they have lived in the streets for so long and in big shelters, and I just assure them that they can do it, and that they deserve a place like this.
>
> We had one client I'm very impressed with. He never has had any affect in three years he has been here. . . . Since he has been a part of this study, his hygiene has improved, his general demeanor.

However, staff at the dual-diagnosis shelter had a much more jaundiced view of the project. Concerns with maintaining sobriety dominated staff remarks (Schutt 2003, 10):

> It [autonomous housing] reminds them of being kids when they first move out of their parents' home. You are on your own and you are in charge and they think, well, I don't have to take my medication; I don't have to go to my doctor; I don't have to go to my program anymore; I'll be able to drink if I want to—that whole freedom issue and that they are independent.
>
> Because we deal with drug and alcohol folks, we spend a lot of time with education and rehab, and keeping people clean and sober. And one of the guests who got the group residence was clean, he had been clean for over a year, and then all of a sudden had a setback around the time of the grant, and then because once the housing came through, like three months later, he again had stabled out, and then been sober, and then we had found out that people could drink in the residences if they chose to, and, um, he is one who needs to be some place dry where there's structure. . . . We take people in and stabilize them, and the grant is moving them out and taking away all their structure and all their supports.

The Boston McKinney Project's overall impact on the shelters was thus to end a sense of operating as a custodial institution and instead to orient staff and guests to make transitions to permanent housing. A comment by one staff member captured this feeling: "I think it is excellent. I think it is outstanding. I think the shelter should take advantage of the fact that these folks are moving out into very, very good homes in great locations."

But not all shelter staff supported this change. Those working at the shelter for homeless persons with a dual diagnosis most often believed that the rapid movement to permanent housing hindered effective service delivery: One explained the basis of this sentiment:

I think it is going to fail within a year because the clients aren't going to last—they are almost encouraged to drink and do their drugs and not go to their day program and make their own judgment and most of their judgment is impaired. They are not capable of that, which is really unfair to them. It is, it is unfair. I just don't think the grant program is going to make it. What is the purpose of it?

These reservations anticipated subsequent problems with substance abuse in the McKinney housing.

Consumer Preferences

Tenants who moved into independent apartments made many enthusiastic comments: "This place is Nirvana compared to the shelter." Some acknowledged being "a little lonely," and one had a problem with noisy neighbors, but there was little indication of dissatisfaction in comments made during meetings with our case management supervisor.

Helen said she would never have moved into an ECH, but "I enjoy every minute of my life now" since she has her own place. Although her apartment was in a building with many elderly tenants, she felt connected: "I talk to everybody. Everybody's very friendly and kind. I make bread. I don't have any trouble."

Another participant remarked happily about her independent apartment and declared: "This is it." Pride in the new apartment was common: "It looks sharp; you can come up and see it if you want."

Some new ECH residents also lauded their new quarters, although they often alluded to initial disappointment about not having gotten an individual apartment. One explained how she came to like the house

much more than the shelter—I like the way it looks, especially the floors. At first, I thought it would be uncomfortable with so many people here. I wanted to get my own apartment. But now I feel much more comfortable, and everybody does their own thing, and it really feels OK.

ECH tenants remarked on the value of staff assistance with chores and other activities. In response to another tenant's question, Andy explained, "No, I don't think they should get rid of the staff: they're good to have around. Ever since I was young, I've always had people like that where I was living, and I look on them as sort of guides in my life, you know?" General anxieties about safety motivated some tenants' continued interest in having house staff. Georgette said that "she did not want staff to leave because at night she hears people calling her and she sees skeletons in her fan."

But not every tenant was happy with his or her housing assignment. Some independent apartment tenants were ambivalent about their new situation because of feeling lonely. Remarks by one tenant captured the tension she felt between not wanting to feel lonely and desiring independence:

> [She] isn't sure that the apartment is better than street life. She used to have a lot of friends, she says, and feels isolated here—doesn't invite people over. [But] the good part about having the apartment is the independence. . . . Homeless people . . . don't get close to each other. . . . I lived my whole life this way.

Many of those who moved into group homes continued to desire independent living. Some ECH tenants asked about openings in independent apartments: Perlina is talking about "wanting to move to her own place." "Everyone is wanting their own place now." Sami says she wants to get on the list for independent living, and Theo remarks that "he couldn't take living at the house anymore" and "will have to go back to the streets" if he doesn't get his own place. "George has gotten his own apartment and is moving." Harvey "wants to move out and has checked on Section 8 housing." Harriett "wants her own apartment, so she can have her own bathroom."

Other tenants who had moved into a group home only wanted their own apartment after they concluded that the group home was functioning poorly: "Tony is looking for an apartment to get away from the tension and disorganization in the house." In contrast, some tenants anticipated disorganization if staff were to depart and so desired a continuing staff presence. When one tenant urged in a meeting that tenants dismiss the entire house staff, reactions were negative:

> Violet said that they do need staff. Jorges said that they need staff for "interpersonal issues." Alice jumped at the occasion and said "we better vote. How many people think the staff should go tomorrow?" When the majority voted against this, she said "staff stays."

Other tenants reacted to difficulties in living in the group homes by deciding to move back to the familiar routines of the shelter.

> Bob . . . wants to move back to [the] shelter because the tenants are too often being hospitalized—"it's an interim program for the hospital." He . . . wants to live in the shelter, going to a day program each day, until he is [older], and then to move permanently into a rest home—liking the structured routine.

Some simply insisted that they could not abide restrictions imposed by the tenant group on their drinking. One of the ethnographers recorded an example:

> Gustaf is drinking and says he is going to move out, wants to drink, and is willing to live on the street again and even die on the street.

These diverse comments indicate that the different residential preferences expressed in the baseline survey continued to be expressed throughout the project. Independent apartment residents tended to like their placement. Many tenants in the group homes continued to prefer an independent
apartment, although in spite of this preference many also liked having
staff. House staff themselves felt that tenants wanted staff to do more to
manage the house, that tenants were resisting "empowerment." A few project participants in both groups decided they would prefer to be back in the
shelter.

Quantitative Analysis of Change

Consumer Preferences

Analysis of the surveys at six-month intervals revealed that desire for staff
support declined over time among tenants in both group homes and independent apartments—by 12–23 percentage points—until after eighteen months
17 percent of ECH tenants and 24 percent of IL tenants believed they needed
staff help (see fig. 4.7). By contrast, preference for living in a group increased
over time for both groups, but more among those living in ECH residences.
Whereas only 12 percent of the participants had expressed a desire for group
living at baseline, 28 percent of the tenants in group homes preferred group
living by the project's conclusion, and 21 percent of those who had been living in independent apartments expressed this preference.

Regression analyses of the predictors of residential preference at the final
eighteen-month follow-up provide some insight into these changes (Schutt
and Goldfinger 2000, 147). The separate analyses in figure 4.8 indicate
that the predictors of residential preference had diverged by eighteen
months. Among independent apartment residents, older, more educated,
male minorities diagnosed with affective or bipolar illness rather than
schizophrenia were more interested in living in a group home; these same
characteristics had little effect among the group home residents. Also,
among independent apartment residents it was now consumers who preferred a staffed group home who tended to be those who had been rated
by clinicians as needing a group home, who had said they couldn't manage the tasks of independent living, and those who had expressed more of
a preference for living in a staffed, group home. Among the group home
residents only those who had fewer negative social contacts were more
interested in living in a group home at a level that was statistically
significant.

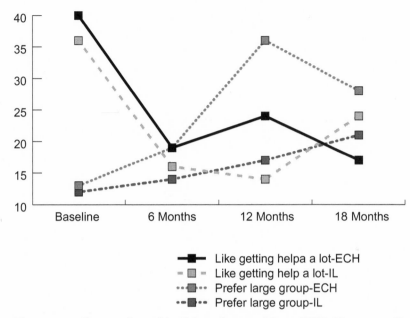

Figure 4.7. Changes in residential preference. Note: ECH $N = 45–53$; IL $N = 35–51$.

Thus, the experience of living independently or in a group changed not only the distribution of residential preferences but also the correspondence of those preferences to clinician recommendations. After experience in independent apartment living, those consumers who had felt initially that they couldn't manage the tasks of independent living and had preferred a staffed group home and whom clinicians had rated as needing more support were now more interested in a group home—in agreement with the initial clinician recommendation. Independent apartment tenants who were male, more educated, older, and African American were also more interested in group homes. After experience in group homes, residents who had had negative social contacts were now more interested in independent living, but the extent to which they believed they could manage the tasks of daily living was no longer related to their desire for independent living.

The changes in the preferences of independent apartment residents generally suggest increased correspondence of preferences and needs, while changes in the preference predictors among group home residents suggest that the experience of group living evened out preexisting differences among individuals in preferences, leaving only the group experience itself—the extent to which social ties had been negative—as the sole differentiator of

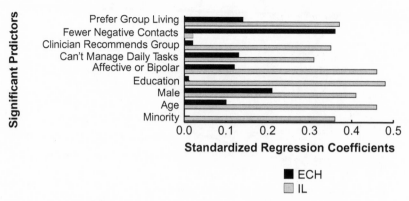

Figure 4.8. Regression analysis of preference at eighteen months for staffed group home. Note: ECH $R^2 = .40$, $N = 52$; IL $R^2 = .71$, $N = 36$. Variables controlled but not statistically significant in IL regression: substance abuse in project, psychiatric symptoms, perceived social support, number of positive social contacts, number of negative social contacts, difficulty with chores. Variables controlled but not statistically significant in ECH regression: race, age, gender, education, diagnosis, substance abuse in project, mean psychiatric symptoms in project, clinician housing recommendation, number of positive social contacts, baseline residential preference, difficulty with chores.

desire to live independently. Participants with a diagnosis of schizophrenia or schizoaffective disorder who had been living in independent apartments were now less interested in a group home, but if they had been living in an ECH they did not differ from others in their residential preferences. Women who had been living in an ECH had changed their preferences from baseline and no longer were more likely than men to choose independent living, but this change had not occurred among women in the IL housing; they were still more likely than men to prefer independent living.

Satisfaction

Residential satisfaction was also influenced by the housing experience—but in a markedly different pattern (Schutt, Goldfinger, and Penk 1997, 189). The move from the shelter into housing was associated with increased satisfaction with the residence overall (and with specific housing features) for IL residents by six months but not for ECH residents. The average level of housing satisfaction did not improve further after six months for either group.

Overall, these findings suggest that the move into independent apartments was more satisfying than the move into group homes, but further experience with residential living did not multiply that difference.

Housing Loss

Obtaining housing that matched participants' baseline preferences did not lead to higher rates of spending time housed during the project. On the contrary those who strongly desired independent living but had been rated by clinicians as needing group support proved to be much less likely to spend all their nights in housing than others—even if they were assigned to the IL that they had preferred (see fig. 4.9). On average, it was the partici- pants who expressed some interest in group housing at baseline who were least likely to experience homelessness again, even if they were assigned to independent apartments (as long as the clinicians had rated them as ready for independent living). Thus, the strong desire for independence among those whom clinicians judged as needing support predicted heightened risk of reexperiencing homelessness, whereas the desire for a more sup- portive group living situation was a predictor of greater ability to remain housed. IL living itself also increased housing loss.

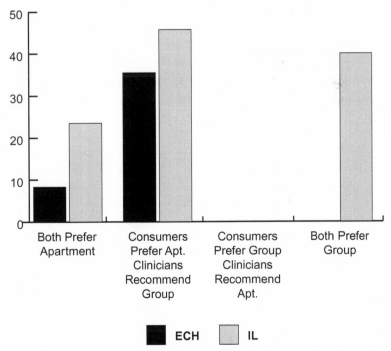

Figure 4.9. Percentage of days homeless by housing preferred, recom- mended, and received. Note: *N* = 108.

Conclusions

The sentiment that being randomized to an independent apartment was "winning the lottery" was widely shared and very strong among project participants. Those who most strongly preferred an independent living situation were also most certain that they could manage on their own, so from their perspective they were making a "rational choice." But the two clinicians who independently reviewed the participants' records disagreed. Not only did the clinicians recommend group homes for most participants, their ratings of participants' support needs bore no relationship to participants' own residential preferences. Professional evaluation of need led to different recommendations than consumers' housing choices. Although this divergence has been identified previously in research about mentally ill homeless persons' housing and service preferences, our research design provides unusually persuasive evidence of the existence and extent of the clinician-consumer gap.

However, in spite of this stark contrast apparent in our baseline survey results, further project findings support a nuanced interpretation of the meaning of consumer residential preferences and the value of adhering to clinician recommendations. Many project participants were interested in staff help in their new residence, so their overall preference for independent living did not preclude recognition by some of a need for ongoing support. In addition, as suggested by Pescosolido's (1992) social organization strategy, the meaning of a preference for independence became clear only in the context of interaction—in relation to clinicians' support recommendations. A desire for independent living when clinicians recommended a group home was first and foremost a rejection of support, and it was associated with a greater risk of a return to homelessness. Whether a desire to avoid clinical services, maintain social isolation, or return to the streets to drink is truly "rational" is open to question, but our analysis indicates unequivocally that a strong *preference* for independence did not indicate more *ability* to live independently. In contrast, consumers who were less confident in their own abilities and more interested in receiving support services were more likely to retain their housing. Clinician concerns about need for support and shelter staff worries about a return to substance abuse proved to be well founded.

Consumers who remained housed throughout the project became more confident in their own abilities but also became somewhat more interested in living in group, staffed housing. After eighteen months, the housing preferences of those who had been living in an IL also were more likely to be related to the clinicians' baseline housing recommendations. These changes support a social structural interpretation of consumer preferences but with the qualification of contingent rationality: consumers who experienced independent living seemed to base their later housing preferences on a more realistic assessment of their own abilities, whereas the experience of living in a group seemed to erase the effect of initial differences on housing preferences.

Homeless mentally ill individuals are not a homogeneous group, and their residential preferences are not all subject to the same interpretation. For about half of our homeless consumers, the strong desire at baseline to live independently foretold less ability to maintain housing. From the standpoint of the consumers, the preference for independent living had a rational basis, as it was associated positively with confidence in ability to manage the tasks of independent living. However, this self-confidence proved ill-founded, as it predicted poorer outcomes (Schutt and Goldfinger 2000, 151).

A central tenet of the health belief model is that interest in help for health problems will increase with the perceived severity of the disease for which help is needed. This tenet was not supported by our analysis at baseline, as indicators of health problems were not associated positively with a desire for more support. This calls into question the applicability of rational choice assumptions. Instead, as predicted by a social structural perspective on help-seeking, both the distribution of housing preferences and their predictors changed with experience. By the end of our eighteen-month project, consumers who had lived independently seemed to take into account problems of their health and functioning in their preference for group or independent living. This change over time supports the hypothesis of *contingent* rationality: the way in which consumers understood residential situations was situated within consumer experiences (Lovell and Cohen 1998; Schutt and Goldfinger 2000, 151).

The project's impact on the shelters indicated situational influence on both guests and staff. Once shelter guests could realize their desire to leave the shelter for permanent housing, staff reported guests becoming more confident and assertive. The mentality characterized by Bob Desjarlais (1997) as "struggling along" seemed to be on the wane. Staff also reported a change in their own work orientations as they began to emphasize the transitional character of the shelters.

The analysis of satisfaction among our participants at baseline and as the project progressed provides another perspective on the impact of housing. Although subjects tended to be satisfied overall with their housing (and even with the shelter), satisfaction varied with actual experience. The consumers were more satisfied with living in permanent housing than with living in a shelter and with independent apartments rather than group living. These differences occurred for the specific housing features—level of privacy and the presence of other residents—that diverged from those in shelters and that differed between group and independent living.

But individuals who expressed a strong preference at baseline for independent living were no more satisfied with their accommodations if they actually received an independent apartment than if they moved into a group home. Where the situation mattered was in how they reacted to their dissatisfaction: participants who were dissatisfied with their housing were more likely to move out if they had been assigned to an independent apartment but not if they were in a group home. The group living situation provided a measure of protection against a return to homelessness.

Although clinician responsibility for residential placement is a guiding principle for many mental health professionals, it is at odds with calls for consumer empowerment. Our research confirms the existence of a marked divergence in consumer and clinician housing preferences. Although the extent of this divergence varies among clinicians and with the specific aspect of housing considered, this is dwarfed by the discrepancy between clinicians' and consumers' overall preference for group or independent living.

The greater willingness of consumers to live with others after they had gained experience with group living is an indication that the marked discrepancy between consumer and clinician preferences identified in most surveys need not be taken as a barrier to the success of efforts to develop supportive group homes. Although we do not know whether the attitudinal changes we observed depended on the type of group housing we provided, we suspect that the basic rationale for the change was that identified by Segal, Kotler, and Holschuh (1991): consumer acceptance of other persons with mental illness increases with their own identification-enhancing experiences with persons who are mentally ill. The engagement of some of our consumers in the management of the group homes provided such experiences.

CHAPTER FIVE

Social Relations

WOULD PLACEMENT IN GROUP homes rather than independent apartments result in more social ties and more supportive social ties? What does prior research suggest about the possibility of shifting from service staff to other residents as a primary source of social connection? Could the "same strokes" be obtained "from different folks?" (Wellman and Wortley 1990). Would it matter that the group homes were managed to build a sense of community among residents? Would social relations in our group homes have such a beneficial effect?

Social isolation is often a concomitant of chronic mental illness, and its exacerbation can contribute to the continuation or worsening of psychiatric symptoms (Link et al. 1987; Sharfstein 2005). Social isolation is particularly severe among persons with serious mental illness who are homeless and have often withdrawn from others (Hawkins and Abrams 2007). Social support can provide resources for effective functioning and a foundation for coping with stress and loss (Mirowsky and Ross 1986; Schutt, Meschede, and Rierdan 1994; Rosenfield and Wenzel 1997), yet this potential is often not achieved for those whose friends are themselves substance abusers and lack resources of their own (Padgett et al. 2008).

Programs that attempt to increase social ties among homeless persons like those in the Boston McKinney Project thus encounter numerous obstacles. Social networks are likely to shrink due to high rates of death and illness (Hawkins and Abrams 2007). Attempts to improve social functioning through medication or professionally run programs can reinforce segregation from the larger community (Hogarty and Wieland 2005). Yet simply discharging inpatients to community settings without proactive efforts to decrease social isolation can result in very minimal patterns of social interaction—"virtual relations" with TV characters and "venturing forth" simply to have casual contact with people in settings like stores and parks (Beal et al. 2005; Liberman and Silbert 2005).

Some mental health programs have sought to achieve the benefits of social support by developing peer support: "social emotional support, frequently coupled with instrumental support, that is mutually offered or provided by persons having a mental health condition to others sharing a similar mental health condition to bring about a desired social or personal change" (Solomon 2004, 393; and see Toff 1988b; Mead, Hilton, and Curtis 2001; Wong and Solomon 2002). Such programs provide a sense of connection, belonging, and community that is often lacking for individuals receiving services in the mental health system (Davidson et al. 1999; Randall and Salem 2005).

Group homes increase the opportunity for social support, but studies of group home living have not yielded consistent findings about the effect of group home social ties or the role of staff. Nelson, Hall, and Walsh-Bowers (1998) compared residents of group homes and supportive apartments with board-and-care home residents, using a panel design. The housing types differed in resident control, but there was little indication of an effect on individual outcomes. Goering et al. (1997) identified development of a strong working alliance between case managers and residents as contributing to residents' social functioning. Falloon and Marshall (1983) observed social interaction in one large hostel and found that residents with schizophrenia who lacked social skills did not benefit from social interaction in the residence and were less likely than other residents to move on to independent living in spite of staff efforts at engagement. Dayson et al. (1998) compared two group homes and found that the home with a high degree of structured programming (self-management and group therapy) improved social and verbal behavior, but this occurred only with older patients who had a longer illness history. These mixed results suggest that we could not be certain that social support would improve in either our independent or group housing.

Prior research also suggests that creating more opportunities for social ties will not necessarily result in clients experiencing more social ties. At least among young adults, those who feel lonely actually spend no more time alone than others; it is the meaningfulness of their interaction with others, not simply time spent together, that is important in reducing feelings of loneliness (Cacioppo and Patrick 2008, 13, 94). The ethnographic notes will help to reveal the extent to which the ECH residents experienced their social ties with others as meaningful and so will provide some insight into whether they felt included in a community in their homes.

This chapter first describes social ties among study participants at baseline and identifies the characteristics that predicted more or less social support. Then the ethnographic notes are employed to explore how social ties varied among residents, how they differed in relation to house staff, and how they changed over time. The chapter concludes with a quantitative analysis of changes in social ties during the project.

Social Relations at Baseline

Participants answered a series of questions about their social contacts in the baseline interview (Barrera 1981). Several questions focused on how many contacts they had—both positive and negative. For example,

During the past month, who did you talk to about things that were very personal and private?

During the past month, who are the people you have had run-ins or disagreements with, or who made you angry and upset?

Many participants had some social contacts. Just 6 percent had no positive social contacts, 15 percent had just one contact, and 10 percent had eight contacts or more. However, these contacts were more likely to be with service staff than with relatives or friends. Fewer negative social contacts were named, with 55 percent reporting none and 25 percent reporting just one; the largest number of negative contacts reported was five. Again, these negative ties were more often with staff than with relatives or friends.

The average number of positive social ties at baseline was 3.7: 0.7 for relatives, 1.0 for friends, and 1.8 for staff. Although these numbers do not comport with a picture of complete social isolation, the average number of positive ties with relatives and friends—1.7—was considerably lower than the 2.94 positive ties found among a representative sample of all Americans in 1985 (McPherson, Smith-Lovin, and Brashears 2006). The average number of negative social ties among our participants was 0.8: 0.05 for relatives, 0.2 for friends, and 0.2 for staff (with the source of other negative contacts unspecified).

At baseline, those with more positive social ties were more likely to have a lifetime substance abuse diagnosis and to have expressed a preference

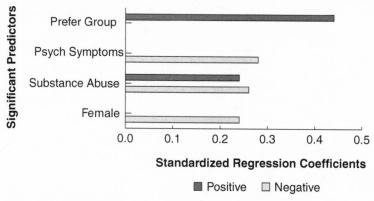

Figure 5.1. Regression analysis of positive and negative social ties at baseline. Note: Positive ties $R^2 = .26$, $N = 100$; negative ties $R^2 = .23$, $N = 100$. Variables included in the equation but not having statistically significant effects: race, age, education, diagnosis, ability to manage tasks, clinician residential recommendation.

for living in a group home rather than independently (see fig. 5.1). Women and substance abusers were likely to report more negative social ties, as were individuals reporting more psychiatric symptoms. Thus, substance abusers were more socially engaged—both positively and negatively—at baseline, whereas those who preferred group living had more positive social ties. Women and those with more psychiatric symptoms had more negative social ties. Each of these patterns would appear in social interaction within the group homes.

The Experience of Social Interaction

Residing in the housing our project provided, like all lived experience, involved interacting in various ways with different people over the course of days, weeks, and months. The specific mix of such experiences, intersecting and unfolding over time, created the tenants' social experience of living in the group homes and the independent apartments. This section draws on our rich ethnographic notes about the group homes in order to analyze patterns in social interaction. McKinney tenants assigned to independent apartments in one building met periodically with a project leader, and so the notes from these meetings provide some details about experiences with social interaction in the IL condition.

Most comments about social relations in the building with independent apartments described feelings of isolation:

The privacy's great; it's a little lonely, but you have to get used to that.

When asked whether he had made any friends yet, another independent apartment resident responded:

I wouldn't call them friends. They haven't fixed my smoke alarm yet.

Asked whether he had invited anyone over, he explained, "No. I like being alone."

The ethnographer recorded an interaction with another independent apartment tenant as the tenant explained why she disliked filling her days by going to a day program:

Doesn't like it. Nothing to do. When asked what she would like to do, she replies she would like to have her days free, so she can watch TV.

There were some independent apartment tenants in this building who remarked on visiting with friends back at the shelter in order to relieve their isolation, seeing friends in day programs, or just hanging out with friends in the building's apartment. However, none of the comments by independent apartment tenants indicated the type of intense social interaction that soon emerged in the group homes.

In the group homes, building community involved changing the nature of social interaction among tenants—strengthening "horizontal" social connections. Most research on the value of social ties focuses on this horizontal dimension, and so tenants' experiences as they interacted with their peers are reviewed first. This provides the first indication of the success of the group homes in becoming meaningful communities. But the process of shifting from staff to tenant control also required changing the distribution of power—inverting the "vertical" dimension of social connections. Throughout the project, this requirement proved to be a challenge for both groups and the individuals within them. The project's attempts to shift power in this way are examined more fully in chapter 9.

Interaction among Tenants

It seemed at the start of the project that tenants in the group homes sought, at most, to continue the "detached style of sociability" that had characterized social interaction in the shelters, rather than to develop more supportive social relations. "Staff efforts to impart a sense of community and skills in group process have been met with a generally unenthusiastic response," noted Ware et al. (1992).

As they settled into group home living and left the shelter environment further behind, many tenants developed more intense social relations and began to appreciate positive social experiences. However, there were also many negative social experiences involving other tenants.

Initial Experiences

Social isolation in the group homes was common when tenants first moved in, irrespective of the physical proximity of other tenants and the constant presence of house staff. Rather than engaging in interaction, many tenants chose isolation or passivity and stayed mostly in their own rooms. In one house just two tenants regularly got up and left early; others slept during the day. Watching TV without interacting with others was common, and many tenants attempted to have a TV in their own room (with varying degrees of success). Some continued to feel isolated as others developed some social ties:

> Mary said that she couldn't stand being in the house anymore, that everybody else has chosen who they're with, and she doesn't have anyone to talk to. She said that she wanted to go back to the . . . shelter.

Some tenants remained socially isolated throughout the project and seemed to be rejected by others:

> Boredom seems to be a big issue for Harold. He really does not do anything all day, other than sit around the house and smoke cigarettes. He would like to be friends with [others], but they are not interested. Sammy just keeps to himself, and Jeff is on his own schedule, spending most of his time out of the house on his daily rounds. And Justine is in the hospital. He and Justine have been good friends, and when Justine was secluding herself, Harold was the one who seemed to remain close to her. Harold complained about feeling lonely—"I sit in that kitchen alone at the table and I have nothing to do and nobody to talk to. I'm so lonely."

Some houses lagged persistently in the development of positive social relations. Even when one house had a cookout, there was little social interaction. But the initial pattern of disengagement changed markedly for many tenants and in most houses.

Positive Experiences

Positive social relations emerged gradually but were apparent in multiple behaviors: talking and laughing together, having parties, meetings, and community meals together, and in socializing. A project coordinator noted at the start of one house meeting that "things seem to be turning around." Tenants in some homes started preparing group meals after the weekly tenant meeting. Staff noted more talking together, more of a family feeling, and better behavior among tenants than in most group homes, with tenants watching TV and playing cards together (and with staff). Some tenants went to movies together, barbecues were organized in the summer, and a few cooked for others. Two tenants went apple picking with a staff member. Birthdays were occasionally celebrated together; in one house, a surprise birthday party moved the recipient to make an impromptu speech:

> This place has been good to me; I'm staging a major comeback. I'm doing rather well, I walk five miles a day, I go to Mass every day, and AA every day just about. I go to day treatment and that leaves only the evenings to be in the house. If I sleep all day Saturday, that's just to catch up for the week.

Holidays also proved to be occasions for positive social experiences in some homes. Christmas trees were purchased and tenants in one home added Hanukkah decorations for a new Jewish tenant. Staff remarked on the change since the move-in period and on the difference in some tenants' behavior.

> *Fred:* You know, I just wanna say something. Since before you left, Jane, for the last couple of weeks, I've been feeling that things have really come together, just like you said at the last meeting. You were saying that would be the next phase—it's not like it's all over all of a sudden. Everyone still has issues, but we're working together as a group more. I was thinking when you said it that that'll be months away, or that it'll be over once the holidays are over, but it's still going on.
> *Sam:* You know, Ralph got up early Christmas Day and spent all day making a turkey dinner. He even soaked the turkey in the tub.
> *Abby:* Yeah, he got the table all set and everything.
> *Tom:* He was nervous all day; he said he never made a turkey dinner before. He couldn't eat that night, he was so nervous! I don't think he had anything—I think he just went to bed.
> *Jane [staff]:* You're kidding! Ralph made a turkey dinner? I don't believe it.
> *Sam:* Yeah, he did. And Abby made a ham, and Kathryn made something— she always makes something nice. Ralph was asking people all kinds of advice about what to do—he was saying "Do you know how much help I asked for today? I never did that before!"
> *Jane [staff]* and I [the ethnographer] are staring at each other with our mouths open. The thought of Ralph making a whole dinner for the house and setting the table and asking for help was delightfully shocking.

When a baby was born to a tenant at one house during the holiday season, tenants came together in a remarkable way for the short period the mother and newborn remained in the house. The house ethnographer captured the spirit of that time:

A moving evening tonight. Quiet and almost spiritual—a house filled with the sounds of a newly born baby, the flickering of eight candles in the window, the glistening of a tall pine tree in the living room, the shared camaraderie of a group of former strangers from all walks of life.

Staff commented that "people are really hanging out together—talking, helping each other out." When tenants in one ECH contributed $5 each for a barbecue, some seemed to be motivated by a desire to "be a part of the group more [than] anything else." Some staff felt that a sense of community had been achieved:

It feels much more comfortable than it did a year ago when I first came!
 The group was so different a year ago—it was all individuals in one space. . . .
 Yeah, now nobody's mad at each other—there's like no conflict.
 People will still grumble, but things seem to get resolved now. And I've even heard people apologize. . . .

Daily Activities

Activities of daily living served as a focus for positive social interaction in some homes at some times. In addition to occasional barbecues organized by the project coordinator, other group activities helped tenants interact for constructive purposes: group shopping trips, group meals, and "chore days."

An ethnographer went grocery shopping with two tenants from one house and marveled at the quality of their interaction:

The way in which [they] worked together on preparing lists and selecting items was extraordinary. [She] was the decisive one and [he] cooled impulses. Both remarked on this effect of the other.
 [Group meals] "brought out who was and who was not committed to the group. It brings people together, that's the best part about it. Food is a wonderful way to do that." [Further discussion of the value of eating together.]

The grant sponsored cooking lessons at one house, with all but one tenant participating and then eating together.

Meetings

With a few exceptions, tenants engaged little in house meetings early in the project. A project leader remarked that people might become more of a group during the winter because they wouldn't want to go out as much; she was optimistic because issues were coming out on the table quickly. A house staff member reported that staff encouraged active participation by telling residents with complaints to bring them up at the tenant meeting.

Over time, more tenants participated actively in tenant meetings and expressed their opinions more freely. The weekly tenant meetings began to provide an opportunity to talk through issues concerning tenant behavior, interaction with staff, and house management. Our empowerment coordinator encouraged a participatory democratic meeting style that would lead to a group consensus:

> I'm here to help make the rules that you all wanna have, but to do that, we['ve] got to have what's called consensus thinking. That means that we decide what a problem is here in the meeting we're having, and we discuss all the sides because then it's a real house with a lot of different ideas.

She usually chaired the meetings and began by asking, simply, "Has anyone got anything to bring up?" Her skill in this role was praised by staff in one conversation prior to a meeting:

> [They were] . . . amazed at [her] ability to balance all the concerns of the house while running an effective meeting; and to do this with people yelling back and forth at each other. They were both also quite impressed with [her] ability to put people in their place without their even knowing that it had been done.

A project ethnographer focused attention on the empowerment coordinator's frequent ability to relate to tenants with an informal, egalitarian style:

> [She] came in and started talking with people in her usual casual style, making jokes. . . . It is an important part of the way she constructs her relationship with the tenants because they join with her in laughing about her connection with "the system."

The complex social dynamic that developed in tenant meetings is best illustrated by an ethnographer's verbatim notes of one meeting. Different issues arose, were discussed, and were either resolved or tabled. Different voices were heard and divergent opinions expressed, but the overall tenor of the meeting was friendly and supportive. Tenants shared responsibilities for house management, including voting on a prospective new member of the house staff. Planning group meals and shopping were frequent topics of discussion.

> Doreen [A staff member, since the project coordinator was away] opened the meeting by listing agenda items left from the last meeting: the house fund, door locks, BJ's, food bank, house supplies.
> Sammy is interested in the food bank, and he asked about how to get involved in it as well as some of the other cheap food opportunities. Doreen talked about Project Share, where they can get $40 worth of groceries for $13.

Doreen suggested that they buy that out of the house fund, and then they could cook a group meal. Freddy was asked about cooking, and he said "I can't cook for the masses." Caroline suggested that they have the group meal immediately following the meeting. She mentioned that she and Ben had fed everyone on chicken and dumplings. Freddy said he was not interested in the food program because he wants to deal with his own food: "I want to know where it's from."

House finances were also a frequent focus of discussion.

A staff member asked Ben how he financed the meal he cooked over the weekend, and he said that he paid for it all himself. Alicia was asked what she thought of the proposal, and she said she didn't understand what she was being asked about. When told she said "yes." Sammy said they shouldn't even ask about it, they should just go right ahead and do it. Doreen said that her concern was that if they paid for it out of the house fund, then that is everybody's money so everybody should have a say in the matter. Freddy was interested in the house fund. He asked Doreen to read off all the names and tell how much they paid up or owed.

They then considered that maybe just the people who pitched in for the food would get to partake in the meal. This raised the issue of how they would enforce this. Sammy: "What are you going to do, put a guard in front of the fridge?" He said that already people share quite a bit of their food, and if they did not they would starve.

Excessive noise by some tenants was an occasional problem. Ben and Freddy had issues about Dave's radio, which they brought up. Freddy said he has already told Dave about the cord stretching in front of the door and how he should use another nearby plug. Dave had said he would but didn't change his practice. Dave agreed that he should. Sammy took the opportunity to suggest that the reason Dave did not change was because he is a "day-tripper," which is a pretty good line. Ben complained that Dave plays it too loud at 1:00 in the morning. He did not complain that Dave plays it at ear-splitting volume most of the afternoon and evening though. Sammy suggested earphones. [A staff member] said that in some of the other houses they had quiet hours. Freddy was asked, and he was somewhat annoyed by the question. Freddy: "It's a moot point, it's too loud, you turn it down at night." Ben said it bothered him more than others because his room is on the first floor. Dave said he didn't mind turning it down.

Manny came in at this point, and he added his $10 to the house fund. He has not been around much, although I'm not sure whether he was at the house for the Saturday cleanup. He was trying to spend more time at the house to see if it would do him any good, and to see if it wasn't too boring. He may have given up and taken to just staying there a couple [of] nights a week.

Referring to people paying up their dues, Freddy said it was the shame factor of bringing it out in the open which [sic] worked for him and for Manny. Doreen brought up the phone bill, and Sammy said that he wanted someone to pay the bill before he got sent to jail. There is now enough money in the house fund to pay the bill.

Doreen pushed for volunteers to run the house bank account and to organize the house shopping. Freddy was reluctant to volunteer for more work because he is already on too many committees and this in particular because he does not believe in banks. Doreen tried to get him to volunteer to organize shopping and gave him a hard sell until he agreed to do it. She said it would involve keeping track of the stuff needed in the house and planning when they needed to go on shopping trips to replace it. He did not have to be in charge of the money, only the inventory. Freddy asked what the title for the position was. . . .

Tenants also considered and voted on whether a prospective staff member should be allowed to work in the house.

Doreen asked her [a prospective new staff member] to go into the office while they considered her. Freddy and Sammy were strong advocates for her. Everyone else approved without any discussion. Alicia seemed to not have strong feelings on the matter and made that clear. Manny said he approved, but Caroline told him that he didn't even know her. He said he was just responding to everybody else's sentiment.

Tenants then expressed frustration with the behavior of some current staff members.

The meeting was just about over, but [a staff member] said that Alicia had something to bring up. Alicia said "Oh yeah" and that there was staff smoking in the TV room, which was outside of the designated smoking area, and there was smoking upstairs. Ben added that the staff leave ashtrays in the TV room, and then he has lit up a smoke a couple of times automatically because he saw them. Doreen promised to address the issue in a staff meeting and said she did not know that anyone was smoking in there. She said she did notice that someone had been smoking upstairs.

Of course, tenant meetings were neither entirely nor consistently a positive experience for all participants. Some staff reported to the empowerment coordinator that the tenants did not bring up their underlying conflicts in meetings.

House Staff: But the tenants act a lot different at the meetings than at the house in general. There are two different behaviors. We see them every day! They don't ever complain during the meetings but every day, they do to us.

Empowerment Coordinator: If Sam is taking it on himself to go to the food bank, and if Jim and Karyn are participating in the way they are, and if many of the decisions are made by Sam and tenants aren't complaining, then why is it that the staff has a problem?

Staff: But they are complaining to us!

Coordinator: So you're saying that the tenant meetings aren't real.

Staff: No, they're not real. There are two different behaviors—they complain when you're gone, and everything's fine when you're here!

Discussion could reveal strains between tenants and staff and among tenants, and participants' behaviors sometimes exposed underlying problems that might otherwise have gone unnoticed. Staff participation in meetings was a source of some controversy. Although the project coordinator initially argued for tenant-only meetings with her, she subsequently supported limited staff participation—as tenants felt more comfortable with staff, and meetings became more "homelike" with them present. Tenants told the house manager in one house that they did not want to have any staff participate, and some complained about staff "running the house." Other tenants remarked that tenant meetings were useless—tenants just used them to argue with each other—and the staff should just "lay down the law." Two tenants were "hung over" at one meeting.

The lack of success of some tenant meetings is captured well in notes on a meeting that occurred shortly before the identification of widespread crack cocaine use in one house. Even at this time, however, some tenants looked forward to meeting time.

The empowerment coordinator comments that no one is responding to her. She interrupts the meeting to say that she feels "something is wrong" and asks what the "bad feeling" is due to. No response. [She says] "Does anybody want to talk about why the house seems tense?" She reminded people of the recent discussion of the coffee thing, and how it had helped to "talk it out." "Sometimes when the problems are real severe and you can't talk, it means you're bullshit mad, which is too bad if you feel you can't talk. You have a great house and I like you all. It's going to be a bummer to hang out in this house."

Harvey says, "I hate those meetings. They always get so uncomfortable." Jill opines, instead, "Oh, I love those meetings. It's the only time that we ever get together in this house and talk. Really hash things out."

Even coping with problems could lead to expressions of group spirit.

Empowerment coordinator: I think we've got to figure out who has the cigarette problem. In a couple of other houses the tenants decided that the people who tended to burn things could only smoke in certain areas, like say downstairs.

[Harvey]: Maybe people should decide on restricted areas, so they'll only burn down the furniture in one room!! [People chuckling and laughing.]

The empowerment coordinator said that the staff dealt very well last night with Andrew when he came into the house ranting and they gathered around monitoring him. . . . A staff member had some reasons for hope too. He said "It was good that people felt safe enough to bitch and moan, which was progress." [The empowerment coordinator] agreed. "If [they] continue to see responsiveness among the tenants then the house will continue to improve. But you have to remember the problems. Just when you think things are fine, someone will test [that] thought."

As tenants gained experience with the meeting process, they played an increasingly important role, including planning and chairing meetings. The complete ethnographic notes from a meeting late in the history of one house exemplified the efficient organization of meetings run by some tenants.

George "officially" called the meeting to order and took over responsibility for running the meeting. He said that he had an agenda but that it wouldn't prevent others from bringing up whatever they wanted.

1. Smoking in the soft chairs in the TV room should stop. If they wanted they might bring up moving the smoking area back to the kitchen, but until then, they must follow the rules. George gave a short lecture on how quickly the house would go up in flames and how long a cigarette butt could smolder in the couch.

2. Room Checks. Jeffery brought up that he had heard that someone had been in his room while he was gone and that he didn't want that to happen again. George said he had heard the same thing. Both of them saw it as a "room search" without their permission. Paula also thought this was an invasion of privacy. Dilma explained that the landlord had requested to see all the rooms so they had to use the staff copies of the keys to open them all up. They were just looking to see the condition of the room, not to look through anyone's stuff. They were looking for ways to help people improve the physical condition of the place. It was a maintenance inspection not a room search.

3. Paula brought up the curtains. She had heard that they were going to get curtains put in, and she is personally against the idea. She asked how many people wanted them. No one felt strongly that they should be there, and [a staff member] said it should be up to them to decide. An informal poll showed a majority of those present voting against the curtains.

4. George told how he had come downstairs in the middle of the night to find the coffee machine on without the carafe. He said that putting his hand over the burner he could feel the heat. This was a serious fire hazard which [*sic*] he harangued people about avoiding in the future.

5. Paula said that people shouldn't put dirty dishes into the cabinet or into the dishwasher when it was full of clean dishes.

6. George said that he felt very strongly that people should be keeping the kitchen clean. Not cleaning up after yourself should be "grounds for dismissal."

7. George asked Oscar to tell his story, and Oscar knew immediately what he was talking about. Oscar said that he was in the kitchen when he saw smoke emanating from the trash can and that it had started because someone had emptied an ash tray into it when there still was a cigarette smoldering. Oscar

put water on it to put it out, but wanted to warn people to clean out the ash trays with water before emptying them.

8. George suggested having a smoke out day. One day everyone would agree not to smoke. [Others] expressed interest, but Jeffery and [another tenant] were more concerned that they wouldn't be prohibited from smoking on that day.

9. AA meeting. For at least the third time this was brought up again. Paula restated her objection, which is that the meeting would bring strangers into the house. The empowerment coordinator (who had arrived late and taken a seat in the meeting) said that was a legitimate concern, and she suggested that they could have a closed meeting but invite guest speakers to each meeting. George said that it was a "slowly evolving thing," and they should figure out the details next week, but Paula seemed mostly assuaged.

10. Trip to BJ's. There is plenty of money in the house fund, and the house is low on supplies, so there should be a trip to BJ's soon. The empowerment coordinator said that at most of the other houses the trip is on automatic and doesn't have to be discussed at the tenant meeting. The shopper should just work out a convenient time with staff. Jeffery said he would do this.

Aside: George said there was a problem with the way the house was going because people did not talk about the issues of the tenant meeting outside of the meeting itself. They should try to reach that level of community organization.

11. George asked if they could go to Hi-Lo Foods instead of Flanagan's on the next shopping trip because it is cheaper.

12. AA anniversary party. George announced again that he was getting his third medallion at a meeting on the morning of the 16th. There would be a van going from the house to the meeting, and there would be a cookout afterwards at the house.

13. George said that since the group sent a letter to [another tenant] he has been doing much better at getting along with people. [The other tenant] said "Thank You Mr. George."

14. George suggested that they have a system of rotating chairperson for the meeting. Each week a different tenant would lead the meeting, and the chairperson one week would choose the chair for the next week. George said that he "grabbed it" today, but that from now on they could do it systematically. George said that it was the McKinney belief that they could bring people from diverse backgrounds together and they could form an integrated group. The house, according to George, was not totally integrated yet—there is a lot of "aloofness." George hopes that by the end of summer they will be more cohesive.

15. George picked Oscar to be next week's chairperson.

Clearly, tenant meetings could be productive and positive experiences for those involved.

Romance

In the best of circumstances romantic relationships provide a mixture of positive and negative experiences. When romance arose in the group homes, positive attraction often had, or soon resulted in, negative elements. One of the most intense romantic engagements involved two tenants who married while living in the ECH. The marriage initially seemed to have a positive impact on the two, although they were seen as withdrawing from participation in group events and were criticized for acting as though the house was now their own. The honeymoon did not last long. Their marital spats disrupted others in the house, and the wife began to criticize another tenant for supposedly having an interest in her husband. The couple's initial attempt to move out of the house together faltered, and the relationship soon ended in divorce, with one member of the couple moving out permanently. Romantic engagement in another house between a recovering alcoholic and a very active drinker led to the recovering alcoholic "falling off the wagon." This retrogression only ended when the relationship was severed (and after a stay in an inpatient detox unit). In general, romance seemed to violate the behavioral limits required for successful maintenance of a community of unrelated individuals.

Negative Experiences

In spite of many tenants' positive experiences of interaction with their peers, problems in interaction with others were ubiquitous—so much so that they dominated many meetings, much staff time, and the course of many days, weeks, and months. At times, the empowerment coordinator referred to "tension you can cut with a knife." Some problems seemed to reflect psychiatric symptoms or substance abuse, but many others were better understood as emerging from conflicting personalities, some residents who were "too bossy," scarce resources, and disappointed hopes.

The overt causes of negative interactions ranged from the mundane to the moralistic. Disputes emerged over which TV show to watch at a particular time and over rudeness or other types of inconsiderate behavior. A male tenant was accused of harassing women in the house. Playing loud music, particularly at night, precipitated tension between tenants in several houses and their housemates. Incessant swearing caused complaints about several tenants. One tenant complained because some of the men made derisive comments when she went out at night to meet other men. Some tenants grumbled when others did not pay into the house fund—at times because of *their* dissatisfaction with house affairs.

Negative experiences like these cast a pall over houses at times.

> We meet at the house at 11 am and drive in two cars over to BJ's with a bunch of people from the house. Everybody in a bad mood—complain[ing] the whole time about anything and everything. Hardly anything is purchased at BJ's—just a few household supplies and a little food. After getting back to the house, nobody wants to have a meeting—all "too tired." We hung around for awhile, feeling the tension in the house.

Confronted with escalating complaints in one house, the empowerment coordinator urged tenants to "say something and hope that people listen" when "this kind of stuff" comes up. However, this admonition had little effect.

Symptoms

Symptoms of mental illness interfered with the development of positive social relations on many occasions. Frequent expressions of "bizarre ideas" by one tenant led to tension with others. Another tenant was "loud, abrupt, and screaming in [the] face" of another, while a tenant in another house was noted to "holler and scream in the kitchen and make things known to everybody else if she's upset with one person." One tenant secluded herself in her room as a response to such problems.

Each house had to designate a tenant to serve as the tenant human rights officer. Soon after he assumed this role, the human rights officer in one house informed a staff member that a complaint had been filed against her. The exchange between the tenant human rights officer and the staff member who was the subject of the complaint illustrated how problems in social relations could be magnified by the symptoms of mental illness.

> I have to notify you that Jill [a tenant] has filed a human rights complaint against you for violating her basic human rights, spreading the AIDS virus, threatening hospitalization due to clothing being cleaned out of a closet, and general insensitivity. [The staff member] was silent for a minute, then asked [the complainant] what all that meant as she was sitting on the couch next to [the human rights officer]. [The tenant] got up and said "It means what it says."

The tenant's linking of AIDS, clothing in a closet, and the risk of hospitalization may have had to do with the staff member being insensitive, or perhaps not, but neither the other tenant serving as the human rights officer, the staff member, nor even the tenant seemed to be able to connect the dots in that type of delusional thought process.

Substance Abuse

Tenants often saw drugs or alcohol as a means of improving their social relations. One tenant began to frequent a local bar and talked at home, to a skeptical audience, about how she knew everyone there, the bartenders and the bouncers. Two tenants who were on friendly terms and supported each other's drinking brought drinks to a tenant meeting, where they then sat and complained about another tenant's "out of control" drinking. Tenants in one house voted to allow beer in the house.

But in spite of the efforts of substance users to assert the "normality" of their habits, substance abuse created tension and conflict throughout the project. Meetings were often "filled with tension and emotional outbursts" due to conflict over substance abuse. Some drug users supported their habit in part with theft within the house. In some houses, substance abusers stayed up late at night, playing loud music, bringing in "guests," or consummating drug deals outside of the house. Tenants sought to help each other avoid staff discovery of their drug use.

Over time, these problems led a few tenants to move to structured drug/ alcohol treatment programs and others to be expelled. The resulting reconsideration of the value of rules for living in the houses, reformulation of tenant selection guidelines, and enhancement of the staff role in the houses are elaborated on in the next chapter.

Conflict

The level of conflict among tenants ebbed and flowed throughout the project, varying between specific tenants and different houses. The sources of this conflict were as varied as the people involved and the circumstances they confronted. There was a shouting incident between two tenants, after one took some of the other's milk and didn't want to give back an extra amount as a penalty. Ongoing conflict developed between some specific tenants who had a particular propensity for getting on each other's nerves.

> [A staff member] said it's always when Sammy is around that Dave gets upset. When Sammy is around Dave changes totally. She said she was sitting downstairs with Dave when Sammy came in and "he changed on me, just like that it was like another person, even a different voice, like Sybil." Sammy agitates him and Dave tried to act tough.

Particular tenants functioned in several houses as vortices for conflict, drawing other tenants into negative interactions that spiraled downward with increasing intensity. Erin played her stereo too loud late at night, even after moving it to the basement. She acted aggressively toward other tenants even when she spilled things while cooking or wanted to watch a different TV channel. She also focused attention on a particular tenant who was offended by her behavior—almost assaulting him until a staff member intervened.

> Gene sticks up to Erin in arguments. Gene complains about Erin's loud music keeping him up but won't confront her directly and insists on going to staff—which Erin turns into an attack on him for relying on "the white man." Gene complains about Erin swearing, and Erin protests that she will talk as she wants; gets very upset with Gene. Ralph avers that she has tantrums like a child. Tenants do not develop a strategy for confronting her.

In another house, Walter began heavy drinking and was soon in conflict with other residents.

> Candy complained about harassment (by Walter), and Walter complained about people who would greet him but then not give him a cigarette. Walter said he just wanted a place to live and that if no one else spoke to him it would be fine. Sylvia explained that she had tried to talk to Walter about his drinking and his treatment of staff, and then he got angry. Sylvia said that Walter had become a totally different person than he had been at [the shelter]. Their arguing continued. The project coordinator proposed tabling the issue, but the argument continued. Walter said other tenants were always trying to get him and threatened a lawyer. The project coordinator said that it was okay to talk about anything but that it was not okay to threaten other tenants or use abusive language. Walter finally moved out.

Theft

Thefts by tenants in their own houses emerged as a major problem early in the grant, with supporting of drug habits seeming to be the major impetus. Furniture was carted out of one house and then not replaced for a time due to fear of its being stolen again. A drug user stole fans from one house, and money was even stolen from an office safe. Personal belongings were stolen from bedrooms. Staff complained that "everybody is stealing from everybody else." Some tenants were irate because of thefts of their food kept in separate areas in the communal kitchen:

> *Tenant [in raised voice]:* And forget about labeling your own food! You can have your names written all over until it's red all over the packages—it doesn't matter! It's useless. They're gonna do it anyway. I even tried to give this guy something to eat of mine—but he still goes and takes my food. [turning to him and yelling] But at least ask me! I don't like the taking!
> *Empowerment coordinator:* I can't believe this—that's shelter behavior!
> *Tenant:* Thank you!!! But nothing helps!

Staff agreed to have bedroom locks installed and so the problem of theft from bedrooms subsided. In some houses, the departure of a severely addicted drug user eliminated major thefts.

Overall, social interaction among tenants in the group homes was a mixed bag. Many interchanges were positive, and group meetings could be important opportunities for positive social engagement. Yet negative interactions occurred frequently throughout the project and had a corrosive effect on community-building efforts. There was no easily defined path to a harmonious community, nor can it be assumed that the mixture of positive and negative social interaction that did occur had any lasting benefits. We therefore return to this issue in several subsequent chapters.

Tenant-Staff Relations

Relations between tenants and staff were characterized by much uncertainty in the initial period in each house. Both tenants and staff knew that the balance of power in the houses was to shift toward the tenants, but how much that was to occur, when it was to happen, and how it was happen was a matter of some confusion. When staff in one house announced that they wanted to teach interested tenants how to cook, a program leader told them that it would be inappropriate to do so. When one house held a cookout in response to the empowerment coordinator's suggestion, house staff did not help out, and the coordinator herself had to buy supplies and take charge.

Friction between tenants and house staff occurred throughout the project. There was a "yelling match" during a barbeque when a tenant took more food than what a staff member deemed reasonable. A tenant in another house complained that a project rep talked down to him, so "fuck her." When a tenant made a sarcastic comment about TV commercials, a staff member responded in kind with a sarcastic retort; the tenant in turn urged the staff member that she "should come right out and say it" if the staff member did not like her.

Staff in one ECH complained to the empowerment coordinator about an "us versus them" situation:

House Staff: I feel it's an us versus them situation, staff versus tenants. I feel like an enemy, and I feel embarrassed in the tenant meetings. I just feel like the tenants are blaming us for a lot of things.
Empowerment Coordinator: O yeah, it's like [the house manager] is the father, you're the mother, and the tenants are the kids. . . .

Tenant: Yeah. The last I heard people in this house can come and go late at night. So I came in late one night and [a staff member] said to me why didn't you call first? He's always checking up on me. If I feel like sitting at home I will, and if I feel like leaving late one night, I will. I don't need a mommy and daddy. I left them when I was 15 years old. [The staff member] don't do nothing, and he's always got smart things to say. He's telling me when to play the stereo and how loud. I'll turn the damn system on and wake everybody up if I want to.

One tenant seemed to want to think of herself as simply a friend on an equal level with staff and stopped communicating with staff when she felt they were focusing their attention on another tenant. She also highlighted her dislike of staff control in a complaint about the staff log book in which problems were recorded for the benefit of the next shift:

Everything we do is reported in that book, it's all over-exaggerated, and we can't do anything without being reported on.

An ethnographer who examined a log book found that it contained "commentary using stereotyped images," such as "the house couch potatoes." He concluded that many staff felt themselves in opposition to tenants. Finally, tenant opposition at one house led to termination of the log. As one tenant argued,

If we're supposed to be independent we don't need someone in the background writing things down. In the shelter they did it because it was their job, and it kept you out of the cold. Here we're payin' rent and should be respected.

Yet house staff often felt that they were themselves being treated unfairly by tenants.

[A staff member] said she felt like the staff would never now be able to communicate or support each other and that so often she felt overcome by all the negativity on the part of the tenants as they gathered together and whispered nasty things about staff or complained loudly that they didn't want staff in the house.

A member of the staff in one house was reduced to tears by a tenant's constant criticisms of staff actions and concluded that "normal human relations" were not possible.

I've known all these tenants for so long. This is supposed to be an empowerment household, but these people just don't know how to have normal human relations.

Conflicts became so common that the ethnographer in one house commented that "The house seems like it's falling apart." Staff often found themselves in conflict, with one complaining that she was "railroaded into leaving" after complaints had emerged about the house manager. Another staff member wrote in a letter of resignation to her supervisor that many staff were unhappy and lacked motivation and cohesion.

Staff Office

Physical arrangements enhance or diminish opportunities for social interaction and convey a sense of what type of interaction is expected (Festinger, Schachter, and Back 1950). In one ECH there was no separate room for staff, and so desks were placed in the foyer. From this vantage point, staff could observe much tenant activity, and the two groups had no choice but to interact throughout the day. Another house had one staff desk in an open area and other in a separate room. When there was no physical barrier between staff and tenants, conflicts among staff and instances of staff tardiness and lethargy were also evident to tenants.

By contrast in another ECH the staff office was on the third floor, removed physically from the ongoing social life of the house and allowing tenants to insist on confining staff to that office. Tenants quickly asserted their power by insisting that staff remain in their third-floor office and requiring that staff ask permission to use the facilities elsewhere in the house. Overall, staff-tenant relations seemed more positive in this house. Another house pressured staff to create an office out of sight, so the house would not seem like a group home. The tenants in this house also demanded to have the kitchen knives back in the kitchen instead of being kept in the staff office.

In a house without a separate staff office, some tenants complained about having too many staff around. Some staff spent their time sitting passively on the couch, so as "not to intrude" on the tenant activities. Several staff in this house wanted to move their "office" into the laundry room (and move the washer and dryer to the basement), so they could remove themselves from house activity. However, other staff argued that their close contact with tenants gave the house a more communal feel—"like a family." Tenants were ambivalent and action was delayed. Finally, at the project's end, a staff office was developed in the basement.

Staff-Initiated Activities

Should staff initiate recreational or other activities for tenants? Initially, the empowerment coordinator encouraged staff to get tenants to participate in joint activities, such as going to the library, registering to vote, working on volunteer projects, or walking in the park or reading a book—activities like those in which staff engaged during the day. Eventually, she asserted, "they will wanna go to work." House staff planned outings, announced expressive art activities, and organized a basement recreational center. Staff planned simple birthday celebrations and cooked a Thanksgiving dinner for three of the group homes. One staff member expressed the hope that such activities would keep people in the house more and build relations among them, rather than letting them go "off in their own world." But project staff remained ambivalent about whether house staff should initiate activities to involve tenants.

> *Sam:* I think tenants should enjoy a couple of nights out. We can utilize the van and go out to shows or the movies, or get a little bowling league action. I'll be glad to take them out.
>
> *Jim:* I got an idea. Why don't you get a list together of who wants to go and what you wanna do and which nights. I'll have you come in those nights, and it'll be set.
>
> *Sam:* I see a lot of them not doing anything.
>
> *Empowerment coordinator:* Yeah, but we've had a lot of people telling them what to do, and they enjoy sitting around and relaxing. One of the things about this model is that nobody is telling them what to do—they decide what they want to do.
>
> *Sam:* I'm just looking to enhance their stay here, while they're getting on their feet.

These efforts did not always have the intended effect. One staff member who had taken the initiative to organize activities finally complained that he was "sick of all the tenants never following through on plans they make."

Setting Limits

Were staff members to be friends of the tenants or professionals who set the rules for tenants and monitor their behavior? Both staff and tenants discussed and tested appropriate limits for their interaction. One house manager encouraged staff to avoid being friends with tenants and not to do too much for them, instead maintaining a professional distance. Staff in one house agreed not to tell tenants how late they could stay up or when they should go to bed. However, when a tenant in another house avoided many house meetings, did not contribute to the house kitty, and threatened other tenants, staff agreed to set limits for her. When tenants discussed personal problems in meetings, staff expressed concerns about their violating the right to privacy and the need to restrict clinical issues to professional-tenant interchanges.

Sexual relations were one dimension of social relations that tested the social boundaries between staff and tenants. Some tenants in several houses flirted with staff: a lesbian tenant wrote a largely incoherent love poem to another tenant and tried to get a female staff member to respond to sexual overtures, explaining to a peer, "They're not gonna do anything to me because I'm mentally ill." The staff member was discouraged by another from filing a report on this incident so as not to make the lesbian tenant "even more of an outcast." The project plan to minimize staff intrusion in tenant relations thus had the unintended consequence of letting interpersonal problems fester.

Staff discussed and debated the problem of establishing appropriate boundaries for interaction with tenants in one house meeting:

Bonnie: But staff are supposed to be caretakers! Staff are told the boundaries we have, but tenants should be told too. They have somebody who is caring, and there's a lot of sexualizing associated with that.

Helen: But I thought empowerment is supposed to mean that we tell them what's going on—the boundaries are set by our example. . . .

Butch: Why not tell them that if they're making friends wherever they are, they're gonna lose them if they cross that line?

Lisa: But this program challenges where those boundaries do lie in their mental health. It's a floating kind of feeling . . . there's this not knowing, you know what I mean? It's so loose here, and we're working so closely with them—I don't know—there are so many traditions in this field that are so weird, so bizarre, and so dehumanizing. But the boundaries here are totally different than in the more structured setting. It's almost as if I'd feel more comfortable in the more structured setting. . . .

Lisa: I feel that this is more of a friendship than a working relationship.

Bonnie: But what's more therapeutic? What happens when something big comes along and you have to be staff? Like the other night, me and Matty were gonna go out after work and Sarah wanted to come with us. But we told her she couldn't do that.

Lisa: I don't know . . . I guess it has to be on an individual case basis. We are taking on a lot of responsibility, but I go home and wonder what's happening to my friends here?

Bonnie: I don't know . . . I don't know what's not acceptable! It's always this thing where you don't draw the boundaries. . . .

Lisa: But this project is all about finding your own boundaries. Look, it's true that some settings need to lose their rigidness, but in this area of the grant, there's a suppleness. I like it. You're still moving among the boundaries of the system, but there's movement and flexibility.

Helen: I just try to dwell on the positive rather than the negative. If I concentrated on this floating lostness, I'd get depressed and want to leave! At this [new] next job . . . it's a small set of clients, and you talk to them and tell them what the boundaries are right off the bat.

Lisa: But that's so restrictive!

Bonnie: No it's not. . . . But I think boundaries are always there between staff and tenants. We don't want to stereotype people, but it is convenient to put people into categories . . . When people start saying that's bad and we have to get rid of the whole thing, there's got to be some type of systematizing that takes over. So I think it's utopia to think that everything's gonna be wiped out. . . .

Helen: Right! I know that the model for this project is tenant-directed, but where does this leave staff? We have had to be in this bad position all along, doing the dehumanizing—so where's our input?

This exploration of boundaries between staff and tenants continued throughout the project without ever being clearly resolved.

Staff-Clinician Relations

Across the group homes, role conflict developed between the paraprofessional house staff and the professional Clinical Homeless Specialists (CHS) (case managers). In most houses, staff felt that they understood the tenants better and were more committed to the empowerment model, whereas the CHSs were "too intrusive" and "overly controlling and infantilizing with tenants." Some house staff indicated that they did not know what the CHSs were supposed to do or why there were paid so much more than house staff. The clinicians asserted superior knowledge of clients' psychiatric disabilities and undertook responsibility for major decisions bearing on their care, while noting that many members of the house staff had no prior training or experience about mental illness.

In an effort to reduce tension and to encourage information sharing, the project began to hold joint meetings between house and clinical staff. During a long meeting with staff at one house, several CHSs described their conception of the empowerment goal and distinguished their role from that of house staff.

Bryana started the meeting by bringing up the question of what staff's role in the ECH was supposed to be. She said that it was somewhat different in each house and that to some extent they should respond to what the clients wanted them to do. In general they are not supposed to be problem solvers but to offer activities as alternatives. Bryana termed this "modeling," which she expanded on at length as a legitimate and vital part of staff's job as empowering counselors in the ECH. Modeling was part of their role as teachers. Bryana brought up as an example a client who was difficult to get along with. The other clients in the house were intimidated by the person and did not know how to deal with him. She said that when staff was sitting with clients watching TV and this client walked in the room and just changed the channel, the staff felt that they should not do anything because they had to let the clients settle it themselves. Bryana said that she thought that the staff would be acting within their rights "as healthy people" and within the mandate of the project as modeling for the other clients, in telling the obnoxious client that he was being so.

The staff have the right and obligation to set limits of acceptable behavior with this client. It makes sense that staff had the right to do this because natural human interaction is not forbidden. On the model of a family, it would be open to debate, for instance, which TV show to watch when there were many people watching. There was no obligation to keep fully professional composure including no obligation to pretend that one is not scared or threatened by a client's behavior. Part of the goal of mental health treatment is to get people to act like rational human beings. Sometimes you have to act as if you are not in this job.

Kristen said ". . . from what [staff] understand we have to teach them how to run the house without staff present. We were told to step in if things got dangerous, but not otherwise."

Bryana said that this was not a question of stepping in or not, but that there is a continuum of intervention. She said that she does not like the implications of the parent-child metaphor and doesn't really believe the developmental story but that some of the clients are on a level of children even though they are adults. Some of them have been more adult at some points in their lives, but they have moved back. There is a great temptation to step in and help them when they want it, but we should not jump into that trap. Ideally they should force them into mutual interaction. Even though, sometimes in order to get to a relation of mutuality, they would have to do something to interest the client. One thing Bryana learned in social work school is that you have to start where the client is. Interaction is the key; this is what brings people from where they are, across the "Grand Canyon," to where they can be on their own.

Daniel said that the problem was one of transitions. Hands off does not equal empowerment. It's like teaching a kid to walk, first you have to walk holding him up completely and little by little he progresses toward walking on his own. The process is similar to teaching but is more of using yourself as a positive role model. Showing how to do and say things, not just telling people to do them on their own. They often just don't know how to do the things we tell them to when we expect them to be independent. It's "doing with." Without modeling, it's like expecting someone to prepare a dish when you have just given them the recipe and they don't know how to cook.

Bryana talked about one client who she had worked with and decided to drive her to her doctor appointment for a little while. The client was afraid to ride on the buses, and the ride made her think that Bryana had an interest in her life. All the time, she was orienting the rides toward the eventual time when the client would move out of the car and onto the buses. Now the client takes buses and is generally less withdrawn. Bryana's initial reaction to her was a sense that she had withdrawn from life altogether. Through the whole process she had a clear idea of the goal and of the process of getting there, and she had argued that it was worth a try even though others thought she was infantilizing the woman. Bryana said you could even rationalize cooking a meal for a person in this way.

Daniel said that before he started this job he didn't know how many skills it took to live in a house. These people have been living in shelters all their lives, and they don't know the daily skills. For instance, Geoffrey's move from his way of life to living in a house was a huge step. For others it is not such a huge step, and every individual is very, very different. There is no formula, and role modeling is the best way to way to teach the basis of these skills. (Not everyone has the right habits to live in a house, and it is particularly hard to start them.) Modeling the right behaviors helped clients with this step.

Daniel said that one validating method he used was to say "I understand your feeling"—giving acknowledgment that, for instance, it really sucks to have someone take your mayo, and an explanation of why the fact that he can't just accuse someone was better than just contradicting him. This would seem less like they were going against him.

Bryana said that the CHS as clinicals can come down harder on the clients. Herman said that this was contradicting what he was trying to do in the house which was to bring in the clients into all decisions about their lives.

Bryana said that sometimes they have to decide to drag someone off to the hospital, and that is not fun, but it is their clinical responsibility to make sure they feel safe. Herman was still protesting. He said he understood where they were coming from, but the staff is actually there in the house every day, and they are constantly working on rapport building and that means that they cannot just pass the buck and consent to whatever the CHS wants. Joan said that that was exactly what he would have to do, to say "talk with the person in charge not me."

Another staff member said that they shouldn't tolerate the clients getting upset when dealing with them; they should just walk away if the client was not going to be reasonable. Dealing reasonably with people is what empowerment is all about. Bryana referred to this as frustration management. . . . After the meeting, Harry was still a bit upset about what he had heard, and he talked a bit about his concerns. He wants to be more actively involved in their lives. He wants to reach out to them and move with them. . . . Harry has said to me [the ethnographer] a couple of times that he sees so much potential for the clients, and he feels like his hands are tied preventing him from helping them reach their potential.

In spite of such efforts to increase cooperation between CHS and house staff and to distinguish their responsibilities, house staff continued to express frustration with their poorly defined roles. One announced that she was leaving for another job, due to "no structure, no supervision, no group cohesiveness." Another house staff member interviewed for another job because "[t]here, the staff have something to teach to people—not like here!"

House staff were disadvantaged in their relations with clinicians by their lack of advanced training and concomitant limitations in their responsibilities. This disadvantage was compounded by the project plan to reduce their role as much as possible, as quickly as feasible. A project employee who worked with house staff declared that he might try to find a different position due to the conflicts between house staff and the CHSs. He termed the clinicians "wannabe Freuds" who are "looking for the illness, rather than dealing with the person."

Changes in Social Relations

In spite of the ongoing experience of such intense social interaction in the group homes, the quantitative indicators of social relations changed little during the project for participants as a whole and mostly did not differ between participants in the group homes and those in individual apartments. Only two indicators of social relations indicated differences between social experiences in the two types of residence, and both reflected the final assessments at eighteen months: those who lived in independent apartments reported more contact with their CHS (project case manager) than those who lived in group homes, whereas the project case managers reported that group home residents were more likely to socialize with others in the project and less likely to socialize with individuals who were not part of the project than those living in independent apartments (see fig. 5.2

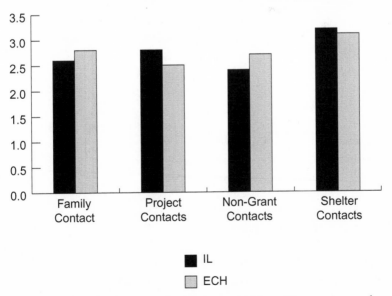

Figure 5.2. Social relations at final assessment. Note: $N = 112$; $p < .05$ for ECH-IL difference in Project Contacts and Non-Grant Contacts. Lower scores indicate more contacts.

for the differences in CHS-reported social relations). Thus, by the project's conclusion, the ECH residents seemed to be relying more on roommates for their social contacts and had less contact with their case manager, whereas IL residents had more contact with nongrant individuals and with their case manager. There was not a statistically significant difference in frequency of contacts with family members or shelter users between the ECH and IL residents.

Conclusions

The project succeeded in setting the stage for intense social interaction to develop among participants in the group homes and for both tenants and staff to engage in significant efforts to redefine roles and reorganize control. Some tenants shouldered key responsibilities in their homes, established themselves as leaders, and took advantage of opportunities to engage in social activities with co-tenants or start new activities in the surrounding community. However, initial expectations that tenants would become a smoothly functioning group, readily take over house management, or start to work or otherwise participate fully in the surrounding community were not met. Although the ethnographic notes contained many instances of productive social relations, these were balanced throughout the project by instances of conflict among tenants and confusion over staff roles. The quantitative analysis identified a few differences in social patterns between the ECH and IL participants but no overall difference or pattern of increase in social ties or feelings of support.

The social control processes identified in chapter 2 were very much in evidence but often ineffective. The success of efforts to develop and enforce behavioral rules was impeded frequently by the uncertain authority of house staff and the prospect of their elimination from ECH management. Although a concerted effort to develop group process through tenant meetings and social activities resulted in many successes, it ultimately achieved only limited success in some homes.

There was some indication in data collected at the end of the project that tenants who were more socially engaged in the ECH housing were more protected from further homelessness. In the independent apartments, by contrast, more social contact with individuals back in the shelter was associated with more risk of housing loss. These different associations are one empirical indication of effects of social processes on housing retention. Overall, these findings support the conclusion of Deborah K. Padgett and colleagues (2008) after their qualitative investigation of social relationships among persons who have experienced serious mental illness, substance abuse, and homelessness:

> Meaningful social relationships—in whatever quantity or quality desired by the individual—remain one of the recovery era's greatest challenges. (p. 338)

Subsequent chapters will explore in much more detail the role of substance abuse, mental illness, and functional capacities in house affairs and housing retention.

CHAPTER SIX

Substance Abuse

A case manager [from the dual-diagnosis shelter] was angry that Linda was moved into the house while she was away and came and said that Linda was a drug abuser. . . . and mentally ill and could not make it on her own. . . . This behavior on the part of the case manager infuriated [a project residential co-ordinator and another case manager]. [The coordinator] said that this kind of thinking and acting planted doubts about the tenants' ability to function in the community in their minds, which sabotaged their success.

LINDA MOVED into McKinney housing and left shelter staff, their concerns, and the many shelter rules in her past. But the problem of substance abuse could not be left behind so easily, either by Linda or many of the two-thirds of project participants with a lifetime history of substance abuse. As the most common health malady among single adult homeless persons and the strongest predictor of poor housing outcomes, substance abuse was not so easily defeated.

There is no more enduring association with homeless persons in the popular mind than that with alcoholism, in no small part because homelessness seems to be the end of the line for those who are "down and out" (Rossi 1989) and "down on their luck" (Jencks 1994) due to excessive drinking or drug use. Yet in spite of widespread recognition of substance abuse's harmful effects and its enduring association with homelessness (Kasprow et al. 2000), the implications of substance abuse for mental health and/or housing policy continue to be debated. Underlying that debate, like others in this investigation, are the theoretical alternatives represented in figure 1.1: Can substance abuse best be understood as a problem with individuals whose dispositions lead to substance abuse, or does it result from troubling situations? If the dispositional explanation is correct, then moving individuals who abuse substances into a new situation will have little effect on their behavior. If the situational alternative is correct, the move to permanent housing could be expected to help individuals end this self-destructive practice.

This chapter begins with an overview of research about substance abuse that has helped to answer questions about cause and effect as well as about substance abuse among homeless persons. The presentation of project findings begins with a description of the prevalence of substance abuse at baseline and its association with participants' characteristics. It continues with a description of the impact of substance abuse in our project, drawing on the ethnographic notes to elaborate its role in the group homes and using the quantitative data to identify changes in its prevalence and the strength of its effects.

The Problem of Substance Abuse

About 10 percent of Americans over the age of twelve abuse or are dependent on illicit drugs or alcohol (SAMSHA 2009a). At some time in their lives between 3 percent and 10 percent of all Americans are alcoholics (Vaillant 1995, 1). These rates are much higher among homeless persons, with about two-thirds having met criteria for alcoholism at some point in their lives and with more severe and long-lasting symptoms than persons who are not homeless (Koegel and Burnam 1988; Booth et al. 2002). As many as one-quarter to one-half of homeless adults use illicit drugs (Velasquez et al. 2000, 396). HUD's 1996 National Survey of Homeless Assistance Providers and Clients identified a total of three-quarters of clients as having had an alcohol or drug problem during their lifetime (The Urban Institute et al. 1999, 24), whereas Lehman and Cordray's (1993) meta-analysis yielded a pooled estimate of 60 percent (47 percent using a weighted average).

The devastating impact of substance abuse among homeless persons with severe mental illness has been identified in many studies (Brunette, Mueser, and Drake 2004, 479). In one sample of former inpatients with schizophrenia, substance abuse increased the risk of homelessness sixfold within the first three months after hospital discharge, whereas symptoms of psychiatric illness had no independent effect (Olfson et al. 1999; and see Folsom et al. 2005).

Multiple investigations among mentally ill persons have found that substance abuse is the personal characteristic most consistently associated with their vulnerability to homelessness (Drake and Wallach 1988; Drake, Wallach, and Hoffman 1989; Linn, Gelberg, and Leake 1990; Hartz, Banys, and Hall 1994). Among homeless individuals who achieved stable housing after entering a substance abuse treatment program, only 50 percent were still stably housed two years later (Orwin, Scott, and Ariera 2003). Substance abuse continues to predict heightened risk of housing loss among homeless persons diagnosed with mental illness even after they are placed in housing and have received extensive substance abuse treatment (Hurlburt, Hough, and Wood 1996; Lipton et al. 2000; Tsemberis and Eisenberg 2000; Gonzalez and Rosenheck 2002; Mares and Rosenheck 2004; Kertesz et al. 2009).

Substance abuse is also associated with high rates of rejection of treatment and lack of motivation for change (Schwartz and Goldfinger 1981; Ridgely, Goldman, and Talbott 1986; Velasquez et al. 2000). Many individuals who are dually diagnosed lack "internal controls and refusal skills to resist cravings and social pressures to use substances," do not have connections with peers who support their recovery, and have trouble "accessing services and maintaining a connection to treatment" (Brunette, Mueser, and Drake 2004, 477).

But recognizing the damaging correlates of substance abuse does not resolve the question implicit in the disagreement over Linda's prospects: Does substance abuse reflect problems with the individual or with her or his social situation? Since Charles Booth's (1969[1902]) research in London, social scientists have recognized that the situation of being homeless is so extreme that it makes drinking and drugs a more acceptable choice.

> A prevailing characteristic of most was the love of drink, but this was, with but little doubt, engendered as often as not by the unhappy circumstances of their surroundings, and it would hardly be fair to state it as a primary cause of failure, except in the 40 cases where it was distinctly ascertained. (218)

Stall's (1984) study of a detoxification center led him to conclude that homeless persons' repeated use of the center could be explained in terms of an adaptation to a life of homelessness. Snow and Anderson (1993) reported a homeless man's "profound demoralization" and then drinking that resulted from feeling trapped in a hopeless situation:

> The boss gave me a check one night and said there wasn't any more work . . . and next thing I knew, I was drinking over in a club on the Eastside. I stayed drunk for three days and blew my whole check. (296)

Another homeless interviewee observed, ". . . they think about it [the situation they're in] and they get depressed, so they get drunk and forget about it. It's just a cycle" (Snow and Anderson 1993).

But it is misleading to consider a medical model focused on the individual pathology of substance abuse as diametrically opposed to a situational explanation. It is certainly true that the social situation shapes the supply of alcohol and drugs as well as individuals' exposure and orientation to addictive substances. The "simplicities and reductionism of the medical model" can easily obscure these realities (Vaillant 1995, 44). Yet medically informed research provides an essential foundation for understanding the effects of addiction. The critical insights come from neurobiological research on the consequences of addiction (Dackis 2005) and from longitudinal research on the development and course of substance abuse (Vaillant 1995).

The most striking finding from the relevant neurobiological research is that addiction can overturn survival-enhancing behaviors that are intended to ensure safety (Amaral 2003). Addictive substances dysregulate dopamine-based endogenous reward systems and so "hijack" the brain's natural protective processes (Dackis and O'Brien 2005), resulting in "an overwhelming desire to obtain the drug, a diminished ability to control drug seeking, and a reduced pleasure from biological rewards" (Kalivas and Volkow 2005, 1408). The "profound effects" of substance abuse (Khantzian et al. 1991) thus include an addictive "pathology of motivation and choice" (Kalivas and Volkow 2005).

This neurobiological process underlies the progression of substance abuse into a profound medical problem—that is, into a "disease." As psychiatrist George Vaillant (1995) explained in his "natural history of alcoholism,"

> The point of using the term disease is simply to underscore that once an individual has lost the capacity consistently to control how much and how often he drinks, then continued use of alcohol can be both a necessary and a sufficient cause of the syndrome. (19)

Before they become addicted to alcohol, alcoholics differ little from their peers—except as their childhood experiences are impacted by their greater likelihood of having had alcoholic parents (Vaillant 1995). However, they tend to be much less physiologically sensitive to alcohol and so may tend to consume more of it to achieve the same effects as others.

Once alcohol dependence develops, depression and poor self-care often ensue, helping to create the type of self-perpetuating cycle of abuse described by Snow and Anderson and ultimately shortening the lifespan by an average of fifteen years (Vaillant 1995). Although it takes years for addiction to develop, effective treatment after that point becomes very difficult. Just 10 percent of alcoholics treated at a low-income clinic in Cambridge, Massachusetts achieved stable remission after the first clinical intervention (Vaillant 1995), and a multisite study of homeless alcohol and drug abusers in treatment programs found that 80 percent in most programs exited prematurely (Orwin et al. 1999).

Abstinence from alcohol is critical for the long-term recovery of most alcoholics (McCarty et al. 1993). Because participation in Alcoholics Anonymous (AA) helps to create social support and personal motivation for abstinence, men who were faithful AA members in Vaillant's sample were more successful. Hospitalization as needed for detoxification purposes combined with AA participation also improved rates of abstinence (Vaillant 1995). Unfortunately, the personal characteristics that predict greater success at abstinence are uncommon among long-term homeless persons—having been residentially and socially stable, married, employed, and never having been jailed. By contrast the situation of homelessness includes many social contexts that support abuse, such as "bottle gangs" (Bahr and Caplow 1968) and "crack houses" (Williams 1992) and other sources for crack cocaine (Jencks 1994).

Research supporting the importance of abstinence is not the most hopeful background for the McKinney project, since our participants were to move from relatively stable "dry" shelters that prohibited substance abuse to housing in which opportunities to abuse substances would inevitably increase. For those among our participants who were recruited from the dual-diagnosis shelter, the contrast was even more extreme: from a situation in which participation in AA and other treatment programs was mandatory and most social interaction was limited to the shelter's isolated island, participants would move to homes without any planned substance abuse treatment programming and urban neighborhoods with the usual rich array of opportunities to nourish addictions.

Yet the contrasting inducements to substance abuse between the environment they were leaving and the nascent communities they were to enter can easily be overdrawn. The formal shelter policies prohibiting substance abuse at the two city shelters did not limit guests' daytime activities, and the rates of substance abuse were no lower in these two city shelters than at the dual diagnosis shelter on the island (see chapter 3). Moreover, the institutional character of the shelters and their guests' prolonged residency at them seemed to nourish the defeatist attitudes that would be conducive to substance abuse. There was reason to think that the move to a permanent home in a community setting would be a sufficient situational change to encourage sobriety.

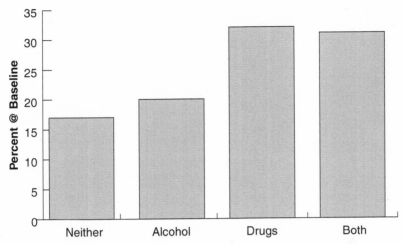

Figure 6.1. Lifetime alcohol and drugs at baseline. Note: *N* = 111.

Baseline Quantitative Analysis

At baseline, 83 percent of our project participants received a classification as having abused either alcohol or drugs (see fig. 6.1). The separate distributions differ for alcohol and drug problems with almost half the sample having had no prior problems with alcohol compared to 37 percent who had had no prior problems with illicit drugs.

In all but two of the group homes, between half and three-quarters of the residents were classified as lifetime substance abusers at baseline. In one of these other two group homes, 90 percent had a substance abuse history, whereas in the other just 44 percent did.

At baseline, participants with a lifetime diagnosis of alcohol abuse or dependence were more likely to be men, and they reported more negative social ties, but they were not distinctive in terms of age, race, or education (see fig. 6.2).

Like alcohol abusers those with a lifetime diagnosis of drug abuse or dependence were more likely to be male, but by contrast, they tended to be younger than those without a drug-abuse problem and reported more positive social ties (see fig. 6.3).

These findings suggest that substance abuse would be a major problem in the McKinney housing. As in other segments of the homeless adult population, many of the project participants, particularly the men, had extensive histories of alcohol and drug abuse. Alcohol abuse was also associated with having more negative social ties, whereas drug abuse was linked to younger

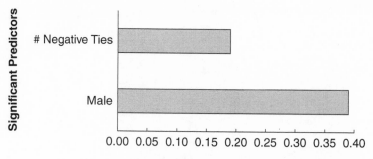

Figure 6.2. Regression analysis of lifetime alcohol abuse at baseline. Note: $R^2 = .32$, $N = 107$. Variables entered in the regression that did not have statistically significant effects: race, age, education, diagnosis, residential preference, clinician recommendation, number of positive social ties.

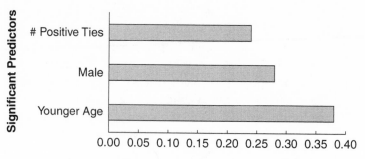

Figure 6.3. Regression analysis of lifetime drug abuse. Note: $R^2 = .33$, $N = 107$. Variables entered in the regression that did not have statistically significant effects: race, education, diagnosis, residential preference, clinician recommendation, negative social ties.

age and involved what users experienced as more positive social ties. Would the situation of living in a group home in which there would be an effort to develop positive social ties to enhance well-being lessen alcohol abuse and the associated problems in dealing with others and reduce the propensity to develop reinforcing social ties among drug abusers?

Initial Alcohol Policy

One of the two house rules mandated by the project was that illicit drugs were not allowed. From the start, however, alcohol policy was subject to agreement by the house tenants, conditional on approval by the housing vendor. After varying degrees of discussion and some dissent, each group home except one began with a permissive alcohol policy—and that one exception was due to a strict policy imposed by the housing vendor. In one home tenants agreed to allow drinking in "moderation" with just beer allowed in the house. The project empowerment coordinator described this as "normal behavior," although a member of the house staff announced that he would refuse to give psychotropic medication to those who had been drinking in the previous four hours. In another house, the coordinator told staff not to do anything when several tenants were drinking but instead to focus on the problem of mixing psychotropic medication and alcohol. The project philosophy was explained to house staff: people "should be free to do what they want," although "at least they could be respectful and not flaunt drinking in front of the alcoholics."

In one house, a new tenant started drinking heavily immediately after moving in. She agreed to drink only in her room but frequently violated this house policy. Several tenants in another house also began drinking heavily upon moving in, and the empowerment coordinator emphasized that the focus should be on problematic behavior, not drinking per se. An exception to this lenient policy was made in a house where one tenant was getting drunk each day and becoming "a royal pain in the ass when drunk"; it was agreed that tenants would give those who were disruptive after an initial warning an ultimatum to go into detox. One prospective tenant declined to move in upon hearing that drinking was allowed.

Escalation of Drinking

The frequency of drinking and troublesome behaviors associated with it escalated rapidly in the group homes. The ethnographic notes were replete with examples. A tenant stole the VCR from one house so that he could buy liquor, and thefts seemed to occur in other houses for the same reason. Harry is "drinking daily" and was "severely drunk at his day program." Sherry is now "drinking all the time," "has no interest in sobriety," has overnight guests repeatedly, and went on a two-week binge after being switched to a more lenient case manager. Sam "came home drunk" and complained when he was not given his medications as a result.

Some staff noted that the drinkers were a "threat to the sobriety of the other residents." Lefty was described as "having real drinking problems," and Phil was "real, real loud," obnoxious, managing "to insult most everyone in the house while drunk." One tenant observed, "The amount of active alcoholism in this house is preposterous," and another complained that "cleaning up vomit in the bathroom" is "simply disgusting." Harvey, who had been sober for several years after many years of active alcoholism, was now getting "psychotic, violent, yelling at voices" when he was drunk. Priscilla "has been drinking up a storm" and disguised her violation of the house rule against open drinking by mixing her alcoholic beverage in punch. Police were called to one house after a tenant threw chairs at a staff member while drunk.

House staff differed in their orientation toward drinking, but disagreements soon arose with the empowerment coordinator about "sticking to the model" that empowered tenants were to set their own policy. At one house, she accused staff of having "jumped on" tenants for drinking after the tenants had agreed to allow drinking on a trial basis for a month. As a result the tenants agreed to another trial month, this time allowing wine as well as beer. A new staff member at another house remarked that, compared to other group homes, "the substance abuse problem in this house is unbelievable." Other staff expressed worries about the interaction of medication and alcohol. Yet the empowerment coordinator urged house staff to let a tenant who had been violent when drunk "make the decision" about this behavior.

> If we intervene now without the tenants processing it in some fashion, we'll all feel insecure that empowerment isn't happening. . . . I think he wants to stay here and the time has come when he has to decide once and for all to drink or not. I'd like him to know that by Monday, he's going to decide that either he's going to drink or not drink.

Tenants who were abusing alcohol and drugs often did not acknowledge any problem. One drinker explained that he "lost his toes [to frostbite] because he was on the street, not because he was drinking." Another argued that "the drinking cures mental illness" and another "says he is drinking because people aggravate him and don't give him the respect he deserves." Samantha "complains about the house alcohol policy," and says that "her drinking is her own business." When house staff told one tenant that he couldn't drink, he protested "that he was thinking about moving out because the house was like a prison because they would not let him drink but other people could drink."

By contrast, tenants who did not have a substance abuse history or who were maintaining their sobriety often complained to staff that they felt threatened by others who were drinking. When one tenant insisted in a meeting that there was not a house drinking problem, another tenant retorted, "I'll disagree with that. Half the people in this house are drunk half the time."

Escalation of Drug Use

Tom has been feeling "pinned to the bed" in the morning. He has enjoyed getting high with Sammy and Ben, although the next day is always bad. Tom has a delusion about the bank putting money into an account for him and says he can think about reality in new ways when he is high.

In spite of the formal prohibition of drug use in the houses, evidence of drug abuse grew soon after several houses opened. One tenant was found to be stealing to support his drug use, and another "lost" $2000 and was believed by staff to have used it to purchase drugs. Staff rationed money for one tenant who seemed to be using his $75 per week to purchase drugs. One tenant explained to an ethnographer that house tenants did not have any money because they were buying crystals of cocaine: "they are all smoking [crack]." Drug sellers arrived routinely for a time late at night outside one home, and tenants went out to make purchases. One ECH tenant was arrested for cocaine possession and so was dropped from a waiting list for an apartment. Several women were observed prostituting in the area or bringing men home to raise funds for illicit drugs. Most of the tenants in another house were sent to detox after they were found to be using crack.

Some house staff worried about how to respond to tenant drug use in the project. The empowerment coordinator cautioned them not to be too quick to expel tenants for this reason. One staff member was so frustrated by the drug problems that she announced she would quit except that she needed the income. By the project's second year, staff in one house with considerable drug use announced that they would start copying down license plate numbers of cars whose drivers seemed to be pulling up to the house to sell drugs. Staff also decided to end their practice of recording all activity notes in a log accessible to tenants, and instead they maintained details about drug use in a confidential log.

Some tenants occasionally expressed remorse over drug use, and non-abusers occasionally urged more staff effort to curb drug use by other tenants.

> *Tenant:* If there's a drug problem, just have those people busted.
> *House Staff:* We will. We will sooner or later, if people keep doing it and they get caught. I don't want to see people evicted over this, but it is in the contract. And if it comes down to that—staff catching people—then we will.

In spite of expressions of concern by some tenants, drug problems were most often denied or rationalized: "Fred says he is bored and has nothing to do instead of drugs." When one house staff member focused on the problem in a meeting with tenants, he found little interest:

> Well, at last week's meeting, I did a little laying down of the rules about drugs in the house, and it was just me talking with a bunch of people looking at me. I just talked, and there was absolutely no discussion. We can't do that in a group.

Cigarette Smoking

Cigarette smoking was common, but it caused fewer problems than alcohol or drug use. Smoking most often came up as a safety and cleanliness problem. Both tenants and staff noted that "people die from careless smoking." But several houses soon had many cigarette burns on the furniture. The empowerment coordinator pleaded with one tenant to avoid smoking in his bedroom.

> Now listen Bob, I'm gonna talk to you now for a minute. You have gotta get your act together about smoking in your bedroom. You know what the rules are in this house. Can you live here without someone reminding you to put out your cigarette, or change your clothes, or clean up after yourself?

Such pleas sometimes fell on deaf ears. When staff told one "unsafe smoker" that he could no longer smoke in the house, he shouted:

> I'm being driven out! . . . What about my smoking rights? . . . I'll see a lawyer because my civil rights have been violated!!

Smoking was also an economic problem for tenants with limited incomes. Several tenants begged others for cigarettes or for food or money after they had spent excessive amounts on cigarettes.

So the group home environment proved to be conducive to smoking as well as drinking and drug use, encouraged by the dispositions of those with a history of addiction. In spite of the formal prohibition of illicit drugs, the staff policy of maintaining only minimal control allowed considerable drug use. Problematic behavior associated with addiction began to increase in intensity.

Redefining Drinking/Drug Policy

Both tenants and staff struggled with the behavioral consequences of substance abuse. When staff in one house reported that tenants had been drinking over the weekend, the empowerment coordinator asked why this was a problem, as long as it was occurring outside the house and "as long as it doesn't disturb someone else." Another house relaxed its rules about drinking in the face of repeated complaints from a forceful and articulate drinker: ". . . it is the tenants' decision to make," Sally argues and declares that she will be able to control her drinking better if she can drink in her room. She insists she knows when it is time for her to go to detox and that no one can tell her what to do.

In a different house, on the other hand, tenants brought up problems with others who were constantly intoxicated, and then the empowerment coordinator suggested that they bar tenants from returning to the house drunk "unless they go immediately to their room." As a result, "in the future, if someone comes in rip- roaring drunk, people have promised to go to their rooms so they won't bother the others."

Restrictions on alcohol and drugs increased with experience in most houses. Tenants at one house insisted that a key criterion for prospective tenants was that they not be using drugs or alcohol. Staff tried in meetings to develop an appropriate response within the context of the empowerment philosophy:

I think we're all concerned about the mental health and drugs, but it is their life, and they should do what they want.
So they go down to the corner and come back to the house high.
The tenants could vote that anybody is drunk or high.
Then we would have to police them and ask them "Are you high?"
Smoking crack is illegal from the view of the program and the liability.
If they are doing it in the house, what do we do? How do we catch them since we never go up to the second or third floors?
Other tenants can catch them and report it to you.
When people approach us, encourage them to bring it up at the meeting. I know Barry gets really freaked out when anything illegal is happening.
That's really empowering too, to have them bring it up themselves.
I think the part about drugs being illegal is scary. There's violence involved and stealing. If it's allowed to continue, I could see it escalating. The illegal nature of it makes it expensive too.
That's what we're gonna focus on—the behavior and consequences. Sometimes things have to escalate and happen before tenants make the decisions that result in some consequences.
What about the guy calling up on the tenant phone and wanting money from Sandy? That affected the house very much. I felt very vulnerable, and it upset people a lot. That was about one or two months back.
It has to come from the tenant group to the people who are doing this. We need to get something in writing to tell them how unsafe the tenants feel.

After many months of experience, the empowerment coordinator emphasized in a house meeting the importance of abstaining from drugs because the ECH model required that people be safe without outside supervision:

"It's not research anymore. We know what doesn't work." As noted by a project ethnographer, ". . . she says she is not going to play any 'mommy-daddy stuff.'"

Treatment for substance abuse increasingly became a part of the house experience. Tenants who had drinking problems often ended up in detox—although often under protest. Examples appear repeatedly in the ethnographic notes. "Sammy fell out of a cab while drunk, sent to detox." "Walter got drunk outside and was jailed due to a complaint for several hours." "Jeff has gone to detox." "Helen admits she has to do something about her drinking, but she refuses to consider detox and rejects all program suggestions by staff." "Althea was to go to a halfway house but refused, . . . saying that she had paid her rent." "Charlie taken to detox by police over the weekend," after coming back to the house drunk and being abusive to staff. "Ronald . . . said that the rules of the house were that he was allowed to drink outside of the house as long as he was not disruptive in the house. He wanted to know, why then did [his case manager] send him to detox?" Harry "hospitalized for drug use." "Charlene hospitalized at [a detox]."

In several houses, tenants who were trying to maintain their sobriety discussed starting AA meetings and increasing rules against substance abuse.

> [A staff member] said that there was a big rift in the house between the drinkers and the non-drinkers. Two major issues divide them. First, the non-drinkers want to have an AA meeting in the house, and the drinkers do not. Second, the non-drinkers have suggested that if people get drunk, they can go to Pine St. for the night rather than coming home and being disruptive.

Some tenants seeking to maintain sobriety began to attend AA meetings in other locations. Fearing ongoing relapses, a few tenants decided to move out to a more structured setting where substance abuse was banned.

Expulsion Due to Substance Abuse

Expulsion from the house became an accepted procedure for dealing with the substance abuse problems after repeated incidents and as the project empowerment coordinator lost her tolerance for destructive substance-abuse-related behaviors.

> Dom [has to leave] after using cocaine in his room with others. Dom is back on the streets, doing drugs again, and [the empowerment coordinator] asks, "Are you starting to get the idea about what kind of people live here?"

Barbara was given a letter requiring her participation in detox. "Finally, [the project coordinator] decides not to allow Barbara to return due to drugs and prostitution. She is in a long-term treatment program." "Bob has been drinking and will be pink-papered soon and moved to a dual-diagnosis residence. He has made some threats."

At a tenant meeting, the empowerment coordinator announced,

> Lisandro should be expelled and asks to get a letter "from the Tenant Association" informing him that he has to move out in thirty days. She notes, as do house staff, that since he came back from the hospital Lisandro has been acting like he is taunting them to throw him out by not complying with rules and continuing to drink and not pay rent. [The empowerment coordinator says] he wants to be a victim; it's like children—they don't want to be held responsible, and they get the parent to step in. He's been upping the ante ever since he got here, and he's kept doing something worse and worse.

In one house, [the empowerment coordinator] announced that if people continued to use crack they would have to move out.

> Arlene returned from [the hospital] and created a scene in the tenant meeting, swearing and making paranoid accusations, and tenants decide that she must leave the house. Arlene is very angry about this with staff and feels it is unjust. Staff agree that Arlene has to leave.

Subsequently, Arlene refused to move to another group home where she would have had to take lithium; instead, she returned to the shelter. She was then expelled from the shelter due to behavioral problems and moved in with a boyfriend.

Change in Substance Abuse

Overall, the prevalence of substance abuse changed little during the eighteen months that subjects were enrolled in the project. Six in ten were identified as lifetime abusers at baseline, and about that many abused alcohol or drugs during the project. Few had given no indications of abuse at baseline, and even this abstinent fraction declined slightly during the project.

But there were changes in the type of substance abused during the project. Drug abuse declined, but alcohol abuse increased (see fig. 6.4).

The relative stability in the overall distribution of substance abuse on a lifetime basis and during the project obscures changes that occurred at the individual level, as some participants increased their level of substance abuse while in the project and others decreased their level of substance abuse. None of the project participants who had not had a lifetime record of substance abuse at baseline increased his or her level of substance use to an abusive level during the project, but two-thirds began to use substances somewhat. Among those who had reported some lifetime substance use

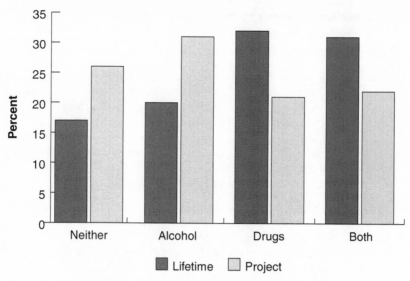

Figure 6.4. Lifetime and project alcohol and drug use. Note: $N = 111$.

problems at baseline, just over one-third increased their level to the point of having symptoms of abuse or dependence during the project. But 18 percent of the participants reduced their substance abuse during the project compared to their lifetime record at baseline.

Neither social background indicators nor participants' orientations to the residential options had much consequence for the propensity to increase substance use during the project. In the ECH housing, the only predictor of increasing substance abuse was a lifetime diagnosis of substance abuse (see fig. 6.5). In other words the group homes seemed to facilitate an increase in abuse by those who had experience with addiction in the past. This did not occur in the independent apartments. Instead, among the IL tenants, those who were African American were more likely to increase their substance abuse.

Substance Abuse and Housing Loss

Substance abuse proved to be a necessary condition for losing housing during the project. None of the participants without a lifetime history of substance abuse lost housing during the project (see fig. 6.6). The rate of housing loss rose to one in five among those with some lifetime substance use and to one in three among those with a lifetime history of abuse or dependence.

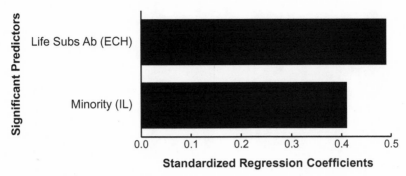

Figure 6.5. Regression analysis of increased substance use. Note: $R^2 = .43$, $N = 38$ (IL); $R^2 = .41$, $N = 53$ (ECH). Variables entered in the regression that did not have statistically significant effects in either housing type: age, gender, education, diagnosis, residential preference, clinician recommendation, positive and negative social ties during the project.

Type of substance mattered. During the project, it was active drug abuse rather than alcohol abuse that predicted housing loss. Although there was a higher rate of housing loss among those who abused alcohol during the project, its impact was statistically significant only among those who also abused drugs. The combination of alcohol and drug abuse led to a particularly high rate of housing loss with almost half of these dual-substance abusers losing their housing at some point.

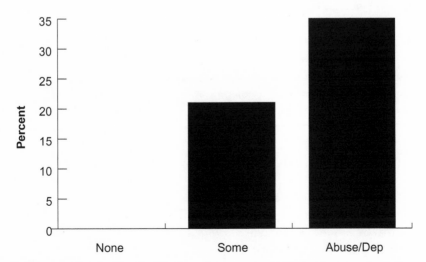

Figure 6.6. Housing loss by lifetime substance abuse. Note: $N = 111$, $\chi^2 = 10.03$, $df = 2$, $p < .01$.

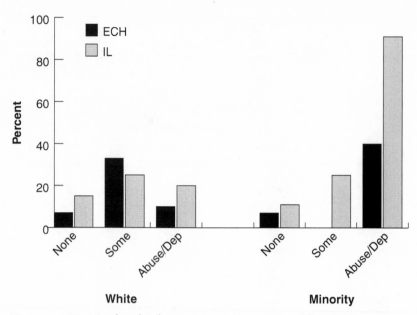

Figure 6.7. Housing loss by drug use in project, race, and housing type. Note: $N = 103$, $\chi^2 = 13.8$, $df = 2$, $p < .001$ for housing loss for minority drug users in IL housing compared to others.

But housing type had a large effect on the risk that drug abuse during the project posed for housing retention. Among all those who abused drugs after assignment to independent apartments, two-thirds experienced housing loss, compared to just 22 percent of those in group homes. Furthermore, this effect of substance abuse on housing loss in the independent apartments occurred primarily among African American tenants, 91 percent of whom experienced homelessness during the project if they were living in independent apartments and abusing drugs (see fig. 6.7). White IL residents who abused drugs while in the project did not experience homelessness much more frequently than whites who did not use drugs.

Conclusions

Most of our project participants had a history of abusing drugs and/or alcohol. These high levels of substance abuse were comparable to those found in other samples of homeless persons and, as in other research, were higher among men than women. In some respects a history of alcohol abuse seemed to connote more problems, since it was associated independently with having more negative social ties, whereas a history of drug abuse was associated with having more positive social ties as well as being younger. However, the negative consequences of both alcohol and drug abuse quickly became apparent after participants moved into their project housing.

Overall level of substance abuse changed little during the project in spite of the acquisition of housing and without regard to the type of housing obtained. Although the level of substance abuse declined among some participants, it increased among others, leaving substance abuse at the end of the project about where it had been among participants at the project's start, in terms of their lifetime diagnosis. Those who had never had problems with substance abuse did not begin to abuse substances during the project, but some engaged in some use of alcohol or drugs that did not meet the threshold for abuse. In the group homes, a background of substance abuse was associated with increasing use during the project.

The high level of substance abuse had a corrosive effect on social processes in the group homes involving conflicts among tenants and between tenants and house staff. The initial goal of letting tenants themselves figure out how to deal with substance abuse was largely abandoned in the face of intensifying problems with behaviors resulting from substance abuse. Although tenants did adopt "rules" about substance abuse in meetings, their decisions were largely shaped by the project empowerment coordinator and initially reflected a trial-and-error approach of constantly trying to accommodate the insistent demands of individuals who were intent on drinking or drugging and did not admit to having a problem.

The fears expressed initially by shelter staff that their guests would "pick up" and deteriorate as soon as they moved into a setting without clear rules against substance abuse were almost immediately realized. Time and again George Vaillant's (1995) caution that persons addicted to alcohol (or drugs) cannot maintain a moderate level of drinking was borne out. By the end of the project the most difficult substance-abusing tenants had been expelled from many of the group homes.

The quantitative analysis of housing loss indicates the devastating effect of substance abuse on the odds of housing retention. The only participants who lost housing during the project had a lifetime history of substance abuse, as assessed at baseline. Substance abuse during the project added to this risk of housing loss. Tenants who abused drugs during the project were more likely to lose their housing, even after taking into account their prior substance abuse history.

This increased risk was primarily experienced by African American tenants in independent housing. Given the positive social ties among those who "picked up" and their high rate of housing loss, it is likely that pressures from substance-abusing peers and pushers in the community were in part responsible.

The needs of substance abusers and non-abusers required markedly different strategies of housing management and service provision. The consequences of the addictive "pathology of motivation and choice" (Kalivas and Volkow 2005) were shaped by the social environment that abusers experienced and required in turn that that environment provide a high level of support for maintaining sobriety (McCarty et al. 1993). It was only after house staff, with the support of some tenants, began to enforce restrictions on substance abuse and emphasized treatment opportunities that the problems associated with substance abuse diminished. Whatever the appeal of empowerment, it could not overcome the force of addiction.

CHAPTER SEVEN

Mental Illness

A WIDE INTELLECTUAL CHASM separates current sociological perspectives on mental illness from the dominant medical model (Pearlin, Avison, and Fazio 2007, 36). On opposite sides of this chasm are contrasting conceptions of mental illness, different explanations of psychiatric symptoms, divergent prognoses for outcomes, and alternative proposals for treatment—competing paradigms, in the language of Thomas Kuhn (1962). Scholars adhering to one perspective often overlook research conducted by adherents of the other, whereas contacts that do occur across the chasm more often generate conflict than build consensus.

Mental illness is in some respects a phenomenon ideally suited to heighten the contrast between medical and sociological perspectives. Whereas many physical illnesses have been linked to a specific pathogen or bodily malfunction, no agent that can be observed under a microscope or found in a defective bodily process has been established as a causal factor in the major mental illnesses such as schizophrenia, bipolar illness, or major affective disorder. Although the internal mechanisms that lead to many physical illnesses can successfully be interrupted by vaccines, drugs, or surgery, there are no vaccines to prevent mental illness, and psychotropic medications are only effective for a portion of patients and often for a limited period of time. Surgical and other invasive treatments for mental illness have been widely discredited.

By contrast such social processes as group disapproval and structural discrimination do not directly cause physical illness, but they do affect how people feel about themselves and perceive the social world. Evaluation by a medical professional is widely accepted as necessary to diagnose a physical illness, but the label of "crazy" is applied all too quickly by persons with no special training whatsoever to others who fail some ambiguous concept of normality. Few would advise friends or loved ones to avoid a medical doctor and simply "shape up" when they seem stricken with a physical malady, but it is a common reaction to symptoms of mental illness.

Elements of the medical perspective have appeared in this book in shelter staff concerns about guests' readiness for housing (chapter 1), in the belief that hospitals, and then medication, were necessary for psychiatric treatment (chapter 3), in the prognostic value of clinicians' evaluations of housing needs (chapter 4) and in genetic and neurobiological explanations of substance abuse (chapter 6). Elements of the dominant sociological perspective appeared in enthusiasm for the transformative impact of voluntary communities (chapter 2), in the nineteenth century expectation that mental illness could be treated with a supportive hospital-based environment and in the twentieth century faith in the value of community integration (chapter 3), in the emphasis on consumer preferences (chapter 4), and positive social relations (chapter 5), and in the expectation that substance abuse problems would diminish as a result of positive environmental change (chapter 6). It is now time to assess the value of these different paradigms for understanding the impact of our housing options.

Medical and Sociological Paradigms

Of course my initial contrast of the medical and sociological paradigms is overdrawn and time bound. Both psychiatry and sociology include alternative perspectives and have attempted at times to meld their divergent conceptions of mental illness. Perspectives such as "community psychiatry," "social psychiatry," "social ecology," and "Gestalt therapy" represent a few of these efforts at disciplinary synergy. Yet the belief that much, if not all, mental illness is socially caused has most often served to demarcate the boundary between sociological and medical perspectives and so has defined the terms of debate between them. This introduction will present some of the complex crosscurrents in both disciplines, but it is in the contrast between the two perspectives that we can locate the most appropriate starting point.

During the late nineteenth century psychiatry included many enthusiasts for biological explanations and drew often on new genetic concepts. However the inability of medical research of that period to investigate the brain and the limited knowledge of the human genome provided a very weak foundation for understanding biological processes. When Sigmund Freud turned to intrapsychic conflicts and frustrations in individual development to explain psychiatric illness, he found a ready audience (Makari 2008, 33). Until about 1980, Freud's psychodynamic perspective dominated academic psychiatry and professional practice and sanctioned the use of psychoanalysis—a nonmedical, interpersonal treatment (Horwitz and Wakefield 2007, 126). Rather than providing a pill to restore an improperly functioning biological process, psychodynamic therapists helped patients take responsibility for their own behavior and then change it (Luhrmann 2000, 115).

In fact during what Klerman (1989, 26–27) terms the "golden age of social epidemiology" after World War II, most mental health researchers accepted the concept of a continuum between mental health and illness and abjured application of a standard medical model of discrete diagnoses and alternative etiologies. The result was a medical perspective on mental illness that had little perceived need for biology, little in common with the practice of other medical specialties, and a natural affinity for sociology and its emphasis on social influence (Eisenberg 1995, 1564–65; Kandel 1998; Luhrmann 2000, 18).

This period also gave rise to *milieu therapy*, a psychiatric perspective that combined sociological and psychoanalytic insights. The *therapeutic community* approach was a popular version of milieu therapy that focused attention on the healing potential of the multiperson environment (Rapaport 1980 [1960]). The origins of mental illness were believed to be related to problematic interactions with others, and so reshaping these interactions could not only improve current functioning but could also remedy interpersonal troubles having their origins in earlier dysfunctional relations (Luhrmann 2000, 19). Psychiatrists and sociologists needed to work as partners to resolve these problems.

A 1981 article presenting a case study of the *social network approach* to treating schizophrenia captured the flavor of this perspective (Pattison and Pattison 1981). Nine members of the psychotic patient's psychosocial network (family and friends) were identified and brought to the hospital for a three-hour evening session.

> The . . . conductor (therapist) is to direct the orchestra (social network) to play a healthy tune (health role definition) instead of playing an unhealthy tune

(psychotic role definition). [After extended emotional discussion among "Jane" and the nine network members about their feelings of hate and love and about the history of their relationships with "Jane," "the dynamic sources of the paranoid symptomatology" are "quickly revealed." The therapist negotiates tasks for each participant.] 1. Relatives to visit mother frequently and decrease her isolation. 2. Family members to take turns visiting Jane in hospital. 3. Sister #3 to write regularly to Jane. 4. Girlfriend and Cousin to remind Jane of lessons learned here. . . . Some four months later, Jane was asymptomatic. (139, 141)

But there was more to effective treatment than this. The authors of this case study acknowledged that "Jane" was also receiving medication and individual therapy (Pattison and Pattison 1981, 141). Research on patient samples had failed to find evidence of much benefit of psychoanalysis, absent psychotropic medication, in cases of severe psychiatric illness (Luhrmann 2000, 220; Horwitz and Wakefield 2007, 183). Hopes for successful drug treatment were encouraged by discoveries of new drugs, by pharmaceutical companies' marketing of these drugs, by the professional appeal of a treatment approach that would enable psychiatrists to intervene "the way doctors are supposed to do" (Luhrmann 2000, 99), and by the potential fiscal benefits of using drugs rather than long-term therapy. By the time Pattison and Pattison (1981) published their case study, the pendulum in psychiatry had already swung back in the biomedical direction (Pearlin, Avuson, and Fazio 2007, 35).

At the same time, sociologists' enthusiasm for increasingly powerful survey research techniques encouraged efforts to explain variable levels of distress in the general population rather than the origins and course of serious mental illness among psychiatric patients (Pescosolido, McLeod, and Avison 2007, 16). Sociologists who had affiliated with medical school psychiatry departments were increasingly isolated from the medical mainstream in those departments. Medical and sociological perspectives on mental illness sharply diverged.

The Medical Model

The American Psychiatric Association's development of the *Diagnostic and Statistical Manual, Third Edition* (DSM-III) marked an unambiguous disciplinary move to a medical model of mental illness (Klerman 1989, 27–28, 31; Luhrmann 2000). Reflecting and encouraging the concept of severe mental illness as a discrete state distinguishable from mental health, the DSM-III provided seemingly clear criteria for diagnosing its presence and for distinguishing maladies with similar symptoms but different etiologies. According to the DSM-III diagnostic criteria, psychiatric symptoms pursuant to organic failure did not indicate mental illness, nor did predictable and transient feelings of distress subsequent to severe stressful experiences. The DSM-III creators reached outside the traditional purview of psychiatry to label substance abuse as a mental illness, but not before carefully distinguishing this disease and its consequences from psychotic and affective disorders. Unlike its predecessor volumes, DSM-I and DSM-II, DSM-III was designed consciously by leaders in psychiatry to establish unambiguous diagnostic criteria.

Continuing this new approach, the next edition of the manual defined a *mental disorder* as (American Psychiatric Association 2000, xxxi):

> a clinically significant behavioral or psychological syndrome or pattern that occurs in an individual and that is associated with present distress (e.g., a painful symptom) or disability (i.e., impairment in one or more important areas of functioning), or with a significantly increased risk of suffering death, pain, disability, or an impaired loss of freedom.

The manual went on to specify instances when an apparent disorder should not be considered to be a "mental disorder" (American Psychiatric Association 2000, xxxi):

- Not merely an expectable and culturally sanctioned response to a particular event.
- Must currently be considered a manifestation of a behavioral, psychological, or biological dysfunction in the individual.
- Not deviant behavior (political, religious, sexual) nor conflicts primarily between an individual and society—unless this is a symptom of a dysfunction in the individual.

A clinician following DSM-III (and then DSM-III-R and DSM-IV) guidelines would thus carefully review a list of symptom-based inclusion and exclusion criteria for a particular diagnostic category and tally up the number of symptoms observed. If the number of symptoms exceeded a designated cutpoint, the clinician would conclude that the patient had that particular illness. Although the number of diagnostic categories multiplied in revisions of the DSM, the basic logic remained: there were a discrete number of severe mental illnesses, and their identification required a skilled clinician. Affective disorders primarily involving emotional symptoms, such as major depression, were distinguished from psychotic disorders primarily involving thought disturbances, such as schizophrenia, and bipolar affective disorder was classified as a disease distinctive from both of these.

In the words of sociologist Allan Horwitz, the DSM had accomplished the *medicalization* of psychiatric disability (2002).

> Medicalization means that problems are considered to be discrete diseases that professionals discover, name, and treat. It also means that psychiatrists and other mental health professionals become the culturally legitimated agents with the greatest authority to deal with conditions that in the past would have been seen as crime, deviance, disruption, sin, or bad habits. (8)

But the evidence for biological influences on mental illness was not just a product of the vigorous efforts of psychiatrists and other medical professionals. An increasing body of research indicates that neurological deficits are associated with the symptoms of severe mental illness. Persons with schizophrenia have, on average, diminished brain volume (Wright et al. 2000). Although there is some debate about the effect of psychotropic medication itself on brain volume, the existence of lower brain volume among first-degree relatives of persons diagnosed with schizophrenia (who are not themselves taking medication) suggests an underlying genetic contribution (Boos et al. 2007). Twin studies and other research on genetic influence estimate the heritability of schizophrenia and bipolar disorder as 80 percent, compared to 40 percent for major depression and 30 percent for generalized anxiety (Rutter 2005). Rajkowska et al. (1999) found that patients with major depressive disorder had smaller neurons and fewer glial cells in the prefrontal cortex that mediate between neurons and their environment.

The Sociological Model

Most sociologists who studied mental illness went in an entirely different direction. Now standing across a chasm, typically measuring symptoms in the general population rather than among persons seeking treatment for mental anguish, sociologists perceived an unbroken continuum from those who manifested few symptoms to those who displayed many—whether or not they had been diagnosed as mentally ill and with little distinction among different diagnostic categories (Horwitz and Wakefield 2007, 129). Although for the purposes of description sociologists sometimes employed symptom inventories to yield discrete diagnoses parallel to those in DSM-III, they emphasized the absence of a clear boundary between particular illnesses as well as between illness and normality. The DSM-III attempt to draw a clear line between mental health and illness seemed from this perspective to be inherently misguided (Mirowsky and Ross 2003, 6, 28–29). Biologically oriented researchers were accused of making "claims of sole causation" by genetic factors (Pearlin, Avison, and Fazio 2007, 37). Thus, "[A] language of categories fits some realities better than others; it fits the reality of psychological problems poorly" (Mirowsky and Ross 1989, 11; Mirowsky and Ross 2002, 155).

Although they have focused most attention on psychological distress as measured in self-report inventories administered to general population samples, sociologists have argued that psychotic symptoms also fall on a continuum, and so "the diagnostic approach does not reflect reality" (Mirowsky and Ross 2002, 165–66).

Research guided by this sociological perspective identified sources of mental distress throughout the social system: lower socioeconomic status, undesirable life changes, being single, having children without having sufficient resources for them, being female, young, or elderly, and living in disordered neighborhoods (Mirowsky and Ross 2003, 151–56). Psychological resources were also important: maintaining a sense of control in life could compensate for having lower levels of social support (Mirowsky and Ross 2003, 201–204).

Identifying structural sources of distress—this "inequality of misery" (Mirowsky and Ross 2003, 6–7)—seemed to establish mental distress as a "social fact," not a medical condition. Distress, or "sadness" in response to external events, was not distinguished from the type of severe and long-lasting depression that psychiatrists tend to see among patients (Horwitz and Wakefield 2007, 205). As Mirowsky and Ross state, "[T]he misery, demoralization, or distress a person feels is not the problem. It is a consequence of the problem. Misery is not only real, it is realistic. Suffering contains a message about the causes of suffering" (2003, 6).

Some sociologists adopted a perspective on mental illness that was even less hospitable to the medical perspective. Following Emile Durkheim (1966 [1895]), the *social constructionist perspective* shifted analysis from "the behavior of individuals to cultural systems of meaning that define various sorts of behavior" (Horwitz 2002, 7). For "constructionists," Allan Horwitz (2002, 6) explained, "mental illnesses do not arise in nature but are constituted by social systems of meaning." The possibility that biological processes may create dysfunctions in the central nervous system, as they do in other parts of the body, seemed beyond the pale.

Bridging the Paradigms

In spite of the stark contrast between the medical and sociological models of the late twentieth century, and regardless of whether sociologists conceived of mental illness as the negative end of a continuum or as a discrete diseased state, both sustained observation and careful measurement suggested a reality that a purely sociological perspective could not explain: some persons evinced thoughts and behaviors that could not be considered normal or healthy. In the words of anthropologist Tanya Luhrmann (2000, 13), "It is hard to describe, to someone who has never seen it, how terrible and intractable madness often is."

Mirowsky and Ross (2003, 29) continued to urge that "Only the most extreme, persistent, or inexplicable distress would get labeled as mental illness," but they did not abjure the use of the "illness" label at this extreme. Sociologist Sue Estroff's (1981) structural analysis viewed some mental health system practices as "making it [perspectives on clients] crazy," but she nonetheless identified symptoms as occurring largely apart from social influence:

> [T]he most potent factors were clients' *subjective experiences with and responses to symptoms,* the meaning attached to these experiences by the client and others, and the degree to which the client was constrained in meeting cultural expectations for health *by the symptoms* and by his or her responses to them. (p. 233) [*emphases added*]

Sociologist Allan V. Horwitz (2002) took a different approach to the medical perspective by arguing for a categorical distinction between psychotic disorders—those that result in bizarre or inappropriate thought, hallucinations, hearing voices, or feeling unjustifiable paranoia—and affective disorders—those involving highly distressed, even paralyzing moods. According to Horwitz (2002, 12–13), distress that arises from stressful social conditions is not a "valid mental disorder[s]," whereas psychotic disorders "seem to be clear dysfunctions of mechanisms that regulate perception, thinking, communication, and other psychological processes." More specifically,

> . . . people whose symptoms fluctuate with the emergence and dissipation of stressful social circumstances are psychologically normal: they do not have internal dysfunctions and so should not be defined as suffering from a mental disorder. (12)

By contrast,

> Biological dysfunctions [distorted thought processes of schizophrenia, massive and continual alcohol consumption, depleted levels of serotonin] can have consequences regardless of the social definitions placed on them. (9)

Horwitz (2002, 36) acknowledged that these "internal dysfunctions" may appear as a "disproportionate" reaction to stressors that have disappeared, but he emphasized a central sociological task is to distinguish between mental disorders and normal reactions to social stressors. There is nothing wrong with people who respond to stressful environments, situations, and relationships with depression, anxiety, and other signs of distress. Their reactions are normal, not abnormal, responses to their environments. (20)

In 2007, Horwitz and Wakefield further distinguished feelings of distress—normal "sadness" in response to troubling events—from depressive disorder that is due primarily to biological imbalance. Horwitz also rejected a simple constructionist interpretation of mental illness by instead distinguishing the etiologies of psychotic and affective disorders:

> Mental disorders are internal dysfunctions that socio-cultural standards define as inappropriate. . . . These functions [e.g., motivation, memory, cognition, arousal, attachment] are not social constructions but properties of the human species that have arisen through natural selection. (Horwitz 2002, 11, 35)

Recent research conducted within the medical paradigm also suggests how an interdisciplinary bridge can be built through investigation of the mounting evidence "of the existence of reciprocal relationships among neurobiological, psychological, and socioenvironmental phenomena" (Schooler 2007, 61). Psychiatrist Carl Cohen (2000, 73) criticized the lack of attention of many biologically oriented psychiatrists to social factors and argued for "overcoming social amnesia." Some research testing various aspects of the medical model since the advent of DSM-III indicates that it is useful to conceive and measure psychiatric symptoms along a continuum, rather than simply using a tally of symptoms to indicate presence or absence of a discrete illness—just as sociologists have urged. Some biologically oriented psychiatrists now urge reformulating the diagnosis of schizophrenia to more accurately describe its underlying dimensions (Tsuang, Stone, and Faraone 2000). Moreover, research provides abundant evidence that the development, course, and outcomes of almost every diagnosable psychiatric illness are influenced by the social environment (Rutter 2005). Genetic studies indicate that "environmental events account for substantial portions of the variance in liability" [to major depression] (Sullivan, Neale, and Kendler 2000, 1559). Such features of the social environment as differences in parental treatment, peer relations, and sibling interaction are important environmental influences on the risk of depression among children (Reiss, Plomin, and Hetherington 1991, 284). As Hyman (2000) has noted, "[t]hroughout development and maturity, genes and environment are involved in a set of complex and almost inextricable interactions. . . . The separation of psychology [and sociology] from biology is a stumbling block to a true understanding of ourselves" (89).

These indications of environmental influence complement findings about biological processes. In the words of Michael Rutter (2005), the many indications of individual variation in response to environmental hazards (both physical and psychosocial) mean that research about genetic susceptibility "for" [his quotes] mental disorder "must include a study of environmental risk mechanism, and there must be study of the several forms of gene-environment interplay."

Psychiatrist Eric Kandel's (1998) "new intellectual framework for psychiatry" included the "central tenet" that "what we commonly call mind is a range of functions carried out by the brain," so that "behavioral disorders that characterize psychiatric illness are disturbances of brain function, even in those cases where the causes of the disturbances are clearly environmental in origin." At the same time, because his framework "makes all bodily functions, including all functions of the brain, susceptible to social influences" through the regulation of gene expression by social factors, Kandel's (1998) framework bridges the chasm between sociology and biologically oriented psychiatry and insists on "multiple causality."

> Behavior and social factors exert actions on the brain by feeding back upon it to modify the expression of genes and thus the function of nerve cells. Learning, including learning that results in dysfunctional behavior, produces alterations in gene expression. Thus all of "nurture" is ultimately expressed as "nature." [Moreover, a]lterations in gene expression induced by learning give rise to changes in patterns of neuronal connections.

In the words of psychiatrist Leon Eisenberg (1995, 1568): "Nature and nurture stand in reciprocity, not opposition."

The Situation of Homelessness

Research provides abundant evidence that severe distress and psychosis are much more common among persons who are homeless than in the general population. Serious psychological distress, including clinical depression, suicidal thinking, and suicide attempts are between two and five times more common among homeless adult individuals than among housed adults (Burt and Cohen 1989; Ritchey et al. 1990). Between one in five and three-quarters of homeless persons in different samples suffer from serious distress, and one-tenth report recent suicidal thoughts (Arce and Vergare 1985; Robertson 1986; Koegel, Burnam, and Farr 1988; Rossi

1989; Tessler and Dennis 1989; Gelberg and Linn 1989; La Gory, Ritchey, and Mullis 1990; Koegel and Burnam 1992; Wong and Piliavin 2001). About one-quarter to one-third have been hospitalized or seen as outpatients at some time in their lives for psychiatric problems (Farr et al. 1986; Roth and Bean 1986; Rossi 1989; Schutt 1989). Half of homeless adults interviewed in St. Louis by Morse and Calsyn (1985–1986) scored above the cutoff for diagnosable mental illness on the Brief Symptom Inventory (Derogatis and Spencer 1982), although in a Boston sample of homeless inpatients at a mental health center, half were found to have a substance abuse disorder, brain disease, or a character disorder rather than a major mental illness (Bennett et al. 1988).

Can research on nonhomeless populations be used to guide understanding of mental illness among homeless persons? Sociologist David Snow and anthropologist Leon Anderson (1993, 211) emphasized the causal role of the homeless situation itself in producing these illnesses:

> ...alcoholism and mental illness sometimes function as means of coping psychologically with the traumas of street life. (208) ...Although such alternative realities frequently invite both folk labels of "nuts" and "crazy" and clinical labels of schizophrenia and paranoia, they may often be quite functional for some individuals who find themselves in a demeaning and inhumane context in which they are the frequent objects of negative attention or attention deprivation.

Focusing specifically on homeless persons, Snow and Anderson referred to "the *so-called* mentally ill" [emphasis added]. In their research, Snow and Anderson classified homeless persons as mentally ill if they met at least two of three criteria: prior institutionalization, "conduct that is so bizarre and situationally inappropriate that it would be likely to be construed as symptomatic of mental illness by most observers," or being labeled as mentally ill by other homeless individuals. Explaining the rationale for this last criterion, Snow and Anderson (1993, 67) argued that "people who share similar sociocultural niches ought to have some sense of who among them is 'crazy' or 'mentally ill.' Accordingly, we listened for such designations and judgments among the homeless and sought to elicit and confirm them in conversational interviewing when appropriate."

Although there have not been large before-and-after studies that could test whether symptoms of mental illness increase with the onset of homelessness, some of the factors associated with the state of being homeless predict distress in both the homeless and housed populations: adverse life events, fewer economic resources, physical disability, self-perceived ill health, and substance abuse (Weissman et al. 1977; Ensel 1986; Tausig

1986; Kaplan et al. 1987; Gelberg and Linn 1989; Rossi 1989; Susser, Conover, and Struening 1989; LaGory, Ritchey, and Mullis 1990; Robins and Regier 1991). Nonetheless, studies that have examined a range of predictors of psychological distress among homeless persons reproduce only some of the usual findings from general population studies (Lin, Dean, and Ensel 1986; Barnett and Gotlib 1988, 119; Mirowsky and Ross 1989).

Demographic correlates of distress among homeless persons do not replicate consistently those found in the general population. Whereas women, minorities, and young adults in the general population are at greater risk for psychological distress (Elpern and Karp 1984; Radloff and Locke 1986; Mirowsky and Ross 1989; Mirowsky and Ross 1992; but see Nolen-Hoeksema 1987), this is not consistently so among homeless populations (Robertson 1986; Gelberg and Linn 1989; La Gory, Ritchey, and Mullis 1990). Findings have been mixed about the association of distress with education in homeless samples (La Gory, Ritchey, and Mullis 1990; Schutt, Meschede, and Rierdan 1994; Wong and Piliavin 2001).

Findings also diverge between studies of the general and homeless populations with respect to social support. Social support often buffers the depressive effect of adverse life events in the general population, but some have argued that adverse life events are so overabundant for homeless persons that it becomes "a condition so devastating that personal ties are almost ineffectual" (La Gory, Ritchey, and Mullis 1990, 99). Research about the relationship of social support to distress among the homeless has yielded mixed results (Gelberg and Linn 1989; La Gory, Ritchey, and Mullis 1990). In a Boston study Schutt, Meschede, and Rierdan (1994) found that those who felt they had more social support were considerably less distressed and suicidal, and those who perceived themselves as lacking social support were particularly prone to the distress-inducing effects of specific adverse life events. In addition, social support interacted with distress in explaining suicidal thinking: distressed individuals who had higher levels of social support were less likely to have had suicidal thoughts than were distressed individuals with less social support. In other words, having more social support benefited homeless people. However, although Wong and Piliavin (2001) also found that perceived support was associated with lesser distress in a homeless sample, they distinguished number of contacts—an objective indicator of social support—and found that it did not vary with distress.

In their study, Wong and Piliavin (2001) investigated distress before and after homeless persons moved into housing. They found that measured distress decreased in their follow-up interviews for those who had moved into housing. However, their study used a naturalistic design that could not ensure baseline equivalence of those who obtained housing from those who did not; nor did they distinguish persons with serious mental illness from others. Only one of nine housing studies reviewed by Nelson, Aubrey, and Lafrance (2007) found any impact of housing on psychiatric symptoms. In general inadequate attention has been given to the potential importance of community context and the available level of social integration (Horwitz 2007, 87).

Our multiple measures allow me to take account of some of these complexities in order to understand the impact and course of mental illness among our project participants. Our structured clinical interviews at baseline distinguish psychotic disorders, bipolar disorder, and major affective disorder. Our self-report measure of symptoms of distress provides a continuous measure like that used in most sociological survey research. Moreover, we are able at baseline to construct counts of the symptoms identified in the diagnosis of both affective and psychotic disorders, thus creating continuous measures that reflect the more rigorous criteria used in a clinical interview. My quantitative analyses can thus compare predictors of, relations among, and consequences of using categorical diagnoses or continuous symptom measures, as well as of using a clinical diagnostic interview as compared to self-report (Horwitz and Wakefield 2007, 203–205).

The McKinney Project's experimental, longitudinal design also aids identification of both changes over time and the impact of living in group rather than independent housing, while the ethnographic notes facilitate intensive examination of the meaning of mental illness to residents and staff and description of the process by which participants responded to mental illness.

Mental Illness at Baseline

We used the Structured Clinical Interview for DSM-III to make DSM-based diagnostic distinctions. Just over two-thirds of the sample members were diagnosed with schizophrenia or schizoaffective disorder, while 12 percent were diagnosed with major affective disorder, and the remaining 17 percent with bipolar disorder.

Questions in the Structured Clinical Interview for DSM-III (SCID) provided the basis for continuous measures of symptoms of distress and psychosis at the threshold or subthreshold levels. Participants reported experiencing an average of 1.4 symptoms of depression, but over half reported no symptoms of distress, and only 19 percent reported more than two. Symptoms of psychosis identified with the SCID as at subthreshold or threshold levels were more common—only 24 percent reported no such symptoms—although most reported only one such symptom. Only four cases reported having had more than two symptoms indicative of psychosis.

We also measured distress with a standard inventory of distressed feelings that is embedded within Lehman's (1991) Quality of Life (QOL) Index. On this four-point scale, participants' scores were approximately normally distributed, with an average distress score of three, indicating considerable distress.

The two continuous measures of depression (based on the SCID and on Lehman's QOL scale) were moderately correlated ($r=.51$, $p<.001$), but neither was associated with the SCID-based measure of psychotic symptoms. Among those diagnosed with major affective disorder and those diagnosed with schizophrenia, the structured clinical interview for DSM (SCID)-based symptom count of depressive symptoms but not the QOL-based depression scale was elevated to a statistically significant degree (and of course it is the count of symptoms that is used in deriving the SCID diagnosis of major affective disorder) (see fig. 7.1).

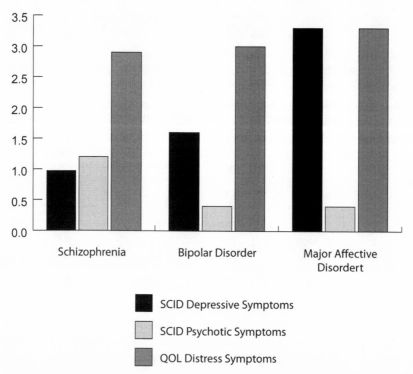

Figure 7.1. Symptoms of depression by SCID diagnosis in baseline interview. Note: $N=111–112$.

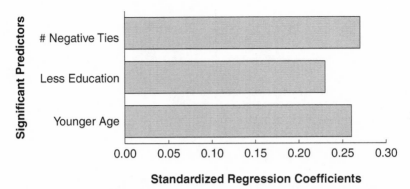

Figure 7.2. Regression analysis of SCID depressive symptoms. Note: $R^2 = .23$, $N = 107$. Other variables included in the analysis that did not have significant coefficients: gender, race, baseline preference for independent living, clinician housing recommendation, lifetime substance abuse, self-reported ability to manage, number of positive social ties.

The correlates of distress at baseline also differed for the two symptom-based measures. Baseline scores on the SCID-based distress measure decreased with age and education, and they increased with reports of more negative social ties (see fig. 7.2). In contrast, there were no differences in distress measured with the continuous QOL index according to sociodemographic characteristics or the other predictors. There were also no independent correlates of the SCID psychotic symptoms index among these potential predictors.

The SCID diagnosis itself did not vary with sociodemographic characteristics, lifetime substance abuse, or the other potential predictors.

The diagnostic distinctions that we made at baseline allow investigation of the relation of diagnosis to housing experience and outcomes, whereas the repeated continuous self-report measure of depressive symptoms permits analysis of the impact of housing experience on symptomatology. Before analyzing these quantitative outcomes, I first examine the ethnographic record to better understand the role of psychiatric symptoms and treatment experience in the group homes.

Mental Illness at Home

A diagnosis of serious mental illness was a criterion for gaining housing through the Boston McKinney project, but it was at the same time a label that some participants sought to escape when they moved out of the shelters.

Both the symptoms and the label continued to shape attitudes and behavior throughout the project.

The Label

"Mentally ill" had been a contested and generally disliked label among DMH shelter residents (Desjarlais 1997, 110). Although they used this label to identify the problems of others, many shelter residents rejected application of the label to themselves.

> [M]any of those staying in the shelter distinguished between those who were "normal" and those who had problems; they did not welcome the awkward identity that came with being considered mentally ill. Most acknowledged that they were "sick" or had specific problems—such as hearing voices, excessive nervousness, or feelings of paranoia—but did not like the idea of being considered "crazy," "schizophrenic," or "psychotic." The difference lay in the nature of the characterizations: diffuse problems were seen as distinct from but combated by oneself, whereas the fixed identity of being "crazy" was held to be integral to a person's existence. . . . The implications were moral: to be psychotic was to be something less than fully human, without control over one's actions, and set apart from the social and ethical realities of others. It came down to a difference between "having" an illness or "being" one. . . . a "Special Persons" pass for the Boston public transportation system (also known as a "crazy card") . . . would make her "different, not normal" and "in need of special consideration." (Desjarlais 1997, 109, 110)

This same rejection of the idea of being mentally ill was also expressed by many participants after they moved into project housing. Some tenants simply rejected the label.

> Cliff refuses the label of mental illness and wants to leave the program, not participate in it.
>
> Millie wants to drop her day program because she doesn't "like it and isn't mentally ill anymore."
>
> Frances "hibernates" in the house—a Haitian staff member explains that Haitians won't accept mental illness.

Upon overhearing another tenant ask a staff member how to obtain discount public transportation fares for persons with disabilities, a tenant interjected,

> Fuck disabled! [yelling] I'm not gonna listen to that! I'm sick of that word. I'm not disabled!! [She leaves the room and slams her bedroom door shut.]

Some participants skirted troubling implications of being labeled "mentally ill" through commitment to an alternative etiology for their symptoms. Jerrold, for example, attributed his "mental illness" to substance abuse:

> Jerrold talked on about how he believes that mental illness is caused by booze and drugs directly at least in his case. He said he has been sober for two years, and when he runs into "his people" with whom he used to party, and they are still using drugs and alcohol, they know better than to offer him any now though. Jerrold said that his doctor changed his diagnosis and he is no longer paranoid schizophrenic. "So long as I don't have drugs I'm not paranoid schizophrenic. I'm on so little Prolixin now that I can function." Jerrold's views of the diagnostic issue were close to saying that it was a status [that] one worked out of through good behavior. There was also an issue that his past psychosis was explained by his drug use and his doctor's agreement with this version of his illness.

Jerrold suggested alternative treatments for others based on this alternative etiology:

> Showing people that you aren't insane, that you can hold a conversation. This is what will take the diagnosis away like mine.

Other tenants proposed different etiologies that also sidestepped the "mental illness" label:

> At the hospital, David explains his stress as having been due to eating spicy Italian food.

When a roommate was hospitalized after he stopped taking his medications and started "acting crazy," Jane was baffled "because she thinks it is the hospital that makes you crazy."

One tenant explained that he had been hospitalized simply for washing his clothes outside.

> I ended up in a mental institution for washing my clothes in a puddle. I had no money and they took me to the [community mental health center]. Did you know that actually if you're an Indian and wash clothes on a rock in the middle of Boston, 'cause that's their culture, don't think about doing it, 'cause they'll put you away for eight days. No kidding. I told the cops I was homeless, and it was an economical thing but they didn't go for it.

Other tenants accepted the diagnosis of mental illness and used it to explain behavioral problems.

> Frank describes his schizophrenia as an illness that has made him do some crazy things.
>
> Ellie describes her problems with feeling everyone was talking about her, and how a man had made fun of her at the bank, and how bad she felt. She agrees that she should take her meds so as to feel better.

Some of the housing staff also rejected initially a medical concept of mental illness and complained that the Clinical Homeless Specialists were "too clinical, judgmental."

> Ron says that [a tenant] should be given control over her money and not be made dependent on the system. Ron sees the system as largely creating mental illness—dependency.

The Symptoms

In spite of these different perspectives on mental illness, psychiatric symptoms were often apparent. Symptoms of depression were common, but they did not often disrupt house functioning.

> Lisa is relatively listless, owes many friends things, and they like her to pay them back with alcohol and drinking with them. Likes to do things with people, but doesn't initiate them.
>
> Al also depressed, sleeping much; refuses to go to a new mind-body program.

The positive symptoms of psychosis—bizarre expressions, seeing things, hearing voices, paranoid thoughts—were displayed by several tenants in each group home, but it was a project participant in an independent apartment who provided the most detailed description of this aspect of having schizophrenia:

> "When I was in the hospital and I felt really bad, I kept thinking about a river. That river kept calling to me, telling me to drown myself in the water. When I went to [one shelter], I was near the river there, and I kept hearing the river calling to me. I told the staff about it there but they said they couldn't help me. But I was all right; I was calm. And then they put me over at [another] shelter and it was much better because I wasn't anywhere near the river. But then they took us for a walk and all of a sudden, there was a pond. And then that water called to me and told me to drown myself, but, I don't know why, but I didn't go in." He laughed then, and told me that he thinks some of the cockroaches in his apartment are schizophrenic too. Why, [the ethnographer] asked? "Because the other day when I was washing my hands in the bathroom sink, I turned on the tap and the water came out. Well, there were a few roaches sitting near the drain, and most of them tried to run away when the water came down. But one of them, a big, fat, long one, started crawling towards the water, kinda looking at it, and then going right into the water, and then it drowned and went down the drain."

Positive symptoms frequently had disruptive effects in the context of the group homes.

> Jill has been acting bizarrely—singing loud to the radio, yelling "fuck you" to tenants.

Sam is doing well, talking about working, but still struggles with hallucinations.

Mary often wrote bizarre notes and called the police to report that people next door were murdering each other. One night Mary started to walk to the store in her socks but was stopped by staff.

She talked about feeling immobile in the house and put it that even if she was sitting in her chair she felt stuck and couldn't move.

In some instances, positive psychotic symptoms were a part of a person's being that had little direct effect.

Harvey is hearing voices, but they are happy voices; he seems to be managing with them, although Mame cautions to keep asking him about them.

Harry had a usual spot at the house, where he often could be found reading the newspaper. But the paper was a mixed blessing, since Harry thought that the problems in the world were his fault. Harry was concerned about having Down syndrome—because he felt "down" all the time. His depressed mood was often punctuated by "mysterious emotional outbursts," with laughing, yelled insults, singing, or talking out loud—and all the while believing others were not aware of these expressions because they were only occurring in his head. At least he was able to take some solace in his accomplishments—writing Abbey Road and other songs for the Beatles.

Positive symptoms were often expressed in the context of problems in the social world.

Walter had come home and was in a bad mood. He was hearing and responding to voices almost continuously, and Jerry was talking aloud also, so Mary was tense. Walter . . . quit his job; hearing loud voices telling him to do bad things. . . . worried that he will lose his room in the house if he is hospitalized. . . . When we were talking about his family he would go between talking with me and talking with his voices quite smoothly—as if his voices were challenging the responses he was giving me [the ethnographer], and he had to convince them, and they do not listen to reason. When he yells at the voices he turns his head to the left and somewhat up in the air, and directs his gaze as if there was someone there he was talking with. He said they were not too bad, and at least he has a good deal of control over them. It is really striking for the combination of florid psychosis and "normal conversation" and the way he went from one into the other and back without blinking.

Walter was sitting at the kitchen table . . . talking loudly and angrily to voices. He was saying that he doesn't need money and that he has balls because he went right into the [shop] and told the mafia off, right to their face. His mannerisms were quite violent, as they usually are, and at one point he threw his glasses down on the table for emphasis. He actually broke the arm of his glasses doing this. But as usual, as soon as anyone addressed him, or when he addressed anyone else, he was as calm and together as ever. We sat there somewhat amazed for a while.

Positive symptoms sometimes had a negative effect on social relations within and outside the houses, particularly when they led to safety concerns.

Frank is aware that what he says often does not make any sense and that he prefaces comments with "you'll think I'm crazy but . . ." He asked [a staff member] to promise she wouldn't send him away if he said something crazy. Miguel agreed that Frank is too paranoid and that the staff "can't touch him." . . . Francine noted how he called everyone a grump at the meeting. Roger said he was right, because they're afraid of him. Whenever he comes around everyone shuts up. He tries to talk with people, but everyone is scared that he might do something rash. When he drinks he is sociable, but the effects of his previous behavior cast a shadow over his interaction, and he is shunned.

Positive symptoms could also hinder interpersonal relations by increasing communication difficulties.

Mary tried to explain some ideas to me, which I [the ethnographer] found very difficult to understand. She started out talking about being alone with oneself and coming to pieces. She said that one could be alone with oneself even if one lived with many people. She said she was very scared of being alone with herself because she feared she might "take herself apart" if there were no people around. Mary expresses paranoid fears frequently. . . . a lot of it I could not even repeat because she talks in circles, using outlandish phrases and hilarious exclamations. . . . She said she "can't stand it" when anybody says "Good Morning" to her when she wakes up, because that means that they're telling her to have a good day, and she's never sure if the day is going to be good or bad.

The progress of meetings could be interrupted by these symptom-based communication difficulties:

Jerry got upset that people were "not recognizing his simple point"—something about making love in his room and then about a guard dog—and got up and left.

Harold "blew up yesterday" about the all-black staff and seems more psychotic, angry.

Disruptions related to insomnia were "the last straw" for some tenants.

Or "you got Bob with his videos all night when he couldn't sleep for five nights in a row. And of course, Jack over here doesn't ever stay in his room when he can't sleep." [screaming] "You don't belong down here watching TV all night when you can't sleep. I'm sick of it!"

Bipolar illness was less common among project participants, but symptoms of mania could be as disruptive as the positive symptoms of schizophrenia.

> Arthur has not taken his Lithium in 2.5 months. . . . The day before yesterday, he left the house and has not been back since. . . . A few days ago, [a staff member] gave him $100 to buy gardening equipment, and he spent all of it on himself, but nobody will ever find out. He was giving quarters to people on the street. Two nights ago, he spent the night in jail because he was arrested for disorderly conduct on Beacon Hill. He was yelling and screaming during the night so that all the rich people would know the truth about the third way of getting AIDS. "I'm the only one who will tell the truth about this. None of the restaurants will ever tell the public but I am. I'm talking about cooks in the back jacking off in the food and spreading AIDS. . . . It's all these immigrants that are fucking up our country." Other things that he said include the following: (1) He came up with another invention that could have prevented the large oil spill from the Exxon Valdez—build an underwater submarine oil tanker, which could have slid right underneath the ice. . . . (3) Animals are much smarter than humans because they can read the minds of humans and plants. (4) Dinosaurs never had blood flowing through them—but rather, crude oil. . . . Throughout all of this, Arthur was very serious, and if we ever smiled or tried to make a joke about what he was saying, he would insist that he was talking seriously.

Responding to Symptoms

Both project and house staff struggled to respond to psychiatric symptomatology in a way that was consistent with the project's empowerment philosophy. Initially staff in one house said they expected that tenants would learn to express and deal with their emotions better after more time away from the shelter environment. When problems persisted, a project representative encouraged tenants in one house to take responsibility for seeking help when their symptoms were intense.

> The key is people asking for help when they need it, and I can give it to you. I'm not gonna criticize you. But if you don't ask for help, then you've got no insight into your illness. Then in that case, I will approach you and tell you I'm referring you elsewhere to live. A chronic illness comes and goes—it's not curable. Chronic illness is like the moon . . . sometimes it's in remission, and sometimes it's not. If I start wearing a lot of makeup, and I buy $400 worth of scratch tickets, and I'm stealing Helen's food and spilling coffee all over the floor and refusing to clean up after myself, then there's a problem, and you all might wanna say to me, "Jane, you're manic, you gotta go and get help." It's up to me as a mature, responsible adult to listen to the residents' input, go to my doctor, and get the help I need. That's called insight into your illness.

At another time house staff reacted to a tenant's suicidal expressions—
"talking about doing away with herself"—by developing a "contract" for
her to sign, stating that she will not harm herself and will talk to staff or
tenants if she feels like doing so.

House staff began to differentiate their role from that of traditional
mental health service staff and to define more severe psychopathology as
the responsibility of the traditional system. A long discussion in a joint
tenant-staff meeting illustrated this process of role differentiation.

Harriet: When you're talking to Pam reasonably, she's not hearing it because
the illness is kicking in. So let's try to find this balance to be understanding
so that you don't wanna add extra pressure but just know that she's
getting the help she needs. When the illness kicks in, either you lose your
home or somebody important in your life or someone steals all your stuff,
instead of working with people before the bad stuff happens. It's only
after you lose your house or whatever that people give you attention.
Nobody ever gave you attention until you were too far gone. So maybe
someone could come and talk to Pam and say—"Have you noticed we're
all avoiding you lately?" And tell her why.

Helen: So how do other people feel—threatened?

Felicity: She shuts all the blinds in the house, turns on the heat all day. Last
night, she turned up all the thermostats.

Helen: How do you feel, Jack?

Jack: I don't know. She buys me cigarettes, and sometimes she has change
and just gives it to me. I don't mind her.

Jeff: I think someone should talk to her. She's a grown female, and she
expects everyone to pamper her. She wants everyone to take care of all her
problems; she thinks she's so special and better than everyone else. . . . I
was very polite, but she was just yelling at me and then she left. That's not
right.

Felicia: Yeah, she is stomping right out every time Nancy comes into the
room. She'll stomp her feet like a little child. I haven't even been able to
yell back at her, I've been so upset. I just quit, and sometimes we'll just
play cards or something. But two weeks and three weeks of this . . . one
night she stayed up all night, making lots of noise, and then it's the
cussing.

Helen: Sounds like it's disruptive to everyone.

Jeff: Sometimes it's the medication that does that.

Jack: But she's not taking her medication!

. . .

Jeff: But we don't have a worker who comes in from the center and talks to
you about your problems. I think she's angry because there is nobody to
talk to about her children.

Helen: Well, we're not illness people—we're all about wellness. But Pam
does have Geraldine and others at the [CMHC] that she feels connected

with. It's probably a very scary thing for her right now, and so she tends to act this way. . . . So we're doing the right thing by contacting staff at the [CMHC], and having those staff contact her. Everything's in place now.

Ultimately, the difficulty of dealing with mental illness slowed progress toward the reduction of staff. As a project leader remarked, "Until we get a grip on when illness is happening, we will need staff."

Medication Compliance

Medication compliance was a continuing concern. Failure to take prescribed medication often exacerbated positive symptoms.

One staff member says that Sally had not taken her meds for three days and was getting really crazy—like saying a staff member was going to murder her. . . .

Harvey went off his meds and became "totally psychotic," by his own recounting—throwing things. Other tenants told a relief staffer that they felt threatened by Harvey and that he had an alliance with the house manager that prevented them from complaining—and this was reported.

Stephanie notes that she was misreading the situation. Stephanie asserts her control in the tenants' meeting, over Harvey, who apologizes for this prior outburst and says he hadn't known that he was on medication for psychosis as well as for manic depression. His doctor explained his medications to him and he agrees 100 percent. From now on Harvey will take his medications because he understands that he needs them to keep from becoming psychotic, and whatever he did, it won't happen again. Stephanie tells Harvey he is out of line [after he talks about calling staff "niggers" at the hospital], and he says "fuck you Stephanie" and walks out, then says he wants to move. There is a plan to write a letter to Harvey about violating alcohol policy and being required to take meds.

Tenants themselves often explained their own and other tenants' behaviors with reference to medication.

Jeff told me what it was like for him to go off his meds. He was in a boarding house and threw all his meds out the window because he hated their side effects. Then a little while later, he was "gripped by a terrible fear—as if somebody put a gun to my head and said if you don't get the answers to my next two questions right, I'm gonna kill you. I knew something was wrong, so I went to the emergency room, and at first I was very paranoid and I didn't want to give my name out, but then I did, and the doctor prescribed my meds again."

Arthur told us that he is worried about Joe. He does not think Joe is taking his meds anymore, because he wakes up in the middle of the night screaming out curses and then he stays up for the rest of the night. . . . Arthur said he has been through similar things himself and that the first bad sign is when somebody thinks they are so well that they do not need to take their meds anymore, and that is what Joe has been saying lately.

. . . Now that Karl is back on his meds, . . . he has completely snapped out of his routine of watching TV all day and not sleeping all night. He goes to bed at 11 every night, is up early, and is out of the house every day, just the way he was when he first moved in. Dana said that "I know that if I went off my meds I'd act strange."

Sam said that when he said something offensive to the staff it had been during a time when he had not been taking his meds. He said that makes him say things which he would not say in his right mind. He said the disease he has inside is touching him.

Project participants living in independent apartments also reported problems due to poor medication compliance.

If Pam does not take her meds, she hears voices telling her the Russians are coming. Then she gets very frightened and hides everywhere, behind bushes, etc. But the meds she takes make her sleepy; she "falls down" during the day (may mean fall asleep) because she is so sleepy.

Later, Pam explained that she "broke down" after stopping her medications, but "everything is OK" now that she resumed taking them.

However, psychotropic medications created problems as well as resolved them. One tenant complained about the effects of one drug for his bipolar illness.

Arthur told me that he has not taken his Stelazine in about two weeks now, and he made me promise not to tell anybody. He quickly told me that he does take his lithium and Ativan; the Ativan helps him to calm down when he feels too high and anxious. He stopped taking the Stelazine because it makes him feel "drugged up like a horse—besides Charlie downstairs is on Stelazine and look at him! He barely moves, lies in bed all day, and can't do nothing for himself. That's not his personality, that's the Stelazine. You know what they're trying to do with this medication? They're trying to close the doors of my mind, and it takes every ounce of fighting power I have in me to keep those doors open. They're trying to crush my creativity and I'm not gonna let them. Every single day they try to come up with something else to close the doors, but I'm keeping up with them."

In spite of the problems with medication compliance, both tenants and staff kept encouraging self-medication, a goal for each of the group homes. Staff discussion illustrated this pressure for self-medication.

He [a tenant] has been more agitated recently, and his thoughts have been less clear. For example, . . . he said that he has not seen his family . . . when he just went and spent a whole week with them about a month ago. Sam asked if he is taking his meds, because this might be a sign that he is not. Carol said he has no history of not taking them, so there is no reason to suspect it. But he did just start holding his own meds so there is a possibility that that is what is going on.

Andy has stopped taking his meds, without telling his doctor. At staff meeting, [there is] discussion of problem with Andy not taking his meds and whether he should be required to do so. There was "enormous tension" among staff and the issue was not resolved.

How, then, could self-medication be achieved? Project representatives met with staff and tenants regularly to discuss procedures. One project representative urged house staff to think of tenants moving toward administration of medication along a family model.

Sally said that she had always thought of community residences on a family model and justified the giving of meds in this way. A family member was ill, and one family member gives the meds to them unless they can take them on their own. They do not need an RN because they are not acutely ill. They do not need intense professional treatment.

Medication policies had a deep symbolism. In another house, a staff member complained that requirements for self-medication undercut client empowerment:

This was one example of not being able to meet the clients where they are because of the requirements of all the paperwork.

A special nurse was then introduced to work with tenants on becoming self-medicating.

A project leader also expressed concerns about slow progress toward achieving self-medication. However, the vendor managing the house was concerned about staff liability in cases of medication-alcohol interactions and other problems.

In another house, staff concluded that tenants who needed to take their medications could not come to the staff office to wait with other tenants, due to privacy concerns, but would have to wait for staff to seek them out individually.

Project staff member Angie feels that staff violated the empowerment policy by not discussing the change in policy with tenants first. Angie says that the staff and tenants have to be mutually respectful, "It's not like our society today which respects the rich and no one else." Discussion [ensues] of how to allow tenants to be self-medicating. Some tenants feel the house is becoming like a hospital, with controls over meds etc. . . . Tenants make the decision to continue taking their meds on an individual basis.

Although self-medication was a goal for all tenants within each of the evolving consumer households, many tenants did not achieve that goal. Noncompliance was common, and in many cases it resulted in hospitalization.

Hospitalization

Psychiatric hospitalization was a frequent experience in the group homes.

Harold is hospitalized after hallucinations telling him to kill himself.

Jeff is to be pink-papered by his Clinical Homeless Specialist, after he came home after drinking, with a bump on his head, and [becoming] increasingly withdrawn and keeping food in his room in an unsanitary manner.

Helen is hospitalized again after acting bizarrely.

Tenants were usually hospitalized after a period of poorly controlled behavior that disrupted house social processes.

Bill is off his medications and starts crying, asks to [be] and is taken to the hospital, where he is evaluated and then released.

Bill is hospitalized, at his request, after having command hallucinations that result in him threatening Jorge with a knife.

Roger and Raymond have been arguing all day, and finally Roger started throwing chairs and ashtrays. Roger told [a female staff member] that he wanted to have sex with her, and she could not calm him down. She finally went into the office and locked the door, called police, and Roger was taken to the hospital. A female friend of another tenant had teased Roger sexually a few days before. There was a strong consensus that Roger had flipped out, but [the ethnographer] viewed Raymond as mercilessly trying to push people over the edge.

Rufus is discharged, seemingly prematurely—acting very manic, from the hospital and gets into a brawl with Tom, who has to be hospitalized for a dislocated shoulder as a result. Rufus is then taken back to the hospital.

Alan avoids the meeting and is talking to himself, apparently angry because he is not able to access his own money any more. Staff discuss hospitalization. Alan is very psychotic.

Staff sometimes anticipated the risk of hospitalization, but they had no strategy for forestalling it.

I'm telling you, . . . the same thing is happening all over again with Claudette. Nobody is addressing the real problem, and this is gonna go on for months until there's a big crisis again.

. . . Claudette has been deteriorating. Another tenant remarks ". . . things were getting even worse than yesterday. I don't mind the things she says that don't make sense, but when she starts talking about slashing throats and watching the blood flow out, that's where I draw the line. That makes me angry." . . . All agree she should be hospitalized, but she has not acted so as to allow involuntary hospitalization.

Claudette had acted bizarre with [a staff member], by continually lighting matches, pointing them at her, and letting them burn down—and not explaining why. Claudette is still in the hospital but is doing better. She had been lying in bed all day, not eating, only coming downstairs for a diet drink.

Some concern [expressed] about Mike—that by letting him drop his meds and not doing anything as he deteriorated, it led to him being involuntarily hospitalized. Some staff agreed that this was the right thing to do so that he would learn from his mistakes.

Some tenants were hospitalized several times in succession before they decided to or were required to move out of the house.

Raymond is doing very well since returning from the hospital; seems grateful to be back. . . . apologetic about yelling in the house (as he has in the past). . . . Raymond has been hospitalized again and is out of the project—cannot handle the house anymore—being around people drinking and not [allowed to] drink himself. He was upset about it but adamant about leaving.

Mary was hospitalized after attacking Jennifer with a hammer, after Jennifer told her to stop her delusion about dogs and their spirits attacking her. Mary had been having trouble with her feelings for [a staff member]. Staff believe she does not have a real friend to talk with at the house. Staff discuss getting her to say when she is getting upset. She had stopped taking her meds.

Arthur grew disillusioned with staff responses to Mary.

"The thing is it won't do any good to tell anybody anything, telling the staff won't help anything. She needs to be hospitalized or something. She needs treatment. I'm afraid that there's going to be violence, not just the verbal but the other kind—like what happened here before. You know what I mean?"

Mary has been hospitalized, at least for 2 weeks . . . at the hospital, Mary is very paranoid and delusional and says she wants to move to [a shelter]. . . . Discussion [at a tenant meeting] about Mary's impending return, and discussion of how she has to take her meds. Hildegaard said that if someone was threatening then they should not be in the house. She said they should be left at [the shelter] where they take care of violent people who cannot live with others. . . . Andy and Alice express willingness to talk to Mary and tell her she is on probation. . . . Mary has been hospitalized again, after feeling she was losing control. Mary was up at night, screaming, yelling at tenant meetings, playing music, upset about not getting money when she wants it. Police called when she started throwing furniture and attacked [staff member] Felicity, biting her on the neck. Calms down after days in the hospital. Does not want to return . . . and is taken to the shelter; returns to day program. . . . General feeling that things were better in the house since Mary left.

An increase in stress in the external environment could result in hospitalization even when the increased stress resulted from a voluntary increase in responsibilities.

> Apparently, being assigned to the committee to review housing proposals had been the "worst thing" for Terry, as he was in another crisis, writing letters to all the higher-ups . . . and filing human rights violation charges against many of them and staff at the house, drinking a lot, and complaining bitterly about other tenants, then finally screaming "fuck you's" . . . during a tenant meeting. He was hospitalized in four-point restraints yesterday or today.

Hospitalization could provide relief from external stressors as well as from internal feelings.

> Fred wants to be hospitalized, due to feeling poorly, stressed, and tired. He thinks "it's better to go now than wait until things get worse." Staff think the real motivation is that Fred is broke—gives all his money away. . . . Fred has been hospitalized, "feeling awful," and has stopped making progress, threatens to cut himself, but was denied admission at [one hospital].
>
> Called Arthur . . . about being at the hospital and whether it was helping: "They're bringing me down to a certain level, you know? The doctor is good, she listens to me, but that's what it seems like, you know? I don't know yet what's really happening. At first they couldn't figure out what was wrong with me, because I wasn't going off on anybody, but now they figure I should slow down a little.

In other cases, hospitalization proved to be a very unpleasant experience.

> Cameron also talked about times when she needs to be hospitalized. She said that there is a certain holiday period when she gets very upset and needs help. Cameron has filed a suit due to being placed in restraints for eight hours. Cameron has been hospitalized, voluntarily. . . . Cameron is just back from the hospital, acting very abusively with others and hearing voices telling her to kill herself. Cameron is suspected of stealing parking money. . . . Cameron pink-papered to hospital after raging and threats, but then calmed down and avoided hospitalization. . . . Cameron was hospitalized after telling her doctor she was hearing voices talking about ways to kill her, but then put in restraints for four hours—so she is suing.
>
> Harold complained about being put in four-point restraints at the hospital, even though he explained "what had been happening at the house." Harold had called the relief staff person a "nigger" and refused to apologize, telling others that they use that language "on yourselves all the time"—and some black people are niggers and some aren't. . . . Harold was barred from the house over the weekend. He had come back from the hospital and had the police accompany him inside, claiming that he was prevented from entering even though he had paid his rent, but the police left when they learned that the house was for mentally ill persons.

Hospitalization was thus neither an unmitigated blessing nor a certain curse in the lives of the McKinney tenants. For some it provided a period of reduced stress and recuperation, whereas for others it was experienced as a humiliating loss of control. Irrespective of these specific effects, the availability of hospitalization as an option provided a critical means of increasing social control and ensuring some psychiatric treatment in each house.

Expulsion

Project staff encouraged tenants to develop expulsion criteria in cases of consistent disruptions. Hospitalization incidents often provided the opportunity for focusing on behavioral criteria for remaining in the house.

> Darcy to return home from the hospital, and if he is still "the same as before" then he will be given a ten-day warning notice, with expulsion in thirty days. He has had a history of deterioration in prior arrangements. But he will definitely be given another chance here.
>
> Darcy was voluntarily hospitalized, and Hildegaard compliments Samantha for having told him that he was not acting himself. ". . . Darcy apologized for his behavior. His illness was bad. But I think we need to give him another chance."
>
> . . . [A]ccording to Darcy, he was very angry the first five days that he was in the hospital. He had a lot of personal issues to resolve. He knew he needed help; he got help, and he feels like he should get another chance. And especially, he is somebody who is willing to take responsibility for what he did. He looks better and sounds better. He told me he is willing to sign a contract with you people that [states] one more time he messes up, he will get a thirty-day notice.
>
> *Hildegaard [staff]:* The problem is what if any of you messed up?
> ". . . The thing is Darcy is willing to make changes, and I believe him—listen,
>   I'm gonna have to be with him every day too."
> *Hildegaard:* So I'll write up a contract and include all the things you all
>   want to say and then he'll sign it.
> *Samantha:* I thought he didn't want to come back.
> *Jim [staff]:* This is the only family he has.
> *Samantha:* This is not a family. We'd be lucky if anybody says hello or
>   goodnight.
> *Jim:* He needs support; people deserve another chance; think about your-
>   selves and whether if you would want another chance.
> Samantha sighs.
> *Helen:* When is he coming back?
> *Hildegaard:* Tuesday. The problem is that we didn't vote on that stuff I
>   passed out at last week's meeting. What you need to do is make something

in writing about when he screws up, he goes. So we don't have a process like we did with Rich; and if he wants another try, then we should today think of all the things that he did that were horrible, write him a letter welcoming him back, and write the conditions he can live here under. So what things were horrible while Darcy was living here?

Samantha: He was spilling coffee all over the floor. He left cups in the living room during the night.

Hildegaard: OK, those things we can call cleaning up after himself.

Samantha: And he was messing with the fire alarm by the front door the other night.

Hildegaard: How do you express that positively? Maybe don't interfere with any electrical equipment. And don't enter anyone else's rooms.

Jim: Hey, Andy, see something that you'd like changed in Darcy's behavior?

Andy: Not really.

Jim: What about cooking after a certain hour? Maybe after 10 pm—that should be late enough.

Samantha: What if you get hungry in the middle of the night?

Hildegaard: So far, I have down here that he should respect everyone in the house and other people's space.

Jim: Yeah, that's good especially for Andy because Darcy was constantly yelling at Andy, right Andy?

Andy: Yeah.

The discussion with other house tenants served to increase awareness of how to respond to symptoms and why it was important to place the interests of the group ahead of the desires of one individual. Before Darcy was released after his hospitalization, staff visited to caution him that his disruptive behaviors could lead to expulsion. Darcy acknowledged the importance of controlling his difficult behaviors and said that returning to the house was his only "viable option."

The ethnographic notes chronicle the importance of recognizing psychiatric symptoms and mental health needs in the development of the group homes. In spite of a common desire to escape the label of being "mentally ill," the group home residents recognized psychiatric symptoms in others and were aware of the importance of treatment with medication and/or hospitalization. Managing medications, dealing with symptoms, and arranging for hospitalization were important foci for housing staff. Although there was little indication of either general progress or retrogression in the symptoms or treatment of mental illness during the project, interaction about illness shaped the housing experience for every participant.

The Process and Outcome of Change

Quantitative data permit more systematic analysis of the delivery of services and the progress of illness during the project.

The likelihood of receiving mental health services during the project varied with baseline diagnosis (see fig. 7.3). Participants who had been diagnosed at baseline with major affective disorder spent more of their time hospitalized during the project and received more direct mental health services from their clinical homeless specialist than those with either bipolar disorder or schizophrenia (or schizoaffective) disorder.

The SCID-based continuous measures of depressive symptoms at baseline also were correlated with the percentage of time hospitalized during the project ($r = .24$, $p < .01$). By contrast the continuous measure of psychotic symptoms at baseline was not associated with either indicator of services received.[1] Neither the QOL-based measure of depressive symptoms at baseline nor the average QOL-based level of depressive symptoms during the project was associated with the amount of time spent in a

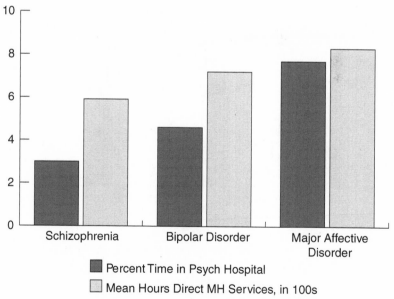

Figure 7.3. Mean hospitalizations and direct mental health service time by diagnosis. Note: $N = 112$. Hospitalization $F = 3.97$, $df = 2$, $p < .05$; service time $F = 4.15$, $df = 2$, $p < .05$.

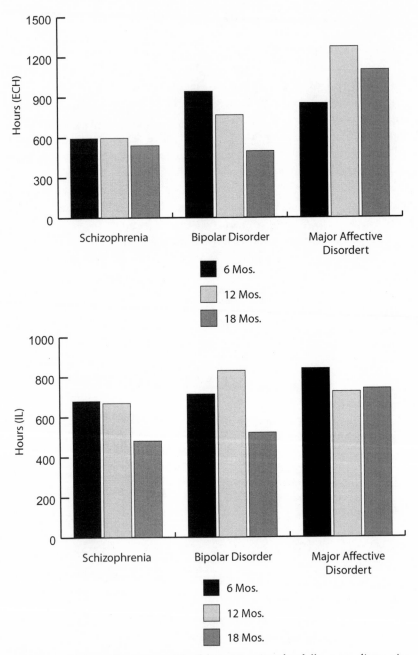

Figure 7.4. Mean direct mental health service time by follow-up, diagnosis, and housing type. Note: Schizophrenia in IL T2–T3, *t* = 2.9, *df* = 33, *p* < .01; bipolar in ECH T2–T3, *t* = 2.3, *df* = 12, *p* < .05; bipolar in IL T2–T3, *t* = 2.8, *df* = 5, *p* < .05.

psychiatric hospital or the number of direct mental health service hours received. Symptoms did not change over time or vary with housing type, irrespective of the symptom measure used. Neither the likelihood of losing housing nor housing satisfaction during the project varied with either categorical diagnosis or the continuous distress measure.

There were some changes in the number of hours of direct mental health services received by participants during the project (see fig. 7.4). In both types of housing, the number of hours of direct mental health service time received from project case managers decreased by the end of the project for those diagnosed with bipolar disorder. By contrast, those diagnosed with major affective disorder received about the same level of direct mental health services from their project case managers throughout the project.[2] Among those diagnosed with schizophrenia, the number of direct mental health service hours remained constant throughout the project for those in ECH housing, but it declined for those in IL housing.

Conclusions

Our multiple measures and sustained observation permit some conclusions about key differences between the medical and sociological models. The importance of the label of mental illness was often apparent in interaction in the group homes and was rejected by many participants as it applied to them. Nonetheless, the symptoms of mental illness were pronounced and continued in spite of changing participants' living situation from shelters to stable housing. Nor did symptoms diverge, on average, between the group and individual settings.

We diagnosed participants using standard DSM-III-R criteria, and we also captured symptomatic variation along continua. The lack of association between distress measured with the type of continuous self-report index popular in sociological research and the categorical diagnosis of affective disorder highlighted the disparity between the sociological and medical models. Moreover it was the symptoms of depression identified with the diagnostic SCID interview that predicted percentage of time subsequently spent in a psychiatric hospital, not the continuous self-report measure. Although the categorical SCID diagnosis was also related to these outcomes, the level of affective symptoms measured in the diagnostic interview was responsible for the effect of diagnosis. Thus, self-report provided a relatively poor basis for predicting service outcomes, whereas a systematic diagnostically oriented clinical interview that allowed a continuous measure of depressive symptoms was a strong predictor of those outcomes.

Psychotic symptoms often disrupted social processes in the group homes, most dramatically when a resident stopped taking psychotropic medication. Rather than being an experience that generated symptoms, hospitalization then often provided a respite from conflict at home and a foundation for symptomatic improvement.

The pattern of change over time in use of mental health case management services raised an important issue for further research. Use of these services did not change over time for participants diagnosed with major affective disorder in either ECH or IL housing, whereas such service use declined for those diagnosed with bipolar disorder in both housing types. The analysis did not identify a possible cause of this overall decline. Use of case manager mental health services also declined for participants diagnosed with schizophrenia in the last six months of the project if they were living in independent apartments—but not if they were living in an ECH residence. It is not possible with our data to determine whether this differential housing effect was due to less need for mental health services by participants with schizophrenia in independent apartments or to their declining interest in and use of services because there was no one on site checking up on their needs, as there was in the ECH housing. However, since there is little basis for expecting that persons living independently were having less need of services, it is quite possible that these patients' needs began to receive less attention over the course of the project.

In spite of these differences in hospitalization and use of mental health case management services, neither psychiatric diagnosis nor self-reported depressive symptoms throughout the project were related to risk of housing loss or to housing satisfaction. Variation in type and symptoms of mental illness within our sample did not directly influence either of these two key outcomes.

Mental illness shaped personal and social experience throughout the project, but neither medical nor sociological predictions about the influence of mental illness were borne out exclusively by our findings. Mental illness did not preclude the development of community, but it also was not remedied through the experience of community. Rather, the experience of mental illness altered the course that community development took by creating additional challenges to overcome and by limiting engagement in community processes. If a medical model of mental illness interprets mental illness as an immutable barrier to the development of community, the participants in our project showed that model to be lacking. If a sociological model presumes that reducing structural strains will have a parallel effect on mental illness, our participants' experiences suggest that model misses the mark. Understanding the course and consequences of mental illness requires both perspectives.

CHAPTER EIGHT

Functioning in the Community

with Larry J. Seidman

R ETURNING TO COMMUNITY settings would have little value if those who made the move could not function in ways required to live in the community. Community living requires performing chores, ordering services, paying bills, shopping for necessities, and using public transportation or other forms of conveyance. Successful community living also involves more general capabilities: maintaining social relations, good health, family ties, and even leisure pursuits. If our project participants could not carry out these functions and demonstrate these capabilities, their quality of life in the community would be severely diminished. Of course for people who have been institutionalized, homeless, and living with a severe mental illness—many also with a co-occurring substance abuse disorder— challenges are likely in both "activities of daily living" and general capabilities (Leary, Johnston, and Owens 1991).

Although positive symptoms—delusions, visual and auditory hallucinations, bizarre behavior, and paranoid thoughts—dominate popular conceptions of psychotic illness, a considerable body of research indicates that functioning can improve in spite of these symptoms. Moreover, symptomatic remission does not necessarily improve functioning (Dixon et al. 1997). The examination of substance abuse and mental illness in the preceding two chapters thus does not provide a sufficient basis for understanding how project participants managed in the community. For this purpose we must focus on the concept of "functioning" itself.

Our task is made more challenging by the multiplicity of ways in which functioning has been conceptually and operationally defined. Functioning has been conceptualized as how people think as well as what people do. It has been measured by self-report and by observation and with both objective and subjective ratings. Each of these definitions is related to the others, and all of the measures overlap. For example cognitive functioning focuses attention on mental processes, but measures of many aspects of cognitive functioning are performance based. Observer ratings are likely to be influenced by what those being rated say about themselves; as a result, observer ratings overlap with self-ratings. Individuals' ratings of their "objective" functioning are likely to be influenced by their subjective feelings. In spite of these areas of overlap, however, research makes it clear that these different approaches to functioning are not interchangeable. In order to understand our participants' functioning during the project, we will have to examine it from several perspectives and then develop an integrated understanding of our results.

We begin this chapter by reviewing prior research about the related constructs of cognitive functioning, self-assessed and observed functioning. We then examine our measures of each of these constructs: their level at baseline, their intercorrelations and predictors, and their change over time. We use our ethnographic data to understand what functioning meant in the environment of the group homes: how evolving consumer household (ECH) tenants and staff carried out chores and otherwise managed their affairs. Finally, we use our quantitative data to explain how housing type and individual factors led to change in cognitive functioning, quality of life, and community functioning.

Research Background

Because everything people do involves "functioning" in some sense, this construct is inherently broad and has been conceptualized and operationalized in many different ways. We focus here on the dimensions of functioning that have most often been a focus of research related to mental health: cognitive functioning, self-assessed functioning (often within "quality of life" instruments), and observed functioning in the community. How people think, how much they think they can do, and what they do in community settings can each influence success in community living. Each of these three dimensions of functioning can in turn be subdivided into more specific aspects.

Neurocognition

Neuropsychology investigates the relationship between brain and behavior, with a focus on the neural structures and mechanisms that can result in brain dysfunction (Seidman, Bruder, and Giuliano 2008, 556). Prior research indicates that neuropsychological deficits accompany chronic psychotic illness and compound its other effects (Goldberg et al. 1993; Kern and Green 1998; Seidman et al. 2002). These deficits are generally associated with impaired community functioning among individuals with chronic mental illness and are unusually severe among those who have become homeless (Lehman and Cordray 1993). Even successful symptomatic treatment does not tend to result in improved cognitive functioning (Helfrich and Fogg 2007).

It appears that the neuropsychological performance of persons with chronic mental illness may improve with participation in supportive programs (Penn, Corrigan, and Racenstein 1998). Spaulding et al. (1997) found that cognitive functioning among stable patients with chronic schizophrenia improved after five to eight months of psychosocial rehabilitation. By contrast the experience of homelessness was associated with IQ decline in a British sample (that was not selected for mental illness) (Bremner et al. 1996).

Prior neuropsychological research identifies a basis for expecting that group living could improve neurocognition: living in a group setting rather than independently can involve participation in group decision making and social interaction, which requires use of the executive ("frontal lobe") functions that are deficient in psychotic illness (Caplan et al. 2006, 78; Seidman 1983). Persons with chronic mental illness who live alone could become isolated and so use their executive functions less and receive less corrective social feedback from others. The risk is likely to be greater for those who are dually diagnosed, since lifetime substance abuse itself predicts cognitive impairment (Moselhy et al. 2001; Kolb and Gibb 2002; Green, Kern, and Heaton 2004) and so may diminish the ability to benefit from environmental stimulation.

Self-Assessed Functioning

Whereas cognitive functioning is assessed with objective neuropsychological tests, self-assessed functioning has also been a focus of concern. Mental health researchers have used self-assessment to evaluate functioning outside of the institutional settings in which it can easily be observed, although clinicians have highlighted the importance of self-assessed functioning as a key dimension of patients' "quality of life" (Lehman, Ward, and Linn 1982; Solomon 1992). "Objective" scales of self-reported functioning and "subjective" scales based on how people feel about their functioning have been distinguished (Lehman 1983; Cramer et al. 2000). However, the popularity of the self-assessment approach and the related concept of "quality of life" have not been matched by consistent findings about the factors that influence them.

Few consistent associations have been identified between self-assessed functioning and demographic variables (Greer Sullivan et al. 2000), although Prince (2006) found that "quality of life" was higher among black as compared to white patients with schizophrenia shortly after their discharge from the hospital. Evidence is mixed concerning effects of psychiatric symptoms and cognitive functioning on self-assessed functioning. Several studies indicate that persons with severe mental illness who evince fewer depressive or psychotic symptoms have better self-assessed quality of life (Greer Sullivan, Wells, and Leake 1992; Lam and Rosenheck 2000; Greer Sullivan et al. 2000; Mares et al. 2002). Mohamed et al. (2008b) found independent effects of both general neurocognition and psychotic symptoms on quality of life in the large eighteen-month multisite CATIE medication trial. Both Ritsner (2007) and Aptekin et al. (2005) found an association between measures of cognitive functioning and some quality-of-life scores among patients with chronic schizophrenia living in the community. By contrast Corrigan and Buican (1995) found that higher verbal intelligence predicted lower subjective quality-of-life ratings, perhaps reflecting a more realistic self-appraisal. Heslegrave, Awad, and Lakshmi (1997) found that neurocognitive deficits among outpatients with schizophrenia had little association with their quality-of-life ratings, whereas symptoms of psychopathology did.

Lehman (1988) presented his Quality of Life Interview as a measure that could distinguish subjective and objective dimensions of functioning and permit meaningful analysis of their separate correlates. Both Lehman (1984) and Corrigan and Buican (1995) concluded that subjective quality-of-life ratings are not redundant with depression because they have different correlates. In contrast Calsyn et al. (1995) concluded that subjective quality of life does not provide a reliable means for assessing objective circumstances: a subjective measure of quality of life was not associated with such objective quality-of-life measures among homeless persons with mental illness as days stably housed, income, and total service utilization. Both Calsyn et al. (1995) and Gladis et al. (1999) concluded that depressed feelings lead to a gloomier self-assessment irrespective of objective conditions.

Better objective living situation has not consistently been associated with better self-assessed functioning. Lehman et al. (1995) found that quality-of-life ratings were considerably lower among homeless mentally ill persons than among domiciled counterparts, particularly in terms of family and other social contacts. Greer Sullivan et al. (2000) also found that homelessness was associated with lower quality of life among persons with mental illness. However although Lehman, Slaughter, and Myers (1991) reported higher quality-of-life ratings among persons with chronic mental illness in residential programs compared to the hospital, there were few apparent differences in quality-of-life ratings between residences offering different levels of independence. Mares et al. (2002) found no associations between residents' quality-of-life ratings and objectively measured characteristics of forty-one board and care homes. Goodwin and Madell (2002) found that quality-of-life ratings tended to be higher among persons with severe mental health problems living in the community as compared to those in the hospital, but this relationship only occurred for three of the six quality-of-life measures they examined (and not for the measure used in the McKinney Project, Lehman's Quality of Life Interview).

Rosenfield (1992) focused attention on features of a community-based program that might empower participants and investigated the contribution of these characteristics to subjective quality of life. Many "empowering" program features, such as vocational services, high work expectations, and perceived empowerment contributed to subjective quality of life, and these effects were explained by the hypothesized mediating variable of mastery. In other words program features that were predicted to increase empowerment were associated with higher levels of a sense of mastery, which in turn predicted better quality of life. However these ratings were only subjective reports from the program clients themselves and thus could have reflected level of depression. In general these findings indicate lower self-assessed functioning among persons with severe mental illness if they are homeless rather than housed but indicate no consistent effects of type of housing or other objective differences in circumstances.

Observed Functioning

Observation provides the most direct method for assessing community functioning. Alan Rosen, Dusan Hadzi-Pavlovic, and Gordon Parker (1989) developed the Life Skills Profile (LSP) as a systematic approach to making such assessments. Whether completed by case managers, house staff, or parents, the LSP seems to provide reliable and valid assessments (Rosen, Hadzi-Pavlovic, and Parker 1989; Parker et al. 1991) of functional disability

(Parker et al. 2002) and to identify change over time (Trauer, Duckmanton, and Chiu 1997).

As assessed with the LSP, persons with schizophrenia who are living in the community evidence less functional impairment than those living in the hospital (Trauer, Duckmanton, and Chiu 1997). Those living in boarding houses score as more functionally impaired than those living in their own homes (Browne and Courtney 2004). However Hobbs et al. (2002) followed patients with long-term illness for six years after the closure of a psychiatric hospital in Sydney, Australia and found no change in observer-rated Life Skills scores in spite of increased scores on Life Satisfaction.

Self-assessed quality of life seems to be associated with LSP observer ratings. Norman et al. (2000) found that psychiatrists' ratings on the LSP were associated with patients' quality-of-life scores, whereas Aki et al. (2008) found that family members' LSP ratings were associated with both subjective and observer-rated quality of life. However when Depp, Scarpelli, and Apostoles (1983, 280) studied candidates for housing in a program for clients of mental health services, they found that clients would often affirm they could do something but were not able to function as they had claimed when their actual performance was observed.

Some evidence suggests that neuropsychological deficits predict impairment in observed community functioning among persons diagnosed with severe mental illness (Green 1996; Penn, Corrigan, and Racenstein 1998; Green et al. 2000; Schutt et al. 2007, 1388). Green's (1996) review of cross-sectional research identified declarative verbal memory as a strong correlate of different types of social ability measures, whereas the Wisconsin Card Sorting Test (a measure of executive function) was a consistent correlate of community functioning. The Green et al. (2000) review of longitudinal research identified fourteen of eighteen published studies and an additional three unpublished studies that found moderate to large effects of baseline cognitive functioning on some aspects of community functioning at least six months post-baseline. However, Norman et al. (1999) found that cognitive measures were not associated with scores on the various dimensions of the LSP. Ertuğrul and Uluğ (2008) found no association between neurocognitive deficits and community functioning in a Turkish sample of patients with schizophrenia.

Findings with respect to the relation between specific cognitive measures and particular dimensions of community functioning have also been inconsistent (Norman et al. 1999; Green, Kern, and Heaton 2004; Milev et al. 2005; Brekke et al. 2005; Cohen et al. 2006; Schutt et al. 2007, 1389). Verbal memory has been identified most often in longitudinal research as a predictor of social functioning (Milev et al. 2005; Cohen et al. 2006), but neither executive functioning nor vigilance has had consistent effects across different diagnostic categories or follow-up periods (Norman et al. 1999; Kurtz et al. 2005; Laes and Sponheim 2006). Correlated influences of such other characteristics as positive and/or negative symptoms (Milev et al. 2005; Addington, Saeedi, and Addington 2005), abuse of alcohol and other substances (Parsons and Leber 1981), and diagnosis (Calvocoressi et al. 1998; Addington and Addington 2000; Laes and Sponheim 2006) may help to explain the variability in these relationships.

The research that we have reviewed suggests that we cannot adequately understand functioning without examining it in terms of both thinking and doing, from the perspectives of both observers and those observed, and using both subjective and objective measures. The diverse findings in this literature also make it clear that we cannot assume a priori any particular pattern of relationship among indicators of these different aspects of functioning. What this literature does establish is that cognitive functioning can influence community functioning, that subjective self-assessments may reflect levels of depression rather than objective functioning, and so observer ratings are important for understanding community functioning.

Baseline Functioning

McKinney subjects' average functioning levels at baseline varied markedly between measures of cognitive functioning, self-assessed functioning, and observed functioning. In terms of cognitive functioning, every neuropsychological test indicated impairment, on average, compared to a group of persons without a psychiatric diagnosis (Seidman et al. 1997, 7). Figure 8.1 reports these comparisons for key measures.

By contrast, self-assessed functioning by the McKinney participants did not yield a consistently negative picture. Overall, two-thirds of the participants rated their functioning at baseline as "excellent" or "good." The most objective measure in the Lehman Quality of Life Interview is the count of activities engaged in within the past week. In terms of this measure, Boston McKinney participants reported having engaged in an average of eight activities, with most having gone for a walk or a ride, watched TV, listened to the radio, attended a meeting, and read something. Hardly any had prepared a meal, played a sport, visited a library, or gone to a movie. Although these positive self-assessments seem more optimistic than the neuropsychological test results, the Boston McKinney participants rated their family and social contact lower than a housed sample of consumers of mental health services in Baltimore (Lehman et al. 1995).

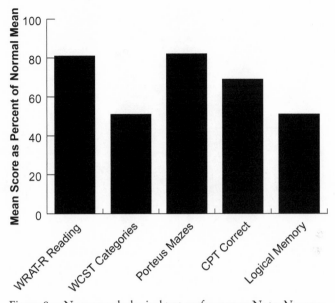

Figure 8.1. Neuropsychological test performance. Note: *N* = 190–91. Adapted from Seidman et al. (1997, 8).

Boston's McKinney Clinical Homeless Specialists first rated their clients' observed functioning with the LSP three months after the clients had moved into project housing (Rosen, Hadzi-Pavlovic, and Parker 1989). At this time case managers rated their clients, on average, as having few problems of self-care: the average (mean) rating at this time was between having "no" problems ("o") and having them to a "slight" degree ("1.0") (see fig. 8.2). Less than 10 percent of the sample seemed to evince these problems to a "moderate" or "extreme" degree. The most impairment was identified in the area of social contact, with an average rating between slightly and moderately impaired.

Correlations among Functional Indicators

Although these results so far indicate a sharp divergence between the impairments indicated in cognitive functioning and the relative lack of impairment in self-assessed and observed functioning, it is only through examination of their empirical correlations that the comparability of these ratings can be established. The use of multiple measures of functioning from each perspective first requires that the correlations among the various indicators included within each battery be examined.

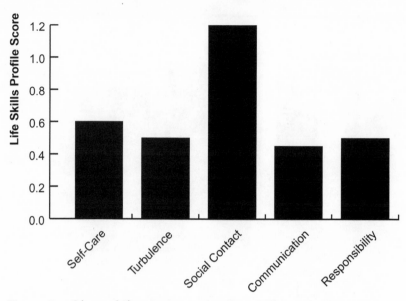

Figure 8.2. Observed functioning at baseline (LSI scores). Note: $N = 101$ ($N = 99$ for "responsibility"). Higher scores mean more impairment.

We focus our analysis of neurocognition on the three dimensions identified by Green (Green 1996; Green et al. 2000) as associated with community functioning: executive functioning (measured with the Wisconsin Card Sorting Test number of categories achieved and Porteus IQ), verbal memory (story recall) and sustained attention (auditory CPT). The neurocognitive dimensions of executive functioning, memory, and attention each had a moderate association with each other at baseline ($r = .20–.31$).

Subjective ratings of functioning were also correlated with each other to a moderate degree ($r = .21–.56$). The strongest relationship was between life satisfaction and satisfaction with leisure activities. The most objective self-assessed measure of functioning—number of daily activities—was not associated with the other "objective" ratings of functioning. Self-assessments of other aspects of functioning had, for the most part, modest intercorrelations ($r = .3–.4$). Correlations among most of the five dimensions of the LSP ratings by case managers were higher at the first three-month assessment ($r = .30–.84$).

Baseline neurocognitive functioning was largely unrelated to variation in self-assessed quality of life. However better performance on Wisconsin Categories and on Logical Delayed Memory were both associated with lower ratings of self-assessed overall functioning (respectively, $r = -.21$, $p < .05$, $r = -.27$, $p < .01$) and lower levels of leisure satisfaction ($r = -.21$, $p < .05$, $r = -.20$, $p < .05$), whereas higher Memory scores were also associated with less satisfaction with family ($r=-.21$, $p<.05$) and with life in general ($r=-.22$, $p<.05$). In other words better cognitive functioning at baseline tended to be associated with poorer self-appraisal at baseline. Baseline neurocognitive scores did not predict any dimension of functioning as observed by project case managers at the first three-month rating point.

Only one of the quality-of-life ratings was associated with most ratings of observed functioning at three months. Self-report of daily activities at baseline predicted better life skill ratings by the case managers at three months in terms of self-care ($r=.21$, $p<.05$), social contact ($r=.30$, $p<.00$), and responsibility ($r=.20$, $p<.05$).

These correlations among the different measures of functioning at baseline (and three months) indicate, first and foremost, the complexity of the concept of *functioning*. Although within the three domains of cognitive, self-report, and observed functioning, different measures tended to be correlated with each other, these correlations were generally of only low to moderate strength. Only the case manager ratings of observed functioning tended to be highly correlated among themselves. Across domains, correlations were much lower. The few significant correlations between cognitive functioning and self-assessed functioning reinforce Corrigan and Buican's (1995) conclusion that those with better cognitive functioning assessed their own community functioning as worse than did others with poorer cognitive functioning. Neither self-assessed functioning nor neurocognitive functioning was associated with observed functioning three months later. There was one interesting exception: subjects' reports of the number of activities they had engaged in within the last week were associated positively with several dimensions of case managers' ratings of their observed functioning three months later. This provides some indication of the construct validity of this one relatively objective dimension of self-assessed quality of life.

Baseline Predictors of Functioning

Personal characteristics predicted little of the variation in the various measures of functioning at baseline. However, multiple regression analyses of daily activities, life skills scales, and neurocognitive functioning add a bit to our understanding of the different measures of functioning.

Several independent correlates of neurocognition at baseline buttress our conclusion from analysis of the correlations among the different functional domains. Positive and independent associations between clinician recommendations of ability to live independently and case manager-assessed ability to self-care at three months provided additional support for our earlier conclusion about clinician recommendations: clinicians at baseline were able to predict subsequent functioning, on average.[1] Finally, the predictors of behavioral turbulence at three months—a lifetime history of substance abuse, and stronger desire to live independently—also support our earlier conclusion about consumers' desire to live independently: it was often a predictor of poor prognosis, not ability to live independently.

Functioning at Home

Many problems in functioning emerged after participants moved into their project housing.

Chores

Chores were a challenge in each group home and in many independent apartments. In the group homes, washing dishes, cleaning, doing laundry, taking out garbage, and grocery shopping were intended to be the responsibility of tenants, rather than staff. However, there was neither an a priori model for organizing chores nor a specific expectation about how staff should facilitate this organization. In each group home some tenants helped to complete chores, and others avoided chores. Discussion and discord about chores occurred throughout the project.

Complaints about chore completion were often a focus of tenant meetings. In one house three tenants complained that they were the only ones doing chores. In another tenants got "pissed" when another left uneaten bread out all day. A staff member reported that tenants would not take garbage to the shed in back but "just throw it off the porch." Bathrooms in one house were termed "disgusting, with water on the floor and a foul smell." A tenant who was drunk and vomiting in the bathroom did not clean up after himself. Another washed himself by splashing water from the sink, getting water on the floor and not cleaning up.

Kitchen cleanliness was a particular concern. One tenant complained,

. . . that everyone is doing it, leaving messes, and it gets left dirty too often.

Tenants frequently pointed fingers at others who were not responsible:

I've noticed there are some self-motivated people here like myself [and two others]. The others don't have respect for the house. They don't do dishes, they don't clean up after themselves.

These are all adults here but they're pigs. And the cleaning is a joke. We're supposed to be cleaning the house on Saturdays. But I'm the only one who does it. If they wanna go back to the shelter, they can.

Tenants who were trying to manage their own affairs and maintain the house often expressed frustration:

> . . . I go to school . . . and when I come back, it's always the same story. I've tried yelling and screaming, but how many times do I have to say these things? It's like we need a mommy here! I don't care—I'll yell until they're so sick of it they move out! I'm always loading up that dishwasher and then unloading it! I can't take this anymore—they're just lazy!!!!
>
> . . . First, we have written down "nobody's doing chores," the second thing is erased, and the third is "don't touch anybody's food." Camy? Did you write all this down?
>
> Cam: How did you know?!! . . . And I would appreciate it if people in this house don't move food that is on the kitchen counters to the downstairs freezer without asking first.
>
> PC: Can we assume we're talking about James here?
>
> Cam: Yes, you can. I am sick of coming into that kitchen and having all my things misplaced.

Staff shared complaints about problems with particular tenants.

> Last night, the kitchen was an absolute mess. It was Camy and Kathy's mess. They talk a good game about everyone else cleaning up after themselves, but they expected us to do it last night! And the really funny thing is that Harvey hasn't been here, and he was the one who always got blamed for messing up the kitchen.

Initially, the empowerment coordinator encouraged the ECH tenants to "figure it out—talk about it among yourselves on each floor and then do it." She emphasized the need to understand different standards of cleanliness.

> This is what having different senses of cleanliness leads up to . . . all of you need to start respecting your differences. These are the kinds of things you'll be working out together during the next few months. But there are some other people who want to have a clean sink when they go to bed each night. And that's what you'll be working out.

She also highlighted the problem posed by different orientations to chore completion.

> When one person is breaking their back keeping things clean, and everybody else watches, they're not participating in this house.

House staff frequently debated how directive they should be about chores.

> [The empowerment coordinator] said that after being in the shelter for a long time, a lot of people are just not used to having to take care of themselves around food. She said that the best thing to do was to tell the person who was

not shopping that they should get someone to teach them how to shop. She said that people would get bullshit, if people continued to take food.

Tenant meeting: only three tenants present. Only two tenants are cleaning in the house. The house has a chore chart, but it is "pretty sketchy."

He said that they should make up a list and have certain people clean up the kitchen on certain days. Paul said that he did not want to go that way. People should do things for the community without expecting money or praise in return. He said that there would also be problems with a fixed schedule because sometimes people have plans which keep them out of the house. But final agreement that they would have a chore list (for the kitchen).

House staff debated with project case managers the right approach to ensuring chore completion.

Some concerns about not cleaning up, in bathroom, and there has been no plan devised. There is a problem in one apartment of three tenants not cleaning at all. Some staff felt the tenants had to decide to clean themselves, but decision [was made]to try a chore schedule. At staff meeting with CHSs, more discussion of what to do about filthy apartment. This has been an ongoing problem, because staff feel the ECH approach does not give them authority to make tenants do chores and some tenants resist. . . . Terry emphasizes, "don't do for, do with." Then a discussion of diet, and one tenant who eats only cold cut sandwiches and candy, but staff were told to let tenants eat the way they want to.

Staff and tenants in each house experimented with ways of allocating responsibility for chores and following up to see that they were completed. One house tried using a lottery for chore allocation, to no avail:

Amy: The cleaning started out with that basket, but then nobody wanted to do it. For a whole month, nothing got done.

Jeff: Yeah, I know that wasn't working out. All of a sudden, nobody would do it anymore.

Amy: Or else they wouldn't pick a chore from the basket. We could do it like we did before—you [staff] choose and put a name next to each thing on a list.

Jeff: Well, if everyone could clean up after themselves in the kitchen.

Joe: I think it should be the opposite way—we each find a chore we like and just do it.

Jeff: But I've seen dishes lying around that kitchen for days.

Amy: That's because I don't do them! I get sick of it.

Joe begins protesting.

Amy: It's like talking with children. It's easier to just yell at him.

Sally: I never see Joe cleaning up after himself.

Frustration with chore completion led some to simply give up:

I know the thing about nobody doing chores is never gonna be fixed so just forget that.

Staff-controlled group homes often use a "chore chart" to allocate responsibilities, but this was initially viewed as having an undesirable "institutional" feel. The project's empowerment coordinator discussed the issue in a house tenant meeting when it appeared that chores were not being completed.

> ... Only one of the seven houses has a chore chart. A chore chart is like living in institutions. The problem wouldn't exist if people were developing considerate behaviors. Are you all interested in chore charts? Is that the only way? I see a lot of shelter behaviors here—it's like being in [the shelter] where everything's abused. All the furniture's beat up from bad smoking behaviors. This place is looking more and more like [the shelter]. I think Helen's right—there are adults here but they're acting like children. So what do you wanna do about the problem?
>
> This is all about keeping the common areas clean, folks. It's really important in a group residence like this. I think this is the one big problem in this house. If you can't handle keeping these areas clean, then maybe a chore chart would work. But I'm not going to tell you what to do. It's not a good environment when people are feeling this tense. I don't know what to do. . . .
>
> Like I said, there's no sense of community here! So the whole idea is to develop a community that can pick up as you go along. I think these rotating chores will get you there.

In spite of these frustrations, a sense of shared responsibility developed in some houses, at least for a time. At one house tenants initially agreed to clean up after themselves, so there was no need for a chore chart. At another the tenants agreed on a distribution of chores.

> Discussion about cleaning the bathroom—and the bath, which was awful and may not have been cleaned in a year. Previous cleaning agreements have been implemented. The garden is going well.
>
> Some tenants insisted they needed to be in control.
>
> Fred asked for help taking out garbage, and when a staff member said staff could help if tenants didn't volunteer, "Fred said, quietly, that "it's our house" implying that some other tenants "should take responsibility."
>
> Tenants reject staff proposal about cleaning schedule—say they have already organized it.

Individual tenants also distinguished themselves as responsible for chore completion.

> Sam's been very helpful. We couldn't fix the sink disposal at all, but Sam came to the rescue and found the reset button underneath that none of us could find anywhere.
>
> Empowerment Coordinator: See, Sam, you're taking all that negative energy taking apart things and turning it into something positive. It's better than taking apart furnaces!

Harry: I can figure things out mentally and Sam can figure them out physically.

Harriet: Sam also figured out how to fix a calculator in the staff office.

Oh, you fixed that, Sam? I was wondering how that got fixed—I broke that, you know, but you figured that out, huh?!!

There was evidence of some tenants increasing their contributions to house upkeep. Sam, who had been an object of opprobrium for his failure to contribute to chores, became an exemplar of success:

Sam is proud of his clean room. . . . stunned himself. He said he never believed that he would be doing as well as he is doing now, and he still does not really believe it. He has quit drinking, quit smoking, quit his day program and is learning some skills, he is lifting [weights] regularly, getting himself in shape, he lives in a nice house. Amazing. . . . "now seems to take it as a point of honor to pay his share" to the house fund.

Initially, staff understood that they were not to simply complete chores for tenants, but the particular role that staff should play and the way in which responsibility for chores should be divided among tenants were frequent topics of conversation at tenant meetings and among staff.

. . . Alice said that she would help by getting staff to remind people to clean and do their chores. Nancy said that it has been dirty for a while. "I mop and it's not my job." Roger said he thinks Alice should let the clients clean the house. Alice agreed in principle but said that since summer was coming up it was even more important than usual to keep the house clean because of how easily pests thrived in the heat. So the staff would not let the house get dirty for the summer.

Staff are keeping a very close watch on the cleanliness of the house. Ray told me that Alice has said that she will give out warnings to staff if she finds the house dirty at any time. . . . He said that the tenants are pretty bad about cleaning, but they are getting better. He also thinks that this is not such a good idea because the tenants will become dependent on them and not learn to keep the house clean on their own.

I did see Ray get people to clean up the kitchen area by pointing at cups out of place for instance and saying "whose is that?"

Increased staff involvement in managing chores led to improvements in one house. The house is split up into nine chores, and everybody picks one out of a hat once a month.

Jeff: And the staff always does one of the chores too.

Jerry: The chores aren't bad—they get done . . .

Jeff: This place is looking cleaner all the time.

Andy: I don't think anybody has been shirking their chore duties. . . . You gotta keep after them because otherwise they'll leave it for the staff to do.

Ernestine: They are not kids. They're not out of it, they're not physically incapable. Everybody wants to be taken care of, and they've gotten used to this and expect it. They know we'll never let the house get to a certain point and we'll just step in. Just break balls with them—they'll respond better to the male approach. Just put it to them! Say to them, "Get out there and clean this up!" . . . Make me the heavy. Tell them Joe, the landlord of the house, will be pissed if they don't clean it up. It will get to the point eventually where they'll say, "Oh, here's the weekend and we gotta clean up."

Jerrod: Well, they sit down in front of that TV and won't move all night.

Ernestine: I'm serious. Shut the TV off and take away the channel selector. They're settling in and testing us out, trying to find out what's the most they can get away with. But this cleaning needs to get done. And the more you take that on, the less time staff will have to hang out with these people. It takes away time we could give them. Make clear the consequences. You could say "Well, the inspector is gonna be coming in and when they see your mess, they will question whether they are capable of living here."

. . . You gotta be straight, clear, direct, real cut and dry. Tell them when you don't like something. Don't be tough with them but just say "What can we do to help?"

Marylou: I really don't agree with the philosophy of cleaning up after them, but don't they have the right to refuse to clean until it gets so bad that they have to clean? Didn't they do that at [another house]?

Ernestine: Yeah, but it didn't work. As soon as someone burned the table, I let everyone know. We have to think what can we do to motivate them to clean their own house. We can't say "every time you clean, we'll buy stuff for you" because we don't have that kind of money. But what it comes down to is that we have to keep the house clean, what with the food bank coming to see the place, and people coming for the federal funding, the inspector, North Suffolk, and the state. All of them need to see the house clean or else we won't get funded. If they come see this mess, they'll be like "Hello! What do you staff do here; can't you work with these people?" It's kind of hard to motivate them but if it's a model that's theirs . . . say something like "I'll do this and you do that." Make it conditional, like you'll sweep if they mop. I would say the bottom line is do it when they're not around. Doing the cleaning in front of them and that visual cue will only encourage them to depend on you. But if when they come home, you can say "Oh, by the way, I did a quick mop on the kitchen floor," that will minimize the chore to get them to think it's not so difficult. Or say to them, if they say "later," then you say "OK, the next time you ask me to go with you to wherever—say, Harvard Square—then I'll say later too." Look, they're gonna get treated like kids if they act like kids. If they start acting up in the living room or yelling at people, then tell them to go to their rooms or go somewhere else where other people can't hear you. That's fair and that's real!

Staff organized "cleaning days" on weekends to ensure chore completion in another house.

Helen had also heard reports that the staff was spending time sitting around reading. "They should not do this." Rather they should spend time interacting more with the tenants. For instance, between 5:00 and 8:00 or so in the evening, when people were preparing dinner, there should always be someone in the kitchen. When cooking is going on there should be staff in the kitchen at all times. This was a temporary measure, because a lot of the tenants do not know how to use the facilities, and it would last until they were orientated to the kitchen. "So if you are in the kitchen while they are cooking, you can help out or just talk with them." This will have the added advantage of getting them to clean up after themselves, because staff will be aware of who is using what and making which mess. If they are on hand when someone is just finishing a meal, then they can suggest that that person clean up their dishes, pots, and pans. They might also try to get a group together to clean up the kitchen, or take out the garbage.

. . . Karen was skeptical that they could keep track about everything and that the clients would own up to using what they actually did. Helen said that this plan was the first line of attack. If this did not work out then they would move to a list of things [that] would have to be done without excuse each day. She said that if the staff is not observing the clients then of course they will not clean up because they can just go up to their rooms and leave stuff in the sink anonymously.

Karen had a question about how to get people to clean. She had spent all of Saturday trying to interest people in cleaning the toilets. They were disgusting.

Paulette said that Saturday was a good day to clean because a lot of people were around in the morning with nothing to do. Karen said that last Saturday she had talked with everyone in the house trying to get them to clean without success. Before she left, she had told Chuck who was coming on about it and told him to keep up the pressure, but still without success. "I'd rather do it myself." Helen said that was the easy way out. She said they should get all the cleaning stuff in their hands, approach the clients and say "let's go." Paulette said that was just what she did, and she got [others] to do some work. She had made it into a cleaning day "It's Saturday, guys, lets clean."

Cleaning has been done by staff and tenants on weekends and has been very effective. Project staff are concerned about whether tenants are initiating this.

One house finally transitioned to what was termed a "group home model," with staff organizing chores, after repeated efforts to encourage tenant control failed. There was general satisfaction with the results.

Pat said that some of the people are not doing their chores. Harriet said the second floor hall [that] Andy was supposed to do was not done. Jane said he had done it after being asked, and Harriet said "right, you had to ask him."

[The project coordinator] said that with staff helping to get people to do their chores things in general would improve.

The people who do their chores without being asked won't mind doing them if others are doing theirs as well. . . . Pat thinks there is a much better attitude in the house now, and 4 tenants had a great time cleaning out the refrigerator.

Chore system is going better, and house is cleaner. Tenants wrote a letter to George requesting that he attend tenant meetings more. Sally is very together and going for a job interview.

This problem was resolved in the meeting by staff suggesting rotation of chores.

Budgeting

Another key goal of the house "empowerment" process was encouraging individuals to manage their funds and developing a system for collective budgeting. Most houses developed a "house kitty" that was to be used to pay for shared expenses, such as coffee, paper towels, cleaning supplies, and other essentials. All houses were encouraged to shop collectively at discount food warehouses. There were some notable successes.

The group has started shopping at BJ's and sees the savings and the selection. [There is s]ome consideration of collective meals and more of a feeling of working together. [There is a p]lan to join the food bank, which is even cheaper.

The house has been approved for the food bank. Group meals are occurring weekly.

Decision [made] to start using the food bank, volunteering to work for food, to save money. Some concern about competing for TV usage, and Isaac says he will buy his own TV.

In spite of some successes, problems with money management occurred in most houses. Staff in one house complained that money was not being collected for supplies, and no tenants wanted to be in charge of that. There was a general sense among staff that tenants live for the moment and do not plan ahead, and do not like responsibility for money.

Staff feel it won't be possible to shift to tenant management as soon as planned because tenants lack the skills for independent living.

Project coordinator: Everybody's gotta pay. That's part of being a member of this household.

Some concern about the phone bill not being paid and who will keep it in their name. A decision to change is delayed.

. . .

Ben: Is there a reason why people aren't paying?

Cessaly: Not that I know of, everybody's getting their checks, and everybody knows what they have to pay for. At first, everybody was paying; then everything went "pooh." It's been five months now, and I've had it.

Empowerment Coordinator: It is a requirement of living here to pay your share. And there'[re] ways around this if you want to do this—there can be a fine for those who don't pay but still eat the food and watch the cable and use the phone. Other houses are doing this—tenants levy a fine against those who don't pay. If it's a problem with checks, then let me know or let staff know, and we can help you with that. But you have to cooperate on each little thing. And if you think about it, it's pretty cheap to live here.

Only one tenant has contributed to the house fund. Much discussion of budgeting issues and money problems, but staff member says "that they could not ask people to contribute to it [the house fund]."

Individual money management also presented frequent challenges.

Dominic is happy and has made a first trip to the bank. . . . Dominic is overspending and begging money from others—exasperating staff.

Complaints about inequities in purchasing and replacing essentials like coffee were common:

Salli: I'm sick and tired of running out the door and down to the supermarket for coffee all week long! I'm getting fed up with it!
I know that the bills have been a problem.
Jodi: Yeah, no one offered to pay anything, for phone or the cable. It's only $17 per month, and it's just in one ear and out the other that they each have to pay into this thing.
Becky: Well, I need to get the rent from people, and that they understand! I just say to them—if you don't pay the bill, [the housing vendor] won't either.

Thefts within the residences, apparently by residents, compounded the budgeting problems.

A clock has been stolen from the house. Also silverware is missing. A picture has been moved out of the living room. No one confesses to stealing or directly saw the thefts.

The incidents of food disappearing are still going on; people are just using up all the money in the house fund at the end of the month. People are raiding each other's food. All I have left are a package of wafers and some sausage. Harvey stays up late and has been taking other tenant's food, although he offers his food to others—but does not understand he cannot take others' food.

Money has been stolen from the office safe. Cautions to keep house safe in the neighborhood, keep an eye on things. [The house manager] encourages staff to walk through the entire house regularly. Staff are to report on each client in meetings.

The theft problem was solved in one house by installing room locks.

Several tenants in one house were accused of not paying back some funds, leading to a decision to issue IOUs.

An agreement to start using IOUs with the house fund. [Two tenants] have decided to manage the loan fund, so that [another] doesn't have to cope with demands from others. Establish very explicit rules for IOUs, etc. The house bank borrowing arrangement is working well.

Nonetheless, sometime after this effort, tenants dissolved the tenant fund, since no one wanted the responsibility.

Phone charges were a particular concern, since rates of usage differed markedly among tenants. In several houses charges appeared on phone bills for calls to 900 numbers (sex services). Initial responses were ineffective.

Phone bill: Several hundred dollars unpaid due to long distance and 900 calls. No one admitted to the 900 calls; [A staff coordinator] offered to pay back bills if a tenant or the whole would take over the bill. No real action to have individual tenants identify and pay their own costs.

Alicia: I'm saying that as staff we can assist you, but we can't make you do anything.

Beatrice: Well, I'm not gonna be in charge of this house fund. Don't look at me!

Hank: If we can't agree on this phone, we are in trouble. This house fund is excellent, but only if we're at a point where we at least don't have to bicker with one another. There it is in the shoebox, and I think it should stay in the office.

By the time one house had a $17,000 bill for "900" calls, staff became more assertive about the problem. Blocks were placed on phones to prevent collect or 900 calls; in one house, the private phone was removed and a pay phone installed in its place.

Empowerment Coordinator: You all do nothing as a group! You're even jeopardizing the phone bill. . . . Look, folks!! It doesn't help to get into this mommy/daddy crap!!! Staff can't get you into this shared residence—the only ones who can are yourselves! In the real world, if someone isn't paying their phone bill, they'd be out the front door. . . . Now either all of you decide to work together as a group, as a team, and make this a shared residence, or this house will fall apart!

Over time, the houses improved their management of financial resources. The Empowerment Coordinator encouraged tenants in each house to register to shop at discount food warehouses and food banks, resulting in a much lower food bill. She explained the benefits in a meeting with a prospective tenant:

Harriet: Let me explain some of the finances to you. You'll pay 30 percent of your income for rent, and then you'll chip in for the food bank, the phone bill, cable, and sometimes BJ's trips.

Tenants agreed to contribute to the house kitty, resulting in successful pooling of resources in some houses for periods of time.

In spite of these improvements, problems with nonpayment into the house funds and lack of interest in collective shopping continued throughout the project.

> Some tenants want to regain control over their own money. Helen is very upset that her CHS does not allow her to manage her own money and feels that she was misled about the McK project allowing tenants to control their own lives—and because she is no longer sick, she should be allowed to manage her own funds.

In spite of these difficulties, the process of organizing and engaging in chores and money management engaged many tenants throughout the project. Many partial successes occurred, as individual tenants assumed responsibility individually for particular chores, as some houses organized and enforced "cleaning days," and as tenants went together on shopping trips to discount warehouses. Some tenants saw their ability to function in the social world increase and the number of their active social relations expand.

Change over Time

Like the ethnographic record, the quantitative data provide a mixed—albeit more precise—picture of change over time. In most domains, the level of functioning remained constant over time, but some domains improved and others deteriorated. There were some important effects of living in group rather than individual housing, although with respect to most domains of functioning, type of residence made little difference.

The most dramatic change in functioning was an across-the-board increase in neuropsychological test scores from the project's start until the final assessment one and one-half years later (see fig. 8.3). Average scores increased on many indicators of cognitive functioning and by an amount that was substantively important as well as statistically meaningful (Seidman et al. 2003). Of course, although the duration of the follow-up periods is long, without a normal control group pretested over the same follow-up periods we cannot definitively rule out a practice effect on the test scores (Goldberg 2007).

On most of these measures the type of housing into which participants moved did not matter; improvements occurred in both. Executive functioning, which did not improve over time for the participants as a whole, was an important exception to this general pattern of no housing type effects. Scores on the Wisconsin Card Sorting Test (Categories Achieved)

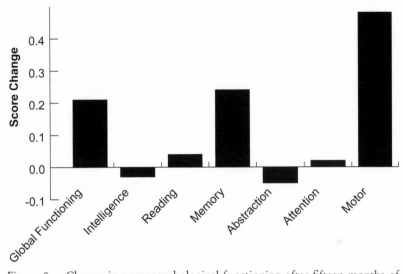

Figure 8.3. Change in neuropsychological functioning after fifteen months of housing. Note: $N = 90$–91. Adapted from Seidman et al. (2003).

improved for those assigned to group housing and deteriorated for those assigned to independent apartments—if they did not have a lifetime substance abuse history (see fig. 8.4). By contrast the WCST scores of those who were assigned to an IL declined sharply during the project and remained lower than at baseline at the three-year follow-up. WCST scores

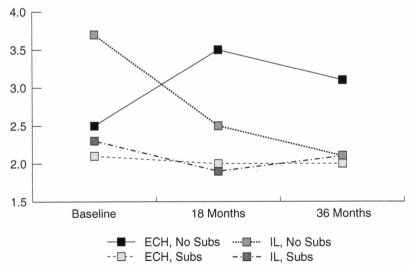

Figure 8.4. Executive functioning (WCST Categories Achieved) by ECH-IL by substance abuse. Note: $N = 62$. Modeled after Caplan et al. (2006).

changed little during and after the project for substance abusers, irrespective of their type of housing. This pattern of differential change is illustrated in figure 8.4 for those subjects who remained in their initially assigned housing throughout the project.

In addition to the effect of housing type, multiple regression analysis identified other predictors of improvement in executive functioning that were specific to one type of housing. Among those living in an ECH, those who gained in executive functioning were more likely to have been judged by the clinician raters at baseline as more ready for an IL (see fig. 8.5). By contrast, among those living in an IL, those with more negative social ties during the project were more likely to gain in executive functioning.

Investigation of case records on the participants who experienced marked declines or gains in the two housing types improves our understanding of the bases of cognitive change. There were seven participants in IL who experienced marked declines in executive functioning during the project. Of these, five had initially preferred to live with others, had severe substance abuse problems, had difficulty developing social relations during the project, and did not acknowledge having a mental illness. By contrast, the three participants in the group homes who experienced marked declines in executive functioning had all initially preferred to live independently and had episodes of severe psychosis after stopping their psychotropic medication. Just one of these regained some behavioral stability after resuming medication at the project's end.

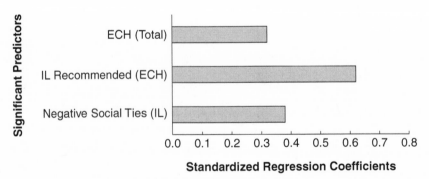

Figure 8.5. Regression analysis of change in executive functioning (WCST Categories Achieved). Note: $R^2 = .22$, $N = 87$ (total); $R^2 = .20$, $N = 51$ (ECH); $R^2 = .60$, $N = 36$ (IL). Variables included in the analysis but not having statistically significant effects in any subsample: gender, race, age, education, diagnosis, in-project substance abuse, clinician recommendation, number of positive social ties at 18 months, number of negative social ties at 18 months.

No participants in ILs improved markedly in executive functioning. Of the five in group homes who improved, four had initially expressed a preference for group living. Nonetheless, three had been relatively independent and functioning relatively well at the outset and left for their own apartment during the project. Of the two who remained in a group home, one was an assertive leader in the group who attended AA sessions regularly and was committed to maintaining his sobriety and encouraging group empowerment. The other took assigned medication faithfully, controlled his drinking, had a girlfriend, and supported other tenants who reported experiencing stigma due to mental illness.

Overall, those who declined in executive functioning found themselves in social situations they had not wanted and had difficulty coping with. Those who gained in executive functioning were more capable at the outset, as reflected in part in their preference for the more supportive group living situation and their ability subsequently to move on from it.

Apparently substance abuse blocked beneficial environmental influence. The executive functioning of individuals with a lifetime diagnosis of substance abuse was insensitive to the difference between living with a group or independently. However, in both types of housing, improvement on story recall and the CPT is consistent with the pattern we identified earlier of general cognitive gains after housing and suggests that, in itself, residential stability benefits both abusers and non-abusers. Our finding of an advantage to group living for non-abusers' executive functioning suggests that executive functioning should be given special attention in research about environmental influence and that it may be uniquely susceptible to social stimulation.

There were no changes in participants' average levels of self-assessed functioning or number of activities during the project's 1.5 years in either the group homes or independent apartments. Changes did occur in the self-reported frequency of participating in some specific types of activities. There were considerable increases in both housing types in the frequency of shopping and meal preparation and moderate gains in the frequency of going to a bar, going for a ride in a bus or car, and watching TV. There were major declines in the frequency of going to a meeting, going to a park, and going to a library and moderate declines in the frequency of going to a movie or play and in playing cards. These changes reflect gains in the activities necessary to live in the community and declines in those that were likely to have been instigated by shelter staff, as well as greater opportunities to go out to drink and to stay home and watch TV after moving into the Boston McKinney Project housing.

The frequency of engaging in only two activities changed more in the group homes than in independent apartments: group home residents were

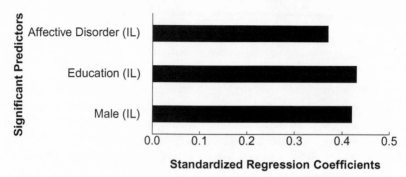

Figure 8.6. Regression analysis of change in behavioral turbulence (LSP scale). Note: $R^2 = .18$, $N = 48$ (ECH); $R^2 = .58$, $N = 36$ (IL). Variables included in the analysis but not having statistically significant effects in any subsample: race, residential preference, in-project substance abuse, clinician recommendation, number of positive social ties at 18 months, number of negative social ties at 18 months.

more likely to participate in meal preparation and to report going to a bar than those in independent apartments.

Clinical Homeless Specialists' ratings of the participants' behavioral turbulence worsened over time. This deterioration was comparable in magnitude in both types of housing. No individual characteristics predicted this deterioration among the ECH residents. Among the IL residents, men, those with more education, and those with affective rather than psychotic disorders fared better (see fig. 8.6).

Housing Loss

Neither cognitive functioning nor self-reported quality-of-life scores were related to housing loss during the project. However functioning as rated by the case managers with the LSI was a strong predictor of housing loss. The problems that case managers observed in participants' ability to interact with others, to take care of themselves, and to act like others in the community were often part of the process of losing housing.

Conclusions

As we anticipated, neurocognition was impaired in our sample across multiple measures. This was less true of participants' self-reported functioning and in the eyes of case managers at the first three-month assessment, but there was some indication of functional impairments on these other measures at baseline compared to a comparable housed sample. In general self-reported functioning was not related to functioning observed by case managers, with the one exception of self-reported daily activities. However, both substance abuse and strength of desire to live independently were related to poorer observed behavioral turbulence after three months in the project. Our results thus add to previous studies (Calsyn et al. 1995) that suggest skepticism about measurements of functioning that rely on self-assessment. In fact better cognitive functioning predicted lower self-assessed functioning, raising the important issue that optimistic self-assessment may reflect a less realistic self-appraisal.

Our most important finding about functioning is that most dimensions of neurocognition improved after the participants moved into project housing. We suspect that the stability associated with being housed was critical for this change. However, the type of housing received did not have a bearing on most measures of cognitive functioning. Although type of housing affected the specific mix of self-reported daily activities, it also did not have other differential effects on self-reported or observed functioning.

Type of housing did have an important effect on executive functioning—a key cognitive dimension. As we predicted, living in group housing improved consumers' executive functioning compared to living independently. The marked improvement in executive functioning we observed for non–substance abusers in the group homes, and the worsening for those in independent apartments who were not substance abusers, suggest that social experience benefits executive functioning when sensitivity to environmental influence is not impaired by substance abuse. This finding emphasizes the importance of substance abuse as a significant moderating factor.

The effects of substance abuse have important implications for mental health services as well as for understanding the processes involved in community functioning. Substance abusers were much more likely to lose their housing during the eighteen-month follow-up period, and they were less likely to gain in cognitive functioning after housing placement. Special addiction treatment programs could help to retain individuals in housing who are otherwise seen as causing trouble for others and behaving irresponsibly. The fact that substance abusers living in group homes themselves reported that they had more positive social relations, compared to substance abusers living alone, is an interesting counterpoint to this broader conclusion. Ethnographic data collected in the group homes recorded frequent conflicts with substance abusers—in part due to their contacts with drug dealers and others from outside the homes. It may be that social relations with other substance abusers are being reported as positive by the substance abusers themselves.

Our ethnographic evidence also provides further insight into the failure of case managers to observe marked improvements in functioning. In many houses and at many times during the project, it seemed that tenants could carry out chores, manage budgeting, and have useful meetings if they had staff support or at least guidance or reinforcement. When there was little staff assistance, however, problems in social interaction and lack of initiative frequently occurred. In addition, cognitive deterioration seemed to be more likely when tenants were assigned to a type of housing that they did not want that did not provide the level of support that they indicated they needed.

Our findings about observed functioning indicate that cognitive functioning generalizes "upward" to actual behavior in the community among individuals with serious mental illness (Drake et al. 2001; Green et al. 2000; Ilonen et al. 2000; Penn, Corrigan, and Racenstein 1998). The variation we found in relationships between specific cognitive indicators and dimensions of community functioning suggests that measurement procedures must be highlighted in explaining disparate findings between studies (Schutt et al. 2007, 1394–95). Most importantly, the interaction effects we identified suggest that lack of attention to social context in research designs may explain some of the variability in prior research and its limited generalizability to real world applications. Social context mattered greatly.

CHAPTER NINE

Empowerment

Kristen said that the staff point of view was that the residents were used to staff doing things for them but that this program wants to give them as much empowerment as possible.

OUR GRANT PROPOSAL had included a statement about how the Evolving Consumer Household (ECH) housing model would put the concept of empowerment into operation (Goldfinger et al. 1990, 51).

Two fundamental principles of operation will be underscored.

1. The locus of control for operating each residence will be centered on the consumers. They, collectively, will help set household routine, establish staff priorities, determine the degree and nature of services they desire, and in collaboration with each residence's program director, set the policies and procedures for their home.
2. The goal of the residence, established at the outset will be to have program residents take over all staff functions. As consumers feel both willing and able, they will systematically assume all house operational responsibilities initially held by paid staff. Early on consumers will begin to take over such functions as shopping, cleaning, and preparing meals. Later they might assume responsibility for their own nighttime coverage, purchasing supplies, arranging for household repairs, and paying utilities and other bills. Finally, with residents working out among themselves how to divide responsibilities, all paid staff will be eliminated, and these residences will be indistinguishable from other groups of adult roommates sharing living quarters in the community.

Conceptualizing Empowerment

As the houses were opening, project staff highlighted the empowerment orientation of the ECH model. The "principles of operation" stated in the grant proposal were read to the incoming tenants. The project's empowerment coordinator emphasized to tenants that the project's philosophy was that, as long-time consumers of mental health services, "you are the experts":

> [N]ow you'll be deciding what you [want to] do. . . . a year from now, staff will be stopping in from time to time and saying 'Hi, how ya doin?' But you all will be taking care of the place on your own. The staff won't be working against you—they'll be trying to help you. . . . As long as it's peaceful and you all don't bash each other over the head, you'll have the freedom to do what you want; but if it starts bothering somebody else, you're gonna have to work it out.

She highlighted key features of the model in one meeting with house staff:

> What's evolving? Each house is evolving to have no staff, to encourage each tenant to make an independent life from all the systems that have been thrown into these people's lives as opposed to a revolving life. [Homeless mentally ill people are] forced to be more independent, "on their own," have a lot of skills we don't. We're not treating disabled people—we're connecting with the wellness of these people because everybody else is looking at their illness. We're connecting with the larger social context of people, not being homeless but rather having the skills to survive. . . . She draws a triangle on the blackboard and puts the homeless at the bottom, and workers at the top. She points out there's a hierarchy in the homeless' lives. The way their world should be is like a circle—nonlinear and nonhierarchical (see fig. 9.1).

The empowerment process was described as developing a sense of community: "learning how to get bunches of people together."

> Eventually, you all will learn to develop a sense of community in this house. In some ways, it is like a family, and it can be kind of dangerous, and sometimes you'll each wanna think about yourselves as a separate person. . . . And eventually all of you will accept each other's faults and gently warn each other not to do certain things that destroy the house. When you're homeless or living in a shelter, you have no ownership in a place, and you don't think about what you're doing to the furniture. It will take a while to get used to having a house, and in the meantime, until you learn that you don't have to wait for other people to do something about a problem, it's probably a good idea to depend on the staff to help you learn this is your house and you're the ones who'll be living in here, forever if you want.

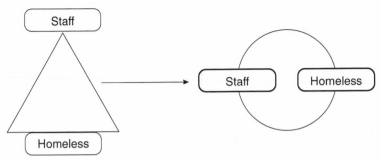

Figure 9.1. The empowerment coordinator's diagram of the empowerment concept.

Tenants were encouraged to assert themselves when service policies were not to their liking:

> We're being forced to do whatever orders are sent but tenants can refuse, write a letter to that effect, and put it in tenants' files. For example, end the [written treatment plans for a tenant] if the objectives are not necessary. "She can do everything fine but she needs to socialize." This sounds so stupid! This is always part of the politics of living in group residences but it's a bunch of crap.

The staff administrator in another house emphasized tenant autonomy and the importance of house upkeep.

> She said: . . . [Staff] should leave the decisions to the folks and only assist in providing them information on what options are available. They have to be able to make the choices. . . . The houses should be the best on the block. Neighbors can't complain about having the facilities in the neighborhood when their own house looks worse! . . . This house is impersonal, and still has a group home feel. As a result the folks here don't feel any ownership of the house, and it won't work as an ECH until that happens, until the barriers are broken down.

Empowerment Scholarship

The proposal's empowerment "principles" and the initial statements of project staff captured the concept of empowerment as it has been developed in the mental health services literature. In this literature, empowerment means engaging consumers and staff in relatively egalitarian, personal relationships and using group process and consumer involvement to develop service plans and make treatment decisions (Rosenfield 1992;

Perkins and Zimmerman 1995; Rappaport 1995). "Empowered" consumers make decisions about their treatment jointly with staff, have the power to act freely, have ultimate authority and control over their treatment, and are able to advocate on their own behalf (Salzer 1997; Ralph 2000). The goals of empowerment processes are to develop community living skills, rather than to treat psychiatric symptomatology, and to shift the locus of control for service decisions to the consumer (Rappaport 1987, 122).

After a comprehensive review of research on self-help and consumer-operated programs, Campbell (2005) concluded that self-help and peer support programs can promote empowerment and recovery (Van Tosh and del Vecchio 2000; Dumont and Jones 2002; but see Corrigan 2006), as well as increase social support, functioning, and activities (Forquer and Knight 2001; Yanos, Primavera, and Knight 2001). However the design of most of this research has been weak (Davidson et al. 1999; Solomon 2004; Campbell 2005; Nelson et al. 2006; Ochocka et al. 2006; Brown et al. 2007). Two studies using more rigorous designs found mixed evidence for beneficial effects of participation in peer support groups. Using an experimental multisite longitudinal design, Rogers et al. (2007) found no effect of participation in traditional or consumer-operated services but a positive relation between individual involvement in peer support and feelings of personal empowerment. Roth and Crane-Ross (2002) found that empowerment had only an indirect effect on symptoms and self-reported quality of life and no association at all with clinician-rated functioning.

Several qualitative investigations have identified some beneficial features of several consumer/survivor initiatives, including engagement with peers and peer control (Ochocka et al. 2006; Salzer and Shear 2002; Schutt and Rogers 2009; Solomon 2004). Overall these findings suggest that there may be some positive benefits of some aspects of empowerment programs, but they may occur only for some participants.

Rules for Empowerment

All the houses began with only two rules that were intended to be inviolable: no illegal drugs in the house and no smoking in bedrooms. Subsequently rules were expanded in tenant meetings beyond these initial prohibitions in response to behaviors that caused problems, but even as these additional rules were being formulated, staff continued to emphasize tenant control:

Empowerment Coordinator (EC): So I have down here that it's important to respect everyone, including no scary talk with neighbors and the community. That goes for the house and the neighborhood, and no screaming or yelling. I also don't think stealing should be tolerated from anybody.

Staff: And about the drinking—Harry wanted to come here because it was a dry house, and Ralph's setting the standard for everybody with his recovery. So it's important that Jeff knows that [this] is a dry house, and there's no liquor allowed.

EC: Would you like to expand the community living guidelines to include no stealing? All right, that's done, and I'll keep it in the book.

Staff: What if he just doesn't change?

EC: Then we can say to him, "Look, we gave you a chance, you did it again, and you're out of here. We don't want you living here anymore." That's all.

A dialogue between the empowerment coordinator and a new tenant in one house captured the emphasis on tenant control and minimal rules:

EC: It's the tenants who run this house, and I'm just the advocate. Hank, did you read the guidelines on this flyer?

Hank: Yeah, I read all that. No smoking, no drinking. I read everything. It's 30 percent rent, keep the kitchen nice and clean, if you eat something throw it in the bucket in the kitchen . . .

EC: What do you think the staff does here?

Hank: They just observe; they're like surveyors.

EC: Well, that's one way of putting it! The staff are here to help people become interdependent so that later they can take care of the house. Eventually the staff won't be here anymore, and you'll be running the place yourselves.

Hank: That will be a long time from now.

EC: It may not be. . . . Would you feel comfortable with that?

Hank: Yes, I would.

A staff member explained the logic of tenant autonomy and contrasted it to the artificiality of traditional residential programs:

He said the residents would do real well, "unless they're absolutely crazy, then they gotta go. They can come and go as they please—do whatever they want. They gotta be on their own in three years, so they gotta learn how to do things for themselves." The ECH is designed to "reflect the real world," with disruptions, not be some contrived world. Residential programs just continue the hospital: "community institutionalization."

A program leader explained to a new tenant that "The group runs by consensus, not like a democracy, and that they divide chores up among themselves." Another program leader explained to staff that "This is not professionals taking care of people with disorders; this is people working together with a common goal."

Defining Roles

These early efforts to explain the goal of empowerment made it clear that both tenant and staff roles would have to change. Staff told tenants that the tenants would be able to make decisions independently, choose their own furnishings, and control their own rooms. A house manager stressed that tenants could stay home during the day (unlike in the shelters) and expected that they eventually would get jobs. But how could control be shifted from staff to tenants? What activities could tenants be responsible for? Should staff give tenants rides to go shopping and for other reasons, since this would not prepare tenants for taking over responsibility once tenants were solely in control? Both groups struggled to define the elements of their new roles.

Defining the Tenant Role

Many tenants were ambivalent and did not rush to exercise control over staff responsibilities. A staff member remarked, "They're so used to staff doing everything for them. They think that if there's a problem, staff will take care of it." Although staff knew that they were expected to shift control to tenants, they often disagreed on which responsibilities could best be reallocated and when it was most appropriate to do so. A house manager told staff they were not to enforce the community guidelines for the house and should let tenants sleep in as they desired—except when they needed to take their medications. Staff members were told not to intervene in disputes between tenants unless the level of conflict was extreme.

Over time the project ethnographers observed that "all the tenants are getting more and more assertive every week" and that staff were more comfortable with letting tenants decide things. Staff encouraged tenants to take over control of the house kitty and developed a ledger to keep track of expenditures on tenant shopping trips. Some tenants began to play a leadership role in tenant meetings, and a house manager suggested that a tenant rep come to staff meetings. Tenants decided to pool their funds in order to be able to afford cable TV. Some tenants agreed to help staff write a grant to get a van. One tenant in each house volunteered to serve as the house human rights officer. Tenants began to take over responsibility for lawn work at one home.

Tenants who engaged actively in house activities often appeared to gain in self-confidence. A tenant who was elected as the house human rights officer provides one example:

> I asked him if he would trust the committee to defend him if his human rights were violated. He said he did, which I was actually surprised to hear. Jerry seems much more comfortable with people in general—and much more talkative. It is really great to see.

The empowerment coordinator spoke to tenants "about the need of working on forming a community" and identified the positions they needed to fill among themselves:

> Two people for BJ's, two people to do treasury duty (so they could check up on each other), two for the food bank, and two for activities.

A staff member again emphasized that it was not the staff's role to work out disputes themselves but to help tenants work out their own disputes.

House managers stressed the importance of respecting tenant rights: staff were supposed to let tenants make decisions (except about illegal drugs and smoking in bedrooms)—whether about alcohol use, medication, or services, encourage them to overcome challenges, and allow time to develop trusting relationships with them. Individual tenants were to be left to do as they saw fit. Tenants at one house complained that their rights were being infringed when staff tried to set behavioral limits; the house supervisor then criticized staff for not following the empowerment philosophy.

One house manager contrasted the ECH approach to tenant rights to what he had observed in "traditional homes":

> Jorge said there were a lot of places where . . . residents who didn't fit into the program get kicked out by staff, that rules and policies don't get reanalyzed as a result of people not being able to make it but rather get more entrenched. Jorge characterized the situation as a "thin line" that everybody has to walk—in the sense that there are always going to be residents or clients or tenants that you know don't "fit," and it is sometimes best to find a way for them to leave; but on the other hand, you want tenants to be able to make decisions about rules that will affect them, and why should everyone have to "fit" anyway and maybe it's better to have people not have to fit any one static or generic form in the first place.

Another project leader encouraged tenants to stick up for themselves in meetings with staff. At one house, tenants asserted their rights by refusing to let staff use one of the house rooms for a staff meeting. At another house, a project leader criticized staff for making a "human rights violation" when they withheld a tenant's check to pressure her into signing up for rep payee status. Tenant money was not to be taken even when tenants were using it to purchase illicit drugs or were engaging in prostitution, as long as they were paying rent and buying food.

The empowerment emphasis seemed to improve some tenants' conceptions of themselves.

> I've been having trouble lately, but I have to say that this place makes me feel more like a person here. In the other halfway house, everything I did was under surveillance. I had to write when I was going out, where I was going, when I was coming back in. Here there's a lot more freedom.

Tenants also began to feel they could complain about staff behavior. When staff in one house began to use the laundry without paying tenants, the tenants complained. Before clear prohibitions were established, some staff used the tenant phone to make long distance calls. The behavior of overnight staff—hired more as monitors than as social service professionals—was a particular focus of complaint. Tenants complained about overnight staff sleeping on the couch, using the laundry all night, and cooking for their families. Some tenants began to complain about staff watching TV in the tenant area or otherwise intruding on the tenants' space. Tenants insisted that night staff had to turn off the TV.

In spite of this emphasis on tenant rights, the empowerment coordinator also pointed out that enhanced freedom for tenants was accompanied by increased responsibilities.

> You all have to get together and say "no" to things you think aren't right. You've all had this money to blow off and now it's gonna be harder to deal with your money because you're paying rent and putting money towards this house fund.
>
> The empowerment coordinator also emphasized that laws had to be obeyed.
>
> If somebody gets violent or there is a crime committed against state law, then this process will be replaced by the police coming over to the house. It would be the same with me in my house—if my sugar bowl was filled with cocaine and somebody finds out—the police would be right over.

The continuation of some staff control meant that the reality experienced by some tenants did not match the project's rhetoric. One complained about the continuation of the requirement that his money be managed by a "rep payee," and other intrusions on his rights.

> He said that he did not see ways of living as being better or worse than one another—only that people should respect other peoples' choices about the way they were living, especially if they were going to try to live together. He said that when he heard from [a housing provider] that they were going to

give tenants housing [that] was designed to allow the tenants to live the way they wanted to, he thought that they would be allowed to move in and start running things. He had found however that they were telling him how he should run his life and that they had put people in the house who were disrespectful of one another's business.

At another house, tenants "became galvanized into a functional unit" when they tried to overturn a vendor prohibition against refrigerators in individual bedrooms. The tenant leader of this effort remarked on how the tenants, with their "different religions, races, and creeds" were showing "a lot more unity . . . generosity, joking, and courtesy"—"exactly what is supposed to happen according to McKinney theology." But this enthusiasm evaporated when the administration declared that the prohibition against bedroom refrigerators could not be lifted. The tenant leader then announced that he had just wanted to "have a nice life" but now felt he had been misled about tenant control, and so,

> I'll withdraw my signature from those documents, and you can just let me out of here.

Defining the Staff Role

If house staff were not to take actions that would infringe on "tenant rights," what could they do? Project leaders explained to house staff that empowerment meant "doing with" tenants, rather than doing things to them. "The key to it was that the environment was not set from the start to make them a certain type of person but, rather, was open to construction by the tenants themselves. The tenants make the rules, not the staff." The residence is about living—social skills—they explained, whereas the clinical focus is outside of the house.

A discussion about overnight guests in one ECH modeled the "doing with" philosophy. The empowerment coordinator tried to encourage tenants to come to a consensus:

> *EC:* So let's be real exact and honest. Do you all mind the guest policy as it is right now? If no one minds having guests stay in the house for between two and thirty days, then that's fine. We make the rules, not the staff. But if a person is unhappy with that, then we have a problem. I don't actually remember whether we ever voted on that guest policy at all.
>
> *Sally:* Why do they have to live here, I mean friends . . . after a while, it becomes excessive. You start to think why is this individual around here for such a long time, especially after fourteen days. The water pressure here is horrible as it is, and it's the little problems that happen . . . it's one of those situations that's hard to talk about, but it gets aggravating.

EC: Yes, Sally, you're on to something here. It's very hard to live in tight quarters like this—no other place has this much sharing of bedrooms and all the rest of the space. Everyone should mutual[ly] respect here, and maybe if this is a problem for some to have friends stay for so long, they should find other places to live.

Andy: I don't know what the big deal is. Thirty days means diddly shit to me. It's just some figure that somebody threw out. Nobody ever stays here for longer than three days.

EC: Andy, you know we just had a situation upstairs that lasted longer than a week. It got to be abusive and excessive. Turned out they were watching the Olympics all the time to the point that nobody else could watch what they wanted. And the toilet constantly broke.

Andy: Oh, you mean Horace? Well, he moved out—he just got a place.

Coordinator: Well, if I were living here I wouldn't like it. That meant there were three men up there and two women. I woulda stayed in my room the whole time.

Sally: It was the little infuriating problems that got to be a pain in the ass. The toilet, him sitting out there when I wasn't expecting it. I didn't feel comfortable enough to say anything. How could it be possible? I thought it was just some problem with a guest, so it seemed infuriating. If he has a problem, that's great but . . .

Coordinator: I really appreciate your talking about your real feelings, especially here. If you all can open up here at these meetings instead of going to staff and telling them, because then you're setting up a split. I want you all to get more comfortable with talking to each other.

There were some staff-imposed behavioral limits. Behavior could be penalized—such as problems due to not taking meds, but not the refusal to take meds itself. Stealing was to be stopped when noticed. Yet when some staff said they felt it was unethical to let a tenant continue to prostitute herself in order to obtain money for illicit drugs, the empowerment coordinator emphasized the importance of adhering to the empowerment model.

A program leader told house staff that they could try to change tenant behaviors through "modeling."

Modeling was part of their role as teachers. . . . The staff have the right and obligation to set limits of acceptable behavior with [an obnoxious] client. It makes sense that staff had the right to do this because natural human interaction is not forbidden. On the model of a family, it would be open to debate, for instance, which TV show to watch when there were many people watching. . . . Part of the goal of mental health treatment is to get people to act like rational human beings.

Modeling could mean different things with different tenants.

. . . taking a client somewhere in a car is not necessarily infantilizing. . . . There is no formula and role modeling is the best way to way to teach the basis of these skills. Not everyone has the right habits to live in a house, and it is particularly hard to start them. Modeling the right behaviors helped clients with this step.

Project leaders distinguished for staff in another house the difference between "doing for" and "doing with":

> There is a great temptation to step in and help them when they want it, but we shouldn't jump into that trap. Ideally [staff] should force them into mutual inter-action. Even though, sometimes in order to get to a relation of mutuality, they would have to do something to interest the client. . . . Interaction is the key.

One project leader explained this philosophy to tenants in one house:

> The idea is what you would like staff to do rather than what we think they should be doing. I pick up on your temperature and do what it feels like you need me to do.

A clinical homeless specialist analogized the appropriate role of ECH house staff to that of a teacher:

> It's like teaching a kid to walk . . . , first you have to walk holding him up completely and little by little he progresses towards walking on his own. The process is similar to teaching but is more of using yourself as a positive role model. Showing how to do and say things not just telling people to do them on their own. They often just don't know how to do the things we tell them to when we expect them to be independent.

The empowerment coordinator emphasized to staff the importance of encouraging tenants to state their concerns openly in meetings.

> The point is we're trying to make a community. So don't you feel bad at the meetings when you might have to say to a tenant "That's not what you told me." Because if we don't force these things out, then we're not having consen-sus thinking. . . . So if a what a tenant is saying during a meeting is far away from the truth, I need to know that, and you all need to bring that up some-how. You all aren't going to be here forever, and they have to learn how to bring up uncomfortable things. . . . The tenants gotta battle these things out because only then will the real house decisions get made, and all this will de-cidedly affect the house vote.

When a staff member at one house felt that she understood the appro-priate staff role, she explained it in a meeting:

> She should tell them [tenants] that they have to police their own issues. "We can take notice, but we cannot enforce the rules." We are here to teach how to enforce their own rules.

In spite of widespread acceptance of the empowerment goal, staff often expressed discomfort with the goal and/or the process of relinquishing control:

> Marty said that the question was who was going to enforce the rule, staff or tenants. Sam said that in his opinion, and he emphasized that this is his opinion; if safety is not an issue then it is up to the tenants, if they do not want to enforce their own rules then so be it. Jane said that this might be a question for the tenants' meeting. Ask what they want in terms of enforcement. Pamela said that it was her interpretation from the other ECHs that tenants do the enforcing themselves. Sam said that the tenants might expect that they will make the rules and that the staff will enforce them, but hopefully they will learn to be their own police.
>
> Marty said that they would sit back and wait. Let the tenants identify the problems and bring them up to staff. Then say "you address it."

House staff talked about the authority inherent in their relationship with the residents and how the limitations on them put staff in a position of not being able to do what is required to achieve what they saw as the great potential for the house. Staff in one house even feared being taken advantage of by "empowered" tenants:

> Tenants have to learn that they can't just do whatever they want to, and they can't have the houses go to pieces, because that will reflect badly on the staff. . . . The tenants can't take advantage of the staff because they have to learn to work together. Staff of course will always put the consumers' interests first.

In these various ways new roles were defined for tenants and staff in the early stages of the project. The common element in the working definitions of empowerment offered by both project leaders and house staff was that in their new role, staff were not to tell tenants what to do. Some staff encouraged a relatively hands-off approach with tenants, whereas others favored a "modeling" approach in which they would help tenants develop their skills by setting a good example of how to do things. No staff argued that staff were responsible for telling tenants what to do.

In spite of the remaining ambiguity over the precise nature of these new roles, and indications that they were not accepted by all tenants and staff, it was clear to the more active tenants and staff (those who appeared frequently in the ethnographic notes) that adopting these new roles would involve a radical shift of the basis of power in the houses from staff to tenants. Many house staff expressed their support for this shift. However, defining the new roles proved to be much easier than implementing them.

Attempting Empowerment

There were some indications that social interaction in tenant meetings facilitated an empowering process—tenants taking over staff functions. Interaction among tenants was often cordial during meetings; groups of tenants in some houses went on joint food-shopping trips; a sense of community seemed to develop. The project's empowerment coordinator helped tenants in some homes recruit new tenants when places opened up. One advertisement for new tenants conveys the spirit of tenants in one ECH as well as the rules they had settled on to prevent continued problems among tenants (see fig. 9.2).

Some tenants also felt empowered due to taking over responsibility for some house purchases.

> Now we can do things without the staff. Now it's like if we wanna buy something, we don't have to wait around for two months for the staff to do it. Cause that's what would happen. If we needed something, it would take a month for us to ask the staff to buy it and then another month before they'd go and get it. Now we can just make a list ourselves and go get it. It's like now they put the responsibility back on us, and we can do what we want.

Tenant empowerment could also result in conflicts with house staff. In some ECHs, tenants were quick to assert their right to do as they wished, and some challenged staff practices that violated their sense of autonomy. One such practice was an "incident log" that staff maintained so that those on the next shift could get oriented to ongoing issues. A dialogue in a staff meeting about this practice captures the conflict house staff felt between being open with tenants to encourage empowerment and keeping some information to themselves to avoid being perceived as judgmental. The discussion was precipitated by a tenant's complaint that staff had written in the incident log that she was being "hyper":

> *Helen:* So we're supposed to keep our own separate journals? . . . I was thinking that part of being in this house where we're trying to empower people is to see things and point out things that people are not always gonna enjoy hearing. I thought people are supposed to hear us out and take it for what it's worth. I just don't feel it's a good option to keep in our heads things that are going on. . . .
>
> *Mary:* If you think it's real important, or real strange, just try to keep the whole situation in mind. Think about the whole picture.
>
> *Helen:* I did talk to Diedre about what was happening with her. I was trying to explain why I should put down certain things, and I really didn't feel like we should keep a separate log from the real one and then come to the meetings and unload.

FAIRMONT STREET RESIDENCE

HOUSEMATE WANTED!!!
We are a shared-residence of eight adults, men and women, who pay 30% of our income toward rent and an additional amount (5%) toward a House Fund which provides household items and services shared by all the residents. We are now searching for a new housemate. If you fit the qualifications and expectations listed below, please contact The Fairmont Tenant Association to make an appointment for an interview.

YOU ARE: a woman
Without a drug/alcohol abuse history OR sober for at least one year self-controlled, neat and tidy—one who cleans up after herself willing to share in the responsibilities of maintaining the residence and its peaceful environment able to pay your share of the telephone bill, BJ's, Food Bank, cable, etc. willing to show and demonstrate respect for other tenants and our Community Living Guidelines*

*FAIRMONT RESIDENCE COMMUNITY LIVING GUIDELINES:

1. Fairmont Residence is a DRY HOUSE from now until forever. The tenant group has voted that alcohol drinking shall never be allowed and shall never be voted on again (1/07/92). If anyone violates the Dry House rule, the individual must go to Detox.
2. Smoking is allowed everywhere—safely and considerately, EXCEPT in the bedrooms.
3. No stealing is permitted by anyone.
4. Tenant Behavior Warning System: If tenants feel another resident is abusing the Community Living Guidelines, or is behaving in a manner inconsiderate of others, tenants may vote to provide a formal warning in an effort to alter this negative behavior.
5. Quiet Hours of considerate behavior are to be observed from 10:00 p.m. to 10:00 a.m., seven days a week. Radio, stereo, television, and talking are to be quiet enough not to disturb any other resident.
6. Tenants must ALL clean up after themselves, participate in cleaning community living areas, and contribute financially to the group-related House Fund.

Please note: Your illness is your doctor's concern; what's important at Fairmont is your ATTITUDE in the residence and your ability to show respect to the other residents and to the Community Living Guidelines.

Figure 9.2. ECH residents advertise for a roommate.

However, the process of empowerment itself was more a topic of discussion in tenant meetings with the project's empowerment coordinator than a description of daily tenant activities. The coordinator's efforts to maintain a focus on empowerment is reflected in a dialogue in a tenant meeting:

She asked whether or not people felt like they were advancing towards self-empowerment. Her phrases were "your own empowerment," "running your own lives," "we need to know your feelings." . . . Sammy complained about others offering him alcohol, though he was trying not to drink . . . and complained that others don't like him. Jill notes that [Sammy] is responsible for being sent to detox. . . . The coordinator said that giving others support was a part of empowerment because "empowering others is a part of empowering oneself." She highlighted this interaction by bringing it back to empowerment saying that "it was empowering to be direct, person to person." She said the staff wasn't going to help him in interaction with other tenants. . . ." The coordinator went back to the open question about whether or not people were feeling empowered and went around the room asking everyone how they felt about it. Jake said "yah" and talked about taking his pills on his own. . . ."

The attempt to shift control to tenants also created many dilemmas for staff. One dilemma emerged from the variable interest of tenants in acquiring more responsibility. Tenants did not uniformly or consistently favor reducing staff control and many tried to avoid taking on more responsibility, whereas staff complained about tenant disinterest in "becoming empowered." Only one tenant agreed to manage one house's fund that pooled resources for group shopping trips. Tenants at another house asked staff to collect the money from tenants for group shopping trips. Staff felt that tenants were still depending on them, or waiting for them, to deal with problems that arose. Arthur said he "doesn't like empowerment" and feels the staff need to impose rules:

Arthur complained that Alice does not support him. He said they should kick out Charlie and the others. He wants to have more structure and is uncomfortable with dealing with others on his own. He thinks the staff are bad because they don't do anything. "We have thieves, liars, stealers and you don't do anything." He really blames Alice for not supporting him.

House staff complained that their jobs were "adult sitting," that "tenants still don't want to do anything for themselves," and that tenants "do not listen to what staff tell them." Another concluded that, "They're not gonna want to do things unless they're forced to, because they prefer the way it is."

Staff also remarked on the lack of group "togetherness." In some homes tenants resisted group purchases of foods in bulk, insisting on shopping on their own. A project manager decided that "more togetherness [between tenants] is needed" before staffing could be reduced. Lack of tenant interest in "empowerment" was most evident when the project planned special events with outside consultants. An ethnographer who observed the discussion about such an event captured the problem of disinterest:

Each of the officials present tried to make it sound exciting, but they could not stir up any interest among the tenants. Their unease with this fact was apparent and kind of eerie.

The empowerment coordinator complained to tenants after she had tried, unsuccessfully, to engage tenants in preparing a special meal.

We need to start looking at each other as interdependent. If you lived by yourself before—that's fine. But now that you're living in a community you gotta understand you can't do things by yourself. If each of you can make these living arrangements acceptable to each other, if you can live with the rough edges, if you can sit here and say, "Yeah I know I shouldn't do that," and actually stop it, then it can work. . . . Everybody needs to own what they are and what they are not. No one here is a victim, and no one here is a savior. That's not a community—that's a religion. A community has both bad and good. You learn the little things about each other and give each other leeway. Some of it we have to learn to love, and I mean love in a spiritual way. . . . It's your choice. . . . Are you all willing to help? . . . [People nod their heads but remain silent.] The bottom line is you can all live as individuals or you can make a community and start sharing. All it requires is doing it. . . . So let's make it happen before Christmas and then we can all sing a bunch of carols and be happy.

Safety concerns created another dilemma for the attempt to shift control to tenants. Staff in one house felt that they should not go into tenant bedrooms, but an administrator said they needed to do so as necessary to check on safety issues—such as smoking in bed. Staff were also told to ask people when they are going out—as in a family. Some tenants remarked that the presence of staff increased their feeling of being safe.

When staff confronted tenants about problems, results were unpredictable. One house manager explained the problem to the house ethnographer,

[The] house manager describes her job as "hell" these days. Problems with staff who personalize reactions from tenants and so try to avoid adverse reactions by not confronting tenants about problems.

When staff shut off phone service at one house upon discovering that tenants had made many unpaid calls to 900 numbers [pornography services], one tenant charged, "staff think they're [the tenants] morons." Another who had been in frequent conflict about drug abuse was given an ultimatum by staff; she then improved her relations with housemates and began to participate in group meals for a time.

Another dilemma emerged when staff felt that the tenants should have the responsibility to resolve interpersonal conflicts. For example, when one tenant was accused of taking others' food, the house manager announced that staff "can't get involved":

Terry said that they could acknowledge what had happened, but they could not take sides. "That's real important, what this whole model is about." He talked about the model for a while. . . . It's important for the residents to know that they are in charge—they're running the show—and that the staff are just there to "keep them safe."

When Estelle got angry and smashed the VCR, staff did not respond because "they wanted tenants to take action." When some tenants complained that others were not doing chores and asked staff to help out, a project coordinator urged that staff-tenant relations be viewed as a "team approach":

It might be helpful for the relationship between tenants and staff, because there's no division between the two and more of a team approach, like at the Fountain House [an empowerment-oriented program in New York City].

Medication management and medical care created special problems. Staff were legally responsible for ensuring distribution of medication, yet some tenants did not like to be told by staff about their medication needs and resisted staff control in this area. One complained about a staff member calling his doctor and a relative to report on his behavior. The staff member explained in a meeting, "It's my responsibility if I have a concern to talk with the doctor." The tenant "just kept insisting that [the staff member] snuck around behind my back," and that he didn't want her doing it any more. He announced that "I'm taking it [the permission he had given her to contact his doctor] back. You coerced a lot of signatures from me." Reflecting the ongoing ambivalence about shifting control to tenants, a project coordinator then chimed in that the tenant is "going to target anyone who tries to make him a responsible individual." The tenant walked out of the room, muttering, "She violated my rights under the Fifth Amendment."

Other staff sought to include tenants more directly in medical decisions.

Jim: "You should be part of your treatment team. When I see a doctor I want to be part of the treatment. I don't want to think that people are talking about me behind my back. You pay for the services."

Michael joked that they would have the people who rent the parking spaces [outside the house] come to the meeting. Sally said they would have to "pay another $20 to listen to my shit."

Some tenants continued to seek help with managing their medications:

Marybeth said that she would like help with taking meds. "I need encouragement to take it." She said that she became homeless because she stopped taking her meds, because she became paranoid. She learned her lesson and now realizes that she needs to take the meds.

House guests created another major difficulty for tenant control. The "guests" that some tenants brought in for brief, overnight, or more extended stays were seen as a problem by other tenants, but staff were reluctant to intervene.

> *Staff1:* The bottom line is that all of you have to be responsible for your guests and make sure that others feel comfortable with them in the house. If something happens, just tell staff, but what we're gonna do is tell you to tell him to leave.
>
> *Sally:* Well, I'd like to do the right thing. But why don't [*sic*] Claudia do anything to stop him?
>
> *Staff2:* I didn't even know about it, Mame.
>
> *Staff1:* How could she do something if you don't tell her?
>
> *Helen:* Well, I'll just tell staff—they're supposed to be in charge of everybody.
>
> *Staff1:* You can tell us for now, and we'll suggest ways for you to deal with it. But we're trying to get away from you running to us every time there's an issue.
>
> . . . If there's an issue, go to the person who's doing it. Or if it's somebody's guest . . . , tell them what's going on so they can handle the situation. That's really not our role. If there's a problem after you try to deal with it, then we'll step in.

In spite of the reluctance of some tenants to assume new responsibilities, many tenants attempted to exercise control in various ways and complained when they felt staff were trying to hinder these attempts. Tenants in one house decided to let staff pay to use the laundry facilities on certain days, as a way to raise money for the house. One tenant expressed an interest in having a staff member help him learn to cook but concluded that he "would be threatening the job of the staff if they helped them." A group of tenants refused to plan for a group activity (like bowling) suggested by staff. Some tenants complained when a staff member recommended dietary changes to another tenant. One tenant woke up and discovered that a staff member had come into his room during the night and left a note containing some instructions:

> He was very upset about it because he does not want anyone in his room for any reason. . . . [The house manager] said that she did not know who had put the note there and that she agreed it was out of line. She promised to find out who it was and to get back to [the tenant] tomorrow.

Some tenants also took offense when they were not consulted about new tenants. One tenant complained about the model and said he would stop attending tenant meetings because tenants don't get to make decisions. He objected to staff being hired without tenant input and to staff writing about tenants in log books again, without tenant approval and after tenants had voted to stop. Another tenant complained that staff overlooked the important things, like a tenant playing loud music late at night. They demanded more consideration:

> The tenants were concerned that their input was being neglected [in the selection of new tenants] and people were working around them rather than with them. Felice suggested people should come to the tenant meeting before moving in, and Walter and others concurred.

Subsequently, tenants interviewed new staff prior to their being hired.

Some staff became quite bitter as they were frustrated increasingly by their inability to resolve problems in the house.

> *Susan:* We're just there to keep people from killing each other. It sounded
> great at first—empowerment—but now there's nothing to help. We lack
> the power to do anything. We just sit and watch TV and stare at the walls.
> *Alice:* The thing is we're here to treat with empowerment, but we don't feel
> empowered!! But I have a lot to contribute but I can't!!
> *Susan:* I know. There is no leadership here, no expectations, we're almost at
> the whim of what the tenants want!

The empowerment coordinator justified the hands-off approach to staff at one of their meetings:

> The most difficult thing to do is what you guys are doing—and that's not doing anything. You all are empowering individuals who aren't even liked anyway. This is a good group of tenants here, and they've had negative things said to them for a long time. They're really tough people; I couldn't put up with even half of the things they do if I were in their position. But they're doing so well, and for the most part they're bright and cheerful; they're so tough. And you all probably think, "What the hell am I doing here? I sit around all day, and I get paid to play scrabble, or get caught up in all my reading, or get all my homework done . . ." But really, you all are doing a great job!!

But the coordinator also took steps to increase tenants' sense of responsibility for their actions in the house:

> Look, folks, I'm going to make an assessment of the house. And I'm going to write a warning letter to the tenants that I feel should get one. I think the best thing to do sometimes is to tell people what we think; that's what we're here for. We all know that we can't change each other's behavior. But what we can do is maintain the tenants' sense of safety in these houses, and I will do that no matter what. . . . These are residences of wellness! They are not residences for persons on unprescribed drugs! Your illness is your doctor's concern; you are not each other's responsibility! So if someone is telling you, "Listen, Susan, you're not acting like the Susan we know," it's up to you to get some help! Tell your doctor what's going on! If you're not doing that, then this is not the place for you to live.

Reducing Staff

The most tangible result of shifting control from staff to tenants was to be the gradual elimination of staff in each home until there were none left at the project's conclusion (eighteen months after each house opened). At this point tenants would have taken over responsibility for all chores and other functions required for house maintenance and would be collectively making all house management decisions. But in order to achieve this goal the project had to overcome the reluctance of many tenants to terminate staff as well as staff concern about tenants' ability to manage on their own.

> That's the whole goal of this house [taking care of problems among yourselves]—because when this is over, we won't be here.
> Felicity: Ya'll won't be here? What's gonna happen to the house?
> Harry: You'll be taking care of it. I know it's very hard to confront people. But that's what adults do, and it's all in the way you say it. There's a way you can talk to people, it's in the approach. There's always a nice way of being confrontative. And a lot will get done in the process.

Many tenants shared concerns like Felicity's. Billy considered the other tenants to be "a bunch of crazy people," refused to work with them, and feared being left alone with them after staff had all moved out. Some tenants expressed concern about not having a car for rides after staff left, particularly in the winter. Fred said that he liked to have staff accompany him to places. Francine said that the staff were needed to keep people taking their medications, since "if there was no staff she wouldn't take her meds." Andy thought staff were needed to help collect rent from others. Harold simply revealed, "I kind of like having the staff here." Tenants at one house agreed that they wanted at least one staff person in the house all the time.

Other tenants were eager to see staff leave. Harvey, who initially had resisted reducing staff, decided that "We shouldn't be dependent on the staff."

> Helen . . . asked, somewhat impatiently, when they would start to get rid of staff. She said that she did not want to live here the rest of her life with staff. [A staff member] said that she wants to know what they want staff to do. Gloria said that [staff] should do what they do now, which is watch TV. . . . [Three tenants] said that they don't like anything that the staff do. [One] said the staff could come by and make a periodic check and then write notes to the tenants.

The project prepared for staff reduction with several steps designed to ensure that tenants would be able to live safely in the homes without staff. House staff created a phone book with all numbers that might be needed in emergencies and trained tenants in calling clinician beeper numbers. Tenants decided that it was important that the phone book include a contact number for each tenant in case of a medical emergency, in spite of the privacy issue involved in listing that number where other tenants could see it. Taking over responsibility for medication was encouraged, since legal regulations stipulated that staff must continue on-site if any tenants required staff to "hold their meds." House staff assessed tenants with "Home Alone" questions to determine if they knew the procedures needed to manage alone, including how to respond to health emergencies.

The process subsequently developed fitfully. One tenant who had done much cooking for her house "pointed out how no one wanted to do anything" and resisted taking on more responsibility herself, but she finally volunteered to help plan house budgets. Staff and tenants discussed what tenants would have to learn once staff moved out and at one house considered acquiring a car, perhaps as a donation. Staffing levels declined somewhat through attrition, as some left and were not replaced. Staffing in some houses was reduced to just one employee per shift. "Home-alone trials" were begun, in which staff would leave the house for an hour during the day. By the spring of 1993, the first project houses started to reduce staffing by having non-overlapping shifts and some unstaffed times during the day and by reducing night staff so that one night each week was unstaffed.

So concrete steps were taken to shift control from staff to tenants in some ways and to reduce the number of staff, but the process only occurred in fits and starts in some houses and did not lead to independent functioning of the tenants as a group in any houses. Many staff members felt that they served as a buffer between different tenants and believed that tenants would have a hard time once staff left. Staff were not completely eliminated in any ECH before the eighteen-month project period ended, although one ECH became self-managing within the following year (although only a few McKinney tenants were still living in the house).

Reconsidering Evolution

The problems encountered with the empowerment model gradually led to disillusionment by both the empowerment coordinator and house staff.

A dialogue between the empowerment coordinator and two tenants captures the growth of frustration.

> *EC:* Look folks, this is not a group home here. Staff are not here twenty-four hours a day just to watch you all. You all are adults who can self-care, be

safe, self-medicate, cook, and clean for yourselves, without staff telling you what to do. Look Sam, if you can't own that you have a problem, then I'm gonna refer you outa here!

Sam: Don't threaten me.

EC: You have got to have some insight, you've got to be an adult, recognize your problem and ask for help. Does everybody know what an evolving consumer household is? You got to either poop or get off the pot here. If you really want to live in a group home, then just tell me and I can refer you. This is your house, not the staff's, not mine, not anybody else's. This is your furniture, and you gotta take care of it because this is all you got for as long as you live here. This isn't like in some institution where nobody cares a hoot cause nobody wants to be there in the first place. Each of you chose to live here, and you gotta treat this house like that. It's been almost a year since you all moved in, and where's the sharing? A lot of people are pissed off here because this isn't a shared household, where everybody pulls their weight.

Jeff: I'm tired of group home living. . . . The one thing I've learned here is how to cook for myself. And yes, I've had Caroline help me make pancakes, but still, I know how to cook now. But now it's time for me to move forward, not just mark time, or go backwards . . .

EC: But this isn't a group home. . . . People are not owning up to their behavior. We cannot have people remaining in this house after it goes off-line who are unsafe smokers—it's too dangerous. But you all are gonna have to own up to this and change. I can't change anybody's behavior.

Jeff: You know, that would require working as a group, but right now, we're just individuals. We're not working together—we're working away from each other, singly. We're each doing our own thing. That isn't what a group home is about.

EC: We seem to have individuals who are not getting what this model is all about! I can't be coming in here constantly reminding you all what to do. That's not my job! There's apathy here, and people are working against each other!! Everett feels this is a group home, exactly because this isn't a residence where everyone is being independent. I'm glad you all are upset about this smoking ban. And I'm happy that Everett decided to do that, because this has finally got you talking for once!

EC: This is a shared residence. Not a group home. That means you're all interdependent. You each live your life, but you share it with others. You share expenses. At a group home, staff make all the rules and they stay forever. But here, staff will be leaving, and you'll be staying. Now that means that you can't have it both ways—being independent but needing the staff to take care of you. If any of you feel you need more care, just tell me, and I'll set something up with you at another place.

After this interchange, the empowerment coordinator described her disappointment to the ethnographer and revealed that for her, the project had been a complete failure because all the [tenant] leaders of the houses just couldn't own up to their problems.

In a tenant meeting in another house the empowerment coordinator paused, "visibly upset, appearing close to tears, [with] dead silence in the room, everybody looking down," and said,

> *EC:* This is two years now. We're now in the process of phasing out staff, but if we phased out now, we'd have drug people in and out of this house constantly, and you know it! I have not worked as hard as I have for that, and nobody else has either. These are residences for mature adults, who talk out their problems. Staff are not here to tell you what to do or how you're gonna live your life. I'm not your mommy, the mental health center is not your mommy, and you don't need others to take care of you. That's what I spend every day all day long arguing with people like Dr. Christopher about—they don't believe you can make it here, and I'm telling them you can. I'm not playing games with you anymore. Eileen, you're in trouble, you're off the wall, and you got to get some help for your mental illness to get stable again.
>
> *Eileen:* All I want is that the staff get reduced here.
>
> *EC:* I don't think I recommend it; I don't even think you should live here! You are not able to ask for help!

A tenant who had been able to move into a subsidized independent apartment looked back at the empowerment effort in her ECH with disdain.

> . . . feels the tenants will never be able to run the house themselves: "She doesn't think anybody has improved since they've moved in—Sam sits around all day drinking coffee and smoking, Helen stays in her room all day; Dennis still needs someone to go with him every time he walks out of the house; Andy is "all right"; Bill doesn't have a clue about anything; and Duane is "out of it since he stopped taking medication."

House staff also increasingly became disillusioned with the empowerment model.

> Well, it seems to me that this house is falling apart. Those other people who would come to the meetings and participate—now they're not here anymore. It's just not clean—there are unwashed dishes everywhere, the floors aren't swept. Before when you first moved in, it was fine, but now, you don't do it anymore. Even the upstairs is starting to look like downstairs. When you guys cleaned, you did a really good job, but now downstairs, there are roaches again. There's food half-eaten and spilled all over the floor and the counters, there's candy half-eaten—the roaches are gonna thrive here! It seems like a symbol to me that people aren't happy here anymore. We used to have BBQ's and fun things, but that never happens now. Everybody's off in their own little world. I know everybody has illnesses and their own problems and it hurts me to see that. But people are sometimes in bed all day. Sometimes this house feels

like a prison. You know? Like today—it's a beautiful day out and yet no one has been outside all day.

Frustrated by the failure of houses to evolve and by continued uncertainty about their role, some house staff quit.

Helena does feel some frustration with the model as well. Sometimes when she leaves the house she can't stop thinking of all the things she would like to do to get people in the house motivated. She has a lot of trouble sitting around the house doing nothing all day. . . .

One staff member revealed the depth of her frustration a few days before her planned departure date.

It doesn't seem like anyone has learned anything about empowerment. And what's really scary is that I'm just sitting here counting the days until I'm gone. I don't care about anything here anymore and I can't wait to leave. . . . But overall, with this empowerment stuff, I don't think this project has really made a difference with these people in the long run. There's just not enough people doing it on an individual basis.

Some staff felt the ECH model was failing in the houses due to a lack of sufficient structure.

"I think the house needs more structure from the beginning instead of waiting until something comes up. That's like letting people run crazy until they make mistakes." If people knew what the consequences were of doing something, they wouldn't do things.

Other house staff emphasized the corrosive effect of substance abuse.

Consensus on drug use is that it counts as neglect to not restrict someone who is using drugs. It's actually disempowering because they can't make choices when using drugs. No one could quit drugs without a lot of support. Cindy said that they had tried leaving people alone and look what happened: it didn't work.

Two house staff members discussed the "lessons learned":

I think people thought that somehow the house was gonna make everything better, and that hasn't happened. People are finding it's not enough to have a roof over your heads.

The honeymoon's over.

Staff Control

As faith in the empowerment model decreased, the empowerment coordinator suggested methods for increasing staff control. The empowerment coordinator apologized to staff at one house for having previously given mixed messages about empowerment, and said that "empowerment isn't *not* intervening when someone needs help." She explained that tenants would have to be self-medicating and responsible for their own funds and not engage in unsafe behaviors in order to live in the house. A "liaison" was added to the staffing of one house with the responsibility of structuring activities for tenants. At this same house, part of "laying down the law" was distributing bills for the house fund to tenants in order to reduce nonpayment. The house manager and the empowerment coordinator jointly "put the squeeze on the tenants," particularly on one who was identified "as the source of all the problems in the house."

At another house, a project leader told staff that the project's new approach would be "to bring things to put in front of tenants to do, rather than waiting for tenants to suggest activities." The empowerment coordinator encouraged a house manager to intervene with tenants "As much as you want!"

So the project approach to tenant autonomy took a 180-degree turn. Project policy about drug abuse also changed dramatically, as the empowerment coordinator explained.

> She said that if a person is disabled to the point that they [*sic*] can't make good decisions, then they cannot be empowered. Following this line of reasoning, and recognizing that a drug addict has no rational control over their [*sic*] drug use, they have been considering some new possibilities. . . . [the EC] said that she should take some of the responsibility for not helping more to keep people from using drugs. They need more control on this issue and are doing no one a favor by the "live and let live" policy.

The basic message was now that staff had to be proactive in managing the house.

Boundary Management

More intensive boundary management—restricting the types of persons who could live in the ECHs—accompanied increasing staff control. The project's empowerment coordinator explained that ECH tenants had to be able to self-care and called an ECH "a wellness house, not an illness house." She expressed frustration with all the time she had to spend with two particular tenants, when "I want to develop a community group here."

Although the 118 initial project participants who had been randomized to the group homes moved into specific group homes as they became available, restrictions on entry to the homes were developed as the project progressed. Tenants were given the right to interview prospective new tenants and usually were able to make the final decision to admit them. They sometimes gave a newly admitted tenant some readings on empowerment to prepare for living in an ECH.

In spite of this effort to control entry to the houses, expulsion of troublesome tenants became the more significant boundary management strategy. Initially the houses had no clear rules about expulsion and neither house staff nor the empowerment coordinator envisioned the need to exclude any tenant. However as some tenants proved to be disruptive over a period of months, the empowerment coordinator guided tenants at their meetings to develop an expulsion policy and help to ensure that ECH tenants were of the "right type."

The expulsion policy required that the other tenants first discuss and vote on expulsion in a meeting. If they decided to expel a tenant, they first had to sign a letter (which was actually drafted by the EC) stipulating behavioral changes required in order for the offending tenant to remain in the house. The letter was given to the offending tenant. When the stipulated requirements were subsequently violated, the tenant could be expelled. The formal steps were listed in the first house termination policy:

Termination Policy

1. Review guidelines.
2. Issue a formal warning.
3. Put the person on probation.
4. Staff will help plan the consequences of ignoring probation.
5. Tenant group meets to decide whether to recommend termination of the offender from the program.

Not all tenants were comfortable with expelling another tenant, and most tried to avoid active involvement in the process—leaving the actions up to staff. Some tenants who were the object of expulsion efforts became quite angry, although others accepted the process with little protest.

Wayne then lit into a diatribe against the other tenants. He said that he has wanted to move out of the house for a long time, and now he just wants to get the heck out of here. He can't stand the rest of the tenants who have ganged up on him leaving him defenseless. They can make up things together which will go down on his record as truth and then there is nothing he can do about it. He asked rhetorically why everyone was just sitting around silently watching him get framed and railroaded out of the house. "They're not acting like people." He said they won't even talk to him—they just wait for him to be thrown out, taken out of their lives. "They're ungrateful and mean. To me they're just a bunch of losers, nothing more. But I'm helpless. They get together and summon me."

The record of a conversation with a tenant who was about to be expelled captures the way the process unfolded.

Jan: I'm not telling you what to do, I'm asking if it would be in your benefit to move somewhere else.

Harvey: I don't want benefits, don't you get that? I'm the one who started up my friends, so what are you gonna say—I'm a bad influence? I wish you could give me more freedom.

Roni: But there is tension in the house. . . .

Harvey: There's no tension in the house. They're just playing games. Everybody's saying there's tension, but I don't feel it.

Roni: But you're using to a point where you have a hangover, and that's a problem.

Harvey: Last time I didn't have problems.

Lefty: Look, Harvey, the point is that you're going to have to make changes. I'd like to blame somebody, but I know we can't do that. We're only here to help. I'm also worried about mixing cocaine with the medication you're on.

. . .

Lefty: We can't just sit and watch you self-destruct.

Harvey: Why not? It would be fun. I'm just joking. I'm not going to.

Lefty: That's what your behavior shows. What are we going to do about this?

Harvey: Do beer, do lines . . .

[A few minutes of silence.]

Harvey: I guess I say these things but I don't mean them.

Lefty: What's the ultimate punishment?

Harvey: I can't quit!

Lefty: I don't think you'll quit on your own. Helping you isn't . . . it's still gonna be there.

. . .

Lefty: On the path you're on, all three of you are gonna go back to the shelter. If you do anything upstairs, then you're out of here.

Harvey: That's not fair!

Lefty: I don't want to see that happen. But to be fair to yourself, why don't you try detox. We can set that up for you.

Harvey: No, I'll end up with a bad room.

Helen begins describing some detox places. She can think of three good programs, but recommends Bournewood—"it's private, takes Medicare, and people seem really nice there. It's out in the middle of the woods, not institutional. What have you got to lose?"

Jan: Do you wanna try one of these, Harvey?

[Harvey shaking his head no.]

Jan: Maybe you can think about it. I'll call in the morning.

Lefty: Maybe it's the hangover. You'll be able to think more clearly later on. Maybe we're putting you on the spot. Think it over, . . .

Harvey: I don't want to think about that. I'm trying, trying, trying!

Harvey: It's the addiction. I even wrote myself a note and that didn't work.

Lefty: You feel like we're all after you?

Harvey: I don't understand why you think it's a crime. The cops even look away.

Lefty: It is a crime, but it doesn't mean you're a bad person.

Harvey: I think it's just the opposite!

Jack: It's not important whether it's illegal or legal—we're concerned about you, and we're just going by the behavior and what other people are saying. We have to balance everybody's needs and health and safety. So you understand where we're coming from?

[Harvey doesn't say anything, but asks if he can be excused now. He leaves the room.]

Multiple tenants were expelled after they failed to control such behaviors as dealing drugs, stealing to support a drug habit, disrupting others due to drunkenness, or engaging in prostitution in the house. A few tenants simply declared their intention to leave to avoid the conflicts within the house. In spite of their reservations about expulsion, many tenants saw the need for reducing conflict and were reassured by staff promises that expelled tenants would receive professional help elsewhere. One tenant was asked not to attend house meetings because he "sets up an atmosphere in which people cannot feel comfortable" and is "not fixable."

The empowerment coordinator subsequently described the appropriate type of consumer for an ECH:

We have gone over in almost every meeting what kind of person should live in these houses. We need to have individuals living in residences who can do two things—manage their illness and manage their wellness. . . . People [who] do well with their illnesses are the kinds of people you feel safe around. They're people who recognize when their illnesses are flowing, who go to the doctor, and they don't dump all of it on you. They're the kinds of people who can monitor their wellness.

In another house, she explained to tenants:

This is permanent housing for adults who can share. If someone is unsafe in the house, or cannot share with other adults living in the same house, they will not stay because they will not be appropriate for this type of housing. This house will not become a group home, and if someone shows that they [*sic*] are not now capable of meeting the high standards for living in an ECH, then [that person] will be moved to a group home where there is more structure.

Some tenants contributed actively to the boundary management process. In one house several tenants urged expulsion of one African American resident they had labeled as a "crazy bastard" who hated white people (and a project leader decided his excessive paranoia made him inappropriate for an ECH). When housing agency staff requested that they allow a tenant to return to the house after she had been expelled for bizarre and disruptive behavior, tenants objected—even to the proposal to bring her to the next tenant meeting to present her case.

The issue of expulsion came up most frequently in response to problems due to tenant drug abuse. When one tenant reported that someone was smoking marijuana in the house, the empowerment coordinator told tenants that the next time it happened they should tell staff, who would conduct an immediate room search and move the offending person out of the house without question. When two tenants repeatedly used drugs in the house, the empowerment coordinator lost her patience.

> I'm on the phone constantly with people who are telling me these houses are never going to work! And then I hear that there are drugs in the household! Not from staff—from other tenants who know what's going on! And I know what it's all about—I see things and you can't fool me! . . . . [Their psychiatrist] thinks you can't maintain yourself in this house, and I'm sitting there arguing for you, and you're . . . going and doing drugs in the house! Do you know how awful that makes me feel? Now, it's a fact, plain and simple, that these houses don't do well with anyone doing drugs. And I will help you weed those people out. . . . The people we haven't felt safe with are gone, and the people we presently don't feel safe with I'll help you weed out. Now that does not mean they will be out on the street; staff and I will work with them to find alternative housing. . . . This is a residence, not a therapeutic hospital. Right now, I need to take over for you, and I'll be an advocate for your position. I need to make sure this model is successful for you. . . . Each of you is not just living in the community but you're living in the community with each other. There's a difference.

Tenants then wrote a "final warning letter" to the two identified drug users, recommending that they seek treatment for their illness and stop doing any drugs. Staff felt that the only thing holding the tenants back from "being independent" was the two tenants who were using drugs.

When the project coordinator learned that several tenants had not contributed [again] to the house fund, she complained, "This house is a joke and it's gonna stop. . . ." She said that the tenants who could not live up to the model's expectations would be expelled. She then threatened to refer people out of the house "who are pains in the ass" before the project ended in a few more months.

> You're adults with chronic illness, not babies who need to be taken care of. I'll save this model for those people who are adults and can live on their own

and refer the others out. . . . It's poop or get off the pot time. . . . Some are doin' it, some aren't. Those that aren't need to leave.

The empowerment coordinator voiced a similar complaint to two tenants in a meeting at another ECH.

These houses are calling out the wellness in all of us. I don't know if you're happy here, either of you. But to live here, you've got to be able to cook, budget, and take care of your share of running the house. . . . If you wanna be part of the residence, I want you to stay, but if you're saying to yourself, "Gee, I really don't want to cook or shop for myself," then I know a guy that runs a residence that has openings for people like that. . . . But this can't be a pothouse or an unsafe place to live or a place that only one person runs. . . . That's not a shared residence! Now I know this model takes a while to percolate, and it's winter and everybody gets pissy at the end of winter. I know this model asks a lot. I don't want to diminish the horror of chronic illness, but you each have the opportunity to pay rent and determine your own day—you don't have to get up and go to day program . . . that's all you guys are doing!! Staying at home! To have a home is not to mess it up or leave a place looking terrible. You have to learn to take care of yourselves. If you want a place where you're taken care of, then just let us know. . . . Do you wanna live like regular adult people doing a shared residence? It's up to you. I'd be remiss if I wasn't honest with you and told you upfront that I don't think it's gonna help you if you don't get off your butts and do something to make this house run instead of walking around and smoking cigarettes.

As the project approached its end, the empowerment coordinator summarized in a tenant meeting the lessons learned about tenant selection.

To un-license the house, they have to be sure that people can live in an ECH. They have to be "ECH people." She explained that . . . they now know what kind of people live in an ECH. . . . She explained that the ECH is a residence inhabited by adult individuals with chronic illnesses who can and do share a living space and a community—but do so without imposed formal rules. A person who became scary and violent when [his or her] illness "kicks in" cannot make it, and this has been proven in this house. A person needs to be able to listen to another's concerns about [him or her], and a person needs to know when [he or she] is getting sick and needs to be hospitalized.

The empowerment coordinator finished her talk by telling tenants she "would appreciate them letting her know what kind of residence they would like to live in. There will be no 'mommy-daddy stuff,' and they will be treated like adults not kids."

In another house, the empowerment coordinator explained "that the ECH environment requires a certain type of person." She went on to tell tenants "to depend on your 'peers' and on yourself, and if you continue doing drugs, there is nothing [I] can do to keep you from getting into 'deep do-do' with your [mental health] center. The whole model is resting on it."

The Group Home Model

Ongoing problems led the empowerment coordinator to reconsider the advisability of the ECH model.

> Maybe this model is no good anymore. Only some people can do it. It's really upsetting to think that people are openly smoking pot here. This house isn't a group model where everybody is running around telling you what to do, but maybe that's what you'd all prefer. Do you wanna grow up or do you wanna have somebody take care of you? I don't think this is the right place for some of you, because it's driving out the people who do good here. . . . So we need to work on this. Please feel free to talk to staff. If you don't believe you want to do this model, that's *not* failure. Failure is let's pretend this is a shared residence and you do nothing while other people wait on you.

In one ECH an explicit decision was made to restructure the house as a traditional group home. The empowerment coordinator explained that tension in the house had made it impossible for some tenants, one of whom had already left as a result. Other tenants said they were afraid to come into the house's common area because of all the tension. So by changing the management model for the house to that of a traditional group home, the empowerment coordinator explained, all the tenants could now feel comfortable. There would be consequences for negative behavior, and the project's Clinical Homeless Specialists would coordinate more with house staff.

Staff soon reported feeling better about the house, and the empowerment coordinator lauded their new approach.

> "I like what's happening." Staff is "walking tenants through everything," and they will "need reminders until they get in the habit." They have to "catch the house up," because "they're not capable." Once they "get the machine going," the tenants "can oil it" on their own.

When a staff member suggested resolving ongoing problems with shopping by adopting it in "a group home way" in which people are constantly pestered to get a shopping list together, the empowerment coordinator opined that it was a good idea.

Several tenants who had complained about problems in the house responded enthusiastically to the new management strategy: "What works is good."

Tenant Reactions to the Group Home Model

But the group home model did not resolve problems with house management. After several weeks of experience with the new approach, several tenants erupted with angry complaints. Patrick complained vociferously, "ranting very loudly," saying "I hate this house." He complained about other tenants, inadequate heat on the third floor, how the second floor "gangs up" on the third floor, and most stridently about his newly assigned chore.

> His complaint was that his chore, keeping the back staircase clean, was no chore at all. Patrick liked doing the garbage when that was his chore. He felt like it was "a union job." He liked going outside and smelling the air. He felt like it was "in order." [In response to another tenant's complaints about tenant control] Patrick said it was worse than a military installation; they drive you out of your mind, up a flagpole. . . . Patrick got very angry and left the room. He could be heard continuing his monolog in the TV room.

Tenants revolted in a meeting over house policy after staff had discussed the need for tenants to avoid keeping food in their rooms so as not to have a problem with mice. Randy was the most outspoken.

> The staff is "coming down hard." He mentioned that Chuck told him he was seen drinking on Washington Street. "This staff is encroaching." He called it a "communist situation," there are "no freedoms, no rights in the house," just the staff pushing and pushing. The mice were here before he got there, he doesn't care about them. . . . Randy said that the staff keeps coming up to his room, asking him things, and bothering him, trying to get him to come downstairs and socialize. He pointed a finger at Chuck, and called him a policeman. He said that Chuck enjoys stomping up the stairs in his combat boots. "It's like a barracks, not a house." Randy lashed out at Chuck, calling him, "Mr. Military over there." He said the house was like a "military installation," and you "can't do nothing in here." . . . Randy said the house was a "sham, a charade." The staff are getting worse and worse, closer and closer. Next they'll be saying what you can and can't eat. Every time you turn around, there's a new fucking rule. . . . Randy opposed the idea of having rooms checked. He said his room should conform to his standards of life, not the staff's. Randy continued on his rant. He talked about how ridiculous it was for the staff to be telling him to socialize in an environment where everyone is constantly stealing everything.

Another tenant expressed sympathy for Randy's position:

> Helen said that she sympathized with what Randy was saying about the house being a communist state—because they have so many meetings. Now they have a new one every month. . . . She said she wouldn't go.

The house staff member who was the object of particular criticism finally responded in kind.

Chuck talked back to Randy, picking up on some comment about the staff, and the project leader reprimanded him for it, but Chuck continued. The project leader reprimanded Chuck a few times, and Chuck defended himself by saying that Randy shouldn't be able to get away with what he was doing, according to Nick's orders. He tried to get some of the tenants to agree with him, that Randy was being unreasonable and out of line. At one point, Chuck and Randy got into a shouting match saying "can" and "can't" to each other at least ten or fifteen times, until Randy left the room. The project leader told Chuck that whatever Randy was doing, he [Chuck] was making it worse and that when she asks him to stop he should stop.

When Randy returned to the meeting, the empowerment coordinator announced that she could fix some of his problems, if he agreed to work with them, starting with not using the hot plate in his room. Randy said that he was willing to do this, if the staff agreed to ease up on him. The project leader then said it had been good that people felt safe enough to "blow off."

The empowerment coordinator became more critical when another tenant complained about his assigned chore in a subsequent meeting.

Harold said he didn't want to clean out a bathroom any longer. . . . The coordinator lashed out at Harold saying that he only comes to the meetings when he has something to complain about, and he expects people to do what he wants them to. If he wants to live in this house, which is a group of adults living together in a house, he has to be here to discuss issues of importance to the community. In clear terms she said "if you want to stay at this house, you have to attend the meetings."

Harold: "Is that an order?"

EC: "You can take it that way."

Harold was obviously aggravated by this, and said that he was going to move out if he was going to be treated like that. A bit later, Harold attempted to point out the inconsistency of this requirement: The argument between Harold and the coordinator flared up again. Harold asked if she was making the meetings mandatory, and she said that they were not mandatory because if they acted like adults they would not need rules to tell themselves that they should do things that were obviously necessary for the group to stay together.

Jeffrey, another tenant, endorsed Harold's complaint, focusing on the glaring contradiction between the project's supposed empowerment orientation and being told "that he would have to have a case manager against his will." However, the empowerment coordinator would not change her stance.

He said that he had learned a lot over the last year about what he needs to do to live in the community and that at the end of the year he thinks he will not need a case manager telling him what to do. The empowerment coordinator said "This is a residence of wellness." She does not think that it is safe for people to sever their ties with the mental health system. She was quite harsh. Jeffery asked if the tenants are not supposed to tell the staff what to do, and they see a staff person doing something wrong, after having been told not to do it, what do they [tenants] do? The empowerment coordinator said that these things should be brought up to house staff. She told him this in a harsh tone, and Jeffery got up and left the meeting. The empowerment coordinator said that they can't have a consumer be a "negative power person." She summarized again: If staff have a standard of cleanliness that needs to be upheld because of their need for accreditation, then that will be the level of cleanliness the house will be kept at. There will be a time when the tenants become self-initiating enough to maintain that level of cleanliness on their own, but there will be no one tenant running the group telling everyone what to do or not do. "We're trying to get this together where power is used in a positive way."

The empowerment coordinator described her frustration with the "real disorder in the house" that was represented by having a staff cleaning schedule on the bulletin board. She emphasized that the house has been open over a year and that the group still had made no progress. Although tenants seemed to expect staff to clean up after them as if staff were the servants of tenants, "Tenants don't tell staff what to do." She explained that they had been through a process before where the staff did nothing around the house, and the result was that the house did not meet acceptable accreditation standards. Empowerment just did not seem to be working.

The empowerment coordinator also complained about the tenants' lack of motivation.

She said that "You all as tenants are way behind." She said "There is a strange game going on about your running the house. Freedom and responsibility go together. Why not suggest to yourself that you put away your dishes or wash the stove before staff suggest it to you. It's not normal to stay in the house all day doing nothing. It's not healthy to sit on your duff all day." She said that they should consider going to a day program where they could meet people and develop a social set. ". . . Our goal is to get you to live like normal people. You look like all of us." She added that tenants shouldn't be telling staff what their job is. . . . She said that she feels like a broken record when she describes how the house should work. Everyone should take care of their [sic] own messes.

Some tenants agreed with the staff position.

Sally offered her opinion on keeping the house clean. She said that if everyone cleaned up after themselves [sic] there would be no problem. The stove is the big problem. Grease and grime build up there because no one cleans it immediately after cooking.

The empowerment coordinator concurred: "That's what living with people is about. We're only asking you to take care of yourself." Another tenant chimed in:

> Duane spoke up at this point with his theory of why the house was screwed up. He was almost coming out of his chair waving his arm for emphasis. He said that the consumers—he used the term consumers throughout—should not look at staff as the rulers of the house, but as people there to help. The attitude that the staff run the house is what breaks down the whole administration. What is happening because of it is a struggle to outmanipulate the situation and control the house. The struggle will continue until people take on the right attitude toward the staff. Holding meetings with other consumers out on the porch in secret to get them to gang up on staff is what breaks down the house. They should realize that everyone is there for a common goal.

The empowerment coordinator then urged tenants to take a new attitude toward their psychiatric care because they did not have to go to the bad public hospitals they were used to. Some were starting to use the posh private hospitals. She said it was wonderful that one of the tenants finally got hospitalized today. As she continued emphatically on this theme for about five more minutes, she was soon talking to staff and just two of the tenants. All the other tenants had left the room.

The Institutional Environment

Rules and regulations affecting group homes—their institutional environment—created their own barriers to the effort to shift control from staff to tenants. Houses had to post medical information, display prominent EXIT signs above doors, have a human rights officer, and take action in response to a tenant's threat of suicide. Monthly medication forms had to be completed, treatment plans maintained, and activities entered in logs. House managers had to report to the Department of Mental Health and to the nonprofit organization responsible for their house, prepare for site visits by accreditation agencies, and operate according to the rules of vendors and merchants with whom house business had to be conducted. All of these engagements required that the house conform to some degree with established modes of operation. Considered as a whole, these created powerful incentives to maintain a traditional structure.

One staff member imagined that a system could develop in which the house would be run on a family model in which tenants gave medications to their "siblings." She was quickly corrected by an administrator:

> That's a very nice model, but unfortunately we don't have that model here. Here we have to have orders which [*sic*] have to match up with the prescriptions which [*sic*] have to match what the bottles say.

The housing vendor required house staff to pass a test on administration of medication that was based on the DSM-III manual.

Regulations required that tenants complete multiple forms recording their use of medications in order to meet requirements for becoming self-medicating. This requirement was an object of complaint.

[A Clinical Homeless Specialist] said that he hears it from so many clients that this is their home, why should they have to fill out so many forms? He said that he knows that the forms are not such a big deal, but he still feels bad pushing them on clients. [A house manager] said that doing away with the forms was unrealistic. [Another CHS] said that she had to remember that if not for a blip on the computer these people would be living in their own apartments. She said that at one house the tenants had written a letter to [an administrator] saying that the meds issues were between them and their doctor and not of interest to the house. She searched for a word to describe it and said that she was looking for a nice way to say revolt. She said that the clients were trying to reform some situations. [A CHS] said that the McKinney agenda was to listen to them as much as possible—to make them as independent as possible.

Some tenants also complained about sharing their information with clinical staff.

Andy: Hold it, hold it, now we hit something. It's invasion of privacy. How did [clinical homeless specialist] get our phone number? We just got that phone on Tuesday! Even though this is a mental illness facility, we still got rights!

Allan: We do have civil rights.

Sam: I don't know what to say about that; I wasn't here at that time. Jeff is your clinician.

Andy: It's up to us individuals in the group home. It's up to us to give them our phone number if we choose to—we do have privacy!

Sam: Well, but doctors and clinicians have a right to your phone number because they're a part of your treatment plan. And family, if you want them involved, but most of you wrote "No." So we have a right to give your doctors and clinicians because they're different from your family.

These frequent reminders of the rules required to function as part of the larger institutional environment created another impediment to tenant empowerment.

Conclusions

Consumer empowerment is an essential goal for the postinstitutional mental health service system (SAMHSA 2006). In contrast to the dependence and passivity that hospital-based care allows—even encourages—success as a community resident requires independent decision making and self-directed action. By increasing the ability of mental health service consumers to manage their own affairs and giving them responsibility for treatment decisions, the empowerment movement focuses attention on the need to improve community functioning within the context of normalizing treatment.

In spite of this growing recognition of the potential for persons with serious mental illness to take action on behalf of themselves and others (Nelson et al. 2006), the means for developing this potential are not well understood.

In our group homes efforts to empower the ECH tenants focused most often on their ability to handle chores and manage funds, but the path to success proved to be rocky. There was a great deal of trial and error in each of the houses as different strategies were tried and rejected, and as the influence of particular tenants varied over time. Organizational difficulties were common and interpersonal conflict, ongoing. The expectation that tenants would be able to handle chores on their own seemed unrealistic soon after each house opened. It was not until staff assumed an active role in organizing chores and monitoring their completion that chores were reliably completed. Efforts to establish a house fund for group expenses and to organize collective shopping trips also faltered.

Achieving greater consumer control in our group homes would have been a sufficiently difficult goal if it had resulted in residential staff losing some of their status and privilege, particularly as professional clinicians retained theirs. But in order for our group homes to "evolve," they also had to overcome two more specific obstacles in the surrounding environment. At the organizational level, the planned evolution had to find a way around the many regulations emanating from government agencies that equate professional attributes with service quality. At the client level, shifting control away from staff required that recently homeless persons with severe mental illness and, often, substance abuse disorders be motivated and able to take over staff functions. Both obstacles proved to be formidable. In response, staff control increased and boundary management was exercised.

These responses were reflected in a shift in the empowerment coordinator's orientation to empowerment. She now began to emphasize the importance of selecting tenants for ECHs who had the characteristics required to live successfully in this type of house. She also made strong statements in meetings about the need for maintaining effective social control within the houses. The attempt to transfer control from staff to tenants was proving to be exceedingly difficult.

Expulsion became a key management strategy. Once this process lessened the impact of substance abuse in the houses and increased group homogeneity, the process of tenant exercise of control advanced. Nonetheless, the behaviors and orientations of many tenants continued to constrain housing "evolution." Constraints imposed by the institutional environment in the form of rules and regulations played a considerably less important role in slowing down the shift to tenant control.

Donald A. Linhorst (2006, 8) concluded that "empowerment of vulnerable people is highly fragile and can end quickly." Our experience with the ECH model reaffirmed the importance of meeting what he termed the conditions for empowering people with severe mental illness through housing, including managed psychiatric symptoms, participation skills, and psychological readiness. At the same time, the ECH experience confirmed that the development of appropriate structures and processes, resources, and a supportive culture, can increase the likelihood of making significant strides toward empowerment. With improved planning, training, and management, the ECH model might have achieved the empowerment goal that eluded us during the eighteen- month period of federal support.

CHAPTER TEN

Housing Loss

SALLY AND FRED and the other Boston McKinney participants could not develop community connections until they resided physically in a real residence like others in the community (Browne and Courtney 2004, 37). But their initial move into housing did not end the experience of homelessness for all of our participants. Nor has research on other housing programs for homeless persons with mental illness identified any model that "*prevent[s] reentry into homelessness for this high-risk group*" [my emphasis] for all participants (Stefanic and Tsemberis 2007, 268). The oft-repeated mantra that the solution to homelessness is "housing, housing, housing" is understandable—even unarguable—but it is not the whole story about what homeless persons with severe mental illness need (Hayes 1986; Lozier 2006).

This chapter reviews the pertinent literature on housing loss and then extends the findings in chapters 4 through 8 with an integrated analysis of influences on housing loss during our project and for more than 15 years after it ended. The analysis is enriched with qualitative data from participants and clinicians and with comparisons to the other McKinney projects. In its entirety, the chapter provides a better sense of why some of our participants lost housing, how our findings compare to those of other research, and why figure 1.2 helps explain the phenomenon of housing loss.

Prior Research on Housing Loss

Receipt of housing reduces the risk of subsequent homelessness for persons with serious mental illness, particularly if it is accompanied with support services (Ridgway and Rapp 1997; Nelson, Aubry, and Lafrance 2007, 358). However residential instability continues for some individuals even after subsidized housing is obtained (Sosin, Piliavin, and Westerfelt 1990; Wong et al. 2006). The eighteen-month rate of in-project homelessness in the three McKinney projects that moved participants directly into housing (Boston, New York City, and San Diego) was about 30 percent (Shern et al. 1997; Schutt et al. 2009). Between 16 percent and 25 percent of participants in other projects have lost their housing one year after housing placement; after five years, the rate of housing loss has risen to 50 percent (Lipton, Nutt, and Sabatini 1988, 43; Kasprow et al. 2000; Lipton et al. 2000; Padgett, Gulcur, and Tsemberis 2006). Although more intensive services may be able to reduce this five-year risk to about 25 percent, 40 percent seems to be a realistic lower-bound estimate for housing loss within five to twenty years in programs offered in typical circumstances for homeless persons with severe mental illness—even if the focus is restricted to those judged to have left their housing on an "involuntary" basis (Wong et al. 2006, 39–40; Stefanic and Tsemberis 2007; O'Connell, Kasprow, and Rosenheck 2008).

The factors identified in the preceding chapters as influences on housing loss in the McKinney Project are consistent with prior research. The analysis in chapter 4 indicated that the McKinney participants who rejected living with staff and group support when clinicians recommended support were much more likely to experience housing loss once again during the project than were those who did not reject support that clinicians judged they needed. These results are consistent with other research on the rejection of mental health services or other sources of support among persons with schizophrenia. Outpatients with schizophrenia who assessed their own daily functioning skills much more positively than did their case managers actually performed more poorly than did those with more negative self-assessments (Bowie et al. 2007). Persons with schizophrenia (Amador et al. 1994) or bipolar disorder (Pini, Cassano, and Dell'Osso 2001) who did not recognize illness-related impairments in their lives—who lacked "insight" (Flashman 2004)—were less likely to maintain treatment, adhere to prescribed medication (Kikkert et al. 2006), accept professionals' or family members' advice, or function well in the community (Haywood et al. 1995).

Chapter 6 revealed that a lifetime history of substance abuse at baseline predicted subsequent housing loss among our participants, whereas drug abuse during the project was associated uniquely with housing loss among African American participants who were assigned to independent apartments. The effect of substance abuse is consistent with prior research (Folsom et al. 2005; Wong et al. 2006, 42; Kertesz et al. 2009, 519) and the risk associated with drug abuse among African Americans specifies circumstances, at least for our participants, when substance abuse can be even more detrimental for housing retention.

Homelessness also appears to be more common among African American recipients of mental health services in the United States than among those who are white (Folsom et al. 2005)—although the effect of ethnicity has varied across samples (Uehara 1994; Wong and Piliavin 1997; Mares, Kasprow, and Rosenheck 2004). This apparent effect of race may be due to reduced housing opportunities as a result of racial discrimination by housing providers, neighbors, or others (Turner and Reed 1990; Takeuchi and Williams 2003; Yanos, Barrow, and Tsemberis 2004). The analysis in this chapter shows the extent to which the effect of race identified in chapter 6 is explained by other factors.

The analysis in chapter 7 confirmed prior research results indicating that neither psychiatric diagnosis nor symptoms predicted risk of further homelessness. However some prior research suggests that more intensive supports are needed to maintain homeless persons with more severe psychiatric symptoms in housing, compared to those with less intense symptoms (Lipton et al. 2000; Clark and Rich 2003; Schutt et al. 2005). The analysis in this chapter tests this possibility by examining the effect of symptom intensity on housing loss separately for those in the ECH and IL housing.

In order for us to understand the bases of housing loss, the process by which preferences, substance abuse, race and symptoms have their effects must also be elucidated. Social ties vary in response to each of the other influences on housing loss, and they tend to decline in tandem with the process of housing loss itself (Johnson 1991; Rosenheck and Fontana 1994; Baumeister and Leary 1995; Green, Vuckovick, and Firemark 2002). Homeless persons with drinking problems have "subtle interactional problems" (Sosin 2003; Zlotnick, Tam, and Robertson 2003), and substance abuse itself is associated with a substantially elevated rate of antisocial personality disorder (Khantzian et al. 1991). Those who reject support are increasing the likelihood of their social isolation (Haywood et al. 1995). Variation in social supports may thus help to explain the influence of the other factors on the likelihood of housing loss. Qualitative data will be used in this chapter to explore social processes involved in housing loss.

Prior research has not identified a clear advantage of a particular type of housing for reducing housing loss among persons with severe mental illness (Rog 2004). In a meta-analysis of thirty studies Leff et al. (2009) distinguished three housing models: residential care and treatment (often called "board and care" group homes), residential continuum housing (transitional group homes), and permanent supported housing (residents live on their own but receive services as needed). Average residential stability did not differ among these three models,[1] but residents were more satisfied in the permanent supported housing. Leff et al. (2009) also found that the apparent beneficial effect of all three of these types of housing on residential stability was reduced in studies with methodologically stronger designs.[2] Siegel et al. (2006) also found no difference in housing retention between two types of supported housing and "community residences" having on-site support services and sobriety requirements. However, the types of housing were not clearly distinguished in terms of group and individual characteristics or other housing characteristics.[3]

Other research provides some support for an expectation that more socially engaging housing will lead to better rates of housing retention. More socially involving transitional housing in a VA program for dually diagnosed adults predicted greater residential stability (Schutt et al. 2005), as did more social support from friends and family for homeless persons in a rehabilitation program (Calsyn and Winter 2002; and see Dayson et al. 1998; Pilisuk 2001). On balance, prior research raises more questions than it answers about the potential for residential stability in our group and independent living alternatives.

Housing Status and Housing Loss

Some project participants left their originally assigned grant housing within the first month after housing placement. They continued to do so at a more or less constant rate throughout the project, so that by the project's eighteenth and last month, just 34 of the original 118 participants had had uninterrupted stays in their first project residence. The average participant spent 310 of the total 540 project days in his or her original housing before any move. The percentage still living in the original grant housing, whether or not the participant had left it for a time for any reason, dropped from 88 percent at the six-month follow-up, to 70 percent after twelve months and to 60 percent after eighteen months.

Participants left their original grant housing for a variety of destinations, ranging from other housing to hospitals, detox centers or jails, and shelters and the streets. Averaging the total residential experience of the 112 project participants who were still enrolled in the project after the first six months, 77 percent of their time was spent in grant housing and another 6 percent in other community housing (see fig. 10.1). They spent, on average, 11 percent of their nights homeless (7 percent in shelters and 4 percent on the streets) and another 4 percent in hospitals. Another 2 percent of their nights were split between detox facilities and jails.

At the time of the project's conclusion, in its eighteenth month, 75 percent of the 112 participants were living in some type of community housing (61 percent in grant-funded housing), 19 percent were homeless, 3 percent

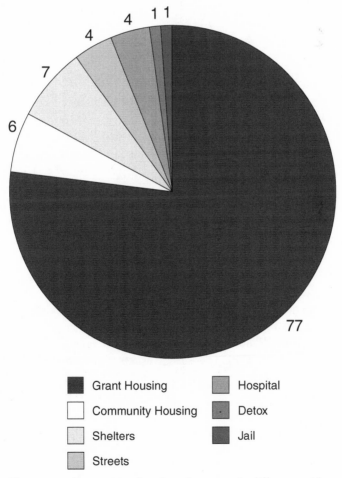

Figure 10.1. Percentage of project time spent in different residential circumstances. Note: N = 112.

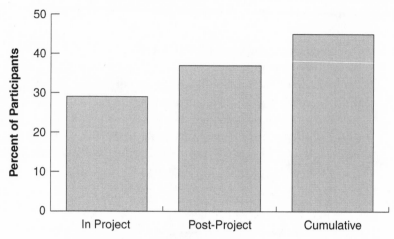

Figure 10.2. Any homelessness during or after the project. Note: $N=75$. Percentages for those located in postproject agency housing records to 2008.

were in a hospital, and 1 percent were in jail; one had died, and the residential status of the rest was unknown. Postproject residential status was evaluated again with mental health agency housing records almost twenty years after the Boston McKinney Project began. Of the original participants, seventy-five had postproject agency housing records. Among these participants, 29 percent had been homeless during the project and at least 37 percent had been homeless after the end of the project (based only on spending nights in shelters, since agency records did not indicate time on the streets). Combining the numbers who spent any nights homeless during and/or after the project, at least 45 percent stayed on the streets or in shelters at some time after they first moved into project housing (see fig. 10.2).

Because the postproject housing records do not indicate time spent on the streets, they underestimate the total time spent homeless by an unknown but probably small fraction (since our participants were accustomed to using the shelter system). Another source of uncertainty in the postproject housing records is missing information about housing status for various periods of time. If time unaccounted for in the records is discounted, our participants spent about as much time homeless after the project as during it (see fig. 10.3). If the time for which location was unknown is assumed to have been time on the streets, the time spent homeless after the project rises from 11 percent to 18 percent. Participants spent more time after the project in staffed group homes (48 percent) than in independent apartments (38 percent). Time spent hospitalized was comparable during and after the project.

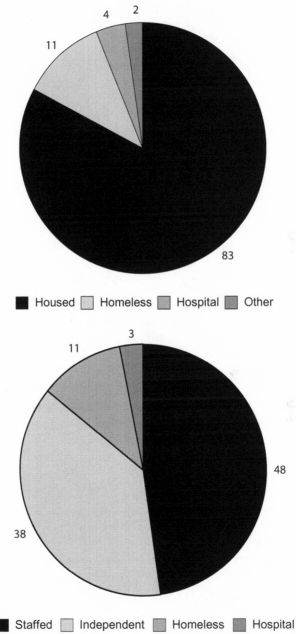

Figure 10.3. Percentage of time spent, by location, during and after project. Note: In-project $N = 112$; postproject $N = 75$. (Base for percentages excludes the 7.8% with location unknown.)

Qualitative Analysis

Project clinicians and the project's residential coordinator recorded unstructured observations for all but 9 of the 112 clients throughout the project and then at the project's formal conclusion, after eighteen months. These comments complement the ethnographic information about the process of housing loss that I have presented in prior chapters, by identifying strengths and weaknesses in functioning for consumers who lost housing and who retained it.

Clinician comments about participants who did not lose housing during the project usually indicated supportive informal social connections and some engagement with professional staff as well as some interest in treatment for substance abuse and/or mental health problems: "gets along well with others," "very friendly, strong verbal skills, assertive but not hostile," "enjoyed group living . . . became more communicative with family," "attended tenant meetings faithfully," sought "help when needed," "had good relationship" with case manager. None of the participants who retained housing received consistently negative comments, although problems were identified in some areas or at some times: "engagingly social but at close range antisocial," or "skittish, . . . but he has a wonderful time out when there is no interpersonal tension." In some cases engagement in treatment appeared to compensate for problems in informal social relations: "antisocial" but "bonded well to staff" or "accepts support when in trouble . . . but barely [when] on his own." In other cases informal social relations appeared to compensate for a lack of treatment motivation: "leadership role . . . easily discursive, comfortable with disagreement" but "intentional neglect of meds resulting in mood downturn. . . ."; "regular contact with children . . . got along with neighbors" but "routinely missed [case manager] appointments . . . history of noncompliance with medications."

In contrast, clinician notes about participants who subsequently became homeless identified many weaknesses in self-care and social interaction: "unable to care for self in IL," "uncontrollability . . . trashed the house . . . battered a staff member," "unable to cope with living alone . . . terrified in residence," "drug trafficking, stealing in the house," "occasionally binges, struggles with substance abuse, paranoia interferes with ability to get along and trust others," "assaultive/obnoxious when drunk," "involvement with dealers, . . . unable to maintain apartment, . . . preferred to be by himself," "goes along with peer pressure . . . difficulty accepting help." One participant who lost housing "let dealers run their business out of the apartment," another had "dealers after him."

Quantitative Analysis

The risk of spending time homeless during the project was higher for project participants who had been randomized to independent living (35 percent) rather than group homes (20 percent) (see fig. 10.4). When this comparison is limited to the seventy-five participants who had postproject mental health agency housing records, the effect of housing type is much stronger, as 45 percent of those assigned to independent living experienced at least some nights homeless during the project, compared to 18 percent of those assigned to group homes. After the project some former participants continued to spend nights in the shelters, and the difference between those assigned to independent living and group homes diminished. The cumulative rate of re-experiencing homelessness from the beginning of the project through the long-term follow-up rose to 36 percent of those initially assigned to the group homes and 58 percent of those originally assigned to independent apartments.

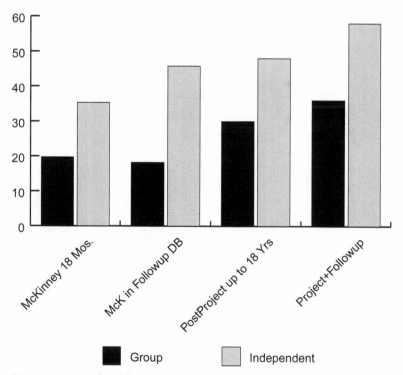

Figure 10.4. Any homelessness by project housing type, by follow-up. Note: Panel 1 $N = 112, p < .05$; Panel 2 $N = 75, p < .01$; Panel 3 $N = 75$, NS; Panel 4 $N = 75, p < .05$. (One-tailed tests.)

The regression of (logged) days homeless by eighteen months (see table 10.1) identifies as significant predictors substance abuse, housing type (with an interaction with race), clinician housing recommendations, and consumer housing preference in interaction with housing type (Goldfinger et al. 1999, 677). African Americans were at high risk of housing loss if they were assigned to independent apartments—a disadvantage that was completely eliminated in the group homes. However, participants who more strongly preferred to live independently were at higher risk of housing loss—if they were assigned to group homes. Poorer life skills, as measured, do not explain the other effects but independently predicted less likelihood of housing retention.[4]

The most striking finding from the analysis of the postproject housing records is that the housing type to which participants were assigned at the project's start was no longer related to time spent homeless after the project ended (see table 10.2). Consumer preference for independent living continued to predict time spent homeless and now this effect occurred in both housing types, rather than being limited to those assigned to group homes.[5] Clinician recommendations of support also predicted more time homeless in the long-term housing records, but only among those assigned initially to an IL; the ECH participants who clinicians had rated at baseline as at greater risk were no longer particularly vulnerable to housing loss. None of the other baseline predictors of time homeless continued to have a statistically significant effect on postproject retention. Two new correlates of time spent homeless appeared in the postproject period: older participants and those with a diagnosis of schizophrenia or schizoaffective

Table 10.1 Regression Analysis of Logged Days Homeless, in Project[1]

Variable	Total[2]	Group	Independent
Independent Apartment	.22*	—	—
Minority	.21*	.01	.48***
Age	.04	−.00	.12
Female	.14	.12	.14
Education	.13	.06	.19
Schizophrenia or SchizAff	.04	.03	−.03
Lifetime Substance Abuse	.29**	.26	.44**
Prefers Independent Living	.19*	.34**	−.00
Clinician Recommends Group	.34***	.33*	.45**
R^2	.31	.30	.44
N	107	59	48

1. Eighteen-month period. 2. Beta coefficients.
*$p<.05$; **$p<.01$; ***$p<.001$.

Table 10.2 Regression Analysis of Logged Time Homeless, Post-Project[1]

Variable	Total[2]	Group	Independent
Independent Apartment	−.05	—	—
Minority	.18	.08	.39
Age	−.24*	−.32	−.26
Female	−.02	−.02	−.12
Education	.07	.11	−.20
Schizophrenia or SchizAff	−.25*	−.20	−.25
Lifetime Substance Abuse	.07	.37	.01
Prefers Independent Living	.32**	.26	.31
Clinician Recommends Group	.17	−.21	.45*
R^2	.30	.36	.51
N	71	41	30

1. Proportion of time with known location, up to 18 years post-project.
2. Beta coefficients.
*$p<.05$; **$p<.01$; ***$p<.001$.

disorder spent less of their time homeless than did those who were younger or who were diagnosed with major affective or bipolar disorder.

The housing records also distinguished time spent in independent living and time spent in group homes in the postproject period. Participants who were assigned to an independent apartment during the project continued to spend more of their housed time living in an independent apartment, as

Table 10.3 Regression Analysis of Independent Living/Total Time Housed, Post-Project[1]

Variable	Total[2]
Independent Apartment (McKinney baseline)	.70**
Minority	.07
Age	−.12
Female	−.05
Education	−.07
Schizophrenia or SchizAff	.01*
Lifetime Substance Abuse	−.19
Prefers Independent Living	.44*
Clinician Recommends Group Home	−.34**
Started In Group & Preferred Group	.92**
R^2	.20
N	72

1. Up to eighteen years post-project. 2. Beta coefficients.
*$p<.05$; **$p<.01$; ***$p<.001$.

did those who had expressed a preference for independent living at base-line (see table 10.3). Those for whom clinicians had recommended a group home at baseline spent less of their time living in independent apartments after the project ended. However, those who had preferred at baseline to live in a group home and had been assigned to live in a group home spent more of their time housed after the project living in an independent apart-ment. In other words it seemed that the experience of living in a group home for those who had initially wanted that level of support ultimately improved their ability to live on their own.

The Multisite McKinney Results

Each of the five McKinney projects tested the value of an enhanced hous-ing intervention for reducing time spent homeless, but the specific housing intervention used varied among projects. Even the three projects that moved some participants directly into housing did so in different ways. All participants in the New York Critical Time Intervention project were moved into housing, but those in the enhanced housing intervention received inten-sive support for their first six months in that housing. In the Boston project, of course, participants were moved into two different types of housing, while in San Diego some participants who moved into housing did so with case management support and some without. In the Baltimore project participants assigned to the housing intervention group received Section 8 vouchers that would pay for the cost of their housing (except for 30 percent of whatever their income was). The New York Street project focused solely on persons liv-ing on the streets—not in shelters—and attempted to increase the use of a transitional shelter through a day program that was offered to those assigned to the enhanced treatment condition. More details are provided in the methodological appendix (also Shern et al. 1997; Schutt et al. 2009).

Individuals assigned randomly to the enhanced treatment condition in each project were less likely to spend project days on streets and/or in shelters than those assigned to the comparison condition in each project, but the specific relationships varied by project, outcome, and substance abuse. Figure 10.5 shows the extent to which the enhanced residential treatment in each project reduced the days spent in shelters for abusers and non-abusers.[6]

In all four projects in which time in the shelters was the primary nega-tive outcome—Baltimore, Boston, the New York Critical Time Interven-tion (CTI) project, and San Diego—enhanced housing was associated with less likelihood of spending time in shelters. However, in Baltimore and San

Figure 10.5. Difference in days in shelters between enhanced residential treatment and comparison condition, by substance abuse, in five McKinney projects. Note: Ns in Table A.4.

Diego—the two projects in which participants were given Section 8 vouchers and then had to secure housing—this positive effect of the enhanced condition occurred for non-abusers. In Boston and the New York CTI project—both projects in which all participants were first placed in housing—it was substance abusers whose residential stability improved with the enhanced residential treatment.

In the New York Street project, spending days in shelters was the positive outcome, since participants had been spending most of their days on the streets. During that project both the substance abusers and the non-abusers who received the enhanced treatment (the day program) spent more of their time in shelters compared to those who did not receive the enhanced treatment.

Conclusions

After initial housing placement, 27 percent of the formerly homeless persons with severe mental illness in our project reexperienced homelessness during the eighteen months they were participants in our project, but up to half did so over a period of up to eighteen years after they had entered the project. For this extended period they spent a total of about 10 percent to 16 percent of their total time homeless. Group home placement reduced subsequent homeless episodes, compared to independent apartments, except for those who most strongly preferred to live independently. African American residents were more vulnerable to housing loss compared to white residents—much more so if they were living in independent apartments and were active drug users. This greater vulnerability of African American tenants is consistent with literature documenting greater structural vulnerability of African Americans at all levels of the housing market, particularly when they are substance abusers.

The reduced vulnerability of African Americans to housing loss when living in one of our group homes can be conceived as "structural deamplification"; that is, roommates and live-in staff in the group homes may have mitigated problems that occurred in connection with the independent apartments—an explanation that is consistent with the clinician notes (Ross, Mirowsky, and Pribesh 2001; see also Rodney Clark et al. 1999; Lincoln, Chatters, and Taylor 2003). The greater vulnerability of African American tenants was not apparent in the posthousing follow-up, perhaps because all the drug users had already left their housing by that time.

Clinician-assessed ratings of need for support at baseline had a strong additive effect on housing loss by eighteen months, apart from the effect they had in interaction with consumers' residential preferences (see chapter 4). Clinician ratings at baseline continued to predict time homeless (in shelters) after the project ended, but they did so only for those who had been assigned to independent living in the project. The clinician ratings also predicted less time spent in independent apartments out of the total time spent housed after the project ended. Thus, clinician ratings had long-term prognostic value in identifying participants who would be less able to live independently.

Substance abuse is a critical individual-level risk factor for housing loss, but this research makes it clear that many formerly homeless substance abusers with severe mental illness can maintain housing if supports are provided. In the words of the report by Yin-Ling Irene Wong and her colleagues (2006) to the U.S. Department of Housing and Urban Development's Office of Policy Development and Research,

> Provision of a long-term housing subsidy is a necessary but not sufficient condition for success. Permanent housing residents have substantial physical and behavioral health needs for which appropriate and continuous support is critical to maintain independent living. (80)

These findings also indicate that consumer preferences in themselves are not meaningful predictors of readiness for independent living. In fact the strong desire for independent living indicated greater vulnerability to housing loss. That relationship was so strong that it persisted in the face of controls for numerous other characteristics and for almost fifteen years after the project ended. On the other hand, our results also indicate that the preference for living independently cannot be ignored by those seeking to maximize housing retention. Participants who wanted to live independently were more likely to spend time homeless if they were randomized to group homes during the project. After the project ended those who had had a stronger baseline preference for independent living spent more of their housed time in independent apartments. In other words preferences predicted behavior, even though they were unrelated to need for support.

The analysis in chapter 4 revealed that individuals assigned to group homes tended to become more favorable to group home living with experience—at least if that experience involved the type of active social engagement that was encouraged in the Boston McKinney Project group homes. This in turn raises the concern that individuals may lose their interest in achieving a greater degree of independence. However, our extended follow-up data indicated an important process that would lessen such an effect: those who had preferred to live in a group home at baseline and were assigned to a group home ended up spending more of their housed time in independent apartments after the project ended. The group living experience seemed to help them prepare for greater independence.

The critical role of social support suggested by our qualitative data is consistent with prior research on the importance of social relationships in the course and outcome of both homelessness and mental illness. By revealing the interplay between social support and engagement with clinicians, our findings also lend support to the framework crafted by Laub and Sampson (2003) for explaining divergent life courses. The effects of strengths and vulnerabilities interact with each other in a process that extends over time and is shaped by changes in social context; examining these factors in isolation will inevitably understate their explanatory power.

Clinicians' qualitative observations of participants' behavior help to explain the process of housing loss. In addition to nearly ubiquitous comments about substance abuse, clinician notes on those who lost housing were rife with observations of problems in social relations and treatment disinterest or even rejection. The frequency with which such problems were mentioned differed dramatically between participants who spent time homeless during the project and those who did not.

Since the risk of renewed homelessness is significant even after formerly homeless persons with severe mental illness are placed in housing, the group home advantage in housing retention is important for policy makers. This advantage is not realized for those who strongly prefer independent living, but those who remain in group homes become more favorable to them, and those who were oriented to them in the first place subsequently seem to become more able to live independently. The group home advantage also was of particular importance in our project for substance abusers and for African American tenants. The group home advantage for substance abusers could be even more pronounced in group homes that offer substance abuse treatment.

These findings suggest that the risk of housing loss can be anticipated so that individualized plans can be developed to reduce that risk. Measurement of housing preferences and careful assessment by clinicians of housing needs are the necessary first steps in order to realize these benefits. Critical additional steps are to make available housing and supports of different types. Providing options for group home living, both with and without on-site substance abuse treatment, offering peer supporters to those who insist on living in independent apartments, and encouraging staff engagement with depressed tenants should each help to lessen the likelihood of homeless persons returning to the shelters and to the streets.

CHAPTER ELEVEN

Community Process in Context

A CHIEVING "COMMUNITY" in different contexts, some McKinney participants remained in the group homes and developed satisfying social relations, whereas some were able to achieve stability in the larger community while living in independent apartments. Others remained isolated within the group housing, quarreled constantly with co-tenants, or left their housing entirely. Divergent reactions to similar experiences occur in any social group; they might even be considered as inherent in the human condition. What remains, in this chapter, is to take account of these diverse experiences and the different dimensions of the analysis in order to reach a conclusion about the book's central questions: Were our project's participants able to become members of the larger communities into which they moved? Did they build communities within the group homes that we designed? Did they cross the boundary, successfully and permanently, between homelessness and housing?

That there is neither a single nor a simple answer to these questions makes an answer no less imperative. In fact it is not until we recognize the complexities that we can reasonably begin to formulate answers. Communities are complicated and changing social entities with many interdependent parts. It is as shortsighted to term communities good or bad for their participants as it is to believe that it is easy to create a community of previously unrelated individuals. Moreover because individuals are as complex as the social world in which they interact, it makes no sense to expect a particular social situation to have a similar effect on all of its participants.

Almost twenty years after he moved into a Boston McKinney Project group home, Wayne Thomas recalled the experience fondly in a follow-up interview:

> It went well. We'd all take turns doing shopping and chores. People did their share—cleaning, cooking, dishes. There were no problems getting them done.

Sandy Telea remembered positive relations with other tenants:

> We got along well together, talked at the meetings, conversed outside meetings, helped each other out, discussed finances of the house (cable and phone). If there [were] any problems with medication (or self-medication) we could discuss and get support from each other.

One of the three former McKinney participants who continued to live in the one remaining evolving consumer household (ECH) recalled the experience in words that evoke an image of stable community living.

> Guests—friends and relatives of residents—would come and have coffee, dinner, talk, walk around, sit on [the] porch. I would have family (we'd do things)—had enjoyable time, went well.

But these positive sentiments were not shared by all of the twenty-eight former ECH tenants who could be reached for an interview. One complained about unproductive meetings:

> Didn't like them—nonsense—didn't make sense; they talked about rooms being clean. I did not like to go. After meetings I wanted to move; didn't feel like things got accomplished. They just talked about rooms being cleaned. That's all.

Another recalled continuing social isolation even within the group home environment.

> I kept to myself, didn't meet anyone—only one time another resident banged on [the] door wanting to use phone—otherwise all was fine—people didn't do much together, but there wasn't any trouble.

At this point, these divergent reactions should come as no surprise, but they are a useful reminder of the complexity of the social world we investigated. Figure 1.2 provides an appropriate model for organizing our thinking about this complexity. The general question posed in chapter 1 was whether individual dispositions or social situations explain behavior. Figure 1.2 also highlights the importance of the social environment—the types of people who participate in a setting, and of the institutional environment—the matrix of organizations and rules that constrain those settings. If we are to understand the interaction between individuals and the communities in which they participate, we must examine each of these elements in figure 1.2 and the relations among them.

Chapter 1's three specific interrelated research questions, modified to refer to the McKinney project, will be the primary focus of this chapter: How do people choose a social environment? How is the social environment constructed? What is the impact of the social environment?

How Did Boston McKinney Project Participants Choose the Social Environment in Which They Lived?

The simple, "methodologically correct" answer to this question is that our participants did not choose their housing environment when they joined our project; instead, they were assigned to group or independent living through a random process. But it is precisely this experimental feature of our research design that allows a worthwhile answer to this important research question. Because those who "got what they wanted" did not differ at baseline from those who did not, we were able to test whether the preference for a particular type of housing was related to the ability to maintain that type of housing. We were also able to compare what our participants preferred for themselves and what clinicians recommended for them and to see whose choices resulted in more favorable outcomes for the participants. Thanks to the long-term housing follow-up data, we can also examine the effect of housing preferences after participants' housing alternatives were no longer constrained by project requirements. To what extent did initial participant preferences and/or clinician recommendations lead to movement over time into the preferred or recommended type of housing?

We learned that from the standpoint of their initial starting point in the shelter, our project participants, like most other shelter guests, gladly chose the move into housing over continued shelter residence. This is itself an important finding, since the DMH shelters were relatively stable and well-maintained environments, compared to many shelters, and most guests seemed to have resigned themselves to living there and "struggling along," as Bob Desjarlais (1997, 19) put it.

So when they were given an opportunity to move directly into permanent community-based housing, over half of the shelter guests who passed the safety screen put words into action and moved. Admittedly some drifted

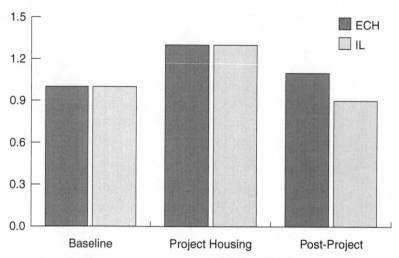

Figure 11.1. Housing satisfaction by housing type by follow-up. Note: ECH *N* = 17, IL *N* = 10 (interviewees in long-term follow-up).

away before their housing opened, some finally received Section 8 certificates that allowed them to move into other housing before the project began, and some may have decided to turn down the housing offer when they failed to "win" the housing lottery with the type of housing they preferred. But most moved, stayed, and felt more satisfied with their housing than they had felt with their prior shelter accommodations. For those who remained in the DMH housing system after the project ended, the McKinney homes represented a high point in their residential experience. For the 27 former McKinney participants who were reinterviewed in my 2008 follow-up, satisfaction had been higher with both types of McKinney housing than with the DMH shelters and also as compared to the last housing they had lived in prior to their 2008 follow-up interview (see fig. 11.1).[1]

But the ending point represented by the McKinney housing for the homelessness of our participants (at least for a time) was the starting point for a much more complex story about housing preferences. Many were disappointed to move into a group home when what they had wanted was an independent apartment. Only a few found themselves in an independent apartment when what they really sought was living in a group and/or with staff. However simply acknowledging this discrepancy does little to identify its meaning. Whereas economists often take consumer preferences as sacrosanct—as being given, or taken for granted with no need for explanation—a sociological analysis of behavior must also investigate the bases for those preferences. We need to identify what shapes peoples' preferences if we are to understand who they are and why they act as they do.

In order to investigate housing preferences, we have to swim upstream against the prevailing policy orthodoxy, which presumes that independent housing will maximize housing retention because that is what most homeless persons with mental illness want. What our empirical investigation revealed about housing preferences is that they are shaped by what has come before in peoples' lives, most importantly by their conclusion about their own abilities to manage on their own. These preferences are often not based on a realistic prediction of what it will take to maintain housing or to improve functioning in the community.

The analysis calls into question the rationality of housing preferences—if by "rationality" we mean a correspondence between what type of housing our participants wanted and what type they needed in order to maximize housing retention and functioning. One finding that suggests this conclusion was that participants' housing preferences had no correspondence to the clinicians' housing recommendations: these preferences and recommendations seemed to have completely different bases, so that participants whose desire to live independently was most pronounced were not rated on average by clinicians as any more able to live independently than those participants who sought to live in a group.

This sharp discrepancy between "client" preferences and clinician recommendations would be of interest only for the sociology of occupations and professions—perhaps suggesting a need for a different model of training for professionals—were it not for another finding about preferences. Participants who strongly preferred to live independently and then moved into their preferred housing type were more, rather than less, likely to re-experience homelessness during and after the project. By contrast, clinicians' recommendations predicted participants' relative vulnerability to losing independent housing: the participants whom clinicians recommended for independent living were less likely to become homeless again, whether they moved into group or independent living. This picture of vulnerability is even starker when participants are grouped by both their own housing preferences and the clinicians' recommendations: participants who strongly desired to live independently but for whom clinicians recommended group homes were at high risk of housing loss, whether they moved into group or independent housing.

The change that we measured in housing preferences from the start to the finish of our project is yet another finding that calls into question the notion that housing type should be determined on the basis of what persons want at any particular point in time. On average, participants who had been randomized to group living grew to like having housemates as they gained experience in the group homes, and those randomized to independent apartments became somewhat more open to the idea of living with roommates. Preferences were shaped by housing experience and so were subject to change as that experience changed. What seemed to be a good idea at one time in an individual's biography might with experience seem to be a bad choice.

We learned two other lessons about residential preferences. One was about the relations among housing preferences, housing experience, and individual characteristics. The experience of living in a staffed group home generally erased the effect of individuals' characteristics on their preference for living in such an environment, while the experience of living in an independent apartment heightened the effect of individual characteristics on residential preferences. Among the factors we assessed, only negative social experience lessened the preference of group home residents for living in a staffed group home. In contrast, the residential preferences of those who moved into independent apartments became more aligned with clinician evaluations of their need for support and remained associated with consumers' ratings of their own ability to manage the tasks of daily living.

The importance of housing preferences and clinician recommendations was underscored in the long-term follow-up interviewing process. The participants who had wanted to live in a group home at baseline were much more likely to be located and to participate in an interview than were others. These were the participants who remained more involved in the DMH housing system and more accessible to DMH staff when I sought to locate them for another interview after so many years.

So participants' baseline housing preferences were shaped by a sense of what they *thought* they could manage but not by what subsequently was learned to be their *ability* to live independently. For most participants group housing reduced the risk of subsequent homelessness whether or not it was what they had initially preferred. In addition, those who initially sought to live in a group home were more likely to retain their housing if this is the type of housing they received.

How Did Project Participants and House Staff
Shape Their Social Environment?

Retrospective comments by those interviewed in the long-term follow-up indicate some of the processes by which participants and staff influenced the social environment of the group homes. Most participants had positive comments about their peers—"I liked having the company of other people"—and remembered group meetings as positive.

> We had house meetings. We would find out what was going on in the house, what needed to be done—cooking, cleaning or outings. Everyone had a turn to cook, . . . we'd let staff know if things were needed for cooking. Things were accomplished most of the time.
>
> I learned about drugs and addiction [at meetings], the difficulty of cutting them loose—that's what got me interested. I felt OK going to meetings; things got accomplished—support to not do drugs.

But some felt the meetings were pointless.

> Didn't like them—nonsense—didn't make sense. They talked about rooms being clean—did not like to go.
>
> Chores were more often, though not always, a source of complaint.
>
> People did their chores; if they didn't, they'd have to the next day—staff would talk to them.
>
> For me, if I had to clean the kitchen or living room, I had no problems—just other clients wouldn't do their chores, staff would have to do it instead.
>
> It was "Useless"—I couldn't buy food that I wanted, no locks on cupboards. You could buy groceries and then they went missing. No one else [other than the respondent and one other] did anything; "it sucks."

Many interviewees remembered fondly social activities outside of the house.

> . . . We would go on outings, cookouts or little trips, movies together. They were fine. I got along with everybody
>
> People got along, talked—went to dances together, baseball fields, we would play home videos. I got along good with people.

One house even formed a band with some staff and tenants, playing every week and going to dances together.
But this feeling of conviviality was not universally shared.

> I kept to myself, didn't meet anyone. . . . People didn't do much together, but there wasn't any trouble.

Some follow-up interviewees also pointed to specific ways in which they had changed as a result of the group home experience. Help with maintaining sobriety was mentioned by several.

I was sober for a long time—I learned how to take care of my own apartment.

Help with becoming responsible was also mentioned by some.

While there I became more responsible—I had been running wild on the streets; there, I had chores, responsibility. I was responsible for getting things done. I still feel responsible to get things done—just without the rules.

I got more independent—can do more things myself, go shopping, joined a day program.

Some participants remembered house staff positively, others negatively; often within the same interview. Positive recollections were common.

We had problems but managed to solve them. We would talk things over with staff. . . . Staff and clients got along. I got along with them good. . . . They were helpful. They had AA books, found activities for us, and took us to appointments.

Others reported a mixed picture of staff in their McKinney group home.

If I needed help, some would help, some were annoying, some treat you like an idiot.

Overall, staff were not that helpful. When I moved in I was using drugs, . . . and staff gave me the third degree; thought I was going to drug rehab. I said I wouldn't use anymore, so they let me off the hook and I kept using; they were too trusting but not supportive.

One respondent expressed more negative views about staff in her house.

They'd be on you all the time—strict. They were too nosy, in your business. I didn't like them—none—were never helpful—I needed help and didn't get it.

Some, but not all, remembered positive social interaction with others from the larger community.

Friends would visit—sometimes we had open house, refreshments were served. There were never any problems.

Nice people—my boyfriend, and a friend—would watch TV and talk.

Some people came in and used drugs and alcohol with one of the residents.

The many positive recollections of social interaction in the group homes resonate with the social activities and positive meeting experiences chronicled with the ethnographic notes in chapter 5. Peer support was a key factor for some residents. One participant gradually engaged in more social activities after moving into a group home, ultimately becoming a respected member and informal leader of the tenant group. A participant in another group home was described by a project leader as finding a milieu of safety in the house, sharing leadership in the house with another participant: leading in a relaxed style "without [being] overwhelming."

Interaction with staff was critical for the stabilization of other participants. One participant who rarely spoke to other participants was an active alcohol abuser but maintained close relations with a case manager and a psychiatrist and managed to avoid housing loss. A participant who used cocaine was reluctant to maintain a regular treatment plan but had a good relationship with his case manager, regularly attended a day program, and kept his housing.

Some group home residents seemed to undergo a "virtuous cycle" of improvement through a combination of interaction with peers and support from staff. An ethnographer described a woman in one group home who changed through this type of process. At first she did not seem to have close relations to anyone in the house, spending her days just sitting in a chair, not going outdoors, expressing apprehension about doing things independently. She attended all tenant meetings but participated only rarely, although her functioning in some areas—maintaining personal hygiene, taking care of her personal effects, managing her money, and taking prescribed medications—was good.

After a time, this reserved woman started to become more involved in the house by cooking a group meal and then participating in a protest demonstration with other homeless persons. She participated in weekly outings for female tenants that were organized by female house staff. She seemed to be getting even more social and started to joke frequently with others. She participated more in meetings and began to go out of the house on her own. Although she had initially been afraid of reducing house staff, before the end of the project she said she was comfortable with the idea. Her personal gains in confidence and autonomy were helping to empower her tenant group.

But the ethnographic records contain many other incidents and cases in which neither group process nor staff action had a beneficial effect. Conflict continued between some tenants and within some group homes throughout the project. Relations between tenants and staff were also rockier than they appeared in the recollections of the tenants interviewed in the long-term follow-up. The effort in most of the houses to minimize staff engagement with tenants and to remove staff, even physically, from a central position in the house led to tension for staff and confusion over roles. As the project progressed, varying combinations of greater staff control and increased boundary management—primarily expulsion of troublesome tenants—reduced this conflict, but it continued to create challenges throughout the project.

Social interaction among group home tenants was able to arrest the process of deterioration related to substance abuse in a few cases. One participant who had been in recovery from alcohol abuse when he moved into the group home was a natural leader in group meetings and was friendly with many other tenants and staff. However, he began to drink abusively after developing a romantic relationship with a female tenant who was an active alcohol abuser. After a period of deterioration in his behavior, staff and his housemates agreed to set clear behavioral limits. Although he resisted initially with angry outbursts, he began to attempt to meet group expectations, terminated his romantic relationship, and gradually returned to a position of group leadership.

More often neither group process nor staff action was successful in improving individual functioning or empowering the group. One tenant had a good relation with his project case manager and began to get involved in the house and its neighborhood. However, when the case manager left the project, this tenant stopped his medications and withdrew socially.

Overall the social environment in the group homes was not sufficiently conducive to tenant control. Heterogeneity of the tenants within homes and problems created by substance abuse and symptoms of mental illness offset the benefits of many positive experiences of social interaction. The reluctance of staff in most homes to take assertive steps to increase constructive social engagement and to deescalate intertenant conflicts, as well as their overarching uncertainty about their appropriate role, also hindered easy resolution of many of the problems that emerged.

An ethnographer described a female tenant in one group home who deteriorated in spite of repeated group and staff efforts and did not adapt to group living. Soon after she moved in, tenants complained that she was not doing her share of the housework, played loud music late at night, drank in the house, and frequently argued with another tenant. She missed many tenant meetings and was very defensive when tenants and staff complained to her about her disruptive behaviors. Most tenants were afraid to confront her. When staff told her that she had to change her behavior, and then when she received a warning letter from the tenants as a group, she blamed her problems on her past. Conflict continued in the house over her drinking, as she insisted that she should have the right to drink as she preferred in spite of rules developed in the house. Finally, she was asked to leave the house.

Larger institutional rules were an additional impediment to the empowerment process, as efforts to make the homes feel less institutional and to provide tenants with more authority over the process of selecting new tenants were thwarted by inflexible system regulations. Destructive intrusions by some outside guests also hindered the process of community development in some homes. But it was primarily within the group homes—in social interaction difficulties among tenants and with staff—that the empowerment process foundered.

The mixed results of project efforts to empower group home residents through encouraging social interaction and shifting control away from staff are consistent with prior research that has identified few positive effects of empowerment programs. Moreover, the Boston McKinney Project's goals were much more ambitious than the peer support programs in this prior research, since we sought to give tenants complete control over the homes in which they lived and to eliminate gradually any role for house staff. It is not surprising that this effort led to many indications of benefits from social interaction but little progress toward independent consumer-run house management.

As the difficulties of shifting to consumer-run house management continued, some staff complained about tenant lethargy and self-destructive habits, and some tenants inveighed against increasing staff control. As the preceding chapters indicate, both charges contained an element of truth. The pull of addiction was the single most significant impediment to developing an empowering group process. Actions to support addictions, ranging from theft and prostitution to unwillingness to contribute to house funds, undermined group spirit, while the effects of substance abuse, whether emotional volatility or reduced functioning, subverted group process. Without a workable strategy for encouraging sobriety, the only viable option for reducing the harm due to substance abuse was expulsion.

Symptoms of mental illness and impaired functioning also hindered group empowerment. Although some houses were quite tolerant of the disconnected speech habits and wandering of some tenants, such tenants in other houses were labeled as crazy and viewed as disruptive in house meetings. The depressed feelings and lethargy that kept some tenants in their rooms or simply sitting in the house for extended periods of time also diminished engagement in empowerment activities.

Interaction with staff was an important aspect of the social environment in the houses, but its course and impact were highly variable. Some staff in some houses engaged tenants in chores and social activities, both modeling needed activities and developing supportive relations with tenants. Other staff withdrew from interaction with tenants and accepted a diminished role. As difficulties with empowerment accumulated, most staff fell back on a more assertive management style.

What is the Impact of the Social Environment?

On average, leaving the shelters for permanent housing led to less subsequent homelessness and improved cognitive functioning. Although the social environment in the DMH shelters was relatively more stable than in many mass shelters, it did not offer the possibilities for permanence and community connections that both the ECH and independent living housing provided. The aimless pattern of just "struggling along" in the shelters appeared in the housing as a more limited problem of depression and lethargy among particular tenants. Community-based housing provided a foundation for enhanced personal functioning and community integration.

But neither the acquisition of housing itself nor its community location ensured improved functioning or community integration. The type of housing McKinney participants received mattered, although not for all outcomes; and it mattered in different ways for different participants. Overall, living in the group home environment was associated with more housing stability and better executive functioning, compared to living in the independent apartments. The experience of living in the McKinney group homes also led to a greater preference for group living.

The higher rates of residential stability achieved by group home residents suggest that living in a type of community at home helped achieve more integration into the larger community outside of the home. Since integration in the larger community could not occur in the first place without location within that community, this group home advantage is a powerful finding in favor of their use as a housing option. The salience of this finding is reinforced by the participants' long-term residential histories: among those with some DMH postproject housing records, those who had been in the McKinney group homes spent more of their postproject time in independent living sites than in group homes. The McKinney group home experience had laid a foundation for greater independence in the future.

The gains in executive functioning in the group homes and the marked deterioration in executive functioning in independent apartments reinforce the value of the group home environment. Social stimulation performed its expected role in extending executive functioning, whereas the dramatic deterioration in executive functioning in the socially isolating independent apartments—even compared to prior residence in the DMH shelters—suggests that rapid placement into independent apartments meant for many participants only physical—not social—integration in the community.

Although most McKinney participants had not wanted to move to a group home, those who did, and who remained there, increased their liking for living with others as they gained experience with it. This attitudinal

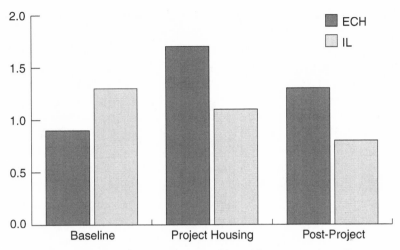

Figure 11.2. Group preference over time. Note: $N = 27$.

change is predictable when viewed in light of research documenting the variability and context dependence of preferences, but it is striking when considered in terms of current policies about housing for homeless persons with severe mental illness.

This finding about changes in housing preferences can be specified further with the responses of those former McKinney participants who were interviewed in the long-term follow-up. As indicated in figure 11.2, preference for living in a group increased during the project for those living in a group home, while it declined for those living in an independent apartment. After the project ended, the former ECH residents' average preference for group living dropped back a bit, but it remained higher than it had been before they entered McKinney housing, whereas preference for group living continued to drop for those initially assigned to an independent apartment.

In spite of these fundamental benefits, housing type had no general effect on levels of substance abuse, psychiatric symptoms, or dimensions of cognitive functioning other than executive functioning. The first two of these null effects are consistent with relevant theory and research; the last adds to a very mixed body of research results about the cognitive impact of the social environment.

Both the strong effect of substance abuse on housing loss and the overwhelming evidence in the ethnographic notes of its detrimental effect on the group homes are consistent with the neurobiological understanding of substance abuse presented in chapter 6. Brains that have been rewired by prolonged substance abuse to prioritize supporting the addictive habit above all other behaviors do not permit rational evaluations of the long-term costs and benefits of repeated substance abuse. When abstinence is not supported and maintained, the urge to "take up" and continue using soon overwhelms the feeble defenses that reasoned calculation creates. Providing independent housing for homeless persons struggling with addictions can lead to exacerbation rather than resolution of the substance abuse problem.

The problems in the houses with drug abuse could be severe, including stealing from and assaulting others in the house, but they also involved the environment outside of the houses. One heavy substance abuser let drug dealers run their business out of his apartment, while another was in constant anxiety because dealers were after him for not paying his bills. The social connections involved in drug use tended to reinforce addiction when they were left to their natural course.

The lack of either direct effects of housing or of housing type on symptoms of mental illness are also consistent with a medical explanation of psychiatric disability. Although social supports and greater security can help persons with serious mental illness to function in the community, they do not in themselves lead to remission of symptoms resulting from the underlying illness. Since we did not measure the extent or type of ongoing treatment our project participants received, we cannot identify the extent to which housing may have made that treatment more efficacious.

Research on the relationship between the social environment and cognitive functioning is not sufficiently developed to provide a clear basis for expecting that verbal memory or attention would have been less, or more, influenced by the social environment than executive functioning. What we do know is that scores on both of these cognitive dimensions improved with housing acquisition and both were associated with subsequent gains in observed community functioning. Considered together, and in light of research that links cognitive functioning to community functioning, these results suggest the importance of considering cognitive effects when designing housing programs.

Fitting Persons and Environments

None of these housing effects can properly be understood until the role of personal characteristics is taken into account. Person-environment fit made a large difference in outcomes. Group homes were much more beneficial for some individuals, whereas independent apartments had benefits for others. Substance abuse was the most important personal characteristic related to housing retention during the project—it proved to be a necessary but not sufficient cause of housing loss (all who lost housing were substance abusers, but not all substance abusers lost housing). However, when coupled with current drug abuse and independent living among African Americans, the risk of housing loss soared. Thus, the greatest benefit of group home living was for African Americans who used drugs during the project. If African American drug users were living independently, almost all reexperienced homelessness during the project, whereas if they were in group homes, there was no racial disadvantage at all—rates of housing loss were minimal for both African American and white ECH tenants whether they used drugs or not. We do not know whether this effect of race represented less tolerance by housing managers of drug use among African American apartment tenants compared to whites, or if it was perhaps an effect of more disruptive connections to drug pushers or different types of drug use among African American tenants, or if it reflected some other process.

Substance abuse also shaped the cognitive effects of housing. Although substance abuse was a risk factor for housing loss in both types of housing, it had a particularly damaging effect on the prospect for cognitive benefit. Those diagnosed as lifetime substance abusers at baseline declined in executive functioning in independent apartments and failed to reap the gains associated with group living. The stimulation of the social environment simply did not seem able to override the effects of the substance abuse.

Housing preferences were another baseline risk factor whose effects varied in interaction with those of housing type. Consumers who preferred to live independently when clinicians recommended support were at high risk of housing loss and cognitive decline in either type of housing. Those who instead preferred group living at baseline but were judged by clinicians as ready for independent living did even better when they were assigned to group homes. The group living environment seemed to be most beneficial for those who were most able to respond to others and develop their capacities. This beneficial effect of the group living experience even extended during the decades after the project concluded, as those who had sought to live in a group home and did so during the project were subsequently able to spend more time living independently.

However, the benefits of group living were not available to those who left that housing soon after entering, and those who strongly preferred independent living were more dissatisfied and likely to leave if they were placed in group homes. Housing preferences can not be ignored if housing placement is to have the optimal value. Instead, assessing housing preferences and comparing them to clinician housing recommendations could inform different strategies of housing preparation and housing placement for particular consumers.

The Multisite Data

Findings from the other McKinney projects help to clarify the limits to generalizability of the Boston findings. The Baltimore project provided more evidence of the importance of housing provision. The Critical Time Intervention project in New York City demonstrated that intensive engagement with tenants within six months after they moved into housing could reduce considerably their risk of housing loss. It is possible that such an approach would yield increased housing retention in our independent apartments. Overall, the other McKinney projects indicated the importance of services—but only in the context of having housing available.

The five McKinney projects also suggested an important interaction between substance abuse and service needs. The pattern of results in the projects indicated that homeless persons who are dually diagnosed with substance abuse and serious mental illness are less likely to lose the housing they receive if extra services are provided, whereas those who do not have the additional diagnosis of substance abuse can maintain their housing with less support. However, if the goal is maximizing placement of homeless persons with serious mental illness in housing, it is those who are not dually diagnosed who benefit the most from additional support services. Both patterns suggest that services matter for homeless persons with serious mental illness but that the impact of services varies with social context (housed or unhoused) and diagnosis (dual or single). The environment mattered for residential stability but in a way that varied with the type of person.

Theoretical Implications

The diverse influences on human behavior are inevitably intertwined, notoriously difficult to distinguish, and undeniably of different appeal to the self-interest of different people at different times and in different places. It is not hard to understand why dispositional and situational explanations underlie opposing theories of human behavior and have enthusiastic supporters as well as fervent detractors. What does the history of the Boston McKinney Project add to this ongoing debate?

Disposition or Situation

Random assignment of our project participants to group homes or independent apartments together with careful measurement of participant housing preferences and clinician housing recommendations allowed us to distinguish the effects of the housing situation from the dispositions that might otherwise have determined which housing situation participants entered. It was because of these methodological features that the beneficial effect of group homes was clear. But this methodology also enables us to demonstrate what we would have seen if we had not used random assignment.

The panel on the right in figure 11.3 shows the difference between the two housing types in housing loss for those who moved into the type of housing they preferred at baseline. In other words it compares housing loss for those in group homes who preferred at baseline to live in a group home with housing loss for those in independent apartments who had strongly preferred to live in an independent apartment. The difference is dramatic: none of the consumers who preferred group homes lost housing if he or she was placed in group homes, whereas more than one-third of those who had preferred to live independently lost their housing if they were placed in an independent apartment.

In other words had we compared rates of housing loss in our two different housing types in a system in which consumer preference determined housing placement, we might have concluded that the housing situation had a very large effect. By contrast, the left panel of figure 11.3 shows that if all participants had moved into the housing type the two clinician raters

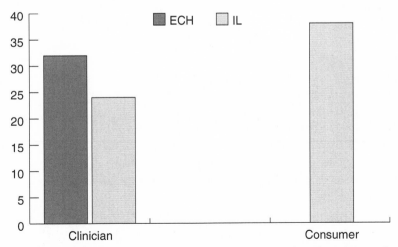

Figure 11.3. Housing loss if consumers receive housing based on their preference or on clinician recommendation, by housing type received. Note: Clinician ECH $N = 28$, IL $N = 25$; consumer ECH $N = 18$, IL $N = 42$.

had recommended for them, we would have observed almost no effect of housing type.

Our conclusions about a situational effect would have been mistaken in both cases. In the first, "preferences regime," the difference in housing loss between the two housing situations was due largely to differences in the dispositions of those who moved into each type, whereas in the second, "clinician knows best regime," the apparent lack of difference in housing loss between the two housing situations was largely due to the clinicians' dispositions cancelling out the effect of the housing itself.

So we have found that in the circumstances and with the people we studied, situation—the environment—made a difference in behavior, but it was a difference that could be magnified or reduced by disposition—the individual. We also learned that dispositions—housing preferences, that is—could change over time in response to the situation—that is, the type of housing experienced. Both findings highlight the complexity of the relation between disposition and situation, their intrinsic interdependence, and the importance of studying their influence over time. Both paths of influence represented in figure 1.1 played an important role in shaping our project participants' behavior.

Medical and Sociological Perspectives

Our findings also suggest that the contrast apparent in medical and sociological perspectives on mental illness specifically, and human behavior generally, is often unduly exaggerated. The continuing problems of alcohol and drug abuse in the McKinney housing reflect the deeply rooted biological and psychological effects of addictive processes on motivation, not the transient effects of situational deprivation. Nor can the ongoing risk of psychiatric hospitalization and the continued displays of psychiatric symptoms be explained as a response to enduring situational difficulties. Individual problems having medical explanations could not be resolved simply by changing the situation an individual experienced, even when that change was as dramatic as moving from a shelter to permanent housing. A purely social explanation seems very inadequate.

Medical explanations also fall short as explanations of the behavioral changes observed in the McKinney project. It was social process that stimulated cognitive gains in the group homes and its lack that led to cognitive deterioration in the independent apartments. The opportunity to engage with peers, the encouragement to solve problems collectively, experiences of social exchange in pursuit of collective objectives represented a radical situational change from the lonely pattern of "struggling along" in the shelters. These features also distinguished the situation in the group homes from that in the independent apartments, and this situational difference, in turn, influenced individual behavior. As we have seen, it was not a difference that mattered for all participants, and it was not a difference that influenced all aspects of behavior, but it was enough of a difference to have a profound impact on many participants' patterns of thinking and acting in the community.

Neither biological vulnerabilities and capabilities nor situational constraints and opportunities influence human behavior in isolation. Both interact with each other's influence and in turn change in response to that influence. A biopsychosocial model recognizes the limitations of both biological and sociological explanations of human behavior. Individual psychology in some respects expresses the mutual influence of these intersecting forces: individual perspectives on and adaptations to the social world in part reflect biologically rooted expressions of perception, mood, and thought and in part the enduring effects of past situations that are retained in memory and fixed in behavioral patterns. It is only through melding these perspectives that researchers can hope to account for divergent responses of similar individuals in different situations as well as for the wide variation in different individuals' responses to similar circumstances.

The rapid progress of genetic and neurobiological research into severe mental illness has led most medically oriented researchers to recognize the limitations of these approaches and the influence of the social environment on both the expression of genes and the functional consequences of neurobiological processes. Sociologists have been slow to recognize the converse importance of taking medical factors into account when attempting to identify situational influence.

Social Interaction

Jonathan Turner's (1988) model provides a useful framework for interpreting project findings about social interaction (see fig. 2.2). Motivational processes had a major influence on the patterning of social interaction throughout the project. Those who were interested in group home living were expressing an openness to support and social interaction that led to improved housing retention, particularly if they were placed in group homes; after the project was over, they also gained in residential independence. By contrast, a strong desire to live independently expressed for many participants rejection of services and disinterest in social support. When this preference was at odds with clinicians' evaluation of need for support, the result was a higher risk of housing loss. However, a strong desire for independence also led to a higher rate of housing loss when participants were assigned to the group homes that they had wanted to avoid. There was also some evidence in the ethnographic notes of prejudicial attitudes shaping interaction between some white and African American tenants. In these ways, participant motivation shaped subsequent experiences in social interaction.

Interactional processes also influenced motivation, in the type of reciprocal process highlighted in Turner's model. Participants who moved into group homes with a strong desire for independence became, over time, more oriented to group home living. Their experiences in interaction changed their motives.

The interactional processes within the group homes were in a state of flux throughout the project. As predicted by Mills (1984), physical proximity and frequent contact facilitated the development of a rich social dynamic in the group homes. However the goal of developing strong group cohesion within the group homes was only partially achieved, and even then only at some times. The lack of homogeneity of members' interests and outlooks was one of the factors that diminished the development of more intense social interaction (Festinger, Schachter, and Back 1950). Lack of commitment to shared group goals also hindered social interaction and undermined the possibility of achieving the more intense social relations characteristic of "intentional communities" (Kanter 1972).

The failure of tenant meetings and other types of empowerment-oriented activities to structure new stable patterns of social interaction was in part due to the preexisting patterns of professional control that shaped both tenant and staff expectations. In general and with some notable exceptions, house staff did not become sources of "bridging" social capital that might have helped to connect the tenants to the larger community and create more accepting reactions to the empowerment model (Almedom 2005). In turn, the resulting relatively low level of social structure in the group homes throughout much of the project often failed to stimulate positive social interaction among tenants.

Organizational Change

The Boston McKinney Project was also an attempt to change the social organization of group homes. What began as traditional group homes with full-time staff and 24/7 staff control were to "evolve" into tenant-run collectives that required no permanent staff presence or direction and would no longer be classified as group homes for disabled adults. During this evolutionary process we had initially expected that tenants would increasingly assert their authority over staff, decide when staff were no longer needed, and, finally, depend only on themselves to seek assistance from clinicians in the larger community on an as-needed basis. In other words, they would begin to function as well as others in the community.

To some extent the failure of this attempt at organizational change can be attributed to the particular characteristics of the group home residents; challenges created by substance abuse, mental illness, and cognitive and social deficits made it difficult for tenant control to "evolve" in the way that had been envisioned in our grant proposal. But there were also larger organizational processes at work. The standard group home model of staff responsibility and control is broadly institutionalized in the mental health service system and reflects the even more widely institutionalized model of professional control. That institutional pattern is reflected in the expectation of staff control within group homes and in common beliefs in the incompetence of group home residents. To challenge this pattern is to undermine vulnerable employees' economic security and self-reinforcing social patterns.

It is possible to shift from hierarchical to egalitarian control within organizations, at least for a period of time, when the employees, volunteers or clients who are meant to assume control have experience with structured group process, abilities in leadership, and supportive ties in the larger community. But when these resources are lacking, the pressure to keep things as they are can overwhelm efforts at change. Without a clear set of goals around which to achieve ideological unity, without high levels of involvement by often withdrawn tenants, without a structure that clarified participants' roles, without clearly defined tactics for stimulating change, the group homes failed to develop an organizational configuration that was conducive to tenant control.

The disadvantages faced by the McKinney group homes are clear when their key dimensions—goals, involvement, structure, and tactics (the "GIST" of these organizations [Schutt 1986])—are compared to the features of the utopian and retreatist groups that have fared somewhat better—and survived longer—in attempts to build face-to-face communities (Vaisey 2007). The successful groups were united by a clear sense of purpose, *goals* that members generally agreed on. They maintained high levels of *involvement* among members, often through activities that kept members engaged throughout the day as well as during meetings. In most cases the group's *structure* was designed to minimize the status differences between leaders and members and to ensure significant responsibilities for members. They adopted *tactics* for achieving their group's goals that were practiced regularly, such as ceremonies, craft rituals, or political activities.

In these and other respects the GIST configuration of these organizations was conducive to building and maintaining a viable community. And in all of these respects the GIST configuration of the ECH homes was lacking.

In spite of the internal reinforcing logic of organizational elements that creates coherent ideal types—whether bureaucratic (Weber 1947) or participatory democratic (Rothschild-Whitt 1979)—organizational processes cannot be understood apart from the environment on which organizations depend for resources and to which they direct influence attempts. The successful communitarian organizations managed their relations with their environments much more systematically than did the McKinney group homes. Successful communitarian organizations minimized disruptive influences from their social environment by restricting entry to members who supported the organization's goals and who shared key characteristics with other members. The McKinney group homes could do nothing of the sort. It was only as they developed procedures for expelling tenants who could not conform to group expectations that they took steps toward the more homogeneous membership composition that characterizes successful communitarian organizations. Successful communitarian organizations also limited contact with persons in the larger social environment, whereas in contrast, participants in McKinney group homes at times brought into the homes drug pushers and users, men seeking sexual liaisons, and other individuals who disregarded group rules.

Successful communitarian organizations reduced the influence of the larger institutional environment of other organizations and public agencies by keeping these bodies at arm's length. Physical isolation was often supplemented by substitution of home-grown foods and home-made goods for dependence on the external economy. Embedded in a matrix of state and federal regulations and oversight, located in established communities that provided necessary goods and services, the McKinney group homes could not even begin to remove themselves from this larger institutional context. Building community within the group homes thus contradicted the established norms and roles in the larger communities outside of them.

So the empowerment effort in the Boston McKinney Project failed to transfer control from staff to tenants in a lasting or comprehensive manner. Tenants' difficulties in feelings and functioning, problems in social relations, particular problems created by substance abusing or otherwise difficult tenants and house guests, as well as constraints imposed by institutional rules and regulations—each hindered the evolutionary process.

Yet in spite of their failure to achieve the goal of self-management, the heightened social interaction and opportunities for decision making and leadership created by the attempt at empowerment benefited many tenants. For some, just having regular staff or peer contact encouraged exercise of social and cognitive capacities; for others, staff and peers helped to inhibit substance abuse and encourage more attention to more constructive pursuits. As one participant in the long-term interviews remarked, "It taught me how to communicate, how to deal with people."

Community

Community is one of sociology's most enduring contributions to explanations of human behavior. Whether describing social dysfunctions stemming from the loss of traditional communities in modern industrial society or identifying the value of community ties in reducing rates of crime, sociologists have called attention to the importance of community processes for individual well-being. Heeding this call, police departments have developed community policing programs, corporations have worked to support team spirit, and urban planners have turned away from building mass housing to designing vibrant communities.

Recognition of the value of traditional communities has competed with identification of the virtues of modernizing processes that result in further individualization. Emile Durkheim's compelling description of the tight bonds achieved through mechanical solidarity—based on likeness among neighbors within face-to-face communities, or *Gemeinschaft* relations, in Tönnies' terminology—is complemented by his argument for the effectiveness of organic solidarity—the bonds among people due to their different but interdependent functions in modern societies; *Gesellschaft* relations.

It is no wonder, then, that calls for direct placement of formerly homeless mentally ill individuals into independent apartments so that they are indistinguishable from other autonomous individuals "in the community" sometimes proceed without recognition of the importance of those individuals' engagement in an identifiable and viable community of peers. Although the Boston McKinney Project did not identify one clear path to building such a community, it provided many examples of the value of starting on such a path.

Policy Recommendations

The many benefits of the empowerment process and the changes made in efforts to move it along suggest that a more carefully planned approach to empowering consumers built on the lessons of the McKinney Project would have considerable potential for success. Offering services to control addiction, including self-help programs, and encouraging a culture of sobriety in each home would be an important first step (McCarty et al. 1993; Brunette, Mueser, and Drake 2004; Kertesz et al. 2009, 520). Limiting substance abuse was the explicit recommendation of many former Boston McKinney participants interviewed in the 2008 long-term follow-up. One participant advised, "Give the residents less freedom regarding their drastic behavior." Another wished that "I hadn't been on drugs." A non-abuser recommended screening clients better, so as to permit only "people who won't bring others down."

More systematic evaluation and preparation prior to housing entry could generate positive orientations among future tenants and social ties between them that could launch group homes in an initially positive direction (Wong et al. 2006, 78).

Although the failure of the empowerment process led to many frustrations with tenants and recriminations among staff—and, in some homes, abandonment of the empowerment effort—it also led, through a trial-and-error process, to identification of some of the prerequisites for success. A constructive and clear role was needed for house staff; substance abuse had to be controlled with a consistent policy; prospective tenants had to have some capacity for autonomous functioning; a plan was needed for the allocation of chores; some type of incentives were required to ensure meeting attendance and contributions to the group.

Planning activities to engage house staff with tenants could stimulate more enduring and supportive social relations and provide the basis for an "early warning system" that would identify those needing more support before they lose their housing. Creating daytime activities, including vocational opportunities, would increase self-reliance and reduce lethargy. Developing individualized plans that take into account tenant housing preferences, clinician insights, medical symptoms, available resources, and external opportunities could increase considerably the value of housing experience (Wong et al. 2006, 79).

But program development cannot be based simply on the recognition of the multiple issues that should be taken into account nor even on the value of tailored approaches for different persons. Thorough assessment of the skill level, support needs, and support preferences of housing residents is only an essential starting point for effective housing programs (Wong et al. 2006, 78). Using such thorough assessment procedures in *Homelessness, Housing, and Mental Illness* within the context of randomized assignment to independent and group living has led to the additional insight that individual living skills and support needs often do not match support preferences.

If consumer preferences are valued as the fundamental bedrock for housing decisions, then the errancy of housing preferences as a guide for maximizing housing retention can be ignored. From this perspective consumers should be given the "dignity and right to fail" (Posey 1988 [1992], 22). This ideological position permits no empirically based argument. But our findings demonstrate that the assumption that every homeless person with mental illness wants to live independently is wrong. If persons who actually would prefer more support than can be provided in an independent apartment setting are nonetheless placed in an apartment, they are more likely to become homeless again. A policy commitment to providing housing based on consumer preferences should at least include a methodological commitment to measure housing preferences rather than assume that independent living is the universal preference.

Once it is recognized that housing preferences can change with experience, it becomes harder to justify the presumption that housing should be provided based solely on expressed preference at the time housing is available. Many McKinney participants who lived in our group homes increased their preference for group living as a result of that experience. Some were pleased to continue to live in that type of environment after the project ended; others decided they were ready to live on their own after the group home experience. In any case, many felt that the group experience had been beneficial in spite of their initial desire to live independently.

Assessing carefully consumer housing preferences and comparing them to the housing recommendations of informed clinicians is an important first step in maximizing the fit between individuals and the type of housing they are offered. The assumption that the housing preferences people express when they are homeless should be the basis for the type of permanent housing to which they are assigned does not account for the shift in preference after prospective tenants experience a socially stimulating and generally supportive group housing environment. Because this change in how people understand their own needs is also associated with improved housing stability and executive functioning, encouraging reexamination of preferences could be considered to be an important element in a responsible housing policy.

Because we know that preferences are malleable and also that they do not identify the type of housing that is most likely to be beneficial for many of the persons seeking housing, it reduces the potential for residential stability to place persons in a particular type of housing without first offering them some housing options and developing a tailored support plan based on the type of housing into which they move and their vulnerability to subsequent housing loss (cf. Chamberlin and Schene 1997; Lovell and Cohen

1998). Consumers who are interested in staff and/or group support are expressing an openness to help that should be the first step in developing an appropriate support network. Consumers who reject any type of peer or professional support are often indicating an unwillingness to accept help or to acknowledge personal difficulties. They should not be placed directly in independent apartments without a careful discussion of their housing preferences and an effort to agree on a meaningful support plan. Mental health agencies should offer an array of alternative forms of service and social supports to those who refuse to consider living for any period in staffed, group homes.

Recent research on a wide variety of housing programs has identified multiple options for enhancing support. In group homes active staff engagement and working with tenants to reduce substance abuse are critical for those who are not ready to live on their own (Fields 1990; McCoy et al. 2003). The Copenhagen Housing Services have developed a successful system of small group homes for mentally ill persons with staff ratios of about 1:3 that encourage resident independence in much the way that was attempted by the Boston McKinney Project (Middelboe 1997). Some former Boston McKinney participants also recommended increasing staff engagement, specifically:

> Have staff get to know clients more, do more than chores and paperwork and telling clients "to do this or that."

Social support can also be provided by community volunteers, who may offer friendship and help with community interaction (Pace and Turkel 1990). Trained landlords can provide instrumental and social support to those living in any type of housing (Kloos et al. 2002), as can peer support programs like multiservice community centers and drop-in centers (Platman 1982; Harp 1990; Ridgway and Zipple 1990a). One former Boston McKinney participant recommended having more staff provide help with medications. These community- and peer-based approaches are similar to those emphasized in the "therapeutic community" movement, in which nonclinical staff participate actively in a residential program alongside mentally ill clients, encouraging and modeling behaviors and developing supportive social relations (Bale et al. 1984).

The most important policy recommendation from the analysis in *Homelessness, Housing, and Mental Illness* is to give community processes their due in housing programs. To expect individuals who have been alienated from established communities for long periods of time to become integrated into a new community because they have been placed in an independent apartment is to ignore the difficulty of reintegration and the value of social support. Policies that presume direct placement into independent apartments ignore deficits in social connections at their peril, with the predictable result being rates of long-term housing loss of 40 to 50 percent. Strategies that expect placement in a community setting to lead to participation in a socially integrating "rhythm of daily life" fail to acknowledge the social complexities of communities, in which opportunities for social support and productive activity often compete with supports for drug abuse and other forms of self-destructive behaviors and the experience of social isolation.

Becoming a contributing member of a meaningful community is a product of collective effort (Carling 1995, 42). Identifying the importance of this effort, setting it in motion, and nurturing its success are vital elements of a successful housing policy. Integration within the larger community will only succeed in the context of participation in a meaningful social community. Neither group homes nor independent apartments provide a simple path along which persons who have been homeless and diagnosed with serious mental illness can return to the community. Building social ties, overcoming social isolation, learning to identify what is needed for sustained community living, and engaging with others to meet these needs are the keys to successful community living.

Research Methods

We see the social world through our own set of lenses—lenses that are shaped by our past experiences and current situation as well as by nature and perhaps an optician. Someone who grew up in a mansion will view a small two-bedroom house differently than someone who grew up in a crowded apartment. An old home may be a turn-off until a realtor's fast-paced sales talk helps a prospective buyer envision the "great potential" in a fixer-upper that is "priced to sell." If we are lucky, what we see will be what we get, but it will not be just what others see—and the feelings it evokes in us are unlikely to be fully shared by others who have not been exposed to the same influences.

We can communicate about our perceptions when we share a language and a culture, overlaid on our common humanity. Because of this common framework, when we engage in everyday discourse and public dialogue, we use unspoken rules for interpreting what other people mean when they describe an experience or a feeling and for imagining what we might have seen and felt if we had been in their shoes. But this natural process only takes us so far. When we seek to learn the perceptions and experiences of a large number of people; when we probe the niceties of social convention to figure out what people really mean; when we try to figure out why people behave as they do, ordinary conversation and everyday observation come up short. For these more ambitious purposes we need to use systematic research methods (Schutt 2009).

Homelessness, Housing, and Mental Illness describes who participated in the Boston McKinney Project, what they wanted, and what they did; it evaluates whether living in group homes or independent apartments influenced participants' desires and actions; it explores how participants interacted with each other and whether they differed in their responses to the same stimuli. For these reasons and more, our project required systematic research methods—not just one method, such as conducting a survey, but multiple methods: different methods to answer different questions and to provide alternative perspectives on similar questions. This appendix introduces these different methods, explains why we used them to answer particular research questions, and acknowledges some of their limitations.

This appendix thus lays the foundation for a balanced perspective on the findings in *Homelessness, Housing, and Mental Illness*. On the one hand the multiple methods we used facilitated investigation of very complex social processes with unparalleled rigor. Some of the findings I report run contrary to currently accepted wisdom, reflecting insights that were possible only because our funding and research arrangements permitted us to use some of the best social science methods available for answering the particular questions we asked. In order to determine the degree of confidence that can be placed in our conclusions, whether in comparison to research results reported by others or in relation to preexisting beliefs, it is essential to understand what our research methods were and why we chose them. On the other hand, however, even the best and most appropriate research methods do not entirely solve the problem of perspective. When we use social science methods, we see farther and probe deeper than we do in our everyday lives; however, no method—whether used alone or in combination with others—gives us perfect vision or infallible insight. Every method we use for investigating the social world will overlook some processes, distort some realities, and confuse some issues. Therefore, this appendix aims to support a critical as well as an appreciative understanding of our project's findings.

Research Questions and Study Hypotheses

Specifying both research questions to answer and hypotheses to test is essential before deciding on methods of investigation. Our primary research question focused attention on the value of group living as compared to independent living: What are the differential outcomes for individuals randomly assigned to independent living or to a meaningful, empowering group-living alternative? We also questioned whether the two different types of housing might have different effects for different types of residents (Goldfinger et al. 1990, 54–55).

We captured our best expectation about our primary question in a formal hypothesis—a tentative proposition about the relationship between two variable phenomena:

> Client outcomes will be more favorable in evolving consumer households than in independent housing.

In other words we believed that the effort to develop a community within our group homes would maximize the benefits of living in the larger community.

We also posed research questions about housing preferences. What is the relationship between housing preference and housing outcome? Would individuals do better if they received the type of housing they wanted? Would they do better if they received the type of housing clinicians recommended? What were the characteristics of clients who favored more independent housing? We posed one specific hypothesis about preferences:

> Client outcomes will be more favorable when both client and clinician choice match the housing obtained than when there is a discrepancy.

Several additional research questions focused on the process of evolution of resident control that we anticipated in the ECHs. What is the process by which group homes can evolve into independent consumer-operated households? What is the natural history of the unfolding of the transition of control and decision making from paid staff to resident consumers?

The research design for our project provided methods with which to answer each of these research questions and to test our two hypotheses. The specific methods we selected also indicated how we would attempt to meet three challenges confronted in social science research: how to identify effects of our treatment (housing type); how to measure the phenomena we considered important (from housing preferences to cognitive functioning); and how to generalize our findings to a larger population (beyond the specific homeless persons we studied).

The Identification of the Effects of Housing Type

The "treatment" that was the focus of our experiment was the type of housing that participants received. The two types of housing to which our participants were assigned represented the two major alternatives used by mental health agencies: staffed group homes and independent apartments. As each group home came "on line" at the start of our project—as quickly as properties could be purchased and rehabilitated to meet codes for disabled persons' housing—they were staffed with several employees during the day and at least one every night and on weekends. Between six and ten former shelter residents then moved into the homes for the project period of eighteen months, with the promise that this would remain their permanent housing as long as they wished to remain and they continued to abide by two basic rules: no illicit drugs in the house and no smoking in bed. Special features planned for our group homes are described below.

Our independent apartments were conventional efficiency units and single-room occupancy (SRO) rooms for single residents in larger buildings that housed other mental health agency clients but provided no special services. All project tenants in both housing types received intensive case management (ICM) services ranging from brokering income benefits to counseling throughout the project. The ICMs were all Master's-level clinicians who had an average caseload of eight, met with clients weekly or more often as needed, and were supervised by a senior project clinician. All tenants had to contribute 30 percent of their income (government benefits) for their housing, but otherwise they did not have to pay rent.

Figure A.1 displays our project's basic experimental design. Participants were recruited from three transitional shelters and screened for safety (more on these features later) and then assigned by a random process (represented by the formatted "R" in figure A.1) to move into either the project's homes or into the independent apartments. Participants' backgrounds

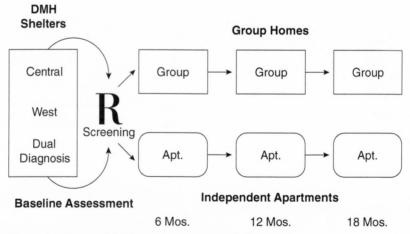

Figure A.1. Boston McKinney Project research design.

and orientations were assessed at the point of recruitment (the project's "baseline") and then every six months until they had spent eighteen months in the project. Data on residential status were collected throughout the project.

Study participants were not required to participate in psychiatric treatment, although they were encouraged by their case managers to use clinical services at their community mental health center (CMHC) that were appropriate to their needs and level of functioning. Through their CMHC, each participant had available to him or her an array of treatments—medication clinics, individual and group therapies, day programs for rehabilitation and social day activities, and, if needed, crisis intervention and hospitalization at the CMHC.

The Problem of Selection Bias

We used experimental methods—assigning individuals randomly to two groups—in order to lessen the problem of selection bias. Selection bias is a technical name for a very common problem in everyday methods of figuring out the social world. When people decide what room to rent or house to buy, they have made a selection. If they have the necessary resources, meet the requirements, and have a bit of luck, they will then realize their preference by renting or buying the selected house. Perhaps they then live happily ever after. But was the new housing responsible for their happiness, even for a bit of it? Would they have lived happily ever after if they had chosen *different* housing? What about people who moved into different housing and who were then unhappy? Does their level of happiness differ because of the different housing *or because they were unhappy people to begin with?* If we ask everyone who moved into one type of housing (let's call it "Type A") and find that they are happier than those who moved into another type of housing ("Type B"), could the greater happiness of the Type A people be due to their having been more happy all along? How can we tell whether the happiness difference between Type A housing and Type B housing is due to the type of housing or to the type of people who "selected" to move into it? That is the problem of selection bias (Schutt 2009, chapter 6).

The problem of selection bias is compounded for persons like those in our project whose housing placements can be determined by others. In many mental health agencies clinicians determine whether service consumers "need" to be placed in a staffed group home or are instead "ready" to live in their own apartments. If clinicians determine in this way the type of housing received by all service consumers, those living in staffed group homes will necessarily differ from those living in independent apartments. If the consumers living in staffed group homes do more poorly than those in independent apartments, we will not know whether it is because of their group home experience or because they were doing more poorly when they moved in. We cannot begin to answer this question until we overcome the problem of selection bias.

The selection bias problem is even more complicated when the type of housing that service consumers receive is shaped by both their own residential preferences and clinicians' recommendations, as well as by such other factors as housing availability. In order to figure out whether the type of housing itself makes a difference in how people do, we have to take account of many influences on housing placement—without being sure that we have identified all the possible influences and without knowing how important each influence is (Van Putten and Spar 1979).

Randomization is the primary method used to reduce the problem of selection bias (Schutt 2009, chapter 7). In a randomized experiment, when two treatments (housing types, in our project) are being compared, nobody who is eligible for the housing can choose the type of housing that she or he receives, nor can clients' clinicians choose their housing for them, nor are housing assignments influenced by age, gender, ability to pay, or any other individual characteristic. So if there is no "selection" of certain people for one type of housing or the other, there can be no selection bias. What determines the type of housing people receive is a coin toss (or random numbers generated by a computer). Assignment to housing type is based solely on chance, so that nobody's preferences or personal characteristics have anything to do with the selection.

If a random assignment process is strictly followed, the characteristics of people in the two types of housing will be more and more similar as more people are assigned to housing. Of course we cannot be 100 percent certain that a difference we subsequently find between our two groups is not due to selection bias—after all, the groups were equated initially by a chance process—but we can be pretty confident as long as we have a number of people in both groups. In fact we can calculate statistics that tell us just how confident we can be.

If random assignment to the two types of housing was successful, participants in the group homes and individual apartments should have been the same, on average, at baseline. If the two types of housing had different effects on participants, then those in the group homes should have come to differ in some ways from those in the independent apartments between the time their participation in the project started and the time it ended. Our comparison of participant characteristics indicated that randomization had been successful. There were no statistically significant baseline differences between the two groups on twenty-seven variables measuring sociodemographic characteristics, homelessness history, diagnosis and symptoms, social support, personality, clinician-assessed need for support, medication, and case manager-rated life skills.

The Process of Evolution

But there was more to the contrast between our two housing alternatives than their initial design. We called our group homes evolving consumer households (ECH) because we sought to transform them over eighteen months into cooperative households managed by the tenants themselves. The project hired a consultant to meet with residents weekly and encourage them to make decisions collectively. Through this process residents were to take responsibility for the tasks of daily living, including budgeting, shopping, cooking, and cleaning, as well as developing supportive relations with each other. As the residents took control, we expected they would have less need for house staff and could begin to lay them off. An ideal process would result in no house staff on site on a regular basis.

Our plan for house "evolution" made the contrast between group and independent living a moving target. We were not comparing one set treatment to no treatment, much less one drug to another drug or to no drug. Instead we had to study carefully the process of evolution in the group homes so that we would know how dissimilar our ECHs had become at any point from traditional staffed group homes.

In order to keep track of changes in our group homes, we turned to the method of ethnography. Ethnographers participate and observe in a setting for an extended period of time in order to develop a holistic understanding of participants' modes of thinking, ways of behaving, and styles of interacting in their culture (Schutt 2009, chapter 9). Anthropologists and sociologists have long used ethnography to study unfamiliar people and places without formalized expectations of what will happen or why (Schutt 2009, chapter 10). Since we did not know just how or when the evolutionary process in our group homes would occur, or even how far it would proceed or what obstacles it would encounter, we decided to have an ethnographer visit each home at least once per week throughout the project.

Figure A.2 represents the key features of our housing alternatives as well as the direction of change—or "evolution"—that we sought in the group homes. The group homes began as shared living facilities controlled by staff, whereas the independent apartments had only a single resident and

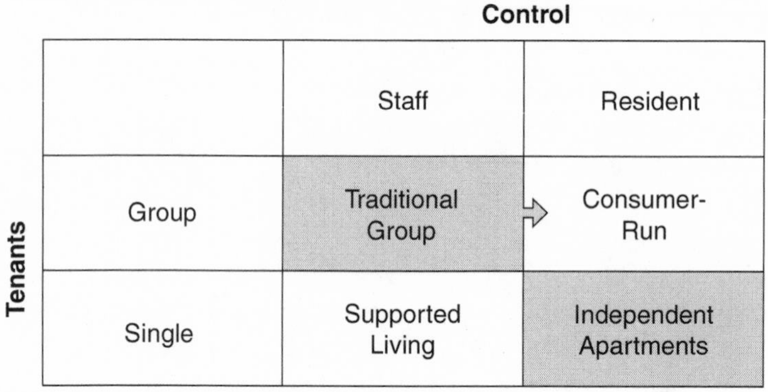

Control

	Staff	Resident
Group	Traditional Group	Consumer-Run
Single	Supported Living	Independent Apartments

Figure A.2. Boston McKinney Project housing types.

no staff on site (but case managers visiting as needed). Over time, the group homes were to continue to be shared residences, but control was to shift from the staff to the tenants. This process of change (represented by the arrow in figure A.2) was to be the primary focus of the project's ethnographers.

Limitations

Although our research design used randomization to reduce the risk of selection bias in the test of our primary hypothesis, the complexity of our study and of the analyses I report in this book require careful attention to many other issues. Several limitations must be considered.

Treatment Process

Researchers who use an experimental design to test the effect of a new treatment often refer to the need to "open the black box" of the treatment in order to understand its effect (Schutt 2009, 410–11). Our eighteen-month effort to engage housing staff and tenants in a process of change created even more uncertainty about the nature of the treatment experience than is the case when simple, structured programs are evaluated. Were benefits of our group homes due to social interaction among the residents, to activities planned by house staff, to a sense of security due to living with others, or to some other process? The ethnographic component of our research design helps us to peer into the black box of our group home treatment, but it does not provide definitive answers about how much the particular social processes identified accounted for the effects we found of living in group homes.

The ethnographic observations assume even greater importance due to the potential for differences between ECHs. Participants were not randomized to particular ECHs, so it is possible that different ECHs could have had somewhat different types of residents. Different house and neighborhood characteristics could also have created different social dynamics within them, thus possibly altering effects. However the similar number of participants assigned to each home and the inability of participants to choose their roommates reduced the potential impact of differences emerging from group composition (Mouw 2006).

Similar questions can be raised about the experience of living in the independent apartments. It was not possible to collect ethnographic data about the daily housing experiences of most IL residents, but in one apartment building having ten project participants, an ethnographer was able to observe regular meetings of tenants with a project leader. The ethnographic notes from these meetings provide further insight about the independent living experience in our project.

Attrition

Participant attrition creates another methodological challenge in program evaluation research (Schutt 2009, 238–39). If some participants drop out of a program before its conclusion, they have had less exposure to whatever the beneficial (or harmful) effects of the program might be. In order to see if the program had a beneficial effect, should these program dropouts be included when program participants are compared to those in the control group? Surely, some of the participants will have dropped out because the program was not "working" for them. If so, including only program participants who received the "full dose" of treatment biases the test in favor of finding a beneficial program effect.

In order to avoid stacking the deck in favor of finding a beneficial program effect, researchers who evaluate program impact usually use what is called an "intention to treat" analysis. That is, everybody who is randomized to the treatment group and the control group is included in a test of the program's impact, whether or not that individual remained in the treatment (or in the control group). This is the analytic approach I have taken in most analyses in *Homelessness, Housing, and Mental Illness*. Overall, 75 percent were housed at the project's end point, with an average tenure for all participants of 310 consecutive days (of a possible 548) in their original housing.

Selection Bias

The randomized experimental design equated the characteristics of those living in the ECH and IL housing, so that comparisons of outcomes between the two housing types are unlikely to be affected by any initial selection bias. However, my comparisons of the characteristics of participants who differed in housing preferences or in symptoms of depression or in levels of cognitive functioning or other orientations or behaviors use a cross-sectional analysis of the data. A cross-sectional analysis can show that people with some characteristics differ in other ways, but it cannot rule out selection bias because people were not randomly assigned to those characteristics. Substance abusers may be more likely to prefer independent living than those who do not abuse substances, but this does not mean that their preferences differ *because* of their substance abuse. Perhaps men are more likely to abuse substances and are also more likely to prefer living on their own. If this were the case, gender would be the factor that shaped housing preference; the relationship between substance abuse and housing preference would be spurious—created by the influence of gender on both of these other factors (Schutt 2009, 209).

The same problem can occur in analyses of change that do not involve the effect of housing type. Was substance abuse associated with higher rates of housing loss? Who was more likely to gain in cognitive functioning during the project? Statistical tests to answer questions like these take advantage of our collection of data at several points in time—the longitudinal feature of our data—but do not involve a simple comparison between the type of housing to which participants were randomly assigned. As a result, these tests do not have the same power as the tests of differences between the housing types.

The problem of selection bias can be lessened in cross-sectional and longitudinal analyses through the technique of statistical control (Schutt 2009, 210–11). If we think that substance abusers may differ in their housing preferences because they are more likely to be men, we can examine the relationship between substance abuse and housing preference for men only—that is, by statistically controlling for gender. We can do the same for women. If substance abuse is no longer related to housing preference when we examine the relationship separately for men and women, then we can conclude that gender explains the apparent effect of substance abuse on housing preference.

Multivariate statistical methods allow a data analyst to statistically control for a number of potential influences simultaneously. I use multiple regression analysis for this purpose in most of the chapters (Schroeder, Sjoquist, and Stephan 1986). Multiple regression analysis allows me to identify the variables that have independent effects on the various outcomes I examine—that is, the variables that are related to the outcomes net of the influence of the other variables in the analysis. It is important to realize that multiple regression and other multivariate statistical methods only control for the influence of the other variables in the model that is tested. In contrast, randomization equates all the characteristics of individuals assigned randomly to the two (or more) experimental groups. This is the primary reason that we can be more confident in conclusions about the effects of housing type than about the effects of other variables.

Multiple Comparisons

This book presents a comprehensive analysis of data collected in the Boston McKinney Project and so includes a great many statistical tests. If this analysis has been successful, the understanding that emerges about the influence of housing type, the role of preferences, the process of evolution in the houses, and the other issues I examine should be much greater than what can be learned from separate analyses of a few relationships of interest. The whole becomes much greater than the sum of its parts. But this approach also creates a statistical problem known as the "multiple comparisons" or "familywise error rate" problem.

A simple experiment may test only one hypothesis—make a single comparison—about a potential influence on the outcome of interest. For example, such a hypothesis might be, "Group home residents will have higher rates of housing retention than individual apartment residents." If we find that the rate of housing retention in the group homes is 10 percent higher than the rate in the independent apartments, should we conclude that our hypothesis has been supported? Could this much of a difference between the two housing types simply have been the result of chance? Fortunately, a statistical test can be used to estimate the probability that the difference we found was due to chance. By convention, statisticians do not conclude that a hypothesis has been supported unless the probability that it is due to chance is less than 5 out of 100 ($p < .05$) (Frankfort-Nachmias and Leon-Guerrero 2008).

But the logic of hypothesis testing becomes more complicated if we hypothesize—as our group of investigators did—that an unspecified number of "client outcomes" will be better for group home residents compared to residents in independent apartments—that is, if we make multiple comparisons. If we test for effects on 20 outcomes, we can expect one of them to meet the requirement of having been no more likely to occur on the basis of chance than 5 times in 100 (1 in 20, or $p < .05$). The more outcomes that are tested in this way, the greater the probability that some of the differences will have been due to chance alone.

When making multiple tests like this, there is no statistical method that identifies which of the "statistically significant" differences ($p < .05$) are due to chance and which reflect actual differences in the phenomena being studied. The usual response to this problem is to reduce the risk of mistakenly concluding that a chance finding actually reflects a relationship in the real world by setting a more stringent criterion, such as $p < .001$ (the possibility that a relationship is due to chance will be rejected only if the odds that it is *not* due to chance are less than 1 in 1000). There are many more specific approaches to specifying what this more stringent criterion should be (Shaffer 1995).

So when many outcomes are tested in relation to some possible influence, and when each of these outcomes was not predicted by an explicit hypothesis, the results of traditional tests of statistical significance should be interpreted with caution. However, for the reasons I explain next, I do not use a more stringent criterion in reporting the "statistical significance" achieved in each of the tests I conduct (I just report the conventional criteria of $p < .05$, $p < .01$, and $p < .001$).

My goal in this book is to present an integrated analysis of the data we collected, within an overarching theoretical model and in relation to the several different areas of theory and research that are relevant to segments of our data (on preferences, social ties, substance abuse, mental illness, cognitive and community functioning, empowerment, and housing loss). By bringing together analyses of parts of the picture into a larger whole, we can better understand the import of the findings about different outcomes. In addition, my combination of findings from analyses based on our experimental design, our longitudinal and cross-sectional data, and our extensive ethnographic data provide multiple perspectives on related issues and so supports a much more sophisticated understanding of our results. But it is important to consider critically whether the many elements of this analysis reinforce each other, and it is critical to realize that some may be chance findings that have emerged from the many "multiple comparisons" I have made. More confidence can be placed in the results of the explicit study hypotheses that I have tested than in the many other statistical tests in this book, but more confidence also can be placed in the interpretation of the particular findings by placing them within the context of my integrated analysis.

When considering the "statistical significance" of the results I present, it is also important to keep in mind that we studied everyone who was able to enroll in our project and move into the housing we provided. The usual purpose of many tests of statistical significance is to determine whether results obtained with a random sample can safely be generalized to the larger population from which the sample was selected. Because we did not draw a random sample from some larger population, this purpose of significance tests is not directly applicable to analyses of our data (see also my section on generalizability in this appendix). Other chance processes such as random measurement error could still have affected our statistical results, but the more important issue is whether our results make sense in relation to each other and in terms of the larger body of theory and research about homeless mentally ill persons that guide my analyses.

The Challenges of Conceptualization and Measurement

A shared understanding of the social world can be developed with systematic research methods only if the meaning of the terms—the concepts—in an investigation is defined (Schutt 2009, chapter 4). Researchers must also specify how they will measure these concepts. These twin processes, conceptualization and measurement, are a critical part of any research project; they are particularly challenging when an investigation focuses on multiple interrelated dimensions of the social world. The chapter titles in *Homelessness, Housing, and Mental Illness* indicate the most important concepts in the Boston McKinney Project: community, housing preferences, social relations, substance abuse, mental illness, functioning, empowerment, and housing loss. There are many details about the conceptualization (definition) and measurement of these concepts in these chapters; here, I highlight the most important conceptual controversies and introduce key measures.

The Concept of Community

"Community"—the overarching concept in this book—provides a good example of the challenges of conceptualization. Although it is a central concept in both sociology and public psychiatry, scholars in these disciplines tend to use "community" in different ways. Many sociologists view community as a form of social organization involving sustained and intimate social ties that has been considerably diminished in modern society (see chapter 2). Investigations of communities from this perspective often chronicle their demise after touting their virtues: *The World We Have Lost,* as a noted social historian (Peter Laslett 1971) put it; or *Gemeinschaft* replaced by *Gesellschaft,* as sociologist Ferdinand Tönnies (2001) observed.

By contrast, many public psychiatrists view "community" as the normative form of social organization to which clients should return after episodes of hospitalization or homelessness. From this perspective clients achieve community integration when they live in their own residences, work at regular jobs, and receive the mental health services that they choose.

Both conceptualizations of community are relevant in *Homelessness, Housing, and Mental Illness,* but they imply different research foci and measures. In the Boston McKinney Project, attempting to develop community in the first sense was the focus of the group homes. Procedures to measure such a development would focus primarily on density of social ties and feelings of closeness. Our ethnographic data provided one way to capture such aspects of social life. If such a community is achieved, individuals would make decisions in part with an eye to the needs and interests of fellow community members. Achieving community integration in the second sense would be reflected in taking on normative roles as autonomous, relatively well-functioning persons who could carry out the tasks of daily living as well as participate in such normal roles as tenant, student, employee, or consumer. Individuals who are integrated in the community in this way would make decisions, like other community members, based on their own preferences. We used multiple measures of individual functioning to evaluate community integration in this sense.

Clinical Measures

Mental illness is itself a highly controversial concept. At least since Erving Goffman's (1961) critique of mental hospitals, some sociologists have conceived of mental illness as a label that is attached to persons whose behavior or attitudes are seen as deviant and who are then stigmatized within and isolated from the larger community. Many psychiatrists instead view mental illness as analogous in some respects to physical illness. An internal process, probably reflecting biologically based defects in or insults to the brain, results in a vulnerability to mental illness (Faraone, Tsuang, and Tsuang 1999). Environmental strains may then interact with this vulnerability to generate the symptoms of mental illness. If the biological defects can be corrected, the insults to the brain avoided, or the environmental strains lessened, prevention or recovery may be possible.

These different conceptualizations of mental illness are not as diametrically opposed as they first appear (see chapter 7), but they lead to different approaches to operationalization (measurement). The psychiatric perspective is reflected in a categorical diagnosis, which we determined with the *Structured Clinical Interview for DSM-III-R—Patient Edition (SCID-P,* 9/1/89 version [Spitzer, Williams, and Gibbon 1989]). We then recoded this diagnosis to a dichotomy that distinguished schizophrenia and schizoaffective disorders from other diagnoses (major affective disorder and bipolar disorder). The *SCID-P* interviews were conducted by doctoral-level clinical psychologists, for whom interrater reliability was established at 100 percent for a subset of seven cases.

Sociologists have preferred continuous measures of symptoms when they operationalize mental illness, rather than categorical diagnoses. We used a standard continuous measure of psychological distress from Lehman's (1988) Quality of Life Index (baseline Cronbach's $\alpha = .82$). The five McKinney projects also used the Colorado Symptom Index (CSI) of Shern et al. (1994) as a common measure of symptoms of mental illness. The CSI is intended to provide a self-report indicator of symptoms of both affective and psychotic disorders and includes questions about frequency of worrying, feeling depressed, hearing voices, being indecisive, trouble concentrating, and feeling like hurting others or oneself (Cronbach's $\alpha = .88$).

We also used a structured clinical assessment—the *SCID-P*—to identify lifetime substance abuse (see table A.1). Drug and alcohol abuse during the project was operationalized as the mean of a composite index based on case manager reports and self-reports, each scored to distinguish abuse, some use, and nonuse, at the three follow-ups (Goldfinger et al. 1996b). McClellan's (1980) popular Addiction Severity Index (ASI) was our self-report measure and, combined with ongoing case manager reports, allowed us to distinguish alcohol and drug use during the project.

The other McKinney projects also assessed lifetime substance abuse with a diagnostic interview at baseline. However, in one project (the New York Street project), these interviews could not be conducted with 111 of the 168 participants. For these participants substance abuse was evaluated with a composite measure of in-project abuse based on McLellan's (1980) ASI. Individuals were coded as having a lifetime substance abuse problem if their composite ASI score indicated possible abuse during the project. Analysis of multiple measures of substance abuse collected in our project in Boston indicated that abuse appeared during the project only among those diagnosed at baseline as having a lifetime substance abuse disorder, although nondisclosure reduced the apparent rate of in-project abuse (Goldfinger et al. 1996b).

Neuropsychological Functioning

Chapter 8 distinguishes the concept of cognitive (neuropsychological) functioning from observed functioning in the community, as well as from self-reported community functioning. Neuropsychological functioning was assessed with a five-hour test battery at baseline and again at the

Table A.1 Boston McKinney Project Substance Abuse Measures and Coding

Code	Label	SCID	ASI	Observer
0	No use	No use or not threshold level for any alcohol dependence criterion; no drug use.	No alcohol or drug use indicated on any question.	No substance use indicated in logs or Life Skills.
1	Possible abuse	Any use or problems reported below abusive level.	Any use or problems reported that are below abusive level.	Any time discussing substance abuse with case manager, in abuser support group, or "rarely" or "occasionally" abuse.
2	Probable abuse	Met abuse criteria: continued use despite knowledge of adverse effects or recurrent use in hazardous situations. Or met dependence criteria: at least three of nine symptoms, at least some of which have persisted for at least one month or occurred repeatedly for a longer period.	Intoxicated at least ten days or experienced alcohol problems at least five days or bothered considerably or extremely by alcohol or drug problems or treatment is considerably or extremely important.	Used detox or rated as "often" abusing.

Table A.2   Neuropsychological Performance of Total Sample at Baseline,
Compared to Normal Population

Variable	Sample (N = 114–16) Mean (s.d.)	Mean or Score Range of Normal Population
WCST Number of Categories	2.8 (2.2)	5–6
WCST Number of Perseverative Responses	45.5 (36.8)	<10
WMS-R Logical Memory Score— Delayed (Percentile)	24.4 (23.4)	50
Auditory CPT Number of Correct Responses	19.8 (7.8)	28–30

Adapted from Seidman et al. (1997)

project's conclusion (Seidman et al. 1997, 5). With additional funding, the battery was also repeated again 2.5 years after the project ended with sixty-six (59 percent) of the original McKinney participants (Caplan et al. 2006).

Participants had significantly lower scores at baseline on each measure when compared to results obtained with samples not selected as being severely mentally ill. For the purposes of this analysis and some of our previous work, however, we focus on the three domains of neuropsychological functioning that prior research has indicated are often related to social functioning: executive functioning, verbal declarative memory, and attention (Green 1996; Dougherty et al. 1998; Kern and Green 1998; Penn, Corrigan, and Racenstein 1998; Ilonen et al. 2000; Green et al. 2000). The specific variables we use as measures of these three domains have been used often in prior research and have been the focus of our previous analyses of neuropsychological functioning in this sample: Categories Achieved on the Wisconsin Card Sorting Test (WCST) to measure executive functions, the delayed condition of the Logical Memory subtest from the Wechsler Memory Scale-Revised to measure verbal memory (LMS), and total number of correct responses out of thirty target spoken letters on an "X" version of an auditory continuous performance test (CPT) to measure sustained attention (vigilance) (see table A.2).

Community Functioning

The construct of "community functioning" itself has at times been used interchangeably with "social functioning" and at times distinguished from it (Schutt et al. 2007, 1390–91). We conceptualize community functioning as a multidimensional construct that includes social functioning as one dimension. The broad construct of community functioning was assessed with the Rosen, Hadzi-Pavlovic, and Parker (1989) multidimensional Life Skills Profile (LSP), which project case managers completed at three, six, twelve, and eighteen months after participants moved into project housing. The LSP uses thirty-nine simple questions about observed functioning to generate index scores for five dimensions: ability to self-care (involving such activities as grooming, hygiene, budgeting, food preparation); turbulent behavior (e.g., degree of offensiveness, violence, intrusiveness, and anger control) (reverse scored); sociability (friendships, interpersonal interests and activities); communication (conversational skills, appropriate gesturing, etc.); responsibility (cooperativeness, responsibility regarding personal property and medication, etc.). Case managers visited participants weekly throughout the project, but when completing the LSP, participants were instructed to focus on the participant's "general state" "over the past month." Case managers met with clients in their residences, in community settings, and on planned shopping trips and other outings, so their LSP ratings should have taken into account functioning outside as well as inside of the project residences. Each index except communication had interitem reliability coefficients (Cronbach's α) between .75 and .88; the α for communication varied between .54 and .59 over the four time points. Prior research has demonstrated high interrater reliability of the LSP between different professional caregivers, although no special tests of interrater reliability were conducted during the training period in this study.

In addition to Rosen's scale, we assessed perceived social support with Barrera's (1981) Arizona Social Support Inventory Schedule (ASSIS), administered to the participants at baseline and at six, twelve, and eighteen months (Schutt et al. 2007, 1390).

We measured self-perceived ability to manage tasks associated with independent living with the average response to nine questions about "things that people may have to do when they live in their own place," such as shopping, cleaning, and cooking. Cronbach's α was .69.

Housing Preferences and Recommendations

It has become commonplace for housing advocates to assert that homeless persons diagnosed with severe mental illness prefer independent living. But what exactly does that mean? Does "independent living" mean living without any staff or just without any roommates? Can it mean having a bed in a room by yourself but sharing kitchen facilities and a living room? Does it apply to people living with friends but without any staff? We will not make any progress in understanding residential preferences unless we can answer such questions.

Since residential preferences and clinician's housing recommendations play a special role in the analysis, I will provide more details here about their measurement. Respondents answered ten questions concerning their residential preferences, with specific questions focusing on interest in moving, interest in staff support, and interest in living with others (Schutt and Goldfinger 1996). The responses to nine of these questions were averaged to create a preference index that had a Cronbach's α of .72 (one of the ten preference questions was not correlated with the others and so was not included in the index).

Two specific index questions are used for analyses of the preference components. To assess desire for staff assistance, consumers were asked:

How would you feel about having someone to help you with the things you have a hard time managing alone?
Responses ranged from "Like the idea a lot" [1] to "Dislike the idea a lot" [5].

To assess desire for living with others as in the ECH, consumers were asked:

If you had a choice of living with six or seven other people, where you had your own bedroom, or living in a small two-room apartment, which would you prefer?
"Group living" [1] or "Apartment" [2].

These responses were then multiplied by the importance attached to this preference (scored from 1 to 3).

We measured clinician residential recommendations for the consumers' housing placements with a similar type of index (Goldfinger and Schutt 1996). Two experienced clinicians (a psychiatric nurse and a psychiatric social worker) who did not know the study participants interviewed these consumers and reviewed their clinical records before the consumers were assigned to project housing. The clinicians answered eight questions regarding the desirability of particular housing features for each consumer and also stated whether, overall, they thought ECHs (group) or apartments (independent living) would be preferable. For example,

1. How likely do you think it is that this client would be able to manage if he/she moved into independent living with intensive case management support?

Extremely likely	1
Likely	2
About 50/50 chance	3
Unlikely	4
Extremely unlikely	5

2. Overall, taking into account all of your sources of information, do you believe that this person will do better clinically living in an evolving consumer household or in an IL?

Much better in an evolving consumer household	1
Better if they stayed in an ECH	2
About equal	3
Better if they stayed in a group home	4
Much better if they stayed in a group home	5

Cronbach's α was a respectable .84.

Satisfaction

Participants' satisfaction with their housing arrangements (including, at baseline, living in a shelter) was one of our key project outcomes. We used two types of measures: satisfaction overall and satisfaction with housing (and shelter) features (Schutt, Goldfinger, and Penk 1997). One question was used to measure overall housing satisfaction: "In general, how satisfied are you with [this shelter/your housing]?" There were four response choices. Satisfaction with housing (and shelter) features was measured with an index that averaged four-point satisfaction ratings of eight features: amount of space, the staff, amount of privacy, safety, kinds of people here, number of people here, your freedom, your comfort. I also use in some analyses Lehman's (1984; 1991) life satisfaction measure: I averaged the responses to two identically worded questions at the beginning and end of his Quality of Life Interview Schedule: "How do you feel about your life as a whole?" (rated on a seven-point scale anchored by "terrible" and "delighted") (baseline $r = .59$).

Housing Loss

Homelessness is conceptualized for the purposes of this book as an experience that can occur repeatedly for vulnerable individuals rather than as a discrete state that may occur once and then be resolved. Prior research on homelessness reveals that maintaining only a dichotomous distinction between being homeless and not being homeless misses the course of homelessness as many persons actually experience it. In the words of Michael Sosin and his colleagues (1990, 171):

> So many transitions occur that the state of homelessness appears to be more a drift between atypical living situations and the street than between normality and street life. In other words, the typical pattern of homelessness seems to be one of residential instability rather than constant homelessness over a long period.

So it would be misleading to examine housing loss only at one point in time, even if that time was indeed the ending point of our project. Instead, I use the proportion of time spent homeless throughout the project as an indicator of risk of homelessness. The more nights participants spent on the streets or in shelters during the project, the more likely they would continue to experience homelessness in the ensuing months and years.[1]

During the project, we constructed a housing timeline using participants' self-report, project housing and DMH records, and weekly case-manager logs. The timeline distinguished the time spent by each participant in project housing, in other community housing, shelters, on the streets, or in institutional settings such as hospitals, detox centers, or jails. These data were compiled even for participants who left project-sponsored housing or withdrew entirely from active participation in follow-up research, allowing an "intention-to-treat" approach to the analysis (Goldfinger et al. 1999). Any client who spent any nights on the streets or in shelters during the project is coded as having experienced housing loss (Lennon et al. 2005). This approach maximizes the identification of risk of housing loss within the context of housing that was available without regard to economic resources or service stipulations (Dworsky and Piliavin 2000). We also calculated the proportion of days spent homeless out of all days not institutionalized.

In an extended residential history follow-up in 2008, Department of Mental Health records were reviewed for the McKinney participants. A total of seventy-five participants had post-McKinney housing records. From these records I then calculated postproject time spent in shelters, in independent living, in group homes, and in the hospital. Time spent living on the streets was not available in the long-term housing records, and an average of 7.8 percent of postproject time was not accounted for.

In the analysis of housing loss in the five McKinney projects, I focus on the likelihood of spending project time in shelters, rather than spending any time homeless, because most projects focused on moving people from shelters into homes (only the New York Street project sought to bring participants directly off the streets into shelters, rather than to move them directly into housing). Spending time on the streets was a very rare occurrence in all the project samples except the New York Street project.

Ethnographic Records

I use our extensive ethnographic records to describe project participants and the experience of living in the group homes. I also refer to limited ethnographic notes that were recorded on participants in one of the apartment buildings used for our IL sites. There were three project ethnographers who each observed social processes and talked with tenants and staff in two of the project's group homes (two ethnographers were engaged in one of the homes for a time). Many of the notes were recorded during weekly meetings of tenants with our project's "empowerment coordinator" (often some staff attended these meetings) or in staff meetings. Other notes reflected conversations with individual tenants or house staff, and some were based on observing social interaction and other behaviors in a house. Ethnographers visited houses weekly for several hours, although sometimes visits were more frequent, and there were some periods of a month or more when ethnographic visits did not occur in some houses. The ethnographers often included lengthy verbatim quotes from conversations and detailed reports of social interaction.

Several graduate research assistants worked with me to categorize and code these notes. We reviewed categories together and gradually refined a system for distinguishing the different topics addressed in the notes. All the notes were also cross-classified by the person(s) and the house involved. I was thus able to easily retrieve notes relevant to the topics of different chapters. However, for this book my primary method of analysis was to read through the notes for each house in chronological order in order to see how issues developed over time and to track the process of "evolution." At times I summarize patterns in the ethnographic notes, but most often I present excerpts from the actual ethnographic notes (replacing actual names with pseudonyms). It is the participants' own words, and the ethnographers' own observations, that provide the most insight into the social processes that they reflected.

Limitations

Our measurement package provided an exceptionally powerful set of tools for investigating our research participants' experiences. For example, measures based on staff observation as well as participant self-report and diagnostic interviews allow a more valid assessment of substance abuse than can be obtained with just one of these measurement approaches (Goldfinger et al. 1996b). Assessing participants' functioning with self-report measures, clinician observation, and neurocognitive tests helps to clarify the discrepant findings of prior studies that have used just one of these approaches (Seidman et al. 1997; Schutt et al. 2007). Our multiple measures of participant satisfaction allow distinguishing effects on satisfaction with housing from those on the broader concept of satisfaction with life (Schutt, Goldfinger, and Penk 1997). Our index of residential preferences allows distinguishing attitudes toward living with staff and with roommates and tracking changes in these attitudes over time (Schutt and Goldfinger 1996, 2000). Our ethnographic notes yield a rich portrait of life in the group homes that our quantitative measures could not capture (Ware et al. 1992).

In spite of the many strengths of our measurement approach, it is important to consider several limitations. Acknowledging different ways of defining the central concepts in this book and the multiple measures that we used may make the methods seem confusing and the analysis arbitrary. But such conclusions are not warranted. The social world that we investigated in the Boston McKinney Project was complex and the individuals within it even more so. From different parts of the brain that are related to different aspects of functioning—whether memory, attention, or reasoning—to different attitudes that undermine or enhance supportive social relations, we have to accept the challenge of conceptualizing and measuring in a way that allows us to begin to understand how these many parts fit together. If we overlook this complexity, we consign ourselves to one-sided perspectives and simplistic conclusions.

Some measures did not perform as we expected, apparently because they were not valid measures in our sample of the concepts they were intended to measure. One such measure was the Interpersonal Support Evaluation List (ISEL), which we selected to capture the concept of perceived social support (Cohen et al. 1985). Two of the thirty-two statements we used in this measure indicate how it was designed:

2. If I needed help fixing a radio or mending my clothes, there is someone who would help me.

Definitely true	1
Probably true	2
Probably false	3
Definitely false	4

4. When I feel lonely, there are several people I can talk to.

Definitely true	1
Probably true	2
Probably false	3
Definitely false	4

Although the ISEL was developed as a measure of social support among college students, it has been used in other research with homeless samples by me and other investigators (Schutt, Meschede, and Rierdan 1994). However, in the McKinney Project, average *ISEL* scores did not vary before and after participants moved into housing; nor did they differ between those in the group homes or independent apartments; nor show a relationship with participants' reports of the number of close friends they had. Of course one interpretation is that perceptions of social support were impervious to major differences in social relationships with others, but the lack of variability in the ISEL between those living with a small group of peers and staff and living alone or in a shelter, even after 1.5 years, makes it more likely that the statements and response choices seemed too vague to our respondents to capture their feelings.

Our measure of clinicians' perceptions of participants' ability to live alone has a very different limitation. We had two clinicians independently assess at baseline the likely ability of each project participant to live on his or her own or in our group homes (Goldfinger and Schutt 1996). The ratings by these two clinicians tended to be similar for the same project participant (baseline $r = .46$), and average response was a very good predictor of participants' ability to retain their housing. However, since we used only two clinician raters, we do not know whether ratings by others might have performed as well or more poorly.

There are also some important concepts and measures that are very relevant to our research questions but that we did not include in our measurement package—in some cases because they had not been developed or adequately tested by 1990. These concepts include negative symptoms—indicating a lack of interest in social affairs that often accompanies schizophrenia; social cognition and related concepts concerning how well people are able to perceive and understand the intentions of others; and insight—the extent of awareness of one's capacities and potential disabilities (Flashman 2004; Sergi et al. 2007).

It is also important to acknowledge that the concept of mental illness itself and thus the most appropriate way to measure such illnesses is itself an area of intense debate and considerable change (Mirowsky and Ross 2003). We used two different approaches—a structured diagnostic interview that captures the logic of the American Psychiatric Association's *Diagnostic and Statistical Manual* and two continuous symptom inventories that are commonly used in surveys about mental illness, but the results obtained with these two approaches were not consistent (Horwitz 2002). Moreover, more recent research on mental illness is leading to new ways of conceptualizing specific mental disorders and thus to new measurement approaches (Horwitz and Wakefield 2007). Our multiple measures enable me in chapter 7 to contribute to this ongoing scholarship and debate, but they cannot resolve different perspectives on the concept of mental illness.

The Prospects for Generalization

Providing housing for 118 formerly homeless persons and learning from their experiences was worthwhile in many respects, but as social scientists we also expected to use our investigation to develop a more general understanding of how people like those we studied benefit from group and individual housing. For this reason, we have to consider the prospects for generalization of our findings (Schutt 2009, chapter 5). We can justify developing implications for social theory and recommendations for public policy only if we can make a convincing case that our specific findings are generalizable to a larger population, to other places, and to other times. By the same token you can only assess the applicability of our results to homeless populations you have read about, encountered, or perhaps plan to work with if we provide information about generalizability.

We did not—and of course, could not—draw a random sample of homeless persons with mental illness from Boston, the Commonwealth of Massachusetts, or the entire United States for our investigation. We only had funds, time, and personnel with which to place eligible people into housing in the Boston area. Rather than drawing what could technically even be termed a "sample" (although I will still use that term), we studied the entire population of persons who were deemed eligible for our study and who were available for our project due to their residence status at the time we began in one of Boston's special shelters for homeless persons with mental illness (funded by the Massachusetts Department of Mental Health). So I cannot provide precise statistical estimates of the degree of confidence with which the results I report can be generalized to a larger population from which the sample was drawn (Schutt 2009, 156).

Instead, in this section I present three other types of evidence about the generalizability of our findings. First, I explain the process through which we selected project participants and describe the characteristics of those who decided to join the Boston McKinney Project. Next, I describe the four other McKinney Projects that were funded at the same time as ours to test different combinations of services and housing in other settings. In chapter 10, I use data from these projects to assess the generalizability of key findings about housing loss in our project. Finally, I describe the process I used to test for differences in effects among different segments of the Boston McKinney sample.

Taken as a whole, this information provides the basis for comparing our participants to those in other research about homeless persons with severe mental illness. Our sample was generally similar to those used in comparable research studies, but some unique features of our recruitment process shaped participants' characteristics in specific ways that must be taken into account when comparing our findings to particular other projects.

Recruitment

Our project's participants were homeless individuals with serious and persistent mental illnesses between the ages of 18 and 65, living in transitional shelters funded by the Massachusetts Department of Mental Health. All English-speaking residents of the transitional shelters who passed a safety screen were asked to participate in the project. Project staff interviewed clients who consented to participate with an initial assessment schedule. Interview results were reviewed with the Project Director and Principal Investigator to ensure that every study participant was homeless, seriously mentally ill, and had given informed and voluntary consent.[2] Potential participants judged to be at imminent risk of harming themselves or others if placed in an independent apartment were excluded and reconsidered after six months (Goldfinger et al. 1996a).

A total of 303 transitional shelter residents were screened. Fifteen individuals were excluded because they were not able to speak and understand English or because they were not mentally ill (Goldfinger et al. 1996a). An additional 110 were deemed imminently dangerous and so were not recruited; of the remainder, 156 individuals provided informed consent to participate in the study (see figure A.3).

Eligible participants entered a period of data collection, education, and training prior to housing placement, including a two-week long

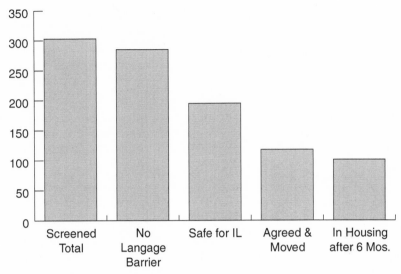

Figure A.3. Project recruitment and attrition.

standardized Housing Education Forum. Client and clinician housing preference questionnaires were also completed prior to housing placement.

Ultimately 118 individuals were randomly assigned into ECH ($N=63$) or IL ($N=55$) sites. The remaining 38 either had found alternative housing during the waiting period before placement or had refused to move into the housing to which they were randomly assigned. Of the 118 participants housed, a total of 6 were excluded from all longitudinal analyses (3 died, 1 had left the state prior to data collection, 2 were not allowed to move into the randomly assigned IL due to laws excluding convicted felons from publicly funded housing).

Sample Characteristics

Our sample had a somewhat higher proportion of women and whites and fewer veterans than most samples of the general homeless population. About one-third were women, about one-third were black (only 5 percent were members of some other minority group), and 15 percent were veterans (see table A.3). Fifteen percent were employed (in part-time or "odd jobs") at the time of the survey. Only 2 percent were currently married, and one-quarter were separated or divorced. About half had less than twelve years of schooling, whereas one in five had some college.

Table A.3   Boston McKinney Project Sample Characteristics

Variable	Statistic
Age	mean 37.6, s.d. 8.1
Gender (Female)	29%
Race (Black)	35%
Veteran Status (Veteran)	15%
Employment Status (Employed)	15%
Years Homeless	2.5
Marital Status	
Never Married	70%
Married	2%
Separated or Divorced	26%
Years of Schooling	
<12	49%
12	30%
>12	21%
Psychiatric Status	
Schizophrenia or Schizoaffective Disorder	62%
Substance Abuse or Dependence	53%
Currently Taking Medications	90%
On SSI/SSDI	84%
Ever Hospitalized	83%
Hospitalized More than 5 Times	28%
Hospitalized Within Last 6 Months	45%

On the basis of the *Structured Interview for DSM-III-R*, the primary diagnosis for 62 percent of the study participants was schizophrenia or schizoaffective disorder. Most of the sample members were current consumers of mental health services. Nine in ten were on psychotropic medication, 97 percent had been in outpatient treatment, and 83 percent had been hospitalized for psychiatric problems—28 percent more than five times and 45 percent within the last six months. About half of the sample members were substance abusers—a proportion typical of studies of homeless mentally ill persons.

Five McKinney Projects

Prospects for assessing generalizability are enhanced because the Boston McKinney Project was one of five projects funded by the National Institute of Mental Health and completed successfully in the early 1990s. Although the specific foci of the five projects varied, they recruited similar samples, used some of the same measures, and they each tested effects of some combination of housing and services. For some purposes it is helpful to compare our sample and findings to the results obtained with the total multisite McKinney sample of 896 persons (Schutt et al. 2009).

The participants in all five McKinney projects were identified as homeless and severely mentally ill, but the projects differed in the segment of the homeless mentally ill population that they recruited. The projects also differed in the cities in which they were located, in the particular housing and service interventions they tested, and in the length of their follow-up period (Center for Mental Health Services 1994).

Providing HUD Section 8 rental vouchers was the primary housing intervention in both Baltimore and San Diego so that participants in the experimental condition could obtain rental housing for 30 percent of their income (see table A.4). Thirty-four (44 percent) of the seventy-seven participants in the Baltimore experimental condition used their housing voucher, reflecting their preference for independent living. The service intervention in the Baltimore experimental group was an Assertive Community Treatment team (Stein and Test 1980), with psychiatrists, medical doctors, social workers, nurses, case managers, consumer advocates, and family liaisons. The San Diego project varied both the provision of comprehensive case management and of Section 8 vouchers in a randomized design (Hurlburt, Hough, and Wood 1996). Some participants could obtain a Section 8 housing certificate,[3] some received comprehensive case management and some received both or neither.

The New York Street Outreach study offered experimental participants a psychiatric rehabilitation program with assertive outreach and engagement activities, preferential access to a drop-in center, respite housing, and counseling (Shern et al. 1997). The New York Critical Time Intervention project (CTI) placed both experimental and control participants in community housing. Experimental participants were then assigned to a special treatment team that provided intensive services for a limited period (up to nine months). The Boston project placed experimental group participants in staffed group homes and the others in independent apartments, with all receiving case management services from a Master's level clinician.

The five projects recruited different segments of the homeless mentally ill population. The New York Street Outreach Project recruited all

Table A.4 Features of Five McKinney Projects

Project (N)	Housing	Services	Recruitment	Follow-up
Baltimore (150)	Vouchers	ACT team	Diverse settings	12 months
Boston (118)	Group (or Independent)	Case Management	MH shelters	18 months
NY CTI (96)	Varied	Transitional help	MH shelters	18 months
NY Street (168)	Varied	Drop-in center	Street	24 months
San Diego (362)	Vouchers	Intensive CM	MH referrals	24 months

Adapted from Schutt et al. (2009, 101).

participants from the street, the Baltimore project recruited from various settings, the CTI and Boston projects recruited only from service-oriented shelters for those diagnosed as mentally ill, and the San Diego project relied on referrals from mental health service providers. Persons who were identified as at high risk for endangering themselves or others if they were to live independently were excluded from the Boston and San Diego projects. Participants were interviewed at six-month intervals over periods ranging from twelve months (Baltimore), to eighteen months (Boston, NY CTI), and twenty-four months (San Diego and NYC Street). In total, the five projects enrolled 896 participants and over eighteen months (twelve months in Baltimore) retained an of 79 percent (Goldfinger et al. 1995).[4]

Characteristics of the total sample are comparable to other studies of homeless mentally ill persons (Tessler and Dennis 1989). Forty-four percent were black or Hispanic, 41 percent were white, and few were Asian American. In the New York CTI Project, however, almost all participants were minority males.

About two-thirds of the participants had had at least two prior psychiatric hospitalizations in Boston, the New York CTI study, and in the San Diego study, but this was true for only about one-third in the New York street sample. Between half (San Diego) and three-quarters (NY CTI) had a primary diagnosis of psychotic illness, between 20 and 40 percent had a primary diagnosis of major affective disorder, and between half and three-quarters had an additional diagnosis of substance abuse.

Tests for Interaction

Throughout the book, I also conduct tests of the generalizability of our findings across different segments of our entire sample. These tests involve what is called *specification* or *moderation* of effects in research methods and *statistical interaction* in statistics (Schutt 2009, chapters 7, 14). That is, I check to see if important relations in the data hold true for different segments of the sample. If group homes tend to reduce subsequent periods of homelessness compared to independent apartments, do they do so only for those persons who wanted to live in group homes? Are independent apartments beneficial for men but not for women? There are many such possibilities that affect the external validity of our findings (Schutt 2009, chapter 5). Although these tests only pertain directly to the persons in our sample, differences in findings for different groups suggest possible limitations to the applicability of our results to others.

Limitations

We could not sample randomly from the general population of homeless persons diagnosed with serious mental illness and then assign them randomly to our two housing alternatives. Our ambitious experimental research design was feasible only within the available time and resources because we were able to offer housing to persons already living in shelters funded by the Massachusetts Department of Mental Health and open only to persons deemed seriously mentally ill. This means that our project participants were not those spending most of their nights on the streets, in the city's mass shelters, or in institutions.

We can identify some of the effects of this sample limitation through comparison to the results obtained with the other four McKinney projects, since some focused on different segments of the homeless population with serious mental illness. However the conclusions from such comparisons can only be tentative and are in themselves limited. Other features of our sample reflect the study's location in Boston, which in 1990 had a lower percentage of minority-group members and persons who did not speak English as their primary language than some other cities—a limitation that was exacerbated by our restriction of the sample to those who could speak English and thus complete our interviews.

It is also important to keep in mind that we included only homeless persons who were diagnosed as having a serious mental illness by the Department of Mental Health and with our systematic assessment. The reactions of our participants to living in a group or independently are unlikely to be

comparable in many respects to others who have not been homeless and/
or diagnosed as mentally ill. Whereas most community members who live
independently are likely to establish social contacts in their community
through sources such as jobs, schooling, or their children's or partner's
friends, these opportunities were not available to our research participants
at the time of their recruitment to our project. The inclusion of many substance abusers in our sample also distinguishes our participants from
many of those in other research (Kertesz et al. 2009). For these and other
reasons any generalizations from the findings I present to other populations must be tentative.

Generalizations from our findings to other types of group homes must
take into account the unique features of the ECH model. Our group home
model created expectations of tenant control of house activities and involved frequent meetings with a grant-funded project empowerment coordinator. These conditions are unusual for group homes designed for persons
with serious mental illness, but to an extent that would vary with the specific features of other group homes. In particular, it is likely that social
processes would have differed in group homes with a planned substance
abuse treatment component.

Of course every research project has such limitations and involves such
trade-offs between the requirements of a particular research design and the
opportunities for research at a given time and place. Specifying important
aspects of our study that limit its generalizability makes it easier to take
these limitations into account when we think about the implications of the
results.

Research Ethics

No research plan is complete until procedures are designed and imple-
mented for protecting the welfare of research participants. Social scientists
do not have an absolute right to conduct research; rather, it is a privilege
they can be granted in order to increase knowledge about the human condition and to advance human welfare. In order to receive the privilege to
intrude in others' lives, researchers must ensure that they will protect research participants; the situation is somewhat analogous to the requirement that highway workers use guards and place traffic cones in order to
protect the driving public as they do roadwork.

A large infrastructure has developed in the United States in order to ensure protection for human subjects in research (Schutt 2009, 70–72). This

infrastructure includes professional associations' codes of ethical practice, National Institutes of Health requirements that researchers must adhere to as a condition of receiving federal funding, and "institutional review boards for the protection of human subjects" at every university and other organization that sponsors research. This infrastructure means, understandably, that there are a lot of "hoops" to go through in order to secure approval for conducting research involving human subjects. In the case of the Boston McKinney Project, we had to seek approval for our research procedures from the Institutional Review Boards (IRB) at Harvard Medical School, the Massachusetts Department of Mental Health, and the Massachusetts Mental Health Center. Later research activities that I initiated were reviewed and approved by the IRBs at the University of Massachusetts Boston, the Massachusetts Department of Mental Health, and the Beth Israel Deaconess Medical Center (a teaching hospital of the Harvard Medical School, which became the formal home of the Massachusetts Mental Health Center psychiatry faculty). These IRBs include a diverse group of institutional members and community representatives, and all members contribute to the review process. Like every IRB, they can only approve research that meets specific guidelines stipulated by the federal government.

Protecting participants—human subjects—in our research project required adhering to three standard requirements: avoiding harm to participants, obtaining informed consent, and maintaining privacy and confidentiality (Schutt 2009, chapter 3). Our research group believed that our research design would alleviate ongoing harm to research participants, rather than increase the risks they faced in their lives. The $10,000,000 we received from HUD for our housing alternatives allowed persons who would otherwise have mostly continued to live in shelters and on the streets to move into their own housing. The National Institute of Mental Health stipulated that this housing had to continue to be available as the participants' permanent housing even after the project ended. Of course we could not guarantee that the housing we provided would launch research participants on a new trajectory involving living in community-based housing, but our procedures created that possibility and encouraged that path.

Living in the community is not itself a risk-free proposition, however, particularly for those who have problems in their daily lives related to severe mental illness or habits developed from years of homelessness. In fact some staff in the transitional shelters from which we recruited our subjects expressed concern that some participants would return to drinking and drugs or otherwise be at risk of harm if they left the shelter environment (see chapter 3). It was a concern that we shared, since all of our participants had an equal chance of being assigned randomly to independent living rather than to one of our staffed group homes.

In order to minimize the risk of harm to participants who moved out of the shelter into independent apartments where they would be living more generally on their own, we added two features to our project plan. First, before any shelter resident could be declared eligible to join the project, he or she was "clinically evaluated as being capable of living safely in an independent apartment" (Goldfinger et al. 1990, 63). Our grant proposal explained the specifics of this plan:

> Potential subjects will be referred by shelter staff to a project housing coordinator. The coordinator will screen the subjects for behavioral or historical evidence that they might not be safely transitioned to an independent apartment. Housing coordinator decisions will be reviewed by one of the co-investigators. (Goldfinger et al. 1990, 63)

This screening process ultimately led to the exclusion of one-third of the shelter residents due to concerns about their ability to live safely on their own (Goldfinger et al. 1996a).

In addition, every research participant was assigned an intensive clinical case manager (Clinical Homeless Specialist) who was to visit the participant, wherever he or she was living, at least weekly—more often when participants' needs seemed to warrant it. These Master's-level case managers had caseloads of about ten participants, so that they were able to provide a more intensive level of support than was available through standard Department of Mental Health services.

Any interview procedure that includes questions about sensitive subjects—ours included questions about psychiatric symptoms, contact with family and friends, and childhood experiences—creates some risk that those who are interviewed will feel uncomfortable while they are being interviewed. This risk is unlikely to be more than what people experience in ongoing social interaction or during visits with health care providers, but it must be evaluated and minimized. We spelled out our plan for responding to participant discomfort in the human subjects section of our grant proposal (Goldfinger et al. 1990):

> Although unlikely [that the interview and other data collection may be difficult or uncomfortable for the subject], interviews will be halted if subjects evidence distress and continued at a later time when the trained, clinical interviewer judges it is appropriate to continue. (p. 64)

We also compensated participants for our intrusion on their time. Every participant received at least a small payment for every interview. Compensation for our full battery of interviews and neuropsychological tests was substantial.

The requirement of obtaining the informed consent of persons invited to participate in research reflects a commitment to allowing individuals to make their own decisions about their activities and welfare. In most social science research, informed consent is obtained by providing potential participants with a detailed statement about the research plans and its possible risks and benefits. Those who agree to participate are then required to sign the informed consent form to indicate their willingness to participate and their understanding of the research plans. Our consent form was signed by each participant before they participated in any research procedures. My interviews with shelter staff and guests before the project began (see chapter 3) required a separate consent form, as did my later follow-up interviews with former McKinney participants (see chapters 10 and 11).

We maintained participants' confidentiality throughout the project by keeping physical project records under lock and key and digitized records in password-protected computer files. Records of participant responses in interviews and other subject-specific records were identified by an ID number only. Participants' names and their match to the ID numbers were kept separately in a file available only to the projects' research directors. No individual participant could be identified in our research reports.

Ethnographic methods create a unique challenge for maintaining participant confidentiality. Because ethnography involves participating and observing in social interaction as it occurs, ethnographers' notes tend to contain a great deal of information about participants' statements, feelings, and actions that would reveal their identity to others involved at the time. One way to minimize the risk of violating confidentiality in ethnographic reports is to describe only general social patterns and avoid use of any direct quotes. This is the approach taken in previous articles from our project that drew on some of its ethnographic data (Ware et al. 1992).

My intensive analysis of social interaction in the group homes throughout *Homelessness, Housing, and Mental Illness* required a different approach. It is not possible to understand what happened in the houses, or to consider possible explanations for particular events, without reading detailed descriptions of what people did and having at least some examples of what people said. But providing such details about specific identified group homes would often reveal who it was who was speaking or acting, at least to former housing staff and participants.

In order to avoid providing intimate and possibly identifiable stories about participants, I have adhered throughout this book to three more specific guidelines. First, I have used arbitrary pseudonyms to refer to everyone whose name appears in the ethnographic notes that I include. Sometimes, I simply refer to individuals by their role, such as "tenant" or "house staff." Second, I have not maintained consistent pseudonyms for individual participants across chapters or even across different incidents that I describe within chapters. This greatly reduces the risk that even a former participant could determine another's identity by gradually being able to imagine the person as I describe different things that individual may have said or done. Third, I do not link the activities or statements I report to the individual houses. Since there were only seven different project group homes (six at any one time), it would be much easier for a former participant to link some actions or statements to another participant if the house in which they occurred were identified. However, every group home in our project experienced many of the same types of incidents and interchanges, so by not distinguishing the houses, I left the statements difficult to connect to particular individuals.

Of course this procedure for maintaining participant confidentiality has a cost for the analysis: I cannot "tell the story" of the development of particular houses with the ethnographic details about the houses. However, review of the notes from all the group homes indicates that the similarities in the issues they confronted far outweighed their differences. Moreover, our three ethnographers varied in their styles of observing, interviewing, and even note-taking, so that explicit comparisons of particular houses could be only partial. So maintaining the confidentiality of the individual group homes seems prudent from a methodological standpoint as well as essential from the standpoint of protecting the confidentiality of our research participants.

There is yet one other ethical issue to discuss, and that has to do with the rationale for this book itself. Although other Boston McKinney Project investigators and I have published a number of articles containing particular project findings, these articles do justice neither to the exceptionally large set of data we collected nor to the larger lessons that can be learned from the project. It is simply not in the nature of academic articles published in journals to provide a multidimensional picture of a large and complex research project. Yet if we do not present this larger picture, I do not think that we have provided appropriate value for the taxpayer dollars we received nor credited the contributions of those courageous project participants who agreed to be interviewed and observed for eighteen months. The publication of *Homelessness, Housing, and Mental Illness* thus represents a concerted effort to satisfy the ethical obligations we incurred when our project began, as well as to make a unique contribution to knowledge about some of society's most needy citizens.

Notes

1. A Point of Departure

1. All personal names and street addresses are fictitious in order to preserve confidentiality.
2. This model draws on concepts and relationships in *A Theory of Social Interaction* (Turner 1988) and in *Organization in a Changing Environment* (Schutt 1986).

2. Community in Theory

1. I am grateful to Kai Erikson for pointing this out.

3. From Back Wards to Dark Hallways

1. There has been a vigorous scholarly debate about the contribution of deinstitutionalization to explaining homelessness, since the largest decrease in the state psychiatric hospital census occurred between 1955 and 1975, before the rise in homelessness in the United States in the 1980s. In a careful analysis of national statistics, sociologist Christopher Jencks (1994, 25) highlighted the impact of further deinstitutionalization between 1975 and 1990. Subsequently, economist Brendan O'Flaherty (1996, 234) reestimated the impact of deinstitutionalization after taking into account the offsetting rise in the number of mentally ill persons in nursing homes and prisons and jails after 1972. O'Flaherty (1996, 235, 240) concluded that "after 1980 homelessness rose among the mentally ill because housing conditions got worse," not because of deinstitutionalization per se. I have sidestepped this debate because both sets of calculations rest on untestable

assumptions, and both scholars agree that substantial numbers of homeless persons with serious mental illness would have been hospitalized before the advent of deinstitutionalization. This was clearly the case for many participants in the Boston McKinney Project, almost all of whom had been treated in a psychiatric hospital but had been released as a result of stringent criteria for long-term admission (and see Rossi 1988, 146).

2. The fraction of the homeless population estimated to be mentally ill has varied among studies and investigators. Some of this variation is due to the particular population sampled, but much reflects differences in measurement procedures. Some researchers have relied on formal diagnostic procedures, whereas others have taken into account use of mental health services, self-reported symptoms, and reports of observed behavior (Rossi 1989, 145–56; Snow and Anderson 1993, 66–69; O'Flaherty 1996, 228). When Hopper (1988) removed symptoms that are inevitably elevated as a result of the situation of being homeless (such as trouble sleeping) from a diagnostic checklist, he found that the estimate of mental illness among homeless adults dropped by one-third. The Boston McKinney Project used a formal diagnostic interview to determine eligibility for the project (see the appendix) but also measured self-reported symptoms. My use of multiple measures of mental illness in chapter 7 allows more insight into the consequences of different measurement strategies.

3. The capacity of the third DMH-funded shelter was much lower. Because of disruptions resulting from a management change at the time of the shelter survey, only seven guests participated in my survey. Their responses would not be representative of the entire shelter's population, and so their responses are not included in this comparison between shelters.

7. Mental Illness

1. The SCID-based measures count the number of symptoms at both subthreshold and threshold levels for both depression and psychosis. When the psychosis measure is restricted to the number of symptoms at threshold, it is inversely correlated with the percentage of time spent in a psychiatric hospital ($r=-.20$, $p<.05$). In other words, severe psychotic symptoms appear to have been associated, on average, with less propensity to spend time in a psychiatric hospital, in spite of the instances captured in the ethnographic notes of exacerbations of psychotic thinking that led to hospitalization.

2. The number of participants diagnosed with major affective disorder in either housing type was too small (ECH = 3; IL = 11) for an interpreter to be confident in the results of the statistical test, but there was no indication of a decline in average direct service hours for this group.

8. Functioning in the Community

Larry J. Seidman, PhD, designed the neuropsychological testing component of the Boston McKinney Project, supervised the neuropsychological testing process, guided the development of project articles focused on neuropsychological functioning, and critiqued this chapter carefully. This chapter would not have been possible without Larry's extraordinary knowledge about neuropsychological functioning and his gifted mentoring of me and others involved in the Project.

1. The clinicians hired as project case managers ("Clinical Homeless Specialists") were not the clinicians who had completed the residential recommendation forms at baseline.

10. Housing Loss

1. Leff et al. (2009) did show that residential stability was higher in all three of these types of housing than in what they termed "non-model housing." However, the non-model category included all forms of "treatment as usual," such as living in shelters and on the streets as well as housing having unknown characteristics and duration. As a result no clear conclusions can be drawn about the effect of type of housing from comparisons to this amorphous assortment of living arrangements.
2. Few of the studies included in the Leff et al. (2009) analysis used randomized designs.
3. Siegel et al. (2006) used a powerful alternative to randomization, propensity scoring, but their propensity scores did not take into account residential preferences.
4. This variable is not included in the regression model presented in table 10.1. Number of symptoms of depression and of psychosis had no effect on housing and are also not included in the regression model in table 10.1.
5. Although this effect is only significant for the combined regression with all the cases, it is similar in strength in the separate regressions with a reduced number of cases.
6. In all the projects except the New York Street project, very few participants spent time on the streets, and so it was reduced shelter use that was the major indicator of a positive residential outcome.

11. Community Process in Context

1. One of the 28 McKinney participants interviewed in the 2008 follow-up did not answer the residential satisfaction questions.

Appendix

1. Wong et al. (2006, 60) found that among homeless persons with serious mental illness, shelter use was a predictor of leaving new, permanent housing. In their project 22 percent of those whom they deemed "non-positive leavers" had an episode of shelter use prior to housing loss, compared to 8 percent of those who remained in their housing (and 16 percent of those considered to be "positive leavers," although this category was not restricted to those who found a better residential option).
2. Institutional Review Boards give special attention to the procedures for obtaining consent for research from persons who have been diagnosed as seriously mentally ill, but they can allow such research if appropriate procedures are followed to

ensure voluntary participation and that risks do not outweigh benefits. With these concerns in mind, our consent procedures were reviewed and approved by the IRBs at the Harvard Medical School and the Department of Mental Health.

3. Twelve percent did not obtain a certificate because they did not complete the application process.

4. The comparison of the results of the five projects is developed in Schutt et al. (2009).

References

Abramowitz, Susan, A. A. Cote, and E. Berry. 1987. "Analyzing Patient Satisfaction: A Multianalytic Approach." *Quality Review Bulletin* 13: 122–130.

Addington, Jean, and Donald Addington. 2000. "Neurocognitive and Social Functioning in Schizophrenia: A 2.5 Year Follow-up Study." *Schizophrenia Bulletin* 44: 47–56.

Addington, Jean, Lynn McCleary, and Heather Munroe-Blum. 1998. "Relationship between Cognitive and Social Dysfunction in Schizophrenia." *Schizophrenia Research* 34: 59–66.

Addington, Jean, Huma Saeedi, and Donald Addington. 2005. "The Course of Cognitive Functioning in First Episode Psychosis: Changes over Time and Impact on Outcome." *Schizophrenia Research* 78: 35–43.

Aki, Hirofumi, Masahito Tomotake, Yasuhiro Kaneda, Jun-ichi Iga, Sawako Kinouchi, Sumiko Shibuya-Tayoshi, Ikuyo Motoki, Kazuhiko Moriguchi, Satsuki Sumitani, Ken Yamauchi, Takahide Taniguchi, Yashuhito Ishimoto, Shuichi Ueno, and Tetsuro Ohmori. 2008. "Subjective and Objective Quality of Life, Levels of Life Skills, and Their Clinical Determinants in Outpatients with Schizophrenia." *Psychiatry Research* 158: 19–25.

Allard, Mary Ann, and Paul J. Carling. 1986. *Providing Housing and Supports for People with Psychiatric Disabilities: A Technical Assistance Manual for Applicants for the Robert Wood Johnson Foundation and U.S. Department of Housing and Urban Development Program for the "Chronically Mentally Ill."* Washington, DC: National Institute of Mental Health.

Almedom, Astier M. 2005. "Social Capital and Mental Health: An Interdisciplinary Review of Primary Evidence." *Social Science & Medicine* 61: 943–964.

Alptekin, Köksal, Yildiz Akvardar, Berna Binnur Kivircik Akdede, Kemal Dumlu, Dogan Isik, Ferdane, Pirincci, Saida Yahssin, and Arzu Kitis. 2005. "Is Quality of Life Associated with Cognitive Impairment in Schizophrenia?" *Progress in Neuro-Psychopharmacology & Biological Psychiatry* 29: 239–244.

Amador, Xavier. F., Michael Flaum, Nancy C. Andreasen, David H. Strauss, Scott A. Yale, Scott C. Clark, and Jack M. Gorman. 1994. "Awareness of Illness in Schizoaffective and Mood Disorders." *Archives of General Psychiatry* 51: 826–836.

Amaral, David G. 2003. "The Amygdala, Social Behavior, and Danger Detection." *Annals of the New York Academy of Sciences* 1000: 337–347.

American Psychiatric Association. 1994. *Desk Reference to the Diagnostic Criteria from DSM-IV: Diagnostic and Statistical Manual of Mental Disorders.* 4th ed. Washington, DC: American Psychiatric Association.

American Psychiatric Association. 2000. *Diagnostic and Statistical Manual of Mental Disorders.* 4th ed. Text Revision. Washington, DC: American Psychiatric Association.

Aneshensel, Carol S. 1992. "Social Stress: Theory and Research." *Annual Review of Sociology* 18: 15–38.

Anthony, William A., and Andrea Blanch. 1989. "Research on Community Support Services: What Have We Learned?" *Psychosocial Rehabilitation Journal* 12: 55–81.

Arce, Anthony A., and Michael Vergare. 1985. "An Overview of Community Residences as Alternatives to Hospitalization." *Psychiatry in North America* 8: 423–436.

Argeriou, Milton. 1992. "Homelessness in Massachusetts: Perception, Policy, and Progress." *New England Journal of Public Policy* 8: 455–470.

Arns, Paul G., and Jean Ann Linney. 1995. "Relating Functional Skills of Severely Mentally Ill Clients to Subjective and Societal Benefits." *Psychiatric Services* 46: 260–265.

Attkisson, C. Clifford, and Rebecca Zwick. 1982. "The Client Satisfaction Questionnaire: Psychometric Properties and Correlations with Service Utilization and Psychotherapy Outcome." *Evaluation and Program Planning* 5: 233–237.

Axleroad, Susan E., and Gail E. Toff. 1987. *Outreach Services for Homeless Mentally Ill People.* Washington, DC: The Intergovernmental Health Policy Project, George Washington University.

Babin, Barry J., and Laurie Babin. 1994. "The Effect of Motivation to Process on Consumers' Satisfaction Reactions." *Advances in Consumer Research* 21: 406–411.

Bachrach, Leon L. 1986. "Dimensions of Disability in the Chronic Mentally Ill." *Hospital and Community Psychiatry* 37: 981–982.

Bahr, Howard M. 1973. *Skid Row: An Introduction to Disaffiliation.* New York: Oxford University Press.

Bahr, Howard M., and Theodore Caplow. 1968. *Old Men, Drunk and Sober.* New York: New York University Press.

Bale, Richard N., Vincent P. Zarcone, William W. Van Stone, John M. Kuldau, Thomas M. J. Engelsing, and Robert M. Elashoff. 1984. "Three Therapeutic

Communities: A Prospective Controlled Study of Narcotic Addiction Treatment: Process and Two-Year Follow-up Results." *Archives of General Psychiatry* 41: 185–191.

Banks, Kira Hudson, Laura P. Kohn-Wood, and Michael Spencer. 2006. "An Examination of the African American Experience of Everyday Discrimination and Symptoms of Psychological Distress." *Community Mental Health Journal* 42: 555–570.

Barber, Bernard. 1963. "Some Problems in the Sociology of Professions." *Daedalus* 92: 669–688.

Barnett, Peter A., and Ian H. Gotlib. 1988. "Psychosocial Functioning and Depression: Distinguishing among Antecedents, Concomitants, and Consequences." *Psychological Bulletin* 104:97-126.

Barrera, Manuel. 1981. "Social Support in the Adjustment of Pregnant Adolescents: Assessment Issues." In *Social Networks and Social Support,* edited by B. H. Gottlieb, 69–96. Beverly Hills: Sage.

Barrow, Susan M., F. Hellman, Ann M. Lovell, J. D. Plapinger, and Elmer L. Struening. 1989. *Effectiveness of Programs for the Mentally Ill Homeless: Final Report.* New York: Community Support Systems Evaluation Program, New York State Psychiatric Institute.

Bassuk, Ellen L., and H. Richard Lamb. 1986. "Homelessness and the Implementation of Deinstitutionalization. *New Directions for Mental Health Services* 30: 7–14.

Bassuk, Ellen L., and Alison Lauriat. 1986. "Are Emergency Shelters the Solution?" *International Journal of Mental Health* 14: 125–136.

Baumeister, Roy F., and Mark R. Leary. 1995. "The Need to Belong: Desire for Interpersonal Attachments as a Fundamental Human Motivation." *Psychological Bulletin* 17: 497–529.

Beal, Georgiana, Georgina Veldhorst, Judy-Lynn McGrath, Sepali Guruge, Parveen Grewal, Rosanna DiNunzio, and Jean Trimnell. 2005. "Constituting Community: Creating a Place for Oneself." *Psychiatry* 68: 199–211.

Becker, Gary S. 1996 *Accounting for Tastes.* Cambridge, MA: Harvard University Press.

Becker, Marshall H., and Lois A. Maimon. 1975. "Sociobehavioural Determinants of Compliance with Health and Medical Care Recommendations." *Medical Care* 13: 10–24.

Bene-Kociemba, Alice, Paul G. Cotton, and Roberta C. Fortgang. 1982. "Assessing Patient Satisfaction with State Hospital and Aftercare Services." *American Journal of Psychiatry* 139: 660–662.

Bennett, Michael I., Jon E. Gudeman, Lynn Jenkins, Alan Brown, and Mona Bleiberg Bennett. 1988. "The Value of Hospital-Based Treatment for the Homeless Mentally Ill." *American Journal of Psychiatry* 145 (10): 1273–1276.

Biegel, David E., and Arthur J. Naparstek. 1982. "Introduction." In *Community Support Systems and Mental Health,* edited by David E. Biegel and Arthur J. Naparstek, xix–xxv. New York: Springer.

Bigelow, Douglas A. 1998. "Supportive Homes for Life versus Treatment Way-Stations: An Introduction to TAPS Project 41." *Community Mental Health Journal* 34 (4): 403–405.

Bird, David. 1981. "Help Is Urged for 36,000 Homeless in City's Streets." *The New York Times,* March 8. Retrieved July 6, 2008 from http://www.nytimes .com/. Based on Baxter, Ellen, and Kim Hopper, "Private Lives/Public Spaces: Homeless Adults on the Streets of New York City."

Blanch, Andrea K., Paul J. Carling, and Priscilla Ridgway. 1988. "Normal Housing with Specialized Supports: A Psychiatric Rehabilitation Approach to Living in the Community." *Rehabilitation Psychology* 33: 47–55.

Blankertz, Laura E., and Ram A. Cnaan. 1994. "Assessing the Impact of Two Residential Programs for Dually Diagnosed Homeless Individuals." *Social Service Review* 68: 536–560.

Boos, Heleen B. M., André Aleman, Wiepke Cahn, Hilleke Hulshoff Pol, and René S. Kahn. 2007. "Brain Volumes in Relatives of Patients with Schizophrenia: A Meta-analysis." *Archives of General Psychiatry* 64: 297–304.

Borgaro, Susan, David L. Pogge, Victoria A. DeLuca, Lale Bilginer, John Stokes, and Philip D. Harvey. 2003. "Convergence of Different Versions of the Continuous Performance Test: Clinical and Scientific Implications." *Journal of Clinical and Experimental Neuropsychology* 25: 283–292.

Bowie, Christopher R., Abraham Reichenberg, Thomas L. Patterson, Robert K. Heaton, and Philip D. Harvey. 2006. "Determinants of Real-World Functional Performance in Schizophrenia Subjects: Correlations with Cognition, Functional Capacity, and Symptoms." *American Journal of Psychiatry* 163: 418–425.

Bowie, Christopher R., Elizabeth W. Twamley, Hannah Anderson, Brooke Halpern, Thomas L. Patterson, and Philip D. Harvey. 2007. "Self-Assessment of Functional Status in Schizophrenia." *Journal of Psychiatric Research* 41: 1012–1018.

Breakey, William R. 1987. "Treating the Homeless." *Alcohol Health & Research World* 11: 42–46, 90.

Brekke, John, D. Diane Kay, Kimmy S. Lee, and Michael F. Green. 2005. "Biosocial Pathways to Functional Outcome in Schizophrenia." *Schizophrenia Research* 80: 213–225.

Bremner, Alexander J., Peter J. Duke, Hazel E. Nelson, and Christos Pantelis. 1996. "Cognitive Function and Duration of Rooflessness in Entrants to a Hostel for Homeless Men." *British Journal of Psychiatry* 169: 434–439.

Brown, George W. 2002. "Social Roles, Context and Evolution in the Origins of Depression." *Journal of Health and Social Behavior* 43: 255–276.

Brown, Louis D., Matthew D. Shepherd, Scott A. Wituk, and Greg Meissen. 2007. "How Settings Change People: Applying Behavior Setting Theory to Consumer-Run Organizations." *Journal of Community Psychology* 35: 399–416.

Browne, Graeme, and Mary Courtney. 2004. "Measuring the Impact of Housing on People with Schizophrenia." *Nursing and Health Sciences* 6: 37–44.

Brunette, Mary F., Kim T. Mueser, and Robert E. Drake. 2004. "A Review of Research on Residential Programs for People with Severe Mental Illness and Co-Occurring Substance Use Disorders." *Drug and Alcohol Review* 23: 471–481.

Bunte, Doris, Gerald J. Morrissey, and Lorna Jones. 1991. Memorandum of Agreement between Boston Housing Authority and Department of Mental Health and Dorchester Counseling Center, Inc. Boston: Mimeographed, August 15.

Burchardt, Tania. 2004. "Capabilities and Disability: The Capabilities Framework and the Social Model of Disability." Disability & Society 19: 735–751.

Burt, Martha. 1992. Over the Edge: The Growth of Homelessness in the 1980s. New York: Russell Sage.

Burt, Martha, Laudan Y. Aron, and Edgar Lee. 2001. *Helping America's Homeless: Emergency Shelter or Affordable Housing?* Washington, DC: The Urban Institute.

Burt, Ronald S. 1982. *Toward a Structural Theory of Action: Network Models of Social Structure, Perception, and Action.* New York: Academic Press.

Busch-Geertsema, Volker. 2005. "Does Re-Housing Lead to Reintegration? Follow-Up Studies of Re-Housed Homeless People." *Innovation* 18: 205–226.

Butcher, James Neal, W. Grant Dahlstrom, John R. Graham, Auke M. Tellegen, and Beverly Kaemmer, B. 1989. *MMPI-2: Manual for Administration and Scoring.* Minneapolis: University of Minnesota Press. .

Bycoff, Sheldon D., and Melanie Powers. 1991. Master Agreement between Department of Mental Health and Vinfen Corporation, Service Contract Renewal. Boston: Mimeographed, July 1.

Cacioppo, John T., and William Patrick. 2008. *Loneliness: Human Nature and the Need for Social Connection.* New York: W. W. Norton.

Calsyn, Robert J., Gary A. Morse, Betty Tempelhoff, Ruth Smith, and Gary Allen. 1995. "Homeless Mentally Ill Clients and the Quality of Life." *Evaluation and Program Planning* 18: 219–225.

Calsyn, Robert J., and Joel P. Winter. 2002. "Social Support, Psychiatric Symptoms, and Housing: A Causal Analysis." *Journal of Community Psychology* 30: 247–259.

Calvocoressi Lisa, Deborah Libman, Sally J. Vegso, Christopher J. McDougle, and Lawrence H. Price. 1998. "Global Functioning Of Inpatients with Obsessive-Compulsive Disorder, Schizophrenia, and Major Depression." *Psychiatric Services* 49: 379–381.

Campbell, Jean. 2005. "The Historical and Philosophical Development of Peer-Run Support Programs." In *On Our Own, Together: Peer Programs for People with Mental Illness,* edited by S. Clay, B. Schell, P. W. Corrigan, and R. O. Ralph, 17–64. Nashville: Vanderbilt University Press.

Campling, Penelope, and Rex Haigh. 1999. *Therapeutic Communities: Past, Present and Future.* Philadelphia: Jessica Kingsley Publishers.

Caplan, Brina, Russell K. Schutt, Winston M. Turner, Stephen M. Goldfinger, and Larry J. Seidman. 2006. "Change in Neurocognition by Housing Type and Substance Abuse among Formerly Homeless Seriously Mentally Ill Individuals." *Schizophrenia Research* 83: 77–86.

Carling, Paul J. 1990. "Major Mental Illness, Housing, and Supports: The Promise of Community Integration." *American Psychologist* 45: 969–975.

——— 1992. "Community Integration of People with Psychiatric Disabilities: Emerging Trends." In *Community Living for People with Developmental and*

Psychiatric Disabilities, edited by John W. Jacobson, Sara N. Burchard, and Paul J. Carling, 20–32. Baltimore: The Johns Hopkins University Press.

———. 1993. "Housing and Supports for Persons with Mental Illness: Emerging Approaches to Research and Practice." *Hospital and Community Psychiatry* 44: 439–449.

———. 1995. Return to Community: Building Support Systems for People with Psychiatric Disabilities. New York: The Guilford Press.

Cartwright Dorwin. 1968. "The Nature of Group Cohesiveness." In *Group Dynamics: Research and Theory,* edited by D. Cartwright and A. Zander, 91–109. London: Tavistock.

Caspi, Avashalom, Karen Sugden, Terrie E. Moffitt, Ian W. Craig, HonaLee Harrington, Joseph McClay, Jonathan Mill, Judy Martin, Antony Braithwaite, and Richie Poulton. 2003. "Influence of Life Stress on Depression: Moderation by a Polymorphism in the 5-HTT Gene." *Science* 301: 386–389.

Center for Mental Health Services. 1994. "Making a Difference: Interim Status Report of the McKinney Research Demonstration Program for Homeless Adults with Serious Mental Illness." Rockville, MD: U.S. Department of Health and Human Services.

Chamberlin, Judi, and Aart H. Schene. 1997. "A Working Definition of Empowerment." *Psychiatric Rehabilitation Journal* 20: 43–46.

Champney, Timothy F., and Laura Cox Dzurec. 1992. "Involvement in Productive Activities and Satisfaction with Living Situation among Severely Mentally Disabled Adults." *Hospital and Community Psychiatry* 43: 899–903.

Child, Irvin L. 1968. "Personality in Culture." In *Handbook of Personality Theory and Research,* edited by E. F. Borgatta and W. W. Lambert, 308–312. Chicago: Rand McNally.

Christian, Julie. 2003. "Homelessness: Integrating International Perspectives." *Journal of Community & Applied Social Psychology* 13: 85–90.

Clapham, David. 2003. "Pathways Approaches to Homelessness Research." *Journal of Community & Applied Social Psychology* 13: 119–127.

Clark, Colleen, and Alexander R. Rich. 2003. "Outcomes of Homeless Adults with Mental Illness in a Housing Program and in Case Management Only." *Psychiatric Services* 54: 78–83.

Clark, David. 1999. "Social Psychiatry: The Therapeutic Community Approach." In *Therapeutic Communities: Past, Present and Future,* edited by Penelope Campling and Rex Haigh, 32–38. Philadelphia: Jessica Kingsley Publishers.

Clark, Rodney, Norman B. Anderson, Vernessa R. Clark, and David R. Williams. 1999. "Racism as a Stressor for African Americans: A Biopsychosocial Model." *American Psychologist* 54: 805–816.

Cleary, Paul D., and Barbara J. McNeil. 1988. "Patient Satisfaction as an Indicator of Quality Care." *Inquiry* 25: 25–36.

Cohen, Alex S., Courtney B. Forbes, Monica C. Mann, and Jack J. Blanchard. 2006. "Specific Cognitive Deficits and Differential Domains of Social Functioning Impairment in Schizophrenia." *Schizophrenia Research* 81: 227–238.

Cohen, Carl I. 2000. "Overcoming Social Amnesia: The Role for a Social Perspective in Psychiatric Research and Practice." *Psychiatric Services* 51: 72–78.

Cohen, Sheldon, Robin Mermelstein, T. Kamarck, and Harry M. Hoberman. 1985. "Measuring the Functional Components of Social Support." In *Social Support: Theory, Research and Applications,* edited by I. G. Sarason and B. R. Sarason, 73–94. Dordrecht: Nijhoff.

Coleman, James S. 1990. *The Foundations of Social Theory.* Cambridge: Belknap, 1990.

Congressional Quarterly. 1985–1988. "A Review of Government and Politics." Congress and the Nation, Volume VII. Washington, DC: Congressional Quarterly.

Cooley, Charles Horton. 1962. *Social Organization: A Study of the Larger Mind.* New York: Schocken Books.

Corrigan, Patrick W. 2006. "Impact of Consumer-Operated Services on Empowerment and Recovery of People with Psychiatric Disabilities." *Psychiatric Services* 57: 1493–1496.

Corrigan, Patrick W., and Brett Buican. 1995. "The Construct Validity of Subjective Quality of Life for the Severely Mentally Ill." *Journal of Nervous and Mental Disease* 183: 281–285.

Coulton, Claudia J., Thomas P. Holland, and Virginia Fitch. 1984. "Person-Environment Congruence and Psychiatric Patient Outcome in Community Care Homes." *Administration in Mental Health* 12: 71–88.

Couture, Shannon M., David L. Penn, and David L. Roberts. 2006. "The Functional Significance of Social Cognition in Schizophrenia: A Review." *Schizophrenia Bulletin* 32: S44–S63.

Coyne, James C., and Geraldine Downey. 1991. "Social Factors and Psychopathology: Stress, Social Support, and Coping Processes." *Annual Review of Psychology* 42: 401–425.

Cramer, Joyce A., Robert Rosenheck, Weichun Xu, Jonathan Thomas, William Henderson, and Dennis S. Charney. 2000. "Quality of Life in Schizophrenia: A Comparison of Instruments." *Schizophrenia Bulletin* 26: 659–666.

Crouse, Joan M. 1986. The Homeless Transient in the Great Depression: New York State, 1929–1949. Albany: State University of New York Press.

Crystal, Stephen, Susan Ladner, and Richard Towbee. 1986. "Multiple Impairment Patterns in the Mentally Ill Homeless." *International Journal of Mental Health* 14: 61–73.

Culhane, Dennis, S. Metraux, T. Hadley. 2002. "Public Service Reductions Associated with Placement of Homeless Persons with Serious Mental Illness in Supportive Housing." *Housing Policy Debate* 13: 107–163.

Dackis, Charles, and Charles O'Brien. 2005. "Neurobiology of Addiction: Treatment and Public Policy Ramifications." *Nature Neuroscience* 8: 1431–1436.

Daniels, L. V., and Paul J. Carling. 1986. *Community Residential Rehabilitation Services for Psychiatrically Disabled Persons in Kitsap County, Washington.* Unpublished manuscript. Boston: Boston University Center for Psychiatric Rehabilitation.

Davidson, Larry, Matthew Chinman, Bret Kloos, Richard Weingarten, David Stayner, and Jacob K. Tebes. 1999. "Peer Support among Individuals with Severe Mental

Illness: A Review of the Evidence." *Clinical Psychology: Science and Practice* 6: 165–187.

Day, Nancy, and Kenneth Leonard. 1985. "Alcohol, Drug Use, and Psychopathology in the General Population." In *Substance Abuse and Psychopathology*, edited by Arthur I. Alterman, 15–43. New York: Plenum Press.

Dayson, David, R. Lee-Jones, K. K. Chahal, and Julian Leff. 1998. "The TAPS Project 32: Social Networks of Two Group Homes . . . 5 Years On." *Social Psychiatry and Psychiatric Epidemiology* 33: 438–444.

Denner, Bruce, and Florence Halprin. 1974. "Measuring Consumer Satisfaction in a Community Outpost." *American Journal of Community Psychology* 2: 13–22.

Depp, Frederick C., Arthur E. Scarpelli, and Frances E. Apostoles. 1983. "Making Cooperative Living Work for Psychiatric Outpatients." *Health and Social Work*, 8: 271–282.

Derogatis, Leonard R., and Phillip M. Spencer. 1982. *Administration and Procedures: BSI. Manual I.* Baltimore: Clinical Psychometric Research.

De Silva, Mary J., Kwame McKenzie, Trudy Harpham, and Sharon R. A. Huttly. 2005. "Social Capital and Mental Illness: A Systematic Review." *Journal of Epidemiology and Community Health* 59: 619–627.

Desjarlais, Robert. 1997. *Shelter Blues: Sanity and Selfhood among the Homeless.* Philadelphia: University of Pennsylvania Press.

Devine, Joel A., and James D. Wright. 1997. "Losing the Housing Game: The Leveling Effect of Substance Abuse." *American Journal of Orthopsychiatry* 67: 618–633.

Diamond, Ronald J. 1993. "The Psychiatrist's Role in Supported Housing." *Hospital and Community Psychiatry* 44: 461–464.

Dickens, Charles. 1996. *American Notes.* 1850. Dowloaded from Project Gutenberg Etext: http://www.gutenberg.org/etext/675.

Dickinson, Dwight, Alan S. Bellack, and James M. Gold. 2007. "Social/Communication Skills, Cognition, and Vocational Functioning in Schizophrenia." *Schizophrenia Bulletin* 33: 1213–1220.

DiMaggio, Paul J., and Walter W. Powell. 1983. "The Iron Cage Revisited: Institutional Isomorphism and Collective Rationality in Organizational Fields." *American Sociological Review* 48: 147–160.

Distefano, M. K., Margaret W. Pryer, and Jesse L. Garrison. 1980. "Attitudinal, Demographic, and Outcome Correlates of Clients' Satisfaction." *Psychological Reports* 47: 287–290.

Distefano, M. K., Margaret W. Pryer, and Jesse L. Garrison. 1981. "Clients' Satisfaction and Interpersonal Trust among Hospitalized Psychiatric Patients." *Psychological Reports* 49: 420–422.

Dixon, Lisa, Nancy Krauss, Patrick Myers, and Anthony F. Lehman. 1994. "Clinical and Treatment Correlates of Access to Section 8 Certificates for Homeless Mentally Ill Persons." *Hospital and Community Psychiatry* 45: 1196–1200.

Dixon, Lisa, Peter Weiden, Michael Torres, and Anthony F. Lehman. 1997. Assertive community treatment and medication compliance in the homeless mentally ill. *American Journal of Psychiatry* 154: 1302–1304.

Donabedian, Avedis. 1980. *Explorations in Quality Assessment and Monitoring: Vol 1: The Definiton of Quality and Approaches to Its Assessment.* Ann Arbor: Health Administration Press.

Dougherty, Donald M., Joel L. Steinberg, Adel A. Wassef, David Medearis, Don R. Cherek, and F. Gerard Moeller. 1998. "Immediate versus Delayed Visual Memory Task Performance among Schizophrenic Patients and Normal Control Subjects." *Psychiatry Research* 79: 255–265.

Dowdall, George W. 1996. The Eclipse of the State Mental Hospital: Policy, Stigma, and Organization. Albany: State University of New York Press.

Downs, Marylou W., and Jeanne C. Fox. 1993. "Social Environments of Adult Homes." *Community Mental Health Journal* 29: 15–23.

Drake, Robert E., and David A. Adler. 1984. "Shelter Is Not Enough: Clinical Work with the Homeless Mentally Ill." In *The Homeless Mentally Ill,* edited by H. R. Lamb, 141–151. Washington, DC: American Psychiatric Association.

Drake, Robert E., Susan M. Essock, Andrew Shaner, Kate B. Carey, Kenneth Minkoff, Lenore Kola, David Lynde, Fred C. Osher, Robin E. Clark, and Lawrence Rickards. 2001. "Implementing Dual Diagnosis Services for Clients with Severe Mental Illness." *Psychiatric Services* 52: 469–476.

Drake, Robert E., and Michael A. Wallach. 1988. "Mental Patients' Attitudes toward Hospitalization: A Neglected Aspect of Hospital Tenure." *American Journal of Psychiatry* 145: 29–34.

Drake Robert E., Michael A. Wallach, and J. Schuyler Hoffman. 1989. "Housing Instability and Homelessness among Aftercare Patients of an Urban State Hospital." *Hospital & Community Psychiatry* 40: 46–51.

Dumont, Jeanne and Kristine Jones. 2002. "Findings from a Consumer/Survivor Defined Alternative to Psychiatric Hospitalization." *Outlook* 3: 4–6.

Dunn, M., Cathy O'Driscoll, David Dayson, Walter Willis, and Julian Leff. 1990. "The TAPS Project. 4: An Observational Study of the Social Life of Long-Stay Patients." *British Journal of Psychiatry* 157: 842–848.

Durkheim, Emile. 1951 [1897]. *Suicide: A Study in Sociology.* New York: Free Press.

Dworsky, Amt L., and Irving Piliavin. 2000. "Homeless Spell Exits and Returns: Substantive and Methodological Elaborations on Recent Studies." *Social Service Review* 74: 193–213.

Earle, Pliny. 1887. *The Curability of Insanity: A Series of Studies.* Philadelphia: J. B. Lippincott.

Earle-Boyer, Elizabeth A., Mark R. Septer, Michael Davidson, and Philip D. Harvey. 1991. "Continuous Performance Tests in Schizophrenic Patients: Stimulus and Medication Effects on Performance." *Psychiatric Research* 37: 47–56.

Earls, Mary and Geoffrey Nelson. 1988. "The Relationship between Long-Term Psychiatric Clients' Psychological Well-Being and Their Perceptions of Housing and Social Support." *American Journal of Community Psychology* 16: 279–293.

Eisenberg, Leon. 1995. "The Social Construction of the Human Brain." *American Journal of Psychiatry* 152: 1563–1757.

Elliott, Susan J., S. Martin Taylor, and Robin A. Kearns. 1990. "Housing Satisfaction, Preference and Need among the Chronically Mentally Disabled in Hamilton, Ontario." *Social Science and Medicine* 30: 95–102.

Elpern, Sarah, and Stephen A. Karp. 1984. "Sex-Role Orientation and Depressive Symptomatology." *Sex Roles* 10:987–991.

Ensel, Walter M. 1986. "Social Class and Depressive Symptomatology." In *Social Support, Life Events, and Depression*, edited by N. Lin, A. Dean, and W. M. Ensel, 249–265. New York: Academic Press.

Eraker, Stephen A., John P. Kirscht, and Marshall H. Becker. 1984. "Understanding and Improving Patient Compliance." *Annals of Internal Medicine* 100: 258–268.

Erikson, Kai T. 1976. *Everything in Its Path: Destruction of Community in the Buffalo Creek Flood*. New York: Simon & Schuster.

Ertuğrul , A., and B. Uluğ. 2008. "The Influence of Neurocognitive Deficits and Symptoms on Disability in Schizophrenia." *Acta Psychiatrica Scandinavica* 105: 196–201.

Etzioni, Amitai. 1988. *The Moral Dimension*. New York: Free Press.

Eyrich, Karin M., David E. Pollio, and Carol S. North. 2003. "An Exploration of Alienation and Replacement Theories of Social Support in Homelessness." *Social Work Research* 27: 222–231.

Fairweather, George. 1980. "Implications of the Lodge Society." In *The Fairweather Lodge: A Twenty-Five Year Retrospective*, edited by George Fairweather, 89–97. San Francisco: Jossey-Bass.

Fakhoury, Walid K. H., Alison Murray, Geoff Shepherd, and Stefan Priebe. 2002. "Research in Supported Housing." *Social Psychiatry and Psychiatric Epidemiology* 37: 301–305.

Falloon, Ian R. H., and Grant N. Marshall. 1983. "Residential Care and Social Behaviour: A Study of Rehabilitation Needs." *Psychological Medicine* 13: 341–347.

Faraone, Stephen V., Ming T. Tsuang, and Debby W. Tsuang. 1999. *Genetics of Mental Disorders: A Guide for Students, Clinicians, and Researchers*. New York: The Guilford Press.

Farr, Rodger K., Paul Koegel, and Audrey Burnam. 1986. *A Study of Homelessness and Mental Illness in the Skid Row Area of Los Angeles*. Los Angeles: Los Angeles Department of Mental Health.

Fehr, Ernst, and Herbert Gintis. 2007. "Human Motivation and Social Cooperation: Experimental and Analytical Foundations." *Annual Review of Sociology* 33: 43–64.

Festinger, Leon, Stanley Schachter, and Kurt Back. 1950. *Social Pressures in Informal Groups: A Study of Human Factors in Housing*. Stanford, CA: Stanford University Press.

Fields, Steve. 1990. "The Relationship between Residential Treatment and Supported Housing in a Community System of Care." *Psychiatric Rehabilitation Journal* 13:105–114.

Fischer, Mary J., and Douglas S. Massey. 2004. "The Ecology of Racial Discrimination." *City & Community* 3: 221–241.

Fjellman, Stephen M. 1976. "Natural and Unnatural Decision-making: A Critique of Decision Theory." *Ethos* 4: 73–94.

Flashman, Laura A. 2004. "Disorders of Insight, Self-Awareness, and Attribution in Schizophrenia." In *Self-Awareness Deficits in Psychiatric Patients: Neurobiology, Assessment, and Treatment*, edited by B. D. Beitman and J. Nair, 129–158. New York: W. W. Norton & Co.

Folsom, David P., William Hawthorne, Laurie Lindamer, Todd Gilmer, Anne Bailey, Shahrokh Golshan, Piedad Garcia, Jürgen Unützer, Richard Hough, and Dilip V. Jeste. 2005. "Prevalence and Risk Factors for Homelessness and Utilization of Mental Health Services among 10,340 Patients with Serious Mental Illness in a Large Public Mental Health System." *American Journal of Psychiatry* 162: 370–376.

Forquer, Sandra, and Ed Knight. 2001. "Managed Care: Recovery Enhancer or Inhibitor?" *Psychiatric Services* 52: 25–26.

Foucault, Michel. 1965. Madness and Civilization: A History of Insanity in the Age of Reason. New York: Random House.

Fox, John. 1991. *Regression Diagnostics: An Introduction*. Sage University paper series on Quantitative Applications in the Social Sciences, series no. 07–079. Newbury Park, CA: Sage.

Franczak, Michael J. 2002. *Final Report: Housing Approaches for Persons with Serious Mental Illness*. Tucson: Community Rehabilitation Division, School of Public Administration & Policy, University of Arizona.

Frank, Richard G., and Mark S. Kamlet. 1989. "Determining Provider Choice for the Treatment of Mental Disorder: The Role of Health and Mental Health Status." *Health Services Research* 24: 83–103.

Frankfort-Nachmias, Chava, and Anna Leon-Guerrero. 2008. *Social Statistics for a Diverse Society*. 5th ed. Thousand Oaks, CA: Pine Forge Press.

Freidson, Eliot. 1988 [1970]. *Profession of Medicine: A Study of the Sociology of Applied Knowledge*. Chicago and London: University of Chicago Press.

Friedkin, Noah E. 2004. "Social Cohesion." *Annual Review of Sociology* 30: 409–425.

Friedman, Alfred S. and Nita W. Glickman. 1987. "Residential Program Characteristics for Completion of Treatment by Adolescent Drug Abusers." *The Journal of Nervous and Mental Disease* 178: 419–424.

Friedman, Alfred S., Nita W. Glickman, and John A. Kovach. 1986. "The Relationship of Drug Program Environmental Variables to Treatment Outcome." *American Journal of Drug and Alcohol Abuse* 12: 53–69.

Friedrich, Rose Marie, Burda Hollingsworth, Elizabeth Hradek, H. Bruce Friedrich, and Kennety R. Culp. 1999. "Family and Client Perspectives on Alternative Residential Settings for Persons with Severe Mental Illness." *Psychiatric Services* 50: 509–514.

Friis, Svein. 1986. "Characteristics of a Good Ward Atmosphere." *Acta Psychiatrica Scandinavica* 74: 469–473.

Gelberg, Lillian S. and Lawrence Linn, 1989. "Psychological Distress among Homeless Adults." *Journal of Nervous and Mental Disease* 177:291–295.

Gelberg, Lillian S., Lawrence Linn, and Barbara D. Leake. 1988. "Mental Health, Alcohol and Drug Use, and Criminal History among Homeless Adults." *The American Journal of Psychiatry* 145: 191–196.

Gladis, Madeline M., Elizabeth A. Gosch, Nicole M. Dishuk, and Paul Crits-Christoph. 1999. "Quality of Life: Expanding the Scope of Clinical Significance." *Journal of Consulting and Clinical Psychology* 67: 320–331.

Goering, Paula, Janet Durbin, Robert Foster, Susan Boyles, Taras Babiak, and Bill Lancee. 1992. "Social Networks of Residents in Supportive Housing." *Community Mental Health Journal* 28: 199–214.

Goering, Paula, Darianna Paduchak, and Janet Durbin. 1990 "Housing Homeless Women: A Consumer Preference Study." *Hospital and Community Psychiatry* 4: 790–794.

Goering, Paula, Donald Wasylinki, Sheryl Lindsay, David Lemire, and Anne Rhodes. 1997. "Process and Outcome in a Hostel Outreach Program for Homeless Clients with Severe Mental Illness." *American Journal of Orthopsychiatry* 67: 607–617.

Goffman, Erving. 1961. *Asylums: Essays on the Social Situation of Mental Patients and Other Inmates.* Garden City, NY: Doubleday.

Goldberg, Richard W., Angela L. Rollins, and Anthony F. Lehman. 2003. "Social Network Correlates among People with Psychiatric Disabilities." *Psychiatric Rehabilitation Journal* 26: 393–402.

Goldberg, Terry E., James M. Gold, Richard Greenberg, Suzanne Griffin, S. C. Schulz, D. Pickar, J. E. Kleinman, and D. R. Weinberger. 1993. Contrasts between patients with affective disorders and patients with schizophrenia on a neuropsychological test battery. *American Journal of Psychiatry* 150: 1355–1362.

Goldberg, Terry E,, Robert S. Goldman, Katherine E. Burdick, Anil K. Malhotra, Todd Lencz, Raman C. Patel, Margaret G. Woerner, Nina R. Schooler, John M. Kane, and Delberg G. Robinson. 2007. "Cognitive Improvement after Treatment with Second-Generation Antipsychotic Medications in First-Episode Schizophrenia: Is It a Practice Effect?" *Archives of General Psychiatry* 64:1115–1122.

Goldfinger, Stephen Mark, Barbara Dickey, Sondra Hellman, Martha O'Bryan, Walter Penk, Russell Schutt, and Larry J. Seidman. 1990. "Apartments v. Evolving Consumer Households for the HMI." Proposal to the National Institute of Mental Health. Boston: Massachusetts Mental Health Center, Harvard Medical School.

Goldfinger, Stephen M., Richard L. Hough, Anthony F. Lehman, David L. Shern, and Elie S. Valencia. 1995. *Recruiting and Retaining Severely Mentally Ill Subjects in Longitudinal Research.* Unpublished report.

Goldfinger, Stephen M., and Russell K. Schutt. 1996. "Comparison of Clinicians' Housing Recommendations and Preferences of Homeless Mentally Ill Persons." *Psychiatric Services* 47: 413–415.

Goldfinger, Stephen M., Russell K. Schutt, Larry J. Seidman, Winston Turner, and George Tolomiczenko. 1996b. "Self-Report and Observer Measures of Substance Abuse, in the Cross-Section and Over Time." *Journal of Nervous and Mental Disease* 184: 667–672.

Goldfinger, Stephen. M., Russell K. Schutt, George S. Tolomiczenko, Winston Turner, N. Ware, Walter E. Penk, Mark S. Ableman, Tara L. Avruskin, Joshua Breslau, Brina Caplan, Barbara Dickey, Olinda Gonzalez, Byron Good, Sondra Hellman, Susan Lee, Martha O'Bryan, and Larry J. Seidman. 1997. "Housing Persons Who Are Homeless and Mentally Ill: Independent Living or Evolving Consumer Households?" In *Mentally Ill and Homeless: Special Programs for Special Needs* edited by William R. Breakey and James W. Thompson, 29–49. Amsterdam: Harwood Academic Publishers.

Goldfinger, Stephen M., Russell K. Schutt, George. S. Tolomiczenko, Larry J. Seidman, Walter E. Penk, Winston M. Turner, and Brina Caplan. 1999. "Housing Placement and Subsequent Days Homeless among Formerly Homeless Adults with Mental Illness." *Psychiatric Services* 50: 674–679.

Goldfinger, Stephen M., Russell K. Schutt, Winston Turner, George Tolomiczenko, and Mark Abelman. 1996a. "Assessing Homeless Mentally Ill Persons for Permanent Housing: Screening for Safety." *Community Mental Health Journal* 32: 275–288.

Goldman, Howard H., Laura Rachuba, and Laura Van Tosh. 1995. "Methods of Assessing Mental Health Consumers' Preferences for Housing and Support Services." *Psychiatric Services* 46: 169–172.

Gonzalez, Gerardo, and Robert A. Rosenheck. 2002. "Outcomes and Service Use among Homeless Persons with Serious Mental Illness and Substance Abuse." *Psychiatric Services* 53: 437–446.

Goodwin, Anne M. and Deborah L. Madell. 2002. "Measuring the Quality of Life of People with Severe and Enduring Mental Health Problems in Different Settings." *Journal of Mental Health* 11: 305–315.

Gouldner, Alvin W. 1954. *Patterns of Industrial Bureaucracy.* New York: The Free Press.

Gounis, Kostas. 1992. "The Manufacture of Dependency: Shelterization Revisited." *New England Journal of Public Policy* 8: 685–693.

Green, Carla A., Nancy H. Vuckovic, and Alison J. Firemark. 2002. "Adapting to Psychiatric Disability and Needs for Home- and Community-Based Care." *Mental Health Services Research* 4: 29–41.

Green, Michael F. 1996. "What Are the Functional Consequences of Neurocognitive Deficits in Schizophrenia." *American Journal of Psychiatry* 153: 321–330.

Green, Michael F., Susan Hellman, and Robert S. Kern. 1997. "Feasibility Studies of Cognitive Remediation in Schizophrenia: Grasping the Little Picture." In *Towards a Comprehensive Therapy for Schizophrenia,* edited by H. D. Brenner, W. Boker, and R. Genner, 79–93. Seattle: Hogrefe & Huber.

Green, Michael F., Robert S. Kern, David L. Braff, and Jim Mintz. 2000. "Neurocognitive Deficits and Functional Outcome in Schizophrenia: Are We Measuring the 'Right Stuff'?" *Schizophrenia Bulletin* 26: 119–136.

Green, Michael F., Robert S. Kern, and Robert K. Heaton. 2004. "Longitudinal Studies of Cognition and Functional Outcome in Schizophrenia: Implications for MATRICS." *Schizophrenia Research* 72: 41–51.

Greene, Roger L. 1991. *The MMPI-2/MMPI: An Interpretive Manual.* Boston: Allyn and Bacon.

Greenfield, Arnold L. 1992. "Evaluating the Quality of Care in Supervised Group Homes for Persons with Mental Illness." *Adult Residential Care Journal* 6: 103–113.

Greenley, James R., and David Mechanic. 1976. "Social Selection in Seeking Help for Psychological Problems." *Journal of Health and Social Behavior* 17: 249–262.

Greenwood, Ronni M., Nicole J. Schaefer-McDaniel, Gary Winkel, and Sam J. Tsemberis. 2005. "Decreasing Psychiatric Symptoms by Increasing Choice in Services for Adults with Histories of Homelessness." *American Journal of Community Psychology* 36: 223–238.

Greisbach, Fred, Adrienne Leban, Jane Benedict, and William Rowen. 1984. "Must We Shoot Society's Losers." *The New York Times*, November 25. Available at www.nytimes.com. Accessed June 20, 2009.

Grob, Gerald N. 1994. *The Mad among Us: A History of the Care of America's Mentally Ill.* New York: The Free Press.

Guest, Avery M., Jane K. Cover, Ross L. Matsueda, and Charles E. Kubrin. 2006. "Neighborhood Context and Neighboring Ties." *City & Community* 5: 363–385.

Gulcur, Leyla, Ana Stefanic, Marybeth Shinn, Sam Tsemberis, and Sean N. Fischer. 2003. "Housing, Hospitalization, and Cost Outcomes for Homeless Individuals with Psychiatric Disabilities Participating in Continuum of Care and Housing First Programmes." *Journal of Community & Applied Social Psychology* 13: 171–186.

Gulcur, Leyla, Sam Tsemberis, Ana Stefancic, and Ronni M. Greenwood. 2007. "Community Integration of Adults with Psychiatric Disabilities and Histories of Homelessness." *Community Mental Health Journal* 43: 211–228.

Gunderson, John G. 1980. "A Reevaluation of Milieu Therapy for Nonchronic Schizophrenic Patients." *Schizophrenia Bulletin* 8: 64–69.

Haigh, Rex. 1999. "The Quintessence of a Therapeutic Environment: Five Universal Qualities." In *Therapeutic Communities: Past, Present and Future*, edited by Penelope Campling and Rex Haigh, 246–257. Philadelphia: Jessica Kingsley Publishers.

Hajema, Klaas-Jan, Ronald A. Knibbe, and Maria J. Drop. 1999. "Social Resources and Alcohol-Related Losses as Predictors of Help Seeking among Male Problem Drinkers." *Journal of Studies on Alcohol* 60: 120–129.

Hampson, Sarah E. 1988. *The Construction of Personality: An Introduction.* 2nd ed. London: Routledge.

Hanson, Glen R. 2002. *Therapeutic Community.* NIH Publication Number 2-4877. Bethesda, MD: National Institute of Drug Abuse.

Hargreaves, William A., Jonathan Showstack, Rinna Flohr, Clair Brady, and Sanford Harris. 1974. "Treatment Acceptance Following Intake Assignment to Individual Therapy, Group Therapy or Contact Group." *Archives of General Psychiatry* 31: 343–349.

Harp, Howie. 1990. "Independent Living with Support Services: The Goal and Future for Mental Health Consumers." *Psychiatric Rehabilitation Journal* 13:85–89.

Hartz Diane, Peter Banys, and Sharon M. Hall. 1994. "Correlates of Homelessness among Substance Abuse Patients at a VA Medical Center." *Hospital & Community Psychiatry*, 45: 491–493,

Hatfield, Elaine. 1983. "Equity Theory and Research: An Overview." In *Small Groups and Social Interaction,* edited by Herbert H. Blumberg, A. Paul Hare, Valerie Kent, and Martin F. Davis, 401–412. New York: John Wiley & Sons.

Hawkins, Robert Leibson, and Courtney Abrams. 2007. "Disappearing Acts: The Social Networks of Formerly Homeless Individuals with Co-Occurring Disorders." *Social Science & Medicine* 65: 2031–2042.

Hayes, Robert M. 1986. "Hope for New York City's Homeless? The Issue Is Housing." *The New York Times,* November 27. Available at http://www.nytimes.com. Accessed February 11, 2009.

Haywood, Thomas W., Howard M. Kravitz, Linda S. Grossman, James L. Cavanaugh, John M. Davis, and Dan A. Lewis. 1995. "Predicting the 'Revolving Door' Phenomenon among Patients with Schizophrenic, Schizoaffective, and Affective Disorders." *American Journal of Psychiatry* 152: 856–861.

Helfrich, Christine A., and Louis F. Fogg. 2007. "Outcomes of a Life Skills Intervention for Homeless Adults with Mental Illness." *Journal of Primary Prevention* 28: 313–326.

Henderson, A. S. 1992. "Social Support and Depression." In *The Meaning and Measurement of Social Support,* edited by Hans O. F. Veiel and Urs Baumann, 85–92. New York: Hemisphere.

Herman, Daniel B., Ezra S. Susser, Lisa Jandorf, Janet Lavelle, and Evelyn J. Bromet. 1998. "Homeless among Individuals with Psychotic Disorders Hospitalized for the First Time: Findings from the Suffolk County Mental Health Project." *American Journal of Psychiatry* 155: 109–113.

Heslegrave, Ronald J., A. George Awad, and Lakshmi N. P. Voruganti. 1997. "The Influence of Neurocognitive Deficits and Symptoms on Quality of Life in Schizophrenia." *Journal of Psychiatry and Neuroscience* 22: 235–243.

Hobbs, Coletta, Lesley Newton, Christopher Tennant, Alan Rosen, and Kate Tribe. 2002. "Deinstitutionalization for Long-Term Mental Illness: A 6-Year Evaluation." *Australian and New Zealand Journal of Psychiatry* 36: 60–66.

Hogan, Michael F., and Paul J. Carling. 1992. "Normal Housing: A Key Element of a Supported Housing Approach for People with Psychiatric Disabilities." *Community Mental Health Journal* 28: 215–226.

Hogarty, Gerard E., and Samuel Flesher. 1999. "Developmental Theory for a Cognitive Enhancement Therapy of Schizophrenia." *Schizophrenia Bulletin* 25: 677–692.

Hogarty, Gerard E., and Melissa Wieland. 2005. "Weak Ties and Schizophrenia: Promise and Problems." *Psychiatry* 68: 230–235.

Hohmann, Ann A. 1999. "A Contextual Model for Clinical Mental Health Effectiveness Research." *Mental Health Services Research* 1: 83–91.

Holley, Heather L., Phyllis Hodges, and Betty Jeffers. 1998. "Moving Psychiatric Patients from Hospital to Community: Views of Patients, Providers, and Families." *Psychiatric Services* 49: 513–517.

Hope, Marjorie, and James Young. 1986. *The Faces of Homelessness.* Lexington, MA: Lexington Books.

Hopper, Kim. 1988. "More Than Passing Strange: Homelessness and Mental Illness in New York City." *American Ethnologist* 15: 155–167.

———. 1990. "Public Shelter as 'a Hybrid Institution': Homeless Men in Historical Perspective." *Journal of Social Issues* 46 (4): 13–29.

———. 2003. *Reckoning with Homelessness.* Ithaca, NY: Cornell University Press.

Hopper, Kim, and Norweeta G. Milburn. 1996. "Homelessness among African Americans: A Historical and Contemporary Perspective." In *Homelessness in America,* edited by J. Baumohl, 123–131. Phoenix: Oryx Press.

Horwitz, Allan V. 1977. "Social Networks and Pathways to Psychiatric Treatment." *Social Forces* 56: 86–105.

———. 2002. *Creating Mental Illness.* Chicago: University of Chicago Press.

———. 2007. "Classical Sociological Theory, Evolutionary Psychology, and Mental Health." In *Mental Health, Social Mirror,* edited by William R. Avison, Jane D. McLeod, and Bernice A. Pescosolido, 67–93. New York: Springer.

Horwitz, Allan V., and Jerome C. Wakefield. 2007. *The Loss of Sadness: How Psychiatry Transformed Normal Sorrow into Depressive Disorder.* New York: Oxford University Press.

Hughes, Everett C. 1963. "Professions." *Daedalus* 92: 655–668.

Humphreys, Keith, and Robert Rosenheck. 1998. "Treatment Involvement and Outcomes for Four Subtypes of Homeless Veterans." *American Journal of Orthopsychiatry* 68: 285–294.

Hurlburt, Michael S., Richard L. Hough, and Patricia A. Wood. 1996. "Effects of Substance Abuse on Housing Stability of Homeless Mentally Ill Persons in Supported Housing." *Psychiatric Services* 47: 731–736.

Huxley, Peter J., and Richard Warner. 1992. "Case Management, Quality of Life, and Satisfaction with Services of Long-Term Psychiatric Patients." *Hospital & Community Psychiatry* 43: 799–802.

Hyman, Steven E. 2000. "The Millennium of Mind, Brain, and Behavior." *Archives of General Psychiatry* 57: 88–89.

Ilonen Tuula, Tero Taiminen, Hasse Karlsson, Pentti Tuimala, Kirsi-Marja Leinonen, Elina Wallenius, and Raimo K. R. Salokangas. 2000. "Impaired Wisconsin Card Sorting Test Performance in First-Episode Severe Depression." *Nordic Journal of Psychiatry* 54: 275–280.

Institute of Medicine, Committee on Health Care for Homeless Persons. 1988. *Homelessness, Health, and Human Needs.* Washington, DC: National Academy Press.

Jencks, Christopher. 1992. *Rethinking Social Policy: Race, Policy, and the Underclass.* New York: HarperPerennial.

———. 1994. *The Homeless.* Cambridge, MA: Harvard University Press.

Johnson, Timothy P. 1991. "Mental Health, Social Relations, and Social Selection: A Longitudinal Analysis." *Journal of Health and Social Behavior* 32: 408–423.

Johnson, Timothy P., Sally A. Freels, Jennifer A. Parsons, and Jonathan B. Vangeest. 1997. "Substance Abuse and Homelessness: Social Selection or Social Adaptation?" *Addiction* 92: 437–445.

Jokela, Markus, Liisa Keltikangas-Järvinen, Mika Kivimäki, Sampsa Puttonen, Marko Elovainio, Riikka Rontu, and Terho Lehtimäki. 2007. "Serotonin Receptor 2A Gene and the Influence of Childhood Maternal Nurturance on Adulthood Depressive Symptoms." *Archives of General Psychiatry* 64: 356–360.

Jones, Peter B., Thomas R. E. Barnes, Linda Davies, Graham Dunn, Helen Lloyd, Karen P. Hayhurst, Robin M. Murray, Alison Markwick, and Shôn W. Lewis. 2006. "Randomized Controlled Trial of the Effect on Quality of Life of Second- vs. First-Generation Antipsychotic Drugs in Schizophrenia." *Archives of General Psychiatry* 63: 1079–1087.

Kadushin, Charles. 1969. *Why People Go to Psychiatrists*. New York: Atherton.

Kahn, Marvin W., Maureen Hannah, Charles Hinkin, Carey Montgomery, and Diane Pitz. 1987. "Psychopathology on the Streets: Psychological Assessment of the Homeless." *Professional Psychology: Research & Practice* 18: 580–586.

Kalivas, Peter W., and Nora D. Volkow. 2005. "The Neural Basis of Addiction: A Pathology of Motivation and Choice." *American Journal of Psychiatry* 162: 1403–1413.

Kandel, Eric R. 1998. "A New Intellectual Framework for Psychiatry." *American Journal of Psychiatry* 155 (4): 457–469.

Kanter, Rosabeth Moss. 1972. *Commitment and Community: Communes and Utopias in Sociological Perspective*. Cambridge, MA: Harvard University Press.

———. 1983. "Commitment and Community: Boundary Problems." In *Small Groups and Social Interaction*, edited by Herbert H. Blumberg, A. Paul Hare, Valerie Kent, and Martin F. Davis. New York: John Wiley & Sons.

Kaplan, George A., Robert E. Roberts, Terry C. Camacho, and James C. Coyne. 1987. "Psychosocial Predictors of Depression: Prospective Evidence from the Human Population Laboratory Studies." *American Journal of Epidemiology* 125: 206–220.

Karnas, Fred. 2006. "Innovation Awardee Models a New State Approach to Ending Homelessness." *Housing Facts & Findings* 8. Available at http://www.fanniemaefoundation.org/programs/hff/v8i3-awardee.shtml. Accessed January 25, 2007.

Kasprow, Wesley J., Robert A. Rosenheck, Linda Frisman, and Diane DiLella. 2000. "Referral and Housing Processes in a Long-Term Supported Housing Program for Homeless Veterans." *Psychiatric Services* 51: 1017–1023.

Katz, Michael B. 1986. *In the Shadow of the Poorhouse: A Social History of Welfare in America*. New York: Basic Books.

Kaufman, Nancy K. 1992. "State Government's Response to Homelessness: The Massachusetts Experience, 1983–1990." *New England Journal of Public Policy* 8: 471–482.

Kawachi, Ichiro, and Lisa F. Berkman. 2001. "Social Ties and Mental Health." *Journal of Urban Health: Bulletin of the New York Academy of Medicine* 78: 458–467.

Keck, Jonathan. 1990. "Responding to Consumer Housing Preferences: The Toledo Experience." *Psychosocial Rehabilitation Review* 13: 51–58.

Kellerman, Sara L., Ronnie S. Helpler, Marybeth Hopkins, and Gail B. Naywith. 1985. "Psychiatry and Homelessness: Problems and Programs." In *Health Care of Homeless People,* edited by Philip W. Brickner, Linda Keen Scharer, Barbara Concanan, Alexander Elvy, and Marianne Savarese, 179–188. New York: Springer.

Kern, Robert S., and Michael F. Green. 1998. "Cognitive remediation in schizophrenia." In *Handbook of Social Functioning in Schizophrenia,* edited by K. T. Mueser and N. Tarrier, 342–354. Boston: Allyn & Bacon.

Kertesz, Stefan G., Kimberly Crouch, Jessy Milby, Robert A. Cusimano, and Joseph Schumacher. 2009. "Housing First for Homeless Persons with Active Addiction: Are We Overreaching?" *The Milbank Quarterly* 87: 495–534.

Kessler, Ronald C., Kristin D. Mickelson, and David R. Williams. 1999. "The Prevalence, Distribution, and Mental Health Correlates of Perceived Discrimination in the United States." *Journal of Health and Social Behavior* 40: 208–230.

Khantzian, Edward J., Margaret Bean-Bayog, Susan Blumenthal, Richard Frances, Marc Galanter, Earl Loomis, Sheldon I. Miller, Robert Millman, Steven Mirin, Edgar Nace, Normal Paul, Peter Steinglass, John Tamerin, Joseph Westermeyer, Alexander D. Kalogerakis, John Menninger, and James Coleman. 1991. "Substance Abuse Disorders: A Psychiatric Priority." *American Journal of Psychiatry* 148: 1291–1300.

Kikkert, Martijin J., Aart H. Schene, Maarten W. J. Koeter, Debbie Robson, Anja Born, Hedda Helm, Michela Nose, Claudia Goss, Graham Thornicroft, and Richard J. Gray. 2006. "Medication Adherence in Schizophrenia: Exploring Patients', Carers' and Professionals' Views." *Schizophrenia Bulletin* 32: 786–794.

Klerman, Gerald L. 1989. "Psychiatric Diagnostic Categories: Issues of Validity and Measurement." *Journal of Health and Social Behavior* 30: 26–32.

Kloos, Bret, Susan O. Zimmerman, Katie Scrimenti, and Cindy Crusto. 2002. "Landlords as Partners in Promoting Success in Supported Housing: 'It Takes More Than a Lease and a Key.'" *Psychiatric Rehabilitation Journal* 25: 235–244.

Knisley, Martha B., and Mary Fleming. 1993. "Implementing Supported Housing in State and Local Mental Health Systems." *Hospital and Community Psychiatry* 44: 456–461.

Koegel, Paul. 1987. "Ethnographic Perspectives on Homeless and Homeless Mentally Ill Women." Proceedings of a two-day workshop sponsored by the Division of Education and Service Systems Liaison, National Institute of Mental Health, October 30–31, 1986. Washington, DC: U.S. Department of Health and Human Services, Public Health Service, Alcohol, Drug Abuse, and Mental Health Administration (ADAMHA).

Koegel, Paul, and M. Audrey Burnam. 1988. "Alcoholism among Homeless Adults in the Inner City of Los Angeles." *Archives of General Psychiatry* 45: 1011–1018.

Koegel, Paul., M. Audrey Burnam, and Rodger K. Farr. 1988. "The Prevalence of Specific Psychiatric Disorders among Homeless Individuals in the Inner-City of Los Angeles." *Archives of General Psychiatry* 45:1085–1092.

Kolb, Bryan, and Robbin Gibb. 2002. Frontal Lobe Plasticity and Behavior." In *Principles of Frontal Lobe Function*, edited by Donalt T. Stuss and Robert T. Knight, 541–556. New York: Oxford University Press.

Kruzich, Jean M. 1985. "Community Integration of the Mentally Ill in Residential Facilities." *American Journal of Community Psychology* 13: 553–564.

Kuhn, Thomas. 1962. *The Structure of Scientific Revolutions*. Chicago: University of Chicago Press.

Kulka, Richard A., Joseph Veroff, and Elizabeth Douvan. 1979. "Social Class and the Use of Professional Help for Personal Problems: 1957–1976." *Journal of Health and Social Behavior* 20: 2–17.

Kurtz, Matthew M., Paul J. Moberg, J. Daniel Ragland, Raquel E. Gur, and Ruben C. Gur. 2005. "Symptoms versus Neurocognitive Test Performance as Predictors of Psychosocial Status in Schizophrenia: A 1- and 4-Year Prospective Study." *Schizophrenia Bulletin* 31: 164–174.

Laes, Joan R., and Scott R. Sponheim. 2006. "Does Cognition Predict Community Function Only in Schizophrenia? A Study of Schizophrenia Patients, Bipolar Affective Disorder Patients, and Community Control Subjects." *Schizophrenia Research* 84: 121–131.

La Gory, Mark, Ferris J. Ritchey, and Jeff Mullis. 1990. "Depression among the Homeless." *Journal of Health and Social Behavior* 31: 87–101.

Lam, Julie A., and Robert Rosenheck. 1999. "Social Support and Service Use among Homeless Persons with Serious Mental Illness." *International Journal of Social Psychiatry* 45: 13–28.

Lam, Julie A., and Robert A. Rosenheck. 2000. "Correlates of Improvement in Quality of Life among Homeless Persons with Serious Mental Illness." *Psychiatric Services* 51: 116–118.

Lamb, H. Richard. 1984. "Deinstitutionalization and the Homeless Mentally Ill." *Hospital & Community Psychiatry* 35: 899–907.

———. 1990. "Will We Save the Homeless Mentally Ill?" *American Journal of Psychiatry* 147: 649–651.

———. 1991. "Community Treatment for the Chronically Mentally Ill." *Hospital and Community Psychiatry* 422: 117.

Larson, Magali Sarfatti. 1977. *The Rise of Professionalism: A Sociological Analysis*. Berkeley and Los Angeles: University of California Press.

Laslett, Peter. 1971. *The World We Have Lost: England Before the Industrial Age*, second edition. New York: Charles Scribner's Sons.

LaTour, Stephen A., and Nancy C. Peat. 1979. "Conceptual and Methodological Issues in Consumer Satisfaction Research." In *Advances in Consumer Research, Volume 6*, edited by William L. Wilkie, 431–437. Ann Arbor: Association for Consumer Research.

Laub, John H., and Robert J. Sampson. 2003. *Shared Beginnings, Divergent Lives: Delinquent Boys to Age 70*. Cambridge, MA: Harvard University Press.

Leary, John, Eve C. Johnston, and David G. C. Owens. 1991. "Disabilities and Circumstances of Schizophrenic Patients — A Follow-up Study. II. Social Outcome." *British Journal of Psychiatry* 159 (Suppl. 13): 13–20.

Lebow, Jay L. 1982. "Consumer Satisfaction with Mental Health Treatment." *Psychological Bulletin* 91: 244–259,

———. 1983. "Research Assessing Consumer Satisfaction with Mental Health Treatment: A Review of Findings." *Evaluation and Program Planning* 4: 211–236.

Lee, Barrett A. 1980. "The Disappearance of Skid Row: Some Ecological Evidence." *Urban Affairs Quarterly* 16: 81–107.

Leff, H. Stephen, Clifton M. Chow, Renee Pepin, Jeremy Conley, I. Elaine Allen, and Christopher A. Seamen. 2009. "Does One Size Fit All? What We Can and Can't Learn from a Meta-analysis of Housing Models for Persons with Mental Illness." *Psychiatric Services* 60: 473–482.

Lehman, Anthony F. 1983. "The Well-Being of Chronic Mental Patients." *Archives of General Psychiatry* 40: 369–373.

———. 1984. "The Effects of Psychiatric Symptoms on Quality of Life Assessments among the Chronic Mentally Ill." *Evaluation and Program Planning* 6: 143–151.

———. 1988. "A Quality of Life Interview for the Chronic Mentally Ill." *Evaluation and Program Planning* 11: 51–62.

———. 1991. *Quality of Life Interview: Core Version Manual.* (January 15, 1991: Draft) Baltimore: Center for Mental Health Services Research, School of Medicine, University of Maryland.

Lehman, Anthony F., and David S. Cordray. 1993. "Prevalence of Alcohol, Drug, and Mental Disorders among the Homeless: One More Time." *Contemporary Drug Problems* 20: 355–386.

Lehman, Anthony F., Eimer Kernan, Bruce R. DeForge, and Lisa Dixon. 1995. "Effects of Homelessness on the Quality of Life of Persons with Severe Mental Illness." *Psychiatric Services* 46: 922–926.

Lehman, Anthony F., Susan Possidente, and Fiona Hawker. 1986. "The Quality of Life of Chronic Patients in a State Hospital and in Community Residences." *Hospital and Community Psychiatry* 37: 901–907.

Lehman, Anthony F., Jean G. Slaughter, and C. Patrick Myers. 1991. "Quality of Life in Alternative Residential Settings." *Psychiatric Quarterly* 62: 35–49.

Lehman, Anthony F., Nancy C. Ward, and Lawrence S. Linn. 1982. "Chronic Mental Patients: The Quality of Life Issue." *American Journal of Psychiatry* 139: 1271–1276.

Lehman, Anthony F., and Thomas R. Zastowny. 1983. "Patient Satisfaction with Mental Health Services: A Meta-Analysis to Establish Norms." *Evaluation and Program Planning* 6: 265–274.

Lennon, Mary Clare, William McAllister, Li Kuang, and Daniel B. Herman. 2005. "Capturing Intervention Effects over Time: Reanalysis of a Critical Time Intervention for Homeless Mentally Ill Men." *American Journal of Public Health* 95: 1760–1776.

Lerman, Paul. 1984. *Deinstitutionalization and the Welfare State.* New Brunswick, NJ: Rutgers University Press.

Levstek, D., and Gary R. Bond. 1993. "Housing Cost, Quality, and Satisfaction among Formerly Homeless Persons with Serious Mental Illness in Two Cities." *Innovations and Research in Clinical Services, Community Support, and Rehabilitation* 2: 1–8.

Levy, Leon H. 1983. "Self-Help Groups: Types and Psychological Processes." In *Small Groups and Social Interaction,* edited by Herbert H. Blumberg, A. Paul Hare, Valerie Kent, and Martin F. Davis, 227–238. New York: John Wiley & Sons.

Liberman, Robert Paul, and Kathy Silbert. 2005. "Community Re-entry: Development of Life Skills." *Psychiatry* 68: 220–229.

Liebow, Elliot. 1993. *Tell Them Who I Am: The Lives of Homeless Women.* New York: The Free Press.

Lin, Nan. 2001. *Social Capital: A Theory of Social Structure and Action.* New York: Cambridge University Press.

Lin, Nan, Alfred Dean, and Walter M. Ensel (eds.). 1986. *Social Support, Life Events, and Depression.* New York: Academic Press.

Lincoln, Karen D., Linda M. Chatters, and Robert J. Taylor. 2003. "Psychological Distress among Black and White Americans: Differential Effects of Social Support, Negative Interaction and Personal Control." *Journal of Health and Social Behavior* 44: 390–407.

Linder-Pelz, Susie. 1982a. "Toward a Theory of Patient Satisfaction." *Social Science and Medicine* 16: 577–582.

———. 1982b. "Social Psychological Determinants of Patient Satisfaction: A Test of Five Hypotheses." *Social Science and Medicine* 16: 583–589.

Linhorst, Donald M. 2006. *Empowering People with Severe Mental Illness: A Practical Guide.* New York: Oxford University Press.

Link, Bruce G., Francis T. Cullen, James Frank, and John F. Wozniak. 1987. "The Social Rejection of Former Mental Patients: Understanding Why Labels Matter." *American Journal of Sociology* 92: 1461–1500.

Link, Bruce G., Francis T. Cullen, Elmer Struening, Patrick E. Shrout, and Bruce P. Dohrenwend. 1989. "A Modified Labeling Theory Approach to Mental Disorders: An Empirical Assessment." *American Sociological Review* 54: 400–423.

Lipset, Seymour Martin, Martin Trow, and James S. Coleman. 1962. *Union Democracy.* New York: Doubleday.

Lipton, Frank R., Suzanne Nutt, and Albert Sabatini. 1988. "Housing the Homeless Mentally Ill: A Longitudinal Study of a Treatment Approach." *Hospital and Community Psychiatry* 39: 40–45.

Lipton, Frank R., Carole Siegel, Anthony Hannigen, Judy Samuels, and Sherryl Baker. 2000. "Tenure in Supportive Housing for Homeless Persons with Severe Mental Illness." *Psychiatric Services* 51: 479–486.

Longshore, Douglas, Cheryl Grills, M. Douglas Anglin, and A. Kiku. 1997. "Desire for Help among African-American Drug Users." *Journal of Drug Issues* 27: 755–770.

Lovell, Anne M., and Sandra Cohen. 1998. "The Elaboration of 'Choice' in a Program for Homeless Persons Labeled Psychiatrically Disabled." *Human Organization* 57: 8–20.

Lozier, John. 2006. "Housing is Health Care." Nashville, TN: National Health Care for the Homeless Council. Available at http://www.nhchc.org/Publications/HousingIsHealthCare.pdf. Accessed February 11, 2009.

Luhrmann, Tanya M. 2000. *Of Two Minds: The Growing Disorder in Psychiatry.* New York: Knopf.

Lysaker, Paul H., Morris D. Bell, and Stephen M. Bioty. 1995. "Cognitive Deficits in Schizophrenia: Prediction of Symptom Change for Participators in Work Rehabilitation." *Journal of Nervous and Mental Disease* 183: 332–336.

Mabry, J. Beth, and K. Jill Kiecolt. 2005. "Anger in Black and White: Race, Alienation, and Anger." *Journal of Health and Social Behavior* 46: 85–101.

Makari, George. 2008. *Revolution in Mind: The Creation of Psychoanalysis.* New York: HarperCollins.

Mapes, Linda V. 1985. "Faulty Food and Shelter Programs Draw Charge That Nobody's Home to Homeless." *National Journal* 9: 474–476.

March, James G. 1978. "Bounded Rationality, Ambiguity, and the Engineering of Choice." *Bell Journal of Economics* 9: 587-608.

Mares, Alvin S., Wesley J. Kasprow, and Robert A. Rosenheck. 2004. "Outcomes of Supported Housing for Homeless Veterans with Psychiatric and Substance Abuse Problems." *Mental Health Services Research* 6: 199–211.

Mares, Alvin S., and Robert A. Rosenheck. 2004. "One-Year Housing Arrangements among Homeless Adults with Serious Mental Illness in the ACCESS Program." *Psychiatric Services* 55: 566–574.

Mares, Alvin S., Alexander S. Young, James F. McGuire, and Robert A. Rosenheck. 2002. "Residential Environment and Quality of Life among Seriously Mentally Ill Residents of Board and Care Homes." *Community Mental Health Journal* 38: 447–458.

Marshall, Grant N., M. Audrey Burnam, Paul Koegel, Greer Sullivan, and Bernadette Benjamin. 1996. "Objective Life Circumstances and Life Satisfaction: Results from the Course of Homelessness Study." *Journal of Health and Social Behavior* 37: 44–58.

Maslow, Abraham. 1943. "A Theory of Human Motivation." *Psychological Review* 50: 370–396.

McBride, Timothy D., Robert J. Calsyn, Gay A. Morse, W. Dean Klinkenberg, and Gary A. Allen. 1998. "Duration of Homeless Spells among Severely Mentally Ill Individuals: A Survival Analysis." *Journal of Community Psychology* 26: 473–490.

McCarty, Dennis, Milton Argeriou, Joseph Vallely, and Christopher Christian. 1993. "Development of Alcohol- and Drug-Free Housing." *Contemporary Drug Problems* 20: 521–539.

McCoy, Marion L., Timothy Devitt, Roy Clay, Kristin E. Davis, Jerry Dincin, Debra Pavick, and Sheila O'Neill. 2003. "Gaining Insight: Who Benefits from Residential, Integrated Treatment for People with Dual Diagnoses?" *Psychiatric Rehabilitation Journal* 27:140–150.

McHugo, Gregory J., Richard R. Bebout, Maxine Harris, Stephen Cleghorn, Gloria Herring, Haiyi Xie, Deborah Becker, and Robert E. Drake. 2004. "A Randomized Controlled Trial of Integrated versus Parallel Housing Services for Homeless Adults with Severe Mental Illness." *Schizophrenia Bulletin* 30: 969–982.

McKinlay, John B. 1972. "Some Approaches and Problems in the Study of the Use of Services—An Overview." *Journal of Health and Social Behavior* 13: 115–152.

McLellan, A. Thomas, Lester Luborsky, George E. Woody, and Charles P. O'Brien. 1980. "An Improved Diagnostic Evaluation Instrument for Substance Abuse Patients: The Addiction Severity Index." *The Journal of Nervous and Mental Disease* 168: 26–33.

McPherson, Miller, Lynn Smith-Lovin, and Matthew E. Brashears. 2006. "Social Isolation in America: Changes in Core Discussion Networks over Two Decades." *American Sociological Review* 71: 353–375.

McQuiston, John T. 1984. "Homelessness Spreading to Bedroom Communities." *The New York Times*, July 15. Available at www.nytimes.com. Accessed June 20, 2010.

Mead, Sherry, David Hilton, and Laurie Curtis. 2001. "Peer Support: A Theoretical Perspective." *Psychiatric Rehabilitation Journal* 25: 134–141.

Middelboe, Thomas. 1997. "Prospective Study of Clinical and Social Outcome of Stay in Small Group Homes for People with Mental Illness." *British Journal of Psychiatry* 171: 251–255.

Milev, Peter, Beng-Choon Ho, Stephan Arndt, and Nancy C. Andreasen. 2005. "Predictive Values of Neurocognition and Negative Symptoms on Functional Outcome in Schizophrenia: A Longitudinal First-Episode Study with 7-Year Follow-Up." *American Journal of Psychiatry* 62: 495–506.

Mills, Theodore M. 1984. *The Sociology of Small Groups.* 2nd ed. Englewood Cliffs, NJ: Prentice-Hall.

Minsky, Shula, Gayle Gubman Riesser, and Mark Duffy. 1995. "The Eye of the Beholder: Housing Preferences of Inpatients and Their Treatment Teams." *Psychiatric Services* 46: 173–176.

Mirowsky, John, and Catherine E. Ross. 1986. "Social Patterns of Distress." *Annual Review of Sociology* 12: 23–45.

———. 1989. "Psychiatric Diagnosis as Reified Measurement." *Journal of Health and Social Behavior* 30: 11–25.

———. 1992. "Age and Depression." *Journal of Health and Social Behavior* 33: 187–205.

———. 2002. "Measurement for a Human Science." *Journal of Health and Social Behavior* 43: 152–170.

———. 2003. *Social Causes of Psychological Distress.* 2nd ed. Hawthorne, NY: Aldine de Gruyter.

Mohamed, Somaia, Robert Rosenheck, Joseph McEvoy, Marvin Swartz, Scott Stroup, and Jeffrey A. Lieberman. 2008a. "Cross-sectional and Longitudinal Relationships between Insight and Attitudes toward Medication and Clinical Outcomes in Chronic Schizophrenia." *Schizophrenia Bulletin* Advance Access, June 26. doi:10.1093/schbul/sbn067.

Mohamed, Somaia, Robert Rosenheck, Marvin Swartz, Scott Stroup, Jeffrey A. Lieberman, and Richard S. E. Keefe. 2008b. "Relationship of Cognition and Psychopathology to Functional Impairment in Schizophrenia." *American Journal of Psychiatry* 165: 978–987.

Mohr, Cynthia D., Susan Averna, David A. Kenny, and Frances K. DelBoca. 2001. "'Getting By (or Getting High) with a Little Help from My Friends': An Examination of Adult Alcoholics' Friendships." *Journal of Studies on Alcohol* 62: 637–645.

Mojtabai, Ramin. 2005. "Perceived Reasons for Loss of Housing and Continued Homelessness among Homeless Persons with Mental Illness." *Psychiatric Services* 56: 172–178.

Monroe, Scott M., and Sheri L. Johnson. 1992. "Social Support, Depression, and Other Mental Disorders: In Retrospect and Toward Future Prospects." In *The Meaning and Measurement of Social Support,* edited by Hans O. F. Veiel and Urs Baumann, 93–105. New York: Hemisphere.

Montgomery, Paul L. 1981. "House Homeless in Armory, Judge Orders City and State." *The New York Times,* October 21. Available at http://www.NYTimes .com. Accessed July 6, 2008.

Moos, Rudolf H. 1997. *Evaluating Treatment Environments: The Quality of Psychiatric and Substance Abuse.* 2nd ed. New Brunswick, NJ: Transaction.

Moos, Rudolf H., and Bernice S. Moos. 2007. "Protective Resources and Long-Term Recovery from Alcohol Use Disorders." *Drug and Alcohol Dependence* 86: 46–54.

Morse, Gary, and Robert J. Calsyn. 1985–86. "Mentally Disturbed Homeless People in St. Louis: Needy, Willing, but Underserved." *International Journal of Mental Health* 14 (4): 74–94.

Morse, Gary A., Robert J. Calsyn, Gary Allen, and David A. Kenny. 1994. "Helping Homeless Mentally Ill People: What Variables Mediate and Moderate Program Effects?" *American Journal of Community Psychology* 22: 661–683.

Moselhy, Hamdy F., George Georgiou, and Ashraf Kahn. 2001. Frontal lobe changes in alcoholism: A review of the literature. *Alcohol and Alcoholism* 36: 357–368.

Mouw, Ted. 2006. "Estimating the Causal Effect of Social Capital: A Review of Recent Research." *Annual Review of Sociology* 32: 79–102.

Mussgay, Lutz, and Ralph Hertwig. 1990. "Signal Detection Indices in Schizophrenics on a Visual, Auditory, and Bimodal Continuous Performance Test." *Schizophrenia Research* 3: 303–310.

Nelson, Geoffrey, Tim Aubry, and Adele Lafrance. 2007. "A Review of the Literature on the Effectiveness of Housing and Support, Assertive Community Treatment, and Intensive Case Management Interventions for Persons with Mental Illness Who Have Been Homeless." *American Journal of Orthopsychiatry* 77: 350–361.

Nelson, Geoffrey, G. Brent Hall, and Richard Walsh-Bowers. 1998. "The Relationship between Housing Characteristics, Emotional Well-Being and the Personal Empowerment of Psychiatric Consumer/Survivors." *Community Mental Health Journal* 34: 57–69.

Nelson, Geoffrey, Joanna Ochocka, Rich Janzen, and John Trainor. 2006. "A Longitudinal Study of Mental Health Consumer/Survivor Initiatives: Part 1— Literature Review and Overview of the Study." *Journal of Community Psychology* 34: 247–260.

Neubauer, Ruth. 1993. "Housing Preferences of Homeless Men and Women in a Shelter Population." *Hospital and Community Psychiatry* 44: 492–494.

Nguyen, Tuan D., C. Clifford Attkisson, and Bruce L. Stegner. 1983. "Assessment of Patient Satisfaction: Development and Refinement of a Service Evaluation Questionnaire." *Evaluation and Program Planning* 6: 299–313.

Nolen-Hoeksema, Susan. 1987. "Sex Differences in Unipolar Depression: Evidence and Theory." *Psychological Bulletin* 101: 259–282.

Norman, Ross M., Ashok K. Malla, Leonardo Cortese, Stephen Cheng, Kristine Diaz, Elizabeth McIntosh, Terry S. McLean, Ann Rickwood, and L. P. Voruganti. 1999. "Symptoms and Cognition as Predictors of Community Functioning: A Prospective Analysis." *American Journal of Psychiatry* 156: 400–405.

Norman, Ross M., Ashok K. Malla, Terry S. McLean, L. P. Voruganti, Leonardo Cortese, Elizabeth McIntosh, Stephen Cheng, and Ann Rickwood. 2000. "The Relationship of Symptoms and Level of Functioning in Schizophrenia to General Well-being and the Quality of Life Scale." *Acta Psychiatrica Scandinavica* 102: 303–309.

Norris, Fran H., Arthur D. Murphy, Charlene K. Baker, and Julia L. Perilla. 2004. "Postdisaster PTSD over Four Waves of a Panel Study of Mexico's 1999 Flood." *Journal of Traumatic Stress* 17: 283–292.

Nuttbrock, Larry H., Daisy S. Ng-Mak, Michael Rahav, and James J. Rivera. 1997. "Pre- and Post-Admission Attrition of Homeless, Mentally Ill Chemical Abusers Referred to Residential Treatment Programs." *Addiction* 92: 1305–1316.

Ochocka, Joanna, Geoffrey Nelson, Rich Janzen, and John Trainor. 2006. A Longitudinal Study of Mental Health Consumer/Survivor Initiatives: Part 3—A Qualitative Study of Impacts of Participation on New Members. *Journal of Community Psychology* 34: 273–283.

O'Connell, Maria J., Wesley Kasprow, and Robert A. Rosenheck. 2008. "Rates and Risk Factors for Homelessness after Successful Housing in a Sample of Formerly Homeless Veterans." *Psychiatric Services* 59: 268–275.

O'Flaherty, Brendan. 1996. *Making Room: The Economics of Homelessness.* Cambridge, MA: Harvard University Press.

O'Hara, Ann. 2007. "Housing for People with Mental Illness: Update of a Report to the President's New Freedom Commission." *Psychiatric Services* 58: 907–913.

Oldham, Greg R., and Benjamin I. Gordon. 1999. "Job Complexity and Employee Substance Use: The Moderating Effects of Cognitive Ability." *Journal of Health & Social Behavior* 40: 290–306.

Olfson, Mark. 1990. "Assertive Community Treatment: An Evaluation of Experimental Evidence." *Hospital and Community Psychiatry* 41: 634–641.

Olfson, Mark, David Mechanic, Stephen Hansell, Carol A. Boyer, and James Walkup. 1999. "Prediction of Homelessness within Three Months of Discharge among Inpatients with Schizophrenia." *Psychiatric Services* 50: 667–673.

Orwin, Robert G., Roberta Garrison-Mogren, Mary Lou Jacobs, and L. Joseph Sonnefeld. 1999. "Retention of Homeless Clients in Substance Abuse Treatment: Findings from the National Institute on Alcohol Abuse and Alcoholism Cooperative Agreemenmt Program." *Journal of Substance Abuse Treatment* 17: 45–66.

Orwin, Robert G., Chris K. Scott, and Carlos R. Arieira. 2003. "Transitions through Homelessness and Factors That Predict them: Residential Outcomes in the Chicago Target Cities Treatment Sample." *Evaluation and Program Planning* 26: 379–392.

Owen, Cathy, Valerie Rutherford, Michael Jones, Christine Wright, Christopher Tennant, and Andrew Smallman. 1996. "Housing Accommodation Preferences of People with Psychiatric Disabilities." *Psychiatric Services* 47: 628–632.

Pace, Suzanne, and William Turkel. 1990. "Participants, Community Volunteers and Staff A: Collaborative Approach to Housing and Support." *Psychiatric Rehabilitation Journal* 13: 81–83.

Padgett, Deborah K., Leyla Gulcur, and Sam Tsemberis. 2006. "Housing First Services for People Who are Homeless with Co-occurring Serious Mental Illness and Substance Abuse." *Research on Social Work Practice* 16: 74–83.

Padgett, Deborah K., Ben Henwood, Courtney Abrams, and Robert E. Drake. 2008. "Social Relationships among Persons Who Have Experienced Serious Mental Illness, Substance Abuse, and Homelessness: Implications for Recovery." *American Journal of Orthopsychiatry* 78: 333–339.

Parker, Gordon, Maryanne O'Donnell, Dusan Hadzi-Pavlov, and Miriam Proberts. 2002. "Assessing Outcome in Community Mental Health Patients: A Comparative Analysis of Measures." *International Journal of Social Psychiatry* 48: 11–19.

Parker, Gordon, Alan Rosen, N. Emdur, and Dusan Hadzi-Pavlov. 1991. "The Life Skills Profile: Psychometric Properties of a Measure Assessing Function and Disability in Schizophrenia." *Acta Psychiatrica Scandinavica* 83: 145–152.

Parsons, Oscar A., and William R. Leber. 1981. "The Relationship between Cognitive Dysfunction and Brain Damage in Alcoholics: Causal, Interactive, or Epiphenomenal?" *Alcohol Clinical Experimental Research* 5: 326–343.

Pascoe, Gregory C. 1983. "Patient Satisfaction in Primary Health Care: A Literature Review and Analysis." *Evaluation and Program Planning* 6: 185–210.

Pattison, E. Mansell, and Myrna Loy Pattison. 1981. "Analysis of a Schizophrenic Psychosocial Network." *Schizophrenia Bulletin* 7: 135–143.

Pearlin, Leonard I., William R. Avison, and Elena M. Fazio. 2007. "Sociology, Psychiatry, and the Production of Knowledge about Mental Illness and its Treatment." In *Mental Health, Social Mirror,* edited by William R. Avison, Jane D. McLeod, and Bernice A. Pescosolido, 33–53. New York: Springer.

Pearlin, Leonard I., and Carmi Schooler. 1978. "The Structure of Coping." *Journal of Health and Social Behavior* 19: 2–21.

Penn, David L., Patrick W. Corrigan, and J. Meg Racenstein. 1998. "Cognitive Factors and Social Adjustment in Schizophrenia." In *Handbook of Social Functioning in Schizophrenia,* edited by K. T. Mueser and N. Tarrier, 213–223. Boston: Allyn & Bacon.

Perkins, Douglas D., and Mark A. Zimmerman. 1995. "Empowerment Theory, Research, and Application." *American Journal of Community Psychology* 23: 569–580.

Pescosolido, Bernice A. 1992. "Beyond Rational Choice: The Social Dynamics of How People Seek Help." *American Journal of Sociology* 97: 1096–1138.

Pescosolido, Bernice A., Jane D. McLeod, and William R. Avison. 2007. "Through the Looking Glass: The Fortunes of the Sociology of Mental Health." In *Mental Health, Social Mirror,* edited by William R. Avison, Jane D. McLeod, and Bernice A. Pescosolido, 3–32. New York: Springer.

Pilisuk, Mark. 2001. "A Job and a Home: Social Networks and the Integration of the Mentally Disabled in the Community." *American Journal of Orthopsychiatry* 71: 49–60.

Pini, Stephano, Giovanni B. Cassano, and Liliana Dell'Osso. 2001. "Insight into Illness in Schizophrenia, Schizoaffective Disorder, and Mood Disorders with Psychotic Features." *American Journal of Psychiatry* 158: 122–125.

Platman, Stanley R. 1982. "The Chronically Mentally Ill: Sharing the Burden with the Community." In *Community Support Systems and Mental Health,* edited by David E. Biegel and Arthur J. Naparstek, 190–201. New York: Springer.

Polowczyk, Dianne, Martin Brutus, Alexandra A. Orvieto, Jackie Vidal, and Donna Cipriani. 1993. "Comparison of Patient and Staff Surveys of Consumer Satisfaction." *Hospital and Community Psychiatry* 44: 589–591.

Portes, Alejandro. 1998. "Social Capital: Its Origins and Applications in Modern Sociology." *Annual Review of Sociology* 24: 1–24.

Portes, Alejandro, and Patricia Landolt. 1996. "The Downside of Social Capital." *The American Prospect* 18. Available at http://www.lexisnexis.com. Accessed May 9, 2008.

Posey, Tom. 1988. In *Orientation Manual for Local Level Supported Housing Staff,* edited by L. Curtis, B. Tanzman, and S. S. McCabe. Burlington, VT: The Centre for Community Change through Housing and Support, Institute for Program Development, Trinity College of Vermont [rev. 1992].

Prince, Jonathan D. 2006. "Ethnicity and Life Quality of Recently Discharged Inpatients with Schizophrenia." *American Journal of Orthopsychiatry* 76: 202–205.

Proteau, Antoinette, Helene Verdoux, Catherine Briand, Alain Lesage, Pierre Lalonde, Nicole Luc, Daniel Reinharz, and Emmanuel Stip. 2004. "The Crucial Role of Sustained Attention in Community Functioning in Outpatients with Schizophrenia." *Psychiatry Research* 129: 171–177.

Radloff, Lenore, and Ben Z. Locke. 1986. "The Community Mental Health Assessment Survey and the CES-D Scale." In *Community Surveys of Psychiatric Disorder,* edited by Myrna M. Weissman, Jerome K. Myers, and Catherine E. Ross, 177-189. New Brunswick, NJ: Rutgers University Press.

Rahav, Michael, James J. Rivera, Larry Nuttbrock, Daisy Ng-Mak, Elizabeth L. Sturz, Bruce G. Link, Elmer L. Struening, Bert Pepper, and Ben Gross. 1995. "Characteristics and Treatment of Homeless, Mentally Ill, Chemical-Abusing Men." *Journal of Psychoactive Drugs* 27: 93–103.

Rajkowska, Grazyna, Jose J. Miguel-Hidalgo, Jinrong Wei, Ginny Dilley, Stephen D. Pittman, James C. Overholser, Bryan L. Roth, and Craig A. Stockmeier. 1999. "Morphometric Evidence for Neuronal and Glial Prefrontal Cell Pathology in Major Depression." *Biological Psychiatry* 45: 1085–1098.

Ralph, Ruth O. 2000. "Recovery." *Psychiatric Rehabilitation Skills* 4: 480–517.

Randall, Katie W., and Deborah A. Salem. 2005. "Mutual-Help Groups and Recovery: The Influence of Settings on Participants' Experience Of Recovery." In *Recovery in Mental Illness: Broadening Our Understanding of Wellness,* edited by R. O. Ralph and P. W. Corrigan, 173–205. Washington, DC: American Psychological Association.

Raphael, Edna E. 1964. "Community Structure and Acceptance of Psychiatric Aid." *American Journal of Sociology* 69: 340–358.

Rapoport, Robert N. 1960/1980. *Community as Doctor: New Perspectives on a Therapeutic Community.* London: Tavistock Publications.

Rappaport, Julian. 1987. "Terms of Empowerment/Exemplars of Prevention: Toward a Theory for Community Psychology." *American Journal of Community Psychology* 15: 121–148.

―――. 1995. "Empowerment Meets Narrative: Listening to Stories and Creating Settings." *American Journal of Community Psychology* 23: 795–808.

Redburn, F. Stevens, and Terry F. Buss. 1986. *Responding to America's Homeless: Public Policy Alternatives.* New York: Praeger.

Reine, G., C. Lançon, S. Di Tucci, C. Sapin, and P. Auquier. 2003. "Depression and Subjective Quality of Life in Chronic Phase Schizophrenic Patients." *Acta Psychiatrica Scandinavica* 108: 297–303.

Reiss, David, Robert Plomin, and E. Mavis Hetherington. 1991. "Genetics and Psychiatry: An Unheralded Window on the Environment." *American Journal of Psychiatry* 148: 283–291.

Ridgely, Susan, Howard Goldman, and John A. Talbott. 1986. *Young Adult Chronics.* Washington, DC: National Institute of Mental Health.

Ridgway, Priscilla, and Charles A. Rapp. 1997. *The Active Ingredients of Effective Supported Housing: A Research Synthesis.* Lawrence, KS: School of Social Welfare, The University of Kansas.

Ridgway, Priscilla, and Anthony M. Zipple. 1990a. "Challenges and Strategies for Implementing Supported Housing." *Psychiatric Rehabilitation Journal* 13: 115–121.

―――. 1990b. "The Paradigm Shift in Residential Services: From the Linear Continuum to Supported Housing." *Psychiatric Rehabilitation Journal* 13: 11–32.

Ritchey, Ferris J., Mark La Gory, Kevin M. Fitzpatrick, and Jefferey Mullis. 1990. "A Comparison of Homeless, Community-Wide, and Selected Distress Samples on the CES-Depression Scale." *American Journal of Public Health* 80: 1384–1386.

Ritsner, Michael S. 2007. "Predicting Quality of Life Impairment in Chronic Schizophrenia from Cognitive Variables." *Quality of Life Research* 16: 929–937.

Roberts, Robert E., Gregory C. Pascoe, and Clifford C. Attkisson. 1983. "Relationship of Service Satisfaction to Life Satisfaction and Perceived Well-Being." *Evaluation and Program Planning* 6: 373–383.

Robertson, Marjorie J. 1986. "Mental Disorder among Homeless Persons in the United States: An Overview of the Empirical Literature." *Administration in Mental Health* 14: 14–27.

Robins, Lee N., and Darrel A. Regier. 1991. *Psychiatric Disorders in America: The Epidemiologic Catchment Area Study.* New York: Free Press.

Rochefort, David A. 1993. *From Poorhouses to Homelessness: Policy Analysis and Mental Health Care.* Westport, CT: Auburn House.

Rog, Debra J. 2004. "The Evidence on Supported Housing." *Psychiatric Rehabilitation Journal* 27: 334–344.

Rogers, E. Sally, William Anthony, and Asya Lyass. 2004. "The Nature and Dimensions of Social Support among Individuals with Severe Mental Illnesses." *Community Mental Health Journal* 40: 437–450.

Rogers, E. Sally., Karen S. Danley, William A. Anthony, Rose Martin, and D. Walsh. 1994. "The Residential Needs and Preferences of Persons with Serious Mental Illness: A Comparison of Consumers and Family Members." *The Journal of Mental Health Administration* 21: 42–51.

Rogers, E. Sally, Gregory B. Teague, Carolyn Lichenstein, Jean Campbell, Asya Lyass, and Ren Chen. 2007. "Effects of Participation in Consumer-Operated Service Programs on Both Personal and Organizationally Mediated Empowerment: Results of Multisite Study." *Journal of Rehabilitation Research & Development* 44: 785–300.

Rosen, Alan, Dusan Hadzi-Pavlovic, and Gordon Parker. 1989. "The Life Skills Profile: A Measure Assessing Function and Disability in Schizophrenia." *Schizophrenia Bulletin* 15: 325–337.

Rosenfield, Sarah. 1992. "Factors Contributing to the Subjective Quality of Life of the Chronic Mentally Ill." *Journal of Health and Social Behavior* 33: 299–315.

Rosenfield, Sarah, and Suzanne Wenzel. 1997. "Social Networks and Chronic Mental Illness: A Test of Four Perspectives." *Social Problems* 44: 200–216.

Rosenheck, Robert, and Alan Fontana. 1994. "A Model of Homelessness among Male Veterans of the Vietnam War Generation." *American Journal of Psychiatry* 151: 421–427.

Rosenheck, Robert A., Julie Lam, Joseph P. Morrissey, Michael O. Calloway, Marilyn Stolar, and Frances Randolph. 2002. "Service Systems Integration and Outcomes for Mentally Ill Homeless Persons in the ACCESS Program." *Psychiatric Services* 53: 958–966.

Rosenheck, Robert, Douglas Leslie, Richard Keefe, Joseph McEvoy, Marvin Swartz, Diana Perkins, Scott Stroup, John K. Hsiao, and Jeffrey Lieberman. 2006. "Barriers to Employment for People with Schizophrenia." *American Journal of Psychiatry* 163: 411–417.

Rosenheck, Robert, Joseph Morrissey, Julie Lam, Michael Calloway, Marilyn Stolar, M. Johnsen, Frances Randolph, M. Blasinsky, and Howard Goldman. 2001. "Service Delivery and Community: Social Capital, Service Systems Integration, and Outcomes among Homeless Persons with Severe Mental Illness." *Health Services Research* 36: 691–710.

Rosenheck, Robert A., and Catherine L. Seibyl. 1998. "Participation and Outcome in a Residential Treatment and Work Therapy Program for Addictive Disorders: The Effects of Race." *American Journal of Psychiatry* 155: 1029–1034.

Ross, Catherine E., John Mirowsky, and Shana Pribesh. 2001. "Powerlessness and the Amplification of Threat: Neighborhood Disadvantage, Disorder, and Mistrust." *American Sociological Review* 66: 568–591.

———. 2002. "Disadvantage, Disorder, and Urban Mistrust." *City and Community* 1: 59–82.

Rossi, Peter H. 1989. *Down and Out in America: The Origins of Homelessness.* Chicago: University of Chicago Press.

Roth, Dee, and Gerald J. Bean. 1986. "New Perspectives on Homelessness: Findings from a Statewide Epidemiological Study." *Hospital & Community Psychiatry* 37: 712–719.

Roth, Dee, and Dushka Crane-Ross. 2002. "Impact of Services, Met Needs, and Service Empowerment on Consumer Outcomes." *Mental Health Services Research* 4: 43–56.

Rothman, David J. 1990. *The Discovery of the Asylum: Social Order and Disorder in the New Republic*. Revised 2nd ed. Boston: Little, Brown.

Rothschild-Whitt, Joyce. 1979. "The Collectivist Organization: An Alternative to Rational Bureaucratic Models." *American Sociological Review* 44: 509–527.

Rule, Sheila. 1984. "A High Tide of Homelessness Washes Over City Agencies." *The New York Times*, March 25. Available at www.nytimes.com. Accessed June 20, 2010.

Russell, Betty G. 1991. *Silent Sisters: A Study of Homeless Women*. New York: Hemisphere Publishing.

Russell, Raymond. 1985. *Sharing Ownership in the Workplace*. Albany, NY: State University of New York Press.

Rutter, Michael. 2005. "Why the Different Forms of Gene-Environment Interplay Matter." *Judge Baker Children's Center Symposium, Children's Mental Health: Genes and Behavior*, October 25. Boston, MA.

Salzer, Mark S. 1997. "Consumer Empowerment in Mental Health Organization: Concept, Benefits, and Impediments." *Administration and Policy in Mental Health* 24: 425–434.

Salzer, Mark S., and Shoshanna Liptzin Shear. 2002. "Identifying Consumer-Provider Benefits in Evaluations of Consumer-Delivered Services." *Psychiatric Rehabilitation Journal* 25: 281–288.

Sampson, Robert J. 2003. "The Neighborhood Context of Well Being." *Perspectives in Biology and Medicine* 46: S53–S64.

Sarason, Barbara R., Gregory R. Pierce, and Irwin G. Sarason. 1990. "Social Support: The Sense of Acceptance and the Role of Relationships." In *Social Support: An Interactional View*, edited by Barbara R. Sarason, Irwin G. Sarason, and Gregory R. Pierce, 97–128. New York: John Wiley & Sons.

Schooler, Carmi. 2007. "The Changing Role(s) of Sociology (and Psychology) in the National Institute of Mental Health Intramural Research Program." In *Mental Health, Social Mirror*, edited by William R. Avison, Jane D. McLeod, and Bernice A. Pescosolido, 55–63. New York: Springer.

Schroeder, Larry D., David L. Sjoquist, and Paula E. Stephan. 1986. *Understanding Regression Analysis: An Introductory Guide*. Beverly Hills, CA: Sage.

Schutt, Russell K. 1986. *Organization in a Changing Environment: Unionization of Welfare Employees*. Albany: State University of New York Press.

———. 1990. "The Quantity and Quality of Homelessness: Research Results and Policy Implications." *Sociological Practice Review* 1: 77–87.

———. 2003. "Shelterization in Theory and Practice." *Anthropology of Work Review* 24: 4–13.

———. 2009. *Investigating the Social World: The Process and Practice of Research*. 6th ed. Thousand Oaks, CA: Pine Forge Press.

Schutt, Russell K., and Gerald R. Garrett. 1992. *Responding to the Homeless: Policy and Practice*. New York: Plenum Press.

Schutt, Russell K., and Stephen M. Goldfinger. 1992. "Mentally Ill Persons in Emergency and Specialized Shelters: Distress and Satisfaction." *New England Journal of Public Policy* 8: 407–418.

——. 1996. "Housing Preferences and Perceptions of Health and Functioning Among Mentally Ill Homeless Persons." *Psychiatric Services* 47: 381–386.

——. 2000. "The Contingent Rationality of Housing Preferences: Homeless Mentally Ill Persons' Housing Choices Before and After Housing Experience." *Research in Community and Mental Health* 11: 131–156.

Schutt, Russell K., Stephen M. Goldfinger, and Walter E. Penk. 1992. "The Structure and Sources of Residential Preferences among Seriously Mentally Ill Homeless Adults." *Sociological Practice Review* 3: 148–156.

——. 1997. "Satisfaction with Residence and with Life: When Homeless Mentally Ill Persons Are Housed." *Evaluation and Program Planning* 20: 185–194.

Schutt, Russell K., Stephen M. Goldfinger, Winston Turner, George Tolomiczenko, and Walter E. Penk. 1993. *Baseline Substance Abuse Indicators: Index Construction and Validation*. Unpublished report. Boston: McKinney Homelessness Project, Department of Psychiatry at the Massachusetts Mental Health Center, Harvard Medical School.

Schutt, Russell K., Richard L. Hough, Stephen M. Goldfinger, Anthony F. Lehman, David L. Shern, Elie S. Valencia, and Patricia A. Wood. 2009. "Lessening Homelessness among Persons with Mental Illness: A Comparison of Five Randomized Treatment Trials." *Asian Journal of Psychiatry* 2: 100–105.

Schutt, Russell K., Tatjana Meschede, and Jill Rierdan. 1994. "Distress, Suicidal Thoughts, and Social Support among Homeless Adults." *Journal of Health and Social Behavior* 35: 134–142.

Schutt, Russell K., and E. Sally Rogers. 2009. "Empowerment and Peer Support: Structure and Process of Self Help in a Consumer-Run Center for Individuals with Mental Illness." *Journal of Community Psychology* 37: 697–710.

Schutt, R. K., Robert E. Rosenheck, Walter E. Penk, Charles E. Drebing, and Catherine L. Seibyl. 2005. "The Social Environment of Transitional Work and Residence Programs: Influences on Health and Functioning." *Evaluation and Program Planning* 28: 291–300.

Schutt, Russell K., Larry J. Seidman, Brina Caplan, Anna Martsinkiv, and Stephen M. Goldfinger. 2007. "The Role of Neurocognition and Social Context in Predicting Community Functioning among Formerly Homeless Seriously Mentally Ill Persons." *Schizophrenia Bulletin* 33: 1388–1396.

Schwartz, Stuart R., and Stephen M. Goldfinger. 1981. "The New Chronic Patient: Clinical Characteristics of an Emerging Subgroup." *Hospital and Community Psychiatry* 32: 470–474.

Segal, Stephen P. 1979. "Sheltered-Care Needs of the Mentally Ill." *Health & Social Work* 4 (2): 41–57.

Segal, Steven P., and Uri Aviram. 1978. *The Mentally Ill in Community-Based Sheltered Care: A Study of Community Care and Social Integration*. New York: John Wiley & Sons.

Segal, Stephen P. and James Baumohl. 1980. "Engaging the Disengaged: Proposals on Madness and Vagrancy." *Social Work* 25: 358–365.

Segal, Stephen P. Jim Baumohl, and Elsie Johnson. 1977. "Falling Through the Cracks: Mental Disorder and Social Margin in a Young Vagrant Population." *Social Problems* 24: 387–400.

Segal, Stephen P. and Jane Holschuh. 1991. "Effects of Sheltered Care Environments and Resident Characteristics on the Development of Social Networks." *Hospital and Community Psychiatry* 42: 1125–1131.

Segal, Stephen P., and Pamela L. Kotler. 1989. "Do We Need Board and Care Homes?" *Adult Residential Care Journal* 3: 24–32.

Segal, Stephen P., Pamela L. Kotler, and Jane Holschuh. 1991. "Attitudes of Sheltered Care Residents toward Others with Mental Illness." *Hospital and Community Psychiatry* 42: 1138–1143.

Seidman, Larry J. 1983. Schizophrenia and brain dysfunction: An integration of recent neurodiagnostic findings. Psychological Bulletin 94: 195–238.

Seidman, Larry J., Gerard E. Bruder, and Anthony J. Giuliano. 2008. "Neuropsychological Assessment and Neurophysiological Evaluation." In *Psychiatry,* 3rd ed., edited by Allan Tasman, Jerald Kay, Jeffrey A. Lieberman, Michael B. First, and Mario Maj, 556–569. New York: John Wiley & Sons.

Seidman, Larry J., Brina Caplan, George S. Tolomiczenko, Winston Turner, Walter Penk, Russell K. Schutt, and Stephen M. Goldfinger. 1997. "Neuropsychological Function in Homeless Mentally Ill Individuals." *Journal of Nervous and Mental Disease* 185: 3–12.

Seidman, Larry J., Geraldine P. Cassens, William S. Kremen, and John R. Pepple. 1992. "The Neuropsychology of Schizophrenia." In *Clinical Syndromes in Adult Neuropsychology,* edited by R. White, 389–449. New York: Elsevier.

Seidman, Larry J., William S. Kremen, Danny Koren, Stephen V. Faraone, Jill M. Goldstein, and Ming T. Tsuang. 2002. "A Comparative Profile Analysis of Neuropsychological Functioning in Patients with Schizophrenia and Bipolar Psychoses." *Schizophrenia Research* 53: 31–44.

Seidman, Larry J., Russell K. Schutt, Brina Caplan, George S. Tolomiczenko, Winston M. Turner, and Stephen M. Goldfinger. 2003. "The Effects of Housing Interventions on Neuropsychological Functions in Homeless Mentally Ill Individuals." *Psychiatric Services* 54: 905–908.

Seilheimer, Thomas A., and Guy T. Doyal. 1996. "Self-Efficacy and Consumer Satisfaction with Housing." *Community Mental Health Journal* 32: 549–559.

Sergi, Mark J., Yuri Rassovsky, Keith H. Nuechterlein, and Michael F. Green. 2006. "Social Perception as a Mediator of the Influence of Early Visual Processing on Functional Status in Schizophrenia." *American Journal of Psychiatry* 163: 448–454.

Sergi, Mark J., Yuri Rassovsky, Clifford Widmark, Christopher Reist, Stephen Erhart, David L. Braff, Stephen R. Marder, and Michael F. Green. 2007. "Social Cognition in Schizophrenia: Relationships with Neurocognition and Negative Symptoms." *Schizophrenia Research* 90: 316–324.

Shaffer, Juliet Popper. 1995. "Multiple Hypothesis Testing." *Annual Review of Psychology* 46: 561–584.

Sharfstein, Steven S. 2005. "The Healing Power of Relationships." *Psychiatry* 68: 212–213.

Shern, David L., Chip J. Felton, Richard L. Hough, Anthony F. Lehman, Stephen M. Goldfinger, Elie Valencia, Deborah Dennis, Roger Straw, and Patricia S. Wood. 1997. "Housing Outcomes for Homeless Adults with Mental Illness: Results from the Second-Round McKinney Program." *Psychiatric Services* 48: 239–241.

Shern, David L., Nancy Z. Wilson, Anita Saranga Coen, and Diane C. Patrick. 1994. "Client Outcomes II: Longitudinal Client Data from the Colorado Treatment Outcome Study." *Milbank Quarterly* 72 (1).

Shinn, Marybeth, Jim Baumohl, and Kim Hopper. 2001. "The Prevention Of Homelessness Revisited." *Analyses of Social Issues and Public Policy* 1: 95–127.

Siegel, Carole E., Judith Samuels, Dei-In Tang, Ilyssa Berg, Kristine Jones, and Kim Hopper. 2006. "Tenant Outcomes in Supported Housing and Community Residences in New York City." *Psychiatric Services* 57: 982–991.

Siskind, Amy B. 2003. *The Sullivan Institute/Fourth Wall Community: The Relationship of Radical Individualism and Authoritarianism.* Westport, CT: Praeger.

Snow, David A., and Leon Anderson. 1993. *Down on Their Luck: A Study of Homeless Street People.* Berkeley: University of California Press.

Snow, David A., Leon Anderson, and Paul Koegel. 1994. "Distorting Tendencies in Research on the Homeless." *American Behavioral Scientist* 37: 461–465.

Solarz, Andrea, and G. Anne Bogat. 1990. "When Social Support Fails: The Homeless." *Journal of Community Psychology* 18: 79–95.

Solomon, Phyllis. 1992. "The Closing of a State Hospital: What Is the Quality of Patients' Lives One Year Post-Release?" *Psychiatric Quarterly* 63: 277–296.

———. 2004. "Peer Support/Peer Provided Services Underlying Processes, Benefits, and Critical Elements." *Psychiatric Rehabilitation Journal* 27: 392–401.

Sorensen, James L., Lyle Kantor, Ronald B. Margolis, and Joseph Galano. 1979. "The Extent, Nature, and Utility of Evaluating Consumer Satisfaction in Community Mental Health Centers." *American Journal of Community Psychology* 7: 329–337.

Sosin, Michael R. 2003. "Explaining Adult Homelessness in the U.S. by Stratification or Situation." *Journal of Community & Applied Social Psychology* 13: 91–104.

Sosin, Michael R., and Susan F. Grossman. 2003. "The Individual and Beyond: A Socio-Rational Choice Model of Service Participation among Homeless Adults with Substance Abuse Problems." *Substance Use & Misuse* 38: 503–549.

Sosin, Michael R., Irving Piliavin, and Herb Westerfelt. 1990. "Toward a Longitudinal Analysis of Homelessness." *Journal of Social Issues* 46: 157–174.

Spaulding, W., D. Reed, D. Elting, M. Sullivan, and D. Penn. 1997. "Cognitive Changes in the Course of Rehabilitation." 106–117 In *Towards a Comprehensive Therapy for Schizophrenia,* edited by H. D. Brenner, W. Boker, and R. Genner, 106—117. Seattle: Hogrefe & Huber.

Spitzer, Robert L., and Janet B. Williams. 1987. *Instruction Manual for the Structured Clinical Interview for DSM-III-R: SCID*. New York: Biometrics Research Department, New York State Psychiatric Institute.

Spitzer, Robert L., Janet B. Williams, and Miriam Gibbon. 1989. *Structured Clinical Interview for DSM-IIIR—Patient Version (SCID-P)*. New York: Biometrics Research Department, New York State Psychiatric Institute.

Srebnik, Debra, Joy Livingston, Lawrence Gordon, and David King. 1995. "Housing Choice and Community Success for Individuals with Serious and Persistent Mental Illness." *Community Mental Health Journal* 31: 139–152.

Stafford, Mai, Mary De Silva, Stephen Stansfeld, and Michael Marmot. 2008. "Neighbourhood Social Capital and Common Mental Disorder: Testing the Link in a General Population Sample." *Health & Place* 14: 394–405.

Stall, Ron. 1984. "Disadvantages of Eclecticism in the Treatment of Alcoholism: The 'Problem' of Recidivism." *Journal of Drug Issues* 14: 437–448.

Stefanic, Ana, and Sam Tsemberis. 2007. "Housing First for Long-Term Shelter Dwellers with Psychiatric Disabilities in a Suburban County: A Four-Year Study of Housing Access and Retention." *Journal of Primary Prevention* 28: 265–279.

Stein, Leonard I., and Mary Ann Test. 1980. "Alternative to Mental Hospital Treatment: I. Conceptual Model, Treatment Program, and Clinical Evaluation." *Archives of General Psychiatry* 37: 392–397.

Stoner, Bradley P. 1985. "Formal Modeling of Health Care Decisions: Some Applications and Limitations." *Medical Anthropology Quarterly* 16: 41–46.

Straw, Roger B., Irene S. Levine, and Fred C. Osher. 1997. "The Federal Role in Developing Solutions for Societal Problems." In *Mentally Ill and Homeless: Special Programs for Special Needs,* edited by William R. Breakey and James W. Thompson, 17–27. Amsterdam: Harwood Academic Publishers.

Substance Abuse and Mental Health Services Administration (SAMHSA). 2009a. *2007 National Survey on Drug Use & Health* (Detailed Tables: Table 5.2B: Substance Dependence or Abuse for Specific Substances in the Past Year, by Age Group; Percentages, 2006 and 2007.). Washington DC: Office of Applied Studies, SAMSHA. Available at http://www.oas.samsha.gov. Accessed April 22, 2009.

———. 2009b. "National Consensus Statement on Mental Health Recovery." Rockville, MD: Center for Mental Health Services, SAMSHA. Available at http://www.samhsa.gov/pubs/mhc/MHC_NCrecovery.htm. Accessed June 10, 2009.

Sullivan, Greer, Audrey Burnam, Paul Koegel, and Jan Hollenberg. 2000. "Quality of Life of Homeless Persons with Mental Illness: Results from the Course-of-Homelessness Study." *Psychiatric Services* 51: 1135–1141.

Sullivan, Greer, Kenneth B. Wells, and Barbara Leake. 1992. "Clinical Factors Associated with Better Quality of Life in a Seriously Mentally Ill Population." *Hospital and Community Psychiatry* 43: 794–798.

Sullivan, Patrick F., Michael C. Neale, and Kenneth S. Kendler. 2000. "Genetic Epidemiology of Major Depression: Review and Meta-Analysis." *American Journal of Psychiatry* 157: 1552–1562.

Susser, Ezra S., Sarah A. Conover, and Elmer L. Struening. 1989. "Problems of Epidemiologic Method in Assessing the Type and Extent of Mental Illness among Homeless Adults." *American Journal of Psychiatry* 40: 261–265.

Susser, Ezra S., Shang P. Lin, and Sarah A. Conover. 1991. "Risk Factors for Homelessness among Patients Admitted to a State Mental Hospital." *American Journal of Psychiatry* 148: 1659–1664.

Susser, Ezra, Elie Valencia, Sarah Conover, Alan Felix, Wei-Yann Tsai, and Richard J. Wyatt. 1997. "Preventing Recurrent Homelessness among Mentally Ill Men: A 'Critical Time' Intervention after Discharge from a Shelter." *American Journal of Public Health* 87: 257–262.

Sutherland, Edwin H., and Harvey J. Locke. 1936. *Twenty Thousand Homeless Men.* Chicago: J. B. Lippincott.

Suto, Melinda, and Geyla Frank. 1994. "Future Time Perspective and Daily Occupations of Persons with Chronic Schizophrenia in a Board and Care Home." *American Journal of Occupational Therapy* 48: 7–18.

Swann, William B., Jr., and Jonathan D. Brown. 1990. "From Self to Health: Self-Verification and Identity Disruption." In *Social Support: An Interactional View,* edited by I. Sarason, B. Sarason, and G. Pierce, 150–172. New York: John Wiley & Sons.

Switzer, Ray, and Ralph B. Taylor. 1983. "Sociability versus Privacy of Residential Choice: Impacts of Personality and Local Social Ties." *Basic and Applied Social Psychology* 4: 123–136.

Takeuchi, David T., and David R. Williams. 2003. "Race, Ethnicity and Mental Health: Introduction to the Special Issue." *Journal of Health and Social Behavior* 44: 233–236.

Tanzman, Beth. 1993. "An Overview of Surveys of Mental Health Consumers' Preferences for Housing and Support Services." *Hospital and Community Psychiatry* 44: 450–455.

Tausig, Mark. 1986. "Prior History of Illness in the Basic Model." In *Social Support, Life Events, and Depression,* edited by N. Lin, A. Dean, and W. M. Ensel, 267–280. New York: Academic Press.

Tessler, Richard C., and Deborah Dennis. 1989. *A Synthesis of NIMH-Funded Research Concerning Persons Who Are Homeless and Mentally Ill.* Washington, DC: U.S. Department of Health and Human Services.

Tessler, Richard C., Gail M. Gamache, Peter H. Rossi, Anthony F. Lehman, and Howard H. Goldman. 1992. "The Kindred Bonds of Mentally Ill Homeless Persons." *New England Journal of Public Policy* 8 (1): 265–280.

The Urban Institute, Martha R. Burt, Laudan Y. Aron, Toby Douglas, Jesse Valente, Edgar Lee, and Britta Iwen. 1999. "Homelessness: Programs and the People They Serve." In *Findings of the National Survey of Homeless Assistance Providers and Clients.* Washington, DC: U.S. Department of Housing and Urban Development.

Thoits, Peggy A. 1983. "Multiple Identities and Psychological Well-Being: A Reformulation and Test of the Social Isolation Hypothesis." *American Sociological Review* 48: 174–187.

Thomas, Elizabeth Marshall. 2006. *The Old Way: A Story of the First People.* New York: Farrar, Straus and Giroux.

Thomas, Jeffrey E. 1987. "A Study of Expatients' Perspectives on Their Housing Experiences and Options." *Smith College Studies in Social Work* 57: 199–217.

Tiernan, Kip. 1992. "Homelessness: The Politics of Accommodation." *New England Journal of Public Policy* 8: 647–667.

Tiffany, Francis. 1890. *Life of Dorothea Lynde Dix*. Boston: Houghton Mifflin.

Timmer, Doug A., D. Stanley Eitzen, and Kathryn D. Talley. 1994. *Paths to Homelessness: Extreme Poverty and the Urban Housing Crisis*. Boulder, CO: Westview Press.

Toff, Gail E. 1988a. *Results from a Survey on State Initiatives on Behalf of Persons Who Are Homeless*. Washington, DC: Intergovernmental Health Policy Project, The George Washington University.

———. 1988b. *Self-Help Programs Serving People Who Are Homeless and Mentally Ill*. Washington, DC: The Intergovernmental Health Policy Project, The George Washington University.

Tönnies, Ferdinand. 2001 [1887]. *Community and Civil Society*, edited by Jose Harris, Translated by Jose Harris and Margaret Hollis. Cambridge: Cambridge University Press.

Trauer, Tom, Robert A. Duckmanton, and Edmond Chiu. 1997. "The Assessment of Clinically Significant Change Using the Life Skills Profile." *Australian and New Zealand Journal of Psychiatry* 31: 257–263.

Tsemberis, Sam, and Ronda F. Eisenberg. 2000. "Pathways to Housing: Supported Housing for Street-Dwelling Homeless Individuals with Psychiatric Disabilities." *Psychiatric Services* 51: 487–493.

Tsemberis, Sam, Leyla Gulcur, and Maria Nakae. 2004. "Housing First, Consumer Choice, and Harm Reduction for Homeless Individuals with a Dual Diagnosis." *American Journal of Public Health* 94: 651–656.

Tsuang, Ming T., William S. Stone, and Stephen V. Faraone. 2000. "Toward Reformulating the Diagnosis of Schizophrenia." *American Journal of Psychiatry* 157: 1041–1050.

Turner, Jonathan H. 1988. *A Theory of Social Interaction*. Stanford, CA: Stanford University Press.

Turner, Margery Austen, and Veronica M. Reed. 1990. *Housing America: Learning from the Past, Planning for the Future*. Washington, DC: The Urban Institute Press.

Turner, R. Jay. 1981. "Social Support as a Contingency in Psychological Well-Being." *Journal of Health and Social Behavior* 22: 357–367.

Tversky, Amos, and Eldar Shafir. 1992. "Choice under Conflict: The Dynamics of Deferred Decision." *Psychological Science* 3:358–361.

Tyler, Kimberly A. 2007. "Social Network Characteristics and Risky Sexual and Drug Related Behaviors among Homeless Young Adults." *Social Science Research* 37: 673–685.

Uehara, Edwina Satsuki. 1994. "Race, Gender, and Housing Inequality: An Exploration of the Correlates of Low-Quality Housing among Clients Diagnosed with Severe and Persistent Mental Illness." *Journal of Health and Social Behavior* 35: 309–321.

U.S. Census Bureau. 2008. "Historical Census of Housing Tables: Recent Movers." Available at http://www.census.gov/hhes/www/ housing/census/historic/movers .html. Accessed July 8, 2008.

U.S. Department of Housing and Urban Development. 1989. *A Report on the 1988 National Survey of Shelters for the Homeless.* Washington, DC: Office of Policy Development and Research, U.S. Department of Housing and Urban Development.

Upshur, Carole C., Paul R. Benson, Elizabeth Clemens, William H. Fisher, H. Stephen Leff, and Russell Schutt. 1997. "Closing State Mental Hospitals in Massachusetts: Policy, Process, and Impact." *International Journal of Law and Psychiatry* 20: 199–217.

Urquhart, Barbara, Barbara Bulow, John Sweeney, M. Katherine Shear, and Allen Frances. 1986. "Increased Specificity in Measuring Satisfaction." *Psychiatric Quarterly* 58: 128–134.

Vaillant, George E. 1995. *The Natural History of Alcoholism Revisited.* Cambridge, MA: Harvard University Press.

Vaisey, Stephen. 2007. "Structure, Culture, and Community: The Search for Belonging in 50 Urban Communes." *American Sociological Review* 72: 851–873.

Van Putten, Theodore. 1973. "Milieu Therapy: Contraindications?" *Archives of General Psychiatry* 29: 640–643.

Van Putten, Theodore, and James E. Spar. 1979. "The Board-and-Care Home: Does It Deserve a Bad Press?" *Hospital and Community Psychiatry* 30: 461–464.

Van Tosh, Laura, and Peter del Vecchio. 2000. *Consumer/Survivor-Operated Self-Help Programs: A Technical Report.* Rockville, MD: U.S. Center for Mental Health Services.

Veiel, Hans O. F., and Urs Baumann. 1992. "The Many Meanings of Social Support." In *The Meaning and Measurement of Social Support,* edited by Hans O. F. Veiel and Urs Baumann, 1–9. New York: Hemisphere.

Velasquez, Mary M., Cathy Crouch, Kirk von Sternberg, and Irene Grosdanis. 2000. "Motivation for Change and Psychological Distress in Homeless Substance Abusers." *Journal of Substance Abuse Treatment* 19: 395–401.

Wagner, David. 1993. *Checkerboard Square: Culture and Resistance in a Homeless Community.* Boulder, CO: Westview.

Walker, Michael E., Stanley Wasserman, and Barry Wellman. 1993. "Statistical Models for Social Support Networks." *Sociological Methods & Research* 22: 71–98.

Ware, John E., and Allyson R. Davies. 1983. "Behavioral Consequences of Consumer Dissatisfaction with Medical Care." *Evaluation and Program Planning* 6: 291–297.

Ware, John E., and Cathy Donald Sherbourne. 1992. "The MOS 36-Item Short-Form Health Survey (SF-36): Conceptual Framework and Item Selection." *Medical Care* 30: 473–483.

Ware, Norma C. 1999. "Evolving Consumer Households: An Experiment in Community Living for Persons with Severe Psychiatric Disorders." *Psychosocial Rehabilitation Journal* 23: 3–10.

Ware, Norma C., Robert R. Desjarlais, Tara L. AvRuskin, Joshua Breslau, Byron J. Good, and Stephen M. Goldfinger. 1992. "Empowerment and the Transition to Housing for Homeless Mentally Ill People." *New England Journal of Public Policy* 8: 297–314.

Ware, Norma C., Kim Hopper, Toni Tugenberg, Barbara Dickey, and Daniel Fisher. 2007. "Connectedness and Citizenship: Redefining Social Integration." *Psychiatric Services* 58: 469–474.

Weber, Max. 1947. *The Theory of Social and Economic Organization,* translated by A. M. Henderson; edited by Talcott Parsons. New York: Free Press.

Weinberg, Richard B., and Herbert Marlowe. 1983. "Recognizing the Social in Psychosocial Competence: The Importance of Social Network Interventions." *Psychosocial Rehabilitation Journal* 6: 25–34.

Weissman, Myrna M., Diane Scholomskes, Margaret Pottenger, Brigitte A. Prusoff, and Ben Z. Locke. 1977. "Assessing Depressive Symptoms in Five Psychiatric Populations: A Validation Study." *American Journal of Epidemiology* 106: 203–214.

Wellman, Barry, and Scot Wortley. 1990. "Different Strokes from Different Folks: Community Ties and Social Support." *American Journal of Sociology* 96: 558–588.

Whitley, Rob, and Martin Prince. 2005. "Is There a Link between Rates of Common Mental Disorder and Deficits in Social Capital in Gospel Oak, London? Results from a Qualitative Study." *Health & Place* 11: 237–248.

Williams, Brian. 1994. "Patient Satisfaction: A Valid Concept?" *Social Science & Medicine* 38: 509–516.

Williams, Brian, and Greg Wilkinson. 1995. "Patient Satisfaction in Mental Health Care: Evaluating an Evaluative Method." *British Journal of Psychiatry* 166: 559–562.

Williams, Terry. 1992. *Crackhouse: Notes from the End of the Line.* New York: Penguin.

Wing, J. K., and George W. Brown. 1970. Institutionalism and Schizophrenia: A Comparative Study of Three Mental Hospitals 1960–1968. Cambridge: Cambridge University Press.

Wolch, Jennifer, and Michael Dear. 1993. *Malign Neglect: Homelessness in an American City.* San Francisco: Jossey-Bass.

Wolf, J., Audrey Burnam, Paul Koegel, G. Sullivan, and S. Morton. 2001. "Changes in Subjective Quality of Life among Homeless Adults Who Obtain Housing: A Prospective Examination." *Social Psychiatry and Psychiatric Epidemiology* 36: 391–398.

Wong, Yin-Ling Irene, Trevor R. Hadley, Dennis P. Culhane, Steve R. Poulin, Morris R. Davis, Brian A. Cirksey, and James L. Brown. 2006. "Predicting Staying in or Leaving Permanent Supportive Housing That Serves Homeless People with Serious Mental Illness." *Final Report Prepared for U.S. Department of Housing and Urban Development, Office of Policy Development and Research.* Philadelphia: Center for Mental Health Policy and Services Research, University of Pennsylvania.

Wong, Yin-Ling Irene, and Irving Piliavin. 1997. "A Dynamic Analysis of Homeless-Domicile Transitions." *Social Problems* 44: 408–423.

Wong, Yin-Ling Irene and Irving Piliavin. 2001. "Stresses, Resources, and Distress among Homeless Persons: A Longitudinal Analysis." *Social Science and Medicine* 52:1029-1042

Wong, Yin-Ling Irene and Phyllis L. Solomon. 2002. "Community Integration of Persons with Psychiatric Disabilities Is Supportive Independent Housing: A Conceptual Model and Methodological Considerations." *Mental Health Services Research* 4: 13–28.

Wright, Ian C., Sophia Rabe-Hesketh, Peter W. R. Woodruff, Anthony S. David, Robin M. Murray, and Edward T. Bullmore. 2000. "Meta-analysis of Regional Brain Volumes in Schizophrenia." *American Journal of Psychiatry* 157: 16–25.

Wright, James. 1989. *Address Unknown: The Homeless in America.* Hawthorne, NY: Aldine de Gruyter.

Wrong, Dennis H. 1961. "The Oversocialized Conception of Man in Modern Sociology." *American Sociological Review* 26: 183–193.

Wykes, Til. 1998. "Social Functioning in Residential and Institutional Settings." In *Handbook of Social Functioning in Schizophrenia,* edited by Kim T. Mueser and Nicholas Tarrier, 20–38. Boston: Allyn & Bacon.

Yablonsky, Lewis. 1989. *The Therapeutic Community: A Successful Approach for Treating Substance Abusers.* New York: Gardner Press.

Yanos, Philip T., Susan M. Barrow, and Sam Tsemberis. 2004. "Community Integration in the Early Phase of Housing among Homeless Persons Diagnosed with Severe Mental Illness: Successes and Challenges." *Community Mental Health Journal* 40: 133–150.

Yanos, Philip T., Louis H. Primavera, and Edward L. Knight. 2001. "Consumer-Run Service Participation, Recovery of Social Functioning, and the Mediating Role of Psychological Factors." *Psychiatric Services* 52: 493–500.

Yeich, Susan, and Carol T. Mowbray. 1994. "The Case for a 'Supported Housing' Approach: A Study of consumer Housing and Support Preferences." *Psychosocial Rehabilitation Journal* 18:75–86.

Ziersch, Anna M., Fran E. Baum, Colin MacDougall, and Christine Putland. 2005. "Neighbourhood Life and Social Capital: The Implications for Health." *Social Science & Medicine* 60: 71–86.

Zinman, Sally. 1982. "A Patient-Run Residence." *Psychosocial Rehabilitation Journal* 6: 3–11.

Zlotnick, Cheryl, Tammy Tam, and Majorie J. Robertson. 2003. "Disaffiliation, Substance Use, and Exiting Homelessness." *Substance Use & Misuse* 38: 577–599.

Index